Frommer's®

4th Edition

Virgin Islands

by Darwin Porter & Danforth Prince

Macmillan • USA

ABOUT THE AUTHORS

A native of North Carolina, **Darwin Porter** was a bureau chief for *The Miami Herald* when he was 21, and later worked in television advertising. A veteran travel writer, he is the author of numerous best-selling Frommer's guides, notably to the Caribbean, England, France, Italy, and Spain. He is assisted by **Danforth Prince,** formerly of the Paris Bureau of *The New York Times.* They have been frequent travelers to the Caribbean for years, and are intimately familiar with what's good there and what isn't. They have also written *Frommer's Caribbean Cruises*, the most candid and up-to-date guide to cruise vacations on the market. In this guide, they share their secrets and discoveries about the Virgin Islands with you.

MACMILLAN TRAVEL

A Simon & Schuster Macmillan Company
1633 Broadway
New York, NY 10019

Find us online at **http://www.mgr.com/travel** or
on America Online at Keyword: **Frommer's**

ISBN 0-02-861641-3
ISSN 1055-5447

Editor: Alicia Scott
Production Editor: Phil Kitchel
Design by Michele Laseau
Digital Cartography by Peter Bogaty

SPECIAL SALES

Bulk purchases (10+ copies) of Frommer's and selected Macmillan travel guides are available to corporations, organizations, mail-order catalogs, institutions, and charities at special discounts. The Special Sales Department can produce custom editions to be used as premiums and/or for sales promotion to suit individual needs. Existing editions can be produced with custom cover imprints such as corporate logos. For more information write to: Special Sales, Macmillan General Reference, 1633 Broadway, New York, NY 10019.

Manufactured in the United States of America

Contents

4   The U.S. Virgin Islands: St. Thomas   59

List of Maps

AN INVITATION TO THE READER

In researching this book, we discovered many intriguing places—hotels, restaurants, shops, and more. We're sure you'll find others. Please tell us about them, so we can share the information with your fellow travelers in upcoming editions. If you were disappointed with a recommendation, we need to know that, too. Please write to:

Darwin Porter & Danforth Prince
Frommer's Virgin Islands, 4th Edition
Macmillan Travel
1633 Broadway
New York, NY 10019

AN ADDITIONAL NOTE

Please be advised that travel information is subject to change at any time—and this is especially true of prices. We therefore suggest that you write or call ahead for confirmation when making your travel plans. The authors, editors, and publisher cannot be held responsible for the experiences of readers while traveling. Your safety is important to us, however, so we encourage you to stay alert and be aware of your surroundings. Keep a close eye on cameras, purses, and wallets, all favorite targets of thieves and pickpockets.

WHAT THE SYMBOL MEANS

✪ Frommer's Favorites

Our favorite places and experiences—outstanding for quality, value, or both.

The following abbreviations are used for credit cards:

AE	American Express	DISC	Discover
CB	Carte Blanche	MC	MasterCard
DC	Diners Club	V	Visa

The Best of the Virgin Islands

Y ou've come to the Virgin Islands to relax—not to wear yourself out searching for the best deals and most eclectic tropical experiences. With this guide in hand, you can plan and enjoy a worry-free vacation and let us do the dirty work. Below you'll find our carefully compiled lists of the islands' superlative beaches, hotels, restaurants, shopping, snorkeling, and nearly everything else your heart might desire.

1 The Best Beaches

Both the U.S. and the British Virgin Islands are known for their white, sandy beaches. This is not true of all islands in the Caribbean, many of which have only jagged coral outcroppings or beaches with black volcanic sand (which heats up fast in the noonday sun). Best of all, every beach in the Virgin Islands is free (except for Magens Bay in St. Thomas) and open to the public, although in some cases, you'll have to walk across the grounds of a resort (or arrive by private boat) to reach them.

- **Magens Bay Beach** (St. Thomas, U.S. Virgin Islands): This $1/2$-mile loop of pebble-free sand and remarkably calm waters is by far the most popular and picturesque beach in the U.S. Virgin Islands. Two peninsulas protect the shore from erosion and strong waves, making Magens an ideal spot for swimming and sunning. Expect a lively crowd here in the high season. See chapter 4.
- **Sapphire Beach** (St. Thomas, U.S. Virgin Islands): Offshore of several luxury resorts, this beach is one of the finest on the island and a favorite with windsurfers. Come here for some of St. Thomas's best shore snorkeling and diving (off Pettyklip Point). And, don't worry about equipment—water sports concessions abound here. Sapphire is the most popular Sunday afternoon gathering place in the East End. Take a moment to enjoy the panoramic view of St. John and other islands. See chapter 4.
- **Trunk Bay** (St. John, U.S. Virgin Islands): Protected by the U.S. National Park Service, this beach is a favorite with cruise-ship passengers. It's famous for its underwater trail, where markers guide beachcombers along the reef lying just off the white, sandy beach. Trunk Bay is consistently ranked among the top 10 Caribbean beaches, most recently by *Condé Nast Traveler*. See chapter 5.
- **Caneel Bay** (St. John, U.S. Virgin Islands): Site of a famous resort, Caneel Bay is a string of seven beaches, stretching around

Durloe Point to Hawksnest Caneel. Against a backdrop of palm trees, these beaches offer sand the color of champagne. Rosewood Hotels, which operates Caneel Bay Resort, admits day guests. See chapter 5.

- **Sandy Point** (St. Croix, U.S. Virgin Islands): The biggest beach in the U.S. Virgin Islands, Sandy Point has shallow, calm waters. It lies in the southwestern part of St. Croix, almost like a small peninsula, directly to the west of Alexander Hamilton Airport. The beach, a protected reserve that is a nesting spot of endangered sea turtles, is open to the public weekends only from 9am to 5pm. Try to concentrate on the sands and not the unattractive zigzagging fences that line the beach. See chapter 6.

- **Cane Garden Bay** (Tortola, British Virgin Islands): Rivaling Magens Bay (see above) for scenic beauty, Cane Garden Bay is the most popular beach in the B.V.I. Its translucent waters and sugar-white sands are reason enough to visit Tortola; it's also the closest beach to the capital at Road Town. See chapter 7.

2 The Best Snorkeling Spots

A readers' poll by *Scuba Diving* magazine confirmed what Virgin Islanders knew all along: The islands of St. Croix, St. John, and St. Thomas are among the top five places to go snorkeling in the Caribbean. Here are some of the best spots:

- **Coki Beach** (St. Thomas, U.S. Virgin Islands): On the north shore of St. Thomas, Coki Beach offers superb year-round snorkeling. Especially enticing are the coral ledges near Coral World's underwater tower, a favorite among cruise-ship passengers. See chapter 4.

- **Trunk Bay** (St. John, U.S. Virgin Islands): This self-guided 225-yard-long trail has large underwater signs that identify species of coral and other marine life. Above water, freshwater showers, changing rooms, equipment rentals, and lifeguards make snorkeling more convenient. See chapter 5.

- **Leinster Bay** (St. John, U.S. Virgin Islands): Easily accessible from land and sea, Leinster Bay, on the northern shore of St. John, offers calm, clear, and uncrowded waters teeming with sea life. See chapter 5.

- **Haulover Bay** (St. John, U.S. Virgin Islands): A favorite with locals, this small bay is rougher than Leinster and is often deserted. The snorkeling is dramatic, with ledges, walls, nooks, and sandy areas set close together. Here, only about 200 yards separate the Atlantic Ocean from the Caribbean Sea. See chapter 5.

- **Buck Island Reef National Monument** (off St. Croix, U.S. Virgin Islands): More than 250 recorded species of fish swim through this 850-acre island and reef system, located 2 miles off St. Croix's north shore. A variety of sponges, corals, and crustaceans also inhabits the monument, which is strictly protected by the National Park Service. See chapter 6.

- **Cane Bay** (St. Croix, U.S. Virgin Islands): One of the island's best diving and snorkeling sites is off this breezy north-shore beach. On a clear day, you can swim out 150 yards to see the Cane Bay Wall that dramatically drops off to deep waters below. Multicolored fish, elkhorn, and brain coral flourish here. See chapter 6.

- **Frederiksted Pier** (St. Croix, U.S. Virgin Islands): Conventional wisdom has designated this pier, located in an old ramshackle town at the west end of St. Croix, the most interesting pier dive in the Caribbean. The original pier was virtually destroyed by Hurricane Hugo in 1989, but a new one opened in 1993. Plunge into a world of exotic creatures, including sponges, banded shrimp, plume worms, and sea horses. See chapter 6.

3 The Best Dive Sites

- **Cow and Calf Rocks** (St. Thomas, U.S. Virgin Islands): Off the southeast end of St. Thomas (about a 45-minute boat ride from Charlotte Amalie), this site is the island's best dive spot. It's also a good bet if you prefer snorkeling. You'll discover a network of coral tunnels riddled with caves, reefs, and ancient boulders encrusted with coral. See chapter 4.
- **Buck Island Reef** (off St. Croix, U.S. Virgin Islands): The only underwater national monument in the United States, this tiny island lies 2 miles off the north coast of St. Croix. With an underwater visibility of some 100 feet, Buck Island is one of the major diving meccas in the Caribbean. There are enough labyrinths and grottoes for the most experienced divers, plus massive gardens of fiery coral inhabited by black sea urchins, barracudas, stingrays, and other creatures. See chapter 6.
- **Davis Bay** (off St. Croix, U.S. Virgin Islands): Davis Bay is the site of the 12,000-foot-deep Puerto Rico Trench, the fifth-deepest body of water in the world. Other sites for deep dives off St. Croix include the drop-offs and coral canyons at Cane Bay and Salt River. See chapter 6.
- **The Wreck of the HMS *Rhone,*** (off Salt Island, British Virgin Islands): The *Rhone* wreck is the premier dive site not only in the Virgin Islands, but also in the entire Caribbean. This royal mail steamer, which went down in 1867, was featured in the murky film *The Deep.* See chapter 7.
- **Chikuzen** (Tortola, British Virgin Islands): Although its not the *Rhone* (see above), this 270-foot steel-hulled refrigerator ship, which sank off the island's east end in 1981, is one of the B.V.I.'s most fascinating dive sites. The hull—still intact under about 80 feet of water—is now home to a vast array of tropical fish, including yellowtail, barracuda, black-tip sharks, octopus, and drum fish. See chapter 7.
- **Alice in Wonderland** (Ginger Island, British Virgin Islands): This brilliant coral wall, offshore of a tiny island, slopes from 40 feet to a sandy bottom at 100 feet. Divers often refer to the site as "a fantasy," because of its monstrous overhangs, vibrant colors, gigantic mushroom-shaped corals, and the wide variety of sea creatures—everything from conch and garden eels to longnose butterfly fish. See chapter 7.

4 The Best Sailing Outfitters

Sailing is big in the U.S. Virgin Islands, but it's even bigger in the British Virgins, lauded for having the best cruising in the Caribbean. Be sure to check individual chapters for the names and numbers of local outfitters. The most reputable companies that we've come across include:

- **American Yacht Harbor** (St. Thomas, U.S. Virgin Islands; ☎ **809/775-6454**): Located in Red Hook Marina, this is one of the best bareboat or fully crewed charter companies on the island, although it still doesn't come close to The Moorings on Tortola (see below). Red Hook itself is home to numerous boat companies, including both fishing and sailing charters. Whatever craft you're looking for, you're bound to find it here. See chapter 4.
- **Yacht Nightwind** (St. Thomas, U.S. Virgin Islands; ☎ **809/775-4110**): Also in Red Hook Marina, this outfit boasts one of the best sailing deals in the Virgin Islands. For $90 (per passenger) you can charter your own state-of-the-art yacht for one day, including a champagne buffet lunch and an open bar on board. See chapter 4.

- **Vacation Vistas and Motor Yachts** (St. John, U.S. Virgin Islands; ☎ **809/ 776-6462**): This is your best bet for half- or full-day charters on St. John. Many boaters head for a day cruise to the famous Baths on Virgin Gorda in the British Virgin Islands. To cut costs, you can go on a regularly scheduled boat charter tour, or if you have a large group, you can charter your own craft. See chapter 5.

- **The Moorings** (Tortola, British Virgin Islands; ☎ **800/535-7289**): Run by Ginny and Charlie Cary, this is the finest charter service in the Virgin Islands. It has done more than any other outfitter to make the British Virgin Islands the destination of choice among the world's yachting class. Their fleet of yachts and boats is staggering—everything from bareboat rentals to fully crewed vessels with skipper, crew, and cook. See chapter 7.

5 The Best Golf Courses

- **Mahogany Run** (St. Thomas, U.S. Virgin Islands; ☎ **800/253-7103**): To the north of Charlotte Amalie, this par-70, 6,022-yard course with breathtaking views of the British Virgin Islands is infamous for its "Devil's Triangle," a tricky trio of holes (13, 14, and 15). The course was designed by Tom and George Fazio and is hailed by golfers as one of the most scenic in the Caribbean. See chapter 4.

- **The Buccaneer** (St. Croix, U.S. Virgin Islands; ☎ **800/255-3881**): This 6,117-yard resort course has some spectacular vistas, especially from its signature third hole, where the seascape stretches from Christiansted to Buck Island. Three new holes have recently been added as a practice area, and a teaching pro is always available for fine-tuning your swing. High season rates are $40 for 18 holes, not including cart fees. See chapter 6.

- **Carambola** (St. Croix, U.S. Virgin Islands; ☎ **809/778-0747**): Known for some decades as Fountain Valley, this par-72 course at Davis Bay was designed by Robert Trent Jones Sr., and is one of the most challenging in the Caribbean. Set near the island's northwestern edge, these well-maintained links are characterized by dangerous water hazards and ravines. See chapter 6.

6 The Best Tennis Facilities

- **Wyndam Sugar Bay Beach Club** (St. Thomas, U.S. Virgin Islands; ☎ **800/ 927-7100**): Several tennis buffs have deserted the Buccaneer on St. Croix (see below) in favor of this resort at Estate Smith Bay. Sugar Bay Plantation offers the U.S. Virgin Islands's first stadium tennis court, as well as six Laykold courts, which are lit at night. There's a pro shop on the premises, and lessons are available. See chapter 4.

- **The Buccaneer** (St. Croix, U.S. Virgin Islands; ☎ **800/255-3881**): This is where Teddy Kennedy plays when he's on St. Croix. The resort's facilities have been touted as the best in the Virgin Islands and have played host to several professional tournaments, including the Virgin Islands Tennis Championships in July. The resort features eight all-weather Laykold courts, two of which are lit at night. Nonresidents can play here for a fee. See chapter 6.

7 The Best Nature Walks

- **The Annaberg Sugar Plantation Ruins Walk** (St. John, U.S. Virgin Islands): The premier route through the 10,000-acre U.S. Virgin Islands National Park, this paved walk is only ¼ mile long. Overlooking the scenic north coast, the self-guided trail traverses the ruins of what was once the most important sugarcane plantation on the island. Slaves' quarters, a windmill tower, and ballast-brick buildings from Danish sailing vessels recapture a long-vanished era. Stunning views look toward Tortola, Great Thatch Island, and Jost Van Dyke on the opposite side of Sir Francis Drake Passage. See chapter 5.

- **The Rain Forest Hike** (St. Croix, U.S. Virgin Islands): The verdant northwestern end of St. Croix is known as the "Rain Forest," although it's actually not a true tropical rain forest. Our favorite trail to explore in this area takes about 2½ hours one-way. Jump in your car and take Route 631, heading north of Frederiksted, to the intersection of routes 63 and 76. Continue along on Route 63 until you reach Creque Dam Road, where you should turn right, park the car, and start walking. About 1 mile past the 150-foot Creque Dam, you'll be deep within the forest's magnificent flora and fauna. Continue along the trail until you come to the Western Scenic Road. Eventually, you reach Mahogany Road (Route 76), near St. Croix Leap Project. Hikers rate this trail moderate in difficulty. See chapter 6.

- **Buck Island Walk** (off St. Croix, U.S. Virgin Islands): A circumnavigation of this national park, which is reached by boat, takes about 2 hours and is rated moderate by most hikers. The mile-long island is an 865-acre park located off the northern coast of St. Croix. Since the island is ringed with white sandy beaches, feel free to take a break for a refreshing swim. There's also a trail that points inland. See chapter 6.

- **Sage Mountain National Park** (Tortola, British Virgin Islands): In 3 to 4 hours, you can experience one of the most dramatic hikes in the British Virgins, all the way from Brewer's Bay to the top of Mount Sage at 1,780 feet, the highest peak in the Virgin Islands. Along the way, you'll see intriguing ruins of old homes, not to mention the beautiful flora and fauna of the park's primeval forest. See chapter 7.

8 The Best Honeymoon Resorts

Many hotels in the U.S. and British Virgins will help plan your wedding, doing everything from arranging the flowers and the photographer to applying for the marriage license (see chapter 3 for more details). Regardless of where you decide to hold your wedding, the Virgin Islands offer some of the most romantic destinations for honeymooners. Here are the most reputable hideaways for newlyweds:

- **Doubletree Sapphire Beach Resort and Marina** (St. Thomas, U.S. Virgin Islands; ☎ 800/524-2090): Located on one of the island's loveliest beaches (see above), this is a huge complex of deluxe suites and villas with facilities for all the water sports you can dream of. An added bonus: You can dine out or test your own culinary specialties on your new bride or groom in one of the fully equipped kitchens. Keep in mind that honeymooners share the resort with vacationing families. See chapter 4.

- **Elysian Beach Resort** (St. Thomas, U.S. Virgin Islands; ☎ 800/753-2554): This Caribbean oasis tempts brides and grooms with its "Honeymoon Get-Away" package, a great value for a deluxe room or a one-bedroom suite, champagne upon arrival, and free use of the tennis courts, fitness center, freshwater pool, and Jacuzzi. Plus, a water sports center with snorkel gear, Sunfish sailboats, kayaks, and other nonmotorized beach equipment is always available to guests, newlyweds or not. See chapter 4.

- **The Buccaneer** (St. Croix, U.S. Virgin Islands; ☎ **800/255-3881**): The Buccaneer boasts the most extensive facilities on the island, including an 18-hole golf course, eight championship tennis courts, a spa and fitness center, a 2-mile jogging trail, and three beaches. In fact, last year *Travel and Leisure* magazine rated the resort as one of the "25 Best Hotels in the Caribbean and Bermuda." We recommend staying in one of the beachside rooms with fieldstone terraces that take you right down to the water. The 1653 sugar mill on the grounds is the most popular wedding spot on St. Croix. See chapter 6.
- **Little Dix Bay** (Virgin Gorda, British Virgin Islands; ☎ **800/928-3000**): The elegance of this luxury resort is understated. It's popular with older couples and honeymooners alike—in fact, the powerfully amorous atmosphere makes single guests feel like wallflowers. Spread out over 500 acres on a secluded bay, this resort offers beautiful beaches and sporting activities galore, or if privacy is what you're after, you'll find plenty of that too. See chapter 7.
- **Biras Creek Estate** (Virgin Gorda, British Virgin Islands; ☎ **800/608-9661**): Private and elegant, this hotel is perched on a narrow promontory of land with signposted nature trails cutting through its lush tropical gardens. It's a secluded 150-acre hideaway, reached only by launch. Honeymooners always enjoy rinsing off in the sensuous open-air showers discreetly located within each bathroom. See chapter 7.

9 The Best Family Resorts

- **Doubletree Sapphire Beach Resort and Marina** (St. Thomas, U.S. Virgin Islands; ☎ **800/524-2090**): Situated on one of the safest and best beaches on the island, this is the family favorite in St. Thomas. The resort's Little Gems Kids Klub plans all sorts of supervised activities (some include the whole family), and there's also a separate toddler program catering to one- to three-year-olds. Children under 12 stay in their parents' accommodations at no extra charge and also eat for free when dining with Mom and Dad. See chapter 4.
- **Bolongo Beach Club** (St. Thomas, U.S. Virgin Islands; ☎ **800/524-4746**): Bolongo Beach is touted as one of the safest spots on St. Thomas and the resort staff here offers a huge roster of family activities; there's also a separate program for kids only, although it's not always divided by age. When booking, ask about the package that allows children to stay and eat for free. See chapter 4.
- **The Buccaneer** (St. Croix, U.S. Virgin Islands; ☎ **800/255-3881**): This hotel is a longtime family favorite located on a 300-acre former sugar estate. It has on-site facilities for just about every sport you can think of, including tennis, golf, swimming, jogging, sailing, scuba diving, and snorkeling. Children's programs include a half-day sail to Buck Island Reef, and nature walks through tropical foliage where kids can taste local fruit in the wild. See chapter 6.
- **Chenay Bay Beach Resort** (St. Croix, U.S. Virgin Islands; ☎ **800/548-4457**): Housed in West Indian–style cottages, families staying here can appease their 3- to 12-year-olds with various organized activities from swimming and snorkeling to nature walks and story hours. In fact, the friendly owners of this barefoot-casual hotel used their own offspring as guinea pigs to design their children's program, which runs during the summer and over holiday periods. See chapter 6.
- **The Bitter End Yacht Club** (Virgin Gorda, British Virgin Islands; ☎ **800/872-2392**): Eco-kids will love this lively resort, located on a sheltered deepwater harbor. They can go snorkeling at Statia Reef, explore the tidal pools and boulders of The Baths, or take an excursion to a bird sanctuary at Anegada Island.

Most programs are geared toward children six and over and involve all the typical water sports: sailing, windsurfing, snorkeling, swimming, and more. Ask about the hotel's packages for families. See chapter 7.

10 The Best Places to Get Away from It All

Although there are tranquil retreats on St. Croix and on St. Thomas, the sometimes frenetic pace on these islands, especially on St. Thomas, may not be what you're after. In that case, head for St. John, or, if even that small, peaceful isle is too much for you, hop over to the British Virgin Islands, and seek out even more remote oases. Below we let you in on some of our best-kept secrets:

- **St. John,** U.S. Virgin Islands: This is one of the most secluded islands you'll find, particularly among the U.S. islands. More than two-thirds of its land has been preserved as a national park, thanks to the generosity of Laurance Rockefeller. That means that unlike St. Thomas and St. Croix, St. John's landscape looks much like it did in the 1950s: white sand beaches and verdant tropical forests. The day-trippers from St. Thomas come over in the morning and usually depart before 5pm. After that, St. John becomes a crowd-free paradise. **Lavender Hill Estates** (☎ 800/562-1901) offers some of the best values here for those who'd like to rent their own private villa (units overlook Cruz Bay Harbor) for a week or so. See chapter 5.

- **The Sandcastle** (Jost Van Dyke, British Virgin Islands; ☎ 284/690-1611): The ultimate escapist's dream. Reached by interisland ferry from Tortola, this little island on White Bay is riddled with good hiking trails, uncrowded sandy beaches, and the ruins of an old military fort. People come to the Sandcastle, a four-villa colony with octagonal-shaped cottages, in search of isolation and relaxation, and that's exactly what they get: intimate gourmet dinners, a beachside bar, hidden hammocks, gas lighting and solar-heated showers, and virtually no cars. See chapter 7.

- **Anegada Reef Hotel** (Anegada, British Virgin Islands; ☎ 284/495-8002): Located some 20 miles north of Virgin Gorda's North Sound on a flat mass of coral and limestone, this hotel is one of the most remote spots in the entire Virgin Island chain. It's not polished or refined in any way, and is loved by the yachting set that cruises through these islands. Chances are you may never meet most of the 250 local residents, although you'll occasionally see snorkelers, fishers, and scuba divers. We recommend this low-maintenance hotel for devotees of deserted beaches: It's the kind of place where if the bartender isn't around, you make your own cocktails and write down what you had. See chapter 7.

- **Peter Island Resort** (Peter Island, British Virgin Islands; ☎ 800/346-4451): This exquisite resort inn sits on an 1,800-acre private island, which comes complete with five pristine beaches, hiking trails, and gorgeous offshore reefs. Guests have free rein here and also enjoy first-rate water sports facilities, elegant candlelight dining, and secluded beachfront accommodations. See chapter 7.

- **Guana Island Club** (Guana Island, British Virgin Islands; ☎ 284/494-2354): The only development on a private 850-acre island, this is one of the most secluded hideaways in the Virgin Islands, maybe in the entire Caribbean Basin. Located off the coast of Tortola, the small, hilltop resort attracts visitors eager to explore the island's nature trails and view its rare species of plant and animal life (look for the rare roseate flamingo). The island, which is a virtual wildlife sanctuary, is also known for its six vacant, virgin beaches. See chapter 7.

11   The Best Restaurants

- **Virgilio's** (St. Thomas, U.S. Virgin Islands; ☎ 809/776-4920): This elegant hide-away boasts the best Italian food on the island. Cheerful and relaxed, Virgilio's lovingly prepares all your favorite Italian classics (try the osso buco or chicken parmigiana), in addition to more than 20 different homemade pasta dishes, and a few surprises too, like *cioppino,* a kettle of savory seafood stew. Savvy diners always save room for one of the flambé desserts. See chapter 4.

- **Eunice's Terrace** (St. Thomas, U.S. Virgin Islands; ☎ 809/775-3975): No one's ever heard of haute cuisine at this airy, bilevel restaurant, but they know how to rattle those West Indian pots and pans. After sampling a lethal rum punch called Queen Mary, dig into broiled fresh fish, conch fritters, herb-stuffed lobster, or savory *callaloo,* a spicy West Indian soup. No one leaves without a slice of Eunice's sweet potato pie, not even President Clinton, who dined here while on vacation with his family in early 1997. See chapter 4.

- **Hervé Restaurant and Wine Bar** (St. Thomas, U.S. Virgin Islands; ☎ 809/777-9703): This newly launched establishment next to the landmark Hotel 1829 has captured much attention, most recently from *Gourmet* magazine. The panoramic view is a minor distraction here, but it's the cuisine that counts, a flavorful American/Caribbean/Continental repertoire that's truly sublime. Nothing beats the black sesame-crusted tuna with a ginger and raspberry sauce. See chapter 4.

- **Asolare** (St. John, U.S. Virgin Islands; ☎ 809/779-4747): The most beautiful and elegant restaurant on St. John is also superlative when it comes to food. Chef Robert Smith roams the world for inspiration and finds it. The result is a fusion French/Asian cuisine that relies on the island's freshest seafood and produce and comes to life in menu items like prawn and coconut milk soup or spicy tuna tartare wrapped in somen noodles. On top of a hill overlooking Cruz Bay, the kitchen prepares dishes with style and flair, and they're served by the most attractive and hippest staff on the island. See chapter 5.

- **Le Château de Bordeaux** (St. John, U.S. Virgin Islands; ☎ 809/776-6611): The view here competes with an exquisite combination of continental and Caribbean cuisine. In our opinion, both are winners. Golden-yellow saffron from the fields of Spain turns pastas into sunbursts, and the West Indian seafood chowder is a perfect blend of fish and spices. Wild game and rack of lamb perfumed with rosemary and a honey-Dijon nut crust appear often on the ever-changing menu. See chapter 5.

- **Indies** (St. Croix, U.S. Virgin Islands; ☎ 809/692-9440): San Francisco–born Catherine Plav-Driggers applies everything she ever learned in California to the rich bounty of the Caribbean. The result is taste and texture unequaled on the island—spicy Caribbean chicken, spring rolls (better than you'll find in Chinatown), and grouper brought to life with coconut milk, shrimp, tomato, ginger, and scallions. The sheltered 19th-century courtyard where meals are served completes this unforgettable dining experience. See chapter 6.

- **Kendricks,** (St. Croix, U.S. Virgin Islands; ☎ 809/773-9199): In a brick building crafted from 19th-century ballast, David and Jane Kendrick bring a light continental touch to richly flavored dishes. You might begin with baked brie smothered in perfectly seasoned wild mushrooms, then move on to coconut shrimp in a chive-studded, jalapeño-peppery aioli. Some of this culinary couple's recipes have been featured in *Bon Appetit* magazine. See chapter 6.

- **Skyworld** (Tortola, British Virgin Islands; ☎ 284/494-3567): With a 360° view of Tortola and its sister isles, sunsets that turn the whole sky a fiery red, and one or two Pascha Coladas (passion fruit juice, rum, and cream of coconut) in hand, who cares about dinner? Here they do. The eclectic cuisine is heavy on fresh fish—mushrooms stuffed with conch and seafood au gratin are two wonderful ways to begin your meal. Don't miss the refreshing key lime pie, touted as the best on the island. See chapter 7.

12 The Best Shopping Buys

The U.S. Virgin Islands are the shopping mecca of the Caribbean, mostly because there's no sales tax and shoppers can take advantage of the $1,200 duty-free allowance. St. Thomas has long been the major destination, and its shops and streetside pushcarts, especially in Charlotte Amalie, continue to soak up visitors' dollars. Look for two local publications, *This Week in St. Thomas* or *Best Buys*—either will steer you toward the goods you want. Also, before you leave home, always check out the price of comparable items you hope to buy in St. Thomas; that way, you'll know if you are really getting a bargain or not (see the shopping section in chapter 4 for more details). St. Croix also offers some discount shopping (see chapter 6), but it's next to nothing compared to St. Thomas.

With that said, your best deals will most likely be found in the following merchandise:

- **Arts and Crafts:** While arts and crafts are not the high-priority items they are on such islands as Haiti and Jamaica, you can find them in the Virgin Islands. The Jim Tillett Gallery (Tillett Gardens; ☎ **809/775-1929**), in St. Thomas, is the premier art gallery and craft studio in the U.S. Virgin Islands. The staff's silk screening has been featured in fashion layouts around the world. In St. John, Mongoose Junction, the woodsy roadside area right at Cruz Bay, offers the best assortment of locally produced arts and crafts (all tax free for U.S. citizens) of any place on the island. Handmade pottery, sculpture, and glass are sold in shops here, along with locally made clothing. In Christiansted on St. Croix, seek out **Folk Art Traders** (☎ **809/773-1900**) for the largest selection of Caribbean arts and crafts. But if you crave handcrafts exclusive to the U.S. Virgin Islands, head for **Many Hands** (☎ **809/773-1990**), also in Christiansted at the Pan Am Pavilion.

- **Fine China and Crystal:** Sometimes (not always) you can find substantial savings on these wares—many shoppers report savings of 30 percent to 50 percent. For example, a Rosenthal place setting (the same pattern Elizabeth Taylor purchased) might go for half the price it sells for on Fifth Avenue. Baccarat goblets, as we recently noted in a price comparison on St. Thomas, went for about a third of the price quoted in the U.S. catalog. Again, know your prices before you land on St. Thomas. That way, you can wander with more knowledge through the vast field of Waterford, Orrefors, Hummel, Wedgwood, Royal Worcester, Royal Doulton, and others.

- **Jewelry:** Watches and gold jewelry are often heavily discounted in St. Thomas and St. Croix, especially during the off-season (mid-April to mid-October), when there aren't 12 cruise ships anchored at Charlotte Amalie. The sheer volume of jewelry offered in St. Thomas is stunning—diamonds, emeralds, rubies, opals, gold, platinum, both world-famous names and one-of-a-kind pieces created by local artists. But you'll want to do comparison shopping even in St. Thomas—that Rolex might be selling for less at a store just around the corner.

- **Liquor:** A recent spot survey showed that prices for liquor in St. Thomas and St. Croix were 50 percent to 60 percent less than in New York City. You're allowed to bring five fifths of liquor back to the United States, or six fifths if the sixth is locally produced. Local liquor nearly always means rum in the Virgin Islands, but it could also mean Southern Comfort, which is also bottled on the island (check the label). Because of the generous U.S. Customs allowances in the Virgin Islands, St. Thomas or St. Croix might be the best place to purchase expensive French brandy, champagne, or an otherwise pricey liqueur.

- **Perfumes and Cosmetics:** Be on the lookout for bargains on imported perfumes and beauty products such as bath gels and makeup, if you know what such merchandise costs at your local discount outlet in the States. How much you save depends on the product. For example, we recently did some comparison shopping between New York City and Charlotte Amalie. An ounce of Yves St. Laurent's Opium was $40 cheaper in St. Thomas than in Manhattan, as was Giorgio. **Tropicana Perfume Shoppes** (☎ 809/774-0010) on Main Street in Charlotte Amalie has the largest selection of fragrances for both women and men in the U.S. Virgin Islands.

13 The Best Nightlife

If you're a serious party animal, you'll want to avoid St. John and virtually all of the British Virgin Islands (with some exceptions) and concentrate on St. Thomas and St. Croix. Below are the latest hot spots in the Virgin Islands:

- **Turtle Rock Bar at the Wyndham Sugar Bay Beach Club** (St. Thomas, U.S. Virgin Islands; ☎ 809/777-7100): Located near Red Hook, this place is known for its burgers and bar scene. There's always something going on here—sometimes it's karaoke, and other nights steel-pan bands or other local talent. Happy hour, from 4 to 6pm, is always happenin' with half-price cocktails. See chapter 4.

- **Walter's** (St. Thomas, U.S. Virgin Islands; ☎ 809/774-5025): As other touristy bars and night dives come and go, this one endures because it attracts a strong local following, not just visitors. It's intimate and dimly lit, and the action spills across two levels. Whatever your sexual preference you're usually assured of a good time here. See chapter 4.

- **Blue Moon** (St. Croix, U.S. Virgin Islands; ☎ 809/772-2222): On Thursday and Friday nights, this little dive/bistro is the hottest spot in Christiansted. Bobby Page, "The Bobby Short of St. Croix," is at the piano on Thursday, and a lively five-piece ensemble usually entertains the following night. The crowd here is predominantly local, along with a few savvy visitors who turn up from time to time. See chapter 6.

- **The Buccaneer** (St. Croix, U.S. Virgin Islands; ☎ 800/255-3881): This deluxe hotel has the best nightlife on the island. Call to see what or who's on stage during your visit. It could be anything from limbo shows to live reggae. See chapter 6.

- **Bomba's Surfside Shack at Cappoon's Bay** (Tortola, British Virgin Islands; ☎ 284/495-4148): This is the most interesting place to hang out on the British Virgin Islands and one of the most famous bars in the West Indies. Bomba's decor consists of junk and Day-Glo graffiti, but it's got the best electronic amplification on the island. The rum punches are always flowing, and the hottest people in town show up here, especially for the notorious all-night Full Moon Parties. See chapter 7.

14 The Most Intriguing Historical Sights

Most travelers in the Virgin Islands aren't terribly interested in history, at least in Caribbean history. But, for those who are, here are our top choices:

- **Fort Christian** (St. Thomas, U.S. Virgin Islands): Named after the Danish king, Christian V, this fort, which stands in the heart of Charlotte Amalie, was built in 1672 after the arrival of the first colonists. The oldest building on the island, it has been vastly altered over the years and has housed a jail, courthouse, town hall, church, and most recently a historical museum. Head to the roof for a stellar view. See chapter 4.

- **Crown House** (St. Thomas, U.S. Virgin Islands): This 18th-century mansion has served as the home of two former governors. Filled with antiques, the stone-built, two-floor house has a Dutch-hipped roof and memorabilia of Peter von Scholten, one of the island's most famous governors, who occupied the premises in 1827. A French chandelier in the mansion is said to have come from Versailles. See chapter 4.

- **Annaberg Ruins** (St. John, U.S. Virgin Islands): The greatest reminder of St. John's plantation heyday, the ruins of this sugar plantation lie at a point opening onto Leinster Bay. At one time, the smell of boiling molasses filled the air, as hard-working slaves turned out sugar for European markets—visitors can explore the remains of former slave quarters. Mother Nature has returned the land to lush vegetation, and the estate, whose ruins have been spruced up rather than restored, dates from 1780. See chapter 5.

- **Fort Frederick** (St. Croix, U.S. Virgin Islands): This fort, completed in 1760, is said to have been the first to salute the flag of the new United States. When an American brigantine anchored at port in Frederiksted hoisted a homemade Old Glory, the fort returned the salute with cannon fire, violating the rules of neutrality. It was also here, in 1848, that Gov. Peter von Scholten read a proclamation freeing the island's slaves. A small museum sits on the site today. See chapter 6.

- **Fort Christiansvaern** (St. Croix, U.S. Virgin Islands): With a facade that hasn't changed very much since the 1820s, this fort is one of the best preserved of its type in the West Indies. Teetering at the edge of picturesque Christiansted Harbor, it was constructed from ballast bricks imported from Denmark, the island's colonial guardian. The first fort on the spot was built between 1732 and 1749, and part of it remains. Today the site hosts the St. Croix Police Museum. See chapter 6.

2 Discovering the Virgin Islands

Former stamping ground of some of history's most famous seafarers, the Virgin Islands are now invaded by thousands of visitors who arrive daily either by cruise ship or plane from Miami or Puerto Rico.

These green, hilly islands, including those owned by both the United States and Great Britain, number about 100 in all, and most are so tiny that they are virtually uninhabited except for a few birds or an adventurous boating party stopping off for a little snorkeling or skinny-dipping. For an ultimate tropical getaway, you can even rent an entire island for yourself and a carefully chosen companion, if you so desire.

Coral reefs often shield the best beaches from the wicked surf of the Atlantic Ocean, which fronts their northern shorelines, and the southern island rims open onto the usually calmer waters of the Caribbean Sea. St. Croix, south of St. Thomas and St. John, is entirely in the Caribbean Sea.

The name "Virgin" came from Christopher Columbus, that great labeler of Caribbean islands who sailed through them in the late 15th century. Impressed by their number, he called them *Las Once Mil Virgenes* in honor of St. Ursula's 11,000 martyred maidens.

Part of the larger archipelago known as the Lesser Antilles, where the Atlantic Ocean meets the calmer Caribbean Sea, the Virgins are for the most part rich in vegetation, and possess the most ideal temperatures (the average annual temperature is 78°F) in the West Indies, thanks to the ever-present trade winds that keep the air from getting unbearably hot. In fact, both the U.S. Virgin Islands and British Virgin Islands report lower humidity levels than many of the other Caribbean isles, making them the quintessential vacation paradise, both in summer and in winter. The greatest number of visitors come between December and April; summer is slower and a bit hotter, but, to compensate, all hotels lower their prices.

Rain showers do come, but they are usually a welcome relief from the sun and pass quickly, except during hurricane season. On nearly any day of the year, you can count on sunshine, at least for part of the day.

Most Virgin Island natives are descendants of African slaves who worked the sugarcane plantations for their European masters until their emancipation in the mid-1800s.

In recent years, the local population has swelled with an influx of "down islanders"—people from other Caribbean islands. Many Puerto Ricans have also moved to the U.S. islands nearby (it's only 30 minutes by air), joined by many "gringo" Americans from the mainland.

The old ways of the islands are all but gone in bustling St. Thomas and St. Croix, but may still be found in St. John and some pockets of the British Virgins, especially on laid-back Virgin Gorda.

1 Choosing the Perfect Island

Peering at the tiny Virgin Islands chain on a world map, you may find it difficult to distinguish the different islands. They vary widely, however, in looks and personality, and so will your vacation depending on which island or islands you choose. If you can only visit one or two of the islands, use this section to select those that best meet your vacation needs. For example, if you're an avid golfer, you don't want spend a week on a remote British Virgin Island with a rinky-dink nine-hole course, or worse, no course at all. But, that same island might be perfect for a young couple contemplating a romantic honeymoon. By providing detailed information about the character of each island in both the U.S. Virgin Islands and the British Virgin Islands, we hope to guide you to your own idea of paradise.

U.S. VS. BRITISH

American and British cultures have left different imprints on the Virgin Islands. The U.S. Virgin Islands, except for St. John, bear the commercial hustle-and-bustle of the mainland, including supermarkets and fast-food chains. In contrast, the British islands to the east are rather sleepy. Except for a few deluxe hotels, mostly on Virgin Gorda, they recall the way the Caribbean was before the advent of high-rise condos, McDonalds, and flotillas of cruise ships.

If you want shopping, a wide selection of restaurants and hotels, and nightlife, head to the U.S. Virgin Islands, particularly St. Thomas and St. Croix. With a little research and effort, you can find peace and quiet on these two islands, most often at outlying resorts.

Among the U.S. Virgin Islands only St. John matches the British Virgins' tranquility. Protected by the Forest Service, it is the least developed of the U.S. islands. St. John is a rugged mixture of bumpy dirt roads, scattered inhabitants, and a handful of stores and services.

As we mentioned earlier, the British Virgin Islands languish in the past, but today even year-round residents can't deny that change is in the air. Tortola, the capital, is the most populated British isle, but its shopping, nightlife, and dining are limited. It's more a spot for boaters of all stripes and is duly considered the cruising capital of the Caribbean. To the east, Virgin Gorda claims most of the B.V.I.'s deluxe hotels. There are also attractive accommodations and restaurants on the smaller islands, such as Jost Van Dyke, Anegada, and Peter Island.

THE MAJOR ISLANDS IN BRIEF
ST. THOMAS

The most developed island in the Virgin Islands, St. Thomas at times resembles a small city. There are peaceful retreats, but you must seek them out. The harbor at **Charlotte Amalie** is the cruise-ship haven of the Caribbean, and many locals and seasonal residents try to avoid it when the greatest concentration of vessels is in port (usually from December to April).

The Caribbean Islands

Charlotte Amalie, the capital, has the widest selection of duty-free shopping in the Caribbean. However, you must browse carefully through the labyrinth of bazaars to find the real bargains.

Like most of the Virgin Islands, there's plenty of opportunity to get outside and get active, although many visitors come here simply to sit, sun, and maybe go for a swim. **Magens Bay Beach,** with its tranquil surf and sugar-white sand, is one of the most beautiful beaches in the world, but it is likely to be packed, especially on heavy cruise-ship days. More secluded beaches include Secret Harbour and Sapphire Beach in East End.

Yachts and boats anchor at Ramada Yacht Haven Marina in and at **Red Hook Marina** on the island's somewhat isolated eastern tip. The serious yachting crowd, however, gathers at Tortola (see below) in the British Virgin Islands.

St. Thomas has only one golf course—Mahogany Run—but it's a gem, with three tricky holes (13, 14, and 15) known throughout the golfing world as "Devil's Triangle."

Sport fishers angle from the American Yacht Harbor at Red Hook, and the island also attracts snorkelers and scuba divers—there are tons of outfitters offering equipment, excursions, and instruction. Kayaking and parasailing are also drawing more and more beach bums away from the water's edge.

St. Thomas has the most eclectic and sophisticated restaurant scene in the Virgin Islands, with special emphasis on French and continental fare. It pays more for its imported (usually European) chefs and secures the freshest of ingredients from mainland or Puerto Rican markets. The wide selection of eateries, from Mexican and Italian to Asian and American, adds an international flavor to the island's limited West Indian fare.

The island St. Thomas boasts a variety of accommodations, from Bluebeard's Castle (a perennial favorite) to more modern beachfront complexes in the East End, including the manicured Elysian Beach Resort. Apartment and villa rentals abound, and there is also a handful of old-fashioned B&B–style guest houses to be found.

If St. Thomas has one drawback, it's that it's no longer as safe a destination. Crime is on the rise, and muggings are frequent. Wandering the island at night, especially on the back streets of Charlotte Amalie, is not recommended.

ST. JOHN

Our personal favorite of all the U.S. Virgin Islands, St. John has only two deluxe hotels but several charming inns and plenty of campgrounds. Its primary attraction is the **U.S. Virgin Islands National Park,** which covers more than half of the island. Guided walks in the wild and safari bus tours are available to help you navigate the park, which is full of pristine beaches, secret coves, flowering trees, and ghostly remains of sugarcane plantations. A third of the park is underwater. The most panoramic submerged trail is at Trunk Bay, which also boasts the island's most coveted beach, despite the pickpockets. It has consistently been named one of the world's 10 best by *Condé Nast Traveler*.

The place to play tennis is **Caneel Bay,** which has 11 courts, a pro shop (complete with teaching pro), and a long-standing tradition of tennis-playing guests. Excellent snorkeling and scuba diving have long lured visitors to St. John, which is also a preferred destination for hikers because of the extensive network of trails covering the national park.

St. John has a handful of posh restaurants, as well as a number of colorful West Indian eateries. Many residents and long-term visitors like to bring cooking supplies over on the ferryboat from St. Thomas, where prices are presumably lower and the selection broader. Nightlife usually means sipping rum drinks in a **Cruz Bay** bar and

---

A Famous Virgin Islander: Dr. Frasier Crane

Born in St. Thomas, Kelsey Grammer is known to TV audiences around the world as Dr. Frasier Crane, the egghead/psychologist at the bar in the long-running TV series *Cheers.* In 1993, he launched his own spin-off series, *Frasier,* which has also proved to be a prime-time hit. Grammer studied acting at New York's Juilliard School, but he was eventually kicked out. He went on to play in *Macbeth* and *Othello.*

---

maybe listening to a local calypso band. After a spending a day outdoors, most visitors to St. John are happy to turn in early.

St. Croix

This island is the second major tourist destination in the Virgin Islands. Like St. Thomas, St. Croix has been grossly overdeveloped, and cruise-ship passengers continue to flood its capital, **Christiansted,** looking for duty-free goods and a handful of white sand to take home in a plastic bag. While parts of it resemble American suburbia, some of St. Croix's true West Indian–style buildings have been preserved, along with some of its rich cultural traditions.

One of the best reasons for a trip to St. Croix, even if only for a day, is **Buck Island National Park,** just 1¹/₂ miles off St. Croix's northeast coast. Its offshore reef is the only underwater national monument and attracts snorkelers and certified divers from around the world. Blue signs posted along the ocean floor guide you through a woodland of staghorn coral that's swarming with flamboyant fish.

Golfers consider St. Croix the premier destination in the Virgin Islands, mainly because it boasts the archipelago's most challenging 18-hole course: Carambola. Designed by Robert Trent Jones Sr., it plays to a length of more than 6,900 yards. St. Croix is also a tennis mecca of sorts. The luxurious Buccaneer Hotel has some of the best courts in the Virgin Islands and hosts several annual tournaments. Other sports for active vacationers include horseback riding, parasailing, sport fishing, waterskiing, snorkeling, and scuba diving.

The restaurants on St. Croix are not as good as those on St. Thomas, although they claim to be. The highly touted Top Hat, for example, prides itself on its Danish dishes, but split-pea soup and *Frikadeller* (meatballs with red cabbage) may not be exactly what you're looking for on a hot Caribbean night. Life after dark is mostly confined to a handful of bars in Christiansted.

St. Croix has only a few real luxury hotels, but there are a lot of small, attractive inns (we highly recommend Pink Fancy). And, as on St. Thomas, it's easy to find villas and condos for rent at reasonable weekly rates.

For the most part life here is laid back; however, St. Croix is certainly not problem-free. Racial tension, even violence, is not uncommon. At night, use discretion and avoid the back streets of Christiansted, and more importantly, Frederiksted.

Tortola

With its capital at **Road Town,** Tortola is the hub of the British Virgin Islands, but not always the best place for visitors, especially if you're planning to spend more than a couple of days here—we think Virgin Gorda (see below) has better hotels and restaurants. Road Town, with its minor shopping, routine restaurants, and uninspired architecture, deserves a couple of hours at the most. Once you leave the capital, however, you'll find Tortola more alluring. The island's best (and most unspoiled) beaches, including Smuggler's Cove with its garden of snorkeling reefs, lie at the

The Virgin Islands

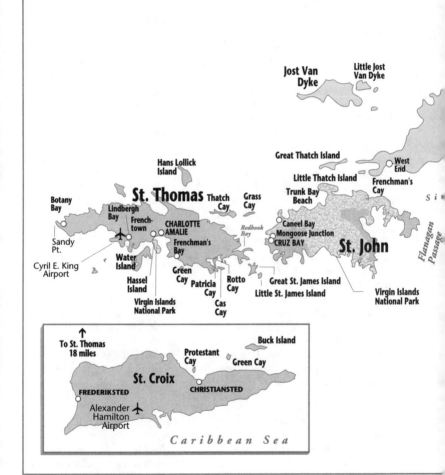

Atlantic

Jost Van Dyke

Little Jost Van Dyke

Hans Lollick Island

St. Thomas Thatch Cay

Grass Cay

Great Thatch Island

West End

Little Thatch Island

Frenchman's Cay

Trunk Bay Beach

Botany Bay

Lindbergh Bay

French-town

CHARLOTTE AMALIE

Frenchman's Bay

Redhook Bay

Caneel Bay

Mongoose Junction

CRUZ BAY

St. John

Si

Sandy Pt.

Cyril E. King Airport

Water Island

Green Cay

Patricia Cay

Rotto Cay

Great St. James Island

Little St. James Island

Flanagan Passage

Hassel Island

Cas Cay

Virgin Islands National Park

Virgin Islands National Park

↑
To St. Thomas
18 miles

Buck Island

Protestant Cay

Green Cay

St. Croix

FREDERIKSTED

CHRISTIANSTED

Alexander Hamilton Airport

Caribbean Sea

0   8.55 km
    5 mi

Anegada

The Settlement

O c e a n

Prickly
Pear
Island

Necker Island

Mosquito
Island

Seal Dogs

*North
Sound*

Eustatia

George Dog

West Dog

South Sound

Guana
Island

Great Camanoe
Little
Camanoe

Scrub
Island

Great Dog

Tortola East
End

Marina Cay

Spanish
Town

Virgin Gorda

Beef
Island

Road
Town

F r a n c i s   D r a k e   C h a n n e l

Fallen
Jerusalem

*Salt
Island
Passage*

Cooper
Island

Round
Rock

Ginger
Island

Salt
Island

Peter
Island

Norman Island

C a r i b b e a n   S e a

British Virgin Islands

U.S. Virgin Islands

Impressions

There could never be lands any more favorable in fertility, in mildness and pleasantness of climate, in abundance of good and pure water. A very peaceful and hopeful place that should give all adventurers great satisfaction.
— Captain Nathaniel Butler, HM *Frigate Nicodemus*, 1637

island's western tip. Tortola's premier beach is **Cane Garden Bay,** a 1½-mile stretch of white sand. Because of its gentle surf, it's one of the most secure places for families with small children.

While many visitors to the Caribbean look forward to fishing, hiking, horseback riding, snorkeling, and surfing, what makes Tortola exceptional is boating. It is *the* boating center of the British Virgin Islands, which are among the most cherished sailing territories on the planet. The island offers some 100 charter yachts and 300 bareboats, and its marina and shore facilities are the most up-to-date and extensive in the Caribbean Basin.

The crystal-clear waters compensate for the island's lackluster bars and restaurants. You can count on the food being simple and straightforward—we suggest any locally caught fish grilled with perhaps a little lime butter.

VIRGIN GORDA

Our favorite British Virgin Island is Virgin Gorda, the third-largest member of the archipelago, with a permanent population of about 1,000 lucky souls. Many visitors come over just for a day to check out **The Baths,** an astounding collection of gigantic rocks, boulders, and tide pools on the southern tip. Shaped by volcanic pressures millions of years ago, they have eroded into shapes reminiscent of a Henry Moore sculpture. With more than 20 uncrowded beaches, the best known of which are Spring Beach and Trunk Beach, Virgin Gorda is a sun worshiper's dream come true.

Unlike Tortola, Virgin Gorda has some of the finest hotels in the Virgin Islands, including Little Dix Bay and Biras Creek, but you must be willing to pay the price for the privilege of staying at these regal resorts. There are more reasonable places to stay, such as Olde Yard Inn, which feels like an old-fashioned retreat. Outside the upscale hotels, restaurants tend to be simple places serving the local West Indian cuisine. No one takes nightlife too seriously on Virgin Gorda—a lucky thing, because there isn't very much of it.

2 The Virgin Islands Past & Present

Dateline

- 1493 Columbus sails by the Virgin Islands and is attacked by Carib Indians on St. Croix.
- 1625 Dutch and English establish frontier outposts on St. Croix.
- 1650 Spanish forces from Puerto Rico overrun English garrison on St. Croix.

A BRIEF HISTORY

Christopher Columbus is credited with "discovering" the Virgin Islands in 1493, but, in fact, they had already been inhabited for 3,000 years. It is believed that the original settlers were the nomadic Ciboney (or Siboney) Indians who migrated from the mainland of South America and lived off the islands' fish and vegetation. The first real homesteaders were the peaceful Arawak Indians, who arrived from Venezuela, presumably in dugout canoes with sails.

For about 500 years, the Arawaks occupied the Virgin Islands until the arrival of the cannibalistic Carib Indians in the 15th century. The Caribs destroyed the Arawaks, either by working them to death as slaves or by eating them. With the advent of European explorers and their diseases, these tribes were completely wiped out.

THE AGE OF COLONIZATION   In November of 1493, on his second voyage to the New World, Columbus spotted the Virgin Islands, naming them *Las Once Mil Virgenes,* after the Christian St. Ursula and her martyred maidens. Short of water, he decided to anchor at what is now Salt River on St. Croix's north shore. Instead of water, his men were greeted by a rainfall of arrows. Embittered, Columbus called that part of the island *Cabo de Flechas* or "Cape of the Arrows" and sailed toward Puerto Rico.

As the sponsor of Columbus's voyage, Spain claimed the Virgin Islands; however, with greater interests in the Greater Antilles, Spain chose not to colonize the Virgin Islands, leaving the door open to other European powers. In 1625, both the English and the Dutch established opposing frontier outposts on St. Croix. Struggles between the two nations for control of the island continued for about 20 years, until the English prevailed.

The islands soon became a virtual battleground, as the struggle among European powers widened. In 1650, Spanish forces from Puerto Rico overran the British garrison on St. Croix. Soon after the Dutch invaded, and in 1653 the island fell into the hands of the Knights of Malta, who gave St. Croix its name. However, these aristocratic French cavaliers weren't exactly prepared for West Indian plantation life, and their debts quickly mounted. By 1674 Louis XIV of France took control of St. Croix and made it part of his kingdom.

The English continued to fight Dutch settlers in Tortola, which was considered the most important of the British Virgin Islands. It wasn't until 1672 that England added the entire archipelago to its growing empire.

A year before, in March 1671, the Danish West India Company made an attempt to settle St. Thomas. They sent two ships, but only one, the *Pharaoh,* completed the voyage with about a third of its crew. Eventually reinforcements arrived, and by 1679, at least 156 Europeans were reported living on St. Thomas, not including their slaves.

- **1671** Danes take over St. Thomas.
- **1672** England adds British Virgin Islands to its empire.
- **1674** Louis XIV of France makes St. Croix part of his empire.
- **1717** Danish planters from St. Thomas cultivate plantations on St. John.
- **1724** St. Thomas is declared a free port.
- **1733** Danish West India Company purchases St. Croix from France; slaves revolt on St. John.
- **1792** Denmark announces plans to abandon the slave trade.
- **1801** England occupies the Danish Virgin Islands for 10 months.
- **1807–15** England reoccupies Danish Virgin Islands.
- **1834** England frees 5,133 slaves living in B.V.I.
- **1848** Under pressure, the governor of St. Croix grants slaves emancipation.
- **1870** U.S. Senate rejects treaty with Denmark for sale of the Virgin Islands.
- **1902** Danish Parliament rejects U.S. offer of $5 million for sale of its islands.
- **1916** Denmark signs treaty with the United States and sells islands for $25 million.
- **1917** U.S. Virgin Islands fall under the control of the U.S. Navy for 14 years.
- **1927** United States grants citizenship to island residents.
- **1936** Under FDR, the first Organic Act is passed, granting voting rights to U.S. Virgin Islanders.
- **1940** Population of U.S. Virgins increases for the first time since 1860.
- **1946** First black governor of the islands is appointed.
- **1954** Revised Organic Act passed; islands under

continues

jurisdiction of Department of the Interior.

- **1966** Queen Elizabeth II visits the British Virgin Islands.
- **1967** B.V.I. get a new constitution.
- **1970** Officials are elected rather than appointed.
- **1989** Hurricane Hugo rips through islands, especially St. Croix.
- **1995** Hurricane Marilyn causes millions in damage, leaving thousands homeless.
- **1996** Water Island, off the coast of St. Thomas, is officially declared the fourth U.S. Virgin Island.
- **1997** Pres. Bill Clinton, along with Hilary and Chelsea Clinton, draw worldwide media attention to St. Thomas and the U.S.V.I. when they vacation here in January.

Captain Kidd, Sir Francis Drake, Blackbeard, and the other legendary pirates of the West Indies continued to use St. Thomas as their base for maritime raids in the area. Its harbor also became notorious for its bustling slave market.

In 1717 Danish planters sailed over to St. John from St. Thomas to begin cultivating plantations, and by 1733 an estimated 100 sugar, tobacco, and cotton plantations were operating on the island. That same year the slaves rebelled against their colonial masters, taking control of the island for about 6 months and killing many Europeans. It took hundreds of French troops to quell the rebellion.

In that same year France sold St. Croix to the Danish West India Company, which divided the island into plantations, boosting the already flourishing slave trade. Some historians say that nearly 250,000 slaves were sold on the auction blocks at Charlotte Amalie before being sent elsewhere, often to America's Deep South. By 1792 Denmark changed its tune and announced that it officially planned to end the slave trade. It was not until 1848, however, that it did so. The British had freed their 5,133 slaves in 1834.

The great economic boom that resulted from the Virgin Island plantations began to wilt by the 1820s. The introduction of sugar beet virtually bankrupted plantation owners, as the demand for cane sugar drastically declined.

Cuba eventually took over the sugar market in the Caribbean. By 1872 the British had so little interest in the British Virgins that they placed them in the loosely conceived and administered Federation of the Leeward Islands.

ENTER THE UNITED STATES   In 1867 the United States attempted to purchase the islands from Denmark, but the treaty was rejected by the U.S. Senate in 1870. The asking price was $7.5 million.

Following its acquisition of Puerto Rico in 1902, the United States expressed renewed interest in acquiring the Danish islands. This time the United States offered to pay $5 million, but the Danish parliament spurned the offer.

Upon the eve of its entry into World War I, the U.S. Navy began to fear a possible German takeover of the islands. The United States was concerned that the kaiser's navy, using the islands as a base, might prey on shipping through the Panama Canal. After renewed attempts by the United States to purchase the islands, Denmark agreed to sell them for $25 million, a staggering sum to pay for island real estate in those days.

By 1917, the United States was in full control of the islands, and Denmark retreated from the Caribbean after a legacy of nearly 2$^{1}/_{2}$ centuries. The U.S. Navy looked after the islands for 14 years, and in 1954 the Virgin Islands came under the sovereignty of the U.S. Department of the Interior.

Some money was diverted to the area during the Prohibition era, as some islanders made rum and shipped it illegally to the United States, often through Freeport, Bahamas. In 1927, the United States granted citizenship to the island residents. In

---

A 51st State?

U.S. Virgin Islanders are not allowed to vote in national elections, a sore spot among some of the local residents. Many hope to see another star added to the flag in the near future, while others prefer not to rock the boat.

When the 1936 Organic Act of the Virgin Islands was passed under the Roosevelt administration, residents 21 and over were granted suffrage and could elect two municipal councils and a legislative assembly for the islands. In 1946, the first black governor of the islands, William Hastie, was appointed, and by 1970 the U.S. Virgin Islanders had the right to elect their own governor and lieutenant governor.

Today, the U.S. Virgin Islands remain an unincorporated territory administered by the U.S. Department of the Interior, and they send a nonvoting delegate to the House of Representatives. Politically speaking, the Virgin Islands, like Puerto Rico, remain outside the family of the United States—their residents continue to elect 15 senators to their own legislature.

Today, islanders are demanding more representation, and they feel that only statehood will provide the respect, power, and influence needed to turn the islands into more than just a "colony." But as of yet Washington doesn't seem to be actively pursuing statehood for the Virgin Islands, and it seems unlikely. The question is raised at each new election of congress or of a president, but progress in this direction moves sleepily along, if at all.

1936, under FDR, the first Organic Act was passed, giving the islanders voting rights. This act was revised in 1954, granting them a greater degree of self-government.

Jobs generated by World War II finally woke the islands from their long economic slumber. Visitors started to appear on the islands, and in the postwar economic boom that swept across America, the Virgin Islands at long last found a replacement for sugar.

The British Virgin Islands were finally freed from the Leeward Islands Federation in 1956, and in 1966 Queen Elizabeth II visited this remote colonial outpost. By 1967 the British Virgin Islands received a new constitution. Tourism was slower in coming to the B.V.I. than to the U.S.V.I., but it is now the mainstay of the economy.

THE ISLANDS TODAY   The United States dominated the Virgins more than any colonial foreign force ever did. As a result, the American way of life prevails today in the U.S. Virgin Islands, and it has even swept across to the British Virgin Islands. The region's traditional recipes and remedies, as well as the self-reliant arts of fishing, boat building, farming, and even hunting, are all but gone. When islanders need something, they have it shipped down from Miami. In clothes, in cars, in food, in entertainment, and in currency, America, not Great Britain, rules the seas around both archipelagos.

These days the news coming out of the Virgin Islands is rarely political. In fact, most often it's about the weather, as it was in 1995 when Hurricane Marilyn ripped through here. Some islanders had barely recovered from the devastation of Hurricane Hugo in 1989 when fiery Marilyn arrived. Following Marilyn's attack, reconstruction efforts in many places have been slow. Even by the end of 1996, some properties—especially those facing difficult insurance adjustments—hadn't fully recovered.

In late 1996, Water Island, off the coast of St. Thomas, became the fourth U.S. Virgin Island when Washington officials agreed to transfer it to the U.S.V.I.

government. About 430 acres of the island, currently owned by the U.S. Department of the Interior, remain to be transferred. The U.S. government also agreed to allocate $3 million for an island-wide clean-up.

The U.S.V.I. drew worldwide media attention in early 1997 when President Clinton, along with Hilary and Chelsea Clinton, vacationed in St. Thomas, an island that's still rebuilding from severe hurricane damage in 1995.

3 The Cuisine: A Taste of the Virgin Islands

Just as food critics were composing eulogies for traditional cooking in the Virgin Islands, there was a last-minute resurgence. Many of the old island dishes have made a comeback, and little taverns, often shanties, offering regional specialties are popping up everywhere. For a price, you can now escape hamburger hell and taste some real Caribbean flavors. In the individual island chapters, we recommend specific restaurants offering the best in West Indian or Virgin Island cuisine.

Still, however, a visit to the Virgin Islands is hardly complete without an indulgence or two in callaloo or conch Creole. The islands are home to some of the Caribbean's best chefs—many hailing from the United States and Europe—and they prepare a variety of sumptuous cuisines, from French and Italian to Mexican and Asian.

When dining in the Virgins, try fresh fish, especially dolphin (not the mammal), wahoo, yellowtail, grouper, and red snapper. These fish, accompanied by a hot lime sauce, are among the tastiest island specialties. Watch out for the sweet Caribbean lobster. It's likely to be overpriced and overcooked, and many diners, especially those from Maine, feel that it's not worth the price.

The major resort hotels often feature elaborate buffets, which inevitably include some West Indian dishes along with more standard continental fare. They're almost always reasonable in price, and you'll most likely enjoy the sounds of a West Indian fungi band while you eat (fungi music is a melodious, usually improvised, blend of African and Spanish sounds). You don't have to be a hotel guest to indulge, but you do need to make a reservation.

THE CUISINE

APPETIZERS   The most famous soup of the islands is *kallaloo,* or callaloo, made in an infinite number of ways with a leafy green vegetable similar to spinach. It's wildly flavored with salt beef, pig mouth, pig tail, hot peppers, ham bone, fresh fish, crab, or perhaps corned conch, along with okra, onions, and spices.

Many soups are sweetened with sugar and often contain fruit; for example, the classic red bean soup, made with pork or ham, various spices, and tomatoes, is sugared to taste. *Tannia* soup is made with its namesake, a starchy root known as the "Purple Elephant Ear" because of its color and shape; it's combined with salt-fat meat and ham, tomatoes, onions, and spices. *Souse* is an old-time favorite made with the feet, head, and tongue of the pig, and flavored with a lime-based sauce.

Salt-fish salad is traditionally served on Holy Thursday or Good Friday in the Virgin Islands and consists of boneless salt fish, potatoes, onions, boiled eggs, and an oil and vinegar dressing.

Herring gundy is another old-time island favorite; it's a salad made with salt herring, potatoes, onions, green sweet and hot peppers, olives, diced beets, raw carrots, herbs, and boiled eggs.

Don't Let the Jumbies Get Ya!

"Don't let the jumbies get ya!" is an often-heard phrase in the Virgin Islands, particularly when people are leaving their hosts and heading home in the dark. Jumbies, capable of good or bad, are supernatural beings that are believed to live around households. It is said that new settlers from the mainland of the United States never see these jumbies and, therefore, need not fear them. But many islanders believe in their existence, and if queried, they may enthrall you with tales of sightings.

No one seems to agree on exactly what a jumbie is. It has been suggested that it is the spirit of a dead person that didn't go where it belonged. Some islanders disagree with this assessment. "They're the souls of live people," one islander told us, "but they live in the body of the dead." The most prominent jumbies are "mocko jumbies," carnival stilt-walkers seen at all parades.

SIDE DISHES Rice—seasoned, not plain—is popular with Virgin Islanders, who are fond of serving several starches at one meal. Most often rice is flavored with ham or salt pork, tomatoes, garlic, onion, and shortening.

Fungi is a simple cornmeal dumpling, made more interesting with the addition of okra and other ingredients. Sweet fungi is served as a dessert, with sugar, milk, cinnamon, and raisins.

Okra (often spelled *ochroe* in the islands) is a mainstay vegetable, usually accompanying beef, fish, or chicken. It's fried in an iron skillet and flavored with hot pepper, tomatoes, onions, garlic, and bacon fat or butter. *Accra* is another popular dish made with okra, black-eyed peas, salt, and pepper, and fried until golden brown.

The classic vegetable dish, some families serve it every night, is **peas and rice.** The dish usually consists of pigeon peas flavored with ham or salt meat, onion, tomatoes, herbs, and sometimes slices of pumpkin. Pigeon peas, one of the most common vegetables in the islands because they flourish in hot, dry climates, are sometimes called congo peas or *gunga.*

FISH & MEAT Way back when, locals gave colorful names to the various fish brought home for dinner, everything from "ole wife" to "doctors," both of which are whitefish. "Porgies and grunts," along with yellowtail, kingfish, and bonito, also show up on many Caribbean dinner tables. Fish is usually boiled in a lime-flavored brew seasoned with hot peppers and herbs and is commonly served with a creole sauce of peppers, tomatoes, and onions, among other ingredients. **Salt fish and rice** is an excellent low-cost dish, the fish flavored with onion, tomatoes, shortening, garlic, and green pepper.

Conch Creole is a savory brew, seasoned with onions, garlic, spices, hot peppers, and salt pork. Another local favorite is chicken and rice, usually made with Spanish peppers. More adventurous diners might try **curried goat,** the longtime classic West Indian dinner, that's prepared with herbs, cardamom pods, and onions.

The famous **johnnycakes** that accompany many of these fish and meat dishes are made with flour, baking powder, shortening, and salt, then fried or baked.

DESSERTS **Sweet potato pie** is a Virgin Island classic, made with sugar, eggs, butter, milk, salt, cinnamon, raisins, and chopped raw almonds (it's been perfected at Eunice's Terrace on St. Thomas). The exotic fruits of the islands lend themselves to various homemade ice creams, including mango. Long ago, islanders invented many new dishes using local ingredients, like orange-rose sherbet made with fragrant rose petal that's mortar-pounded into a paste and flavored with sugar and orange juice. Guava ice cream is our favorite concoction, as are *soursop,* banana, and papaya. Sometimes dumplings, made with guava, peach, plum, gooseberry, cherry, and apple, are served for dessert.

DRINKS

The island's true poison is **Cruzan rum** made with sugarcane. To help stimulate the local economy, U.S. Customs allows you to bring home an extra bottle of Cruzan rum, in addition to your usual 5-liter liquor allowance.

Long before the arrival of Coca-Cola and Pepsi, many islanders concocted their own drinks with whatever was available, mostly from locally grown fruits. From the guavaberry comes an unusual liqueur rum, which is a mixture of sorrel, fruit, ginger, prunes, raisins, cinnamon, and rum.

Water is generally safe to drink on the islands. Much of the water is stored in cisterns and filtered before it's served. Delicate stomachs, however, should stick to mineral water or club soda. All American sodas and beer are sold in both the U.S.V.I. and the B.V.I. Wines have to be imported from either Europe or the United States, and are usually quite expensive.

3

Planning a Trip to the Virgin Islands

VISITOR INFORMATION

IN THE U.S. Before you take off for the U.S. Virgin Islands, contact the **U.S. Virgin Islands Division of Tourism,** 1270 Ave. of the Americas, New York, NY 10020 (☎ **800/372-USVI** or 212/332-2222; fax 212/332-2223). There are additional offices at the following locations: 225 Peachtree St. NE, Suite 760, Atlanta, GA 30303 (☎ **404/688-0906;** fax 404/525-1102); 500 N. Michigan Ave., Suite 2030, Chicago, IL 60611 (☎ **312/670-8784;** fax 312/670-8788); 900 17th St. NW, Suite 500, Washington, DC 20006 (☎ **202/293-3707;** fax 202/785-2542); 2655 Le Jeune Rd., Suite 907, Coral Gables, FL 33134 (☎ **305/442-7200;** fax 305/445-9044); and 3460 Wilshire Blvd., Los Angeles, CA 90010 (☎ **213/739-0138;** fax 213/739-2005). For details on the British Virgin Islands, get in touch with the **British Virgin Islands Tourist Board,** 370 Lexington Ave., Suite 1605, New York, NY 10017 (☎ **800/835-8530** or 212/696-0400; fax 212/949-8254). On the West Coast, contact the **BVI Information Office,** 1804 Union St., San Francisco, CA 94123 (☎ **800/232-7770** or 415/775-0344; fax 415/775-2554).

IN THE U.K. Tourist information for the British Virgin Islands is available at the **BVI Information Office,** 110 St. Martin's Lane, London, England WC2N 4DY (☎ **0171/240-4259;** fax 0171/240-4270). For the U.S. Virgin Islands, information is available at 2 Cinnamon Row, Plantation Wharf, York Place, London, England SW11 3TW (☎ **0171/978-5262;** fax 0171/924-3171).

@VIRGIN ISLANDS

If you have Internet access, "City.net" (**http://www.city.net/regions/Caribbean**) is a great Web site that will point you toward a wealth of travel information on both the U.S. Virgin Islands and the British Virgin Islands. Another good place to start is "Caribbean On-Line" (**http://www.webcom.com/earleltd**), a series of virtual guidebooks packed with information on hotels, restaurants, shopping, beaches, sports outfitters, and more. If you're set on the U.S. Virgin Islands, the best place to go is "America's Caribbean

Paradise: The U.S. Virgin Islands" (**http://www.usvi.net**); for the B.V.I., it's "The British Virgin Islands Welcome Tourist Guide On-Line" (**http://www.bviwelcome.com/**).

ENTRY REQUIREMENTS

U.S. and Canadian citizens are required to present some proof of citizenship—a passport, voter registration card, or birth certificate—to enter the Virgin Islands. While a passport is not necessary, it is the best form of identification and will speed you through Customs and Immigration.

If you do carry a passport, you can take an excursion to the nearby Leeward Islands such as Anguilla or St. Maarten, which are foreign destinations. Entry into one of these little island countries is always easier with a passport, even though some of them don't absolutely require it if your other documentation is acceptable.

Visitors from Europe and other parts of the world do need a passport and a U.S. visa to enter the U.S. Virgin Islands. Those who stay less than 6 months in the B.V.I. need only a passport and a return or onward ticket.

Before you leave, make two copies (leave one at home) of your most valuable documents, including your passport, driver's license, voter registration card (if you're using that instead of a license), airline tickets, and hotel vouchers. If you're on medication, you should also make copies of prescriptions.

CUSTOMS

Because the U.S. Virgin Islands are duty-free ports and U.S. citizens are allowed to bring back $1,200 worth of duty-free goods, Americans must clear Customs when they are leaving the U.S. Virgin Islands. Americans flying directly from the U.S.V.I. do not have to clear Customs when they arrive in the United States. Customs procedures for Canadian, Australian, British, and other foreign travelers to the U.S.V.I. are the same as on the mainland.

In the British Virgin Islands, there is a Customs review upon entry. You can usually bring items intended for personal use into the B.V.I. *No illegal drugs allowed.*

BRINGING IT ALL HOME

U.S. Customs   The government generously allows $1,200 worth of duty-free imports every 30 days, twice the amount allowed for most Caribbean Basin countries (including the British Virgin Islands), and exactly three times the $400 exemption U.S. visitors are allowed returning from most foreign countries and French islands such as Guadeloupe or Martinique. Purchases made in the U.S. Virgin Islands over the duty-free exemption are taxed at a flat rate of 5% (10% in the British Virgin Islands).

Joint declarations are possible for members of a family traveling together: For a husband and wife with two children, the exemption in the U.S. Virgins is $4,800!

Unsolicited gifts of $100 per day from the U.S. Virgin Islands can be sent to friends and relatives, and they do not have to be declared as part of your $1,200 duty-free allowance. Gifts mailed from the B.V.I. cannot exceed $50 per day. U.S. citizens can bring back 5 liters of liquor duty free, plus an extra liter of rum (including Cruzan rum) if one of the bottles is produced in the Islands. U.S. Customs exempts goods made on the island, including perfume, jewelry, clothing, and original paintings; however, if the price of an item exceeds $25, you must show a certificate of origin. If you purchased such an item during an earlier trip abroad, carry proof that you have already paid Customs duty on the item at the time of your previous reentry.

Be sure to collect receipts for all purchases in the Virgin Islands, and beware of merchants offering to give you a false receipt—he or she might be an informer to U.S.

Area Code Change Notice

Please note that, effective October 1, 1997, the area code for the British Virgin Islands will change from **809** to **284.** All of the B.V.I. area codes in this book have been changed to 284. Prior to October 1, you will need to use the 809 area code for all B.V.I. phone numbers.

Customs. Also, keep in mind that any gifts received during your stay must be declared.

If you're concerned about Customs procedures and want more specific guidance, write to the **U.S. Customs Service,** 1301 Constitution Ave., P.O. Box 7407, Washington, DC 20044, requesting the free pamphlet *Know Before You Go.* For information on U.S. Virgin Islands requirements, call **809/774-4554** in St. Thomas.

Canadian Customs   For more information, write for the booklet *I Declare,* issued by **Revenue Canada,** 2265 St. Laurent Blvd., Ontario K1G 4K3 (☎ **613/993-0534**). Canada allows its citizens a $300 exemption, and Canadians can bring back the following items duty free: 200 cigarettes, 2.20 pounds of tobacco, 40 imperial ounces of liquor, and 50 cigars. In addition, Canadian visitors can mail gifts home from abroad at the rate of Can$60 a day, provided they are unsolicited and aren't alcohol or tobacco. Be sure to mark the package "Unsolicited gift, under $60 value." All valuables should be declared on the Y-38 form before leaving Canada; always include serial numbers for more valuable items like cameras that you already own.

Note: The $300 exemption can be used only once a year and only after an absence of 7 days.

British Customs   British travelers can bring home goods up to £136, and you must be 17 or older to import liquor or tobacco. Travelers are allowed 200 cigarettes or 100 cigarillos or 50 cigars or 250 grams of tobacco. In addition, 2 liters of table wine may be brought in, as well as 1 liter of alcohol greater than 22% by volume or 2 liters of alcohol equal to or less than 22% by volume. British Customs policies and procedures are complicated and strictly enforced, so make sure you know the rules before you leave home. For details contact **Her Majesty's Customs and Excise Office,** Dorset House, Stamford St., London, SE1 9NG (☎ **0171/202-4227**).

Australian Customs   The duty-free allowance in Australia is A$400 or, for those under 18, A$200. Personal property mailed back from the Virgin Islands should be marked "Australian Goods Returned," to avoid payment of duty, providing it is what it says on the package. Upon returning to Australia, citizens can bring 250 grams of tobacco and 1 liter of alcohol. If you're returning with valuable goods that you already own, such as expensive foreign-made cameras, you should file form B263. *Customs Information for Travelers* is a helpful brochure available from Australian consulates or Customs offices. For more information, contact Australian Customs Services, GPO Box 8, Sydney NSW 2001 (☎ **02/213-20-00**).

New Zealand Customs   The duty-free allowance is NZ$700. Citizens over 17 years of age can bring in 200 cigarettes or 50 cigars or 250 grams of tobacco (or a mixture of all three if their combined weight doesn't exceed 250 grams), plus 4.5 liters of wine or beer, or 1.125 liters of liquor. New Zealand currency does not carry import or export restrictions. A Certificate of Export listing already-owned valuables taken out of the country allows you to bring them back in without paying duty. Most questions are answered in a free pamphlet available at New Zealand consulates and

Customs offices called *New Zealand Customs Guide for Travelers,* Notice No. 4. For more information, contact New Zealand Customs, 50 Anzac Ave., P.O. Box 29, Auckland (☎ 09/377-35-20).

Irish Customs   Irish citizens may bring in 200 cigarettes or 100 cigarillos or 50 cigars or 250 grams (approximately 9 ounces) of tobacco, plus 1 liter of liquor exceeding 22% by volume (such as whiskey, brandy, gin, rum, or vodka), or 2 liters of distilled beverages and spirits with a wine or alcoholic base of an alcoholic strength not exceeding 22% by volume, plus 2 liters of other wine and 50 grams of perfume. Other allowances include duty-free goods to a value of £34 per person or £17 per person for travelers under 15 years of age. For more information, contact The Revenue Commissioners, Dublin Castle, Dublin 1 (☎ **01/679-27-77**).

MONEY
CASH & CURRENCY

Both the U.S. Virgin Islands and the British Virgin Islands use the U.S. dollar as their form of currency.

British travelers will have to convert their pounds sterling into U.S. dollars. The British pound trades at an average of around 62 pence to one U.S. dollar (or $1.60 = £1). The chart below gives a rough approximation of conversion rates you're likely to find at the time of your trip, but be sure to check them before you leave.

TRAVELER'S CHECKS

It's getting easier each year to find automated-teller machines (ATMs) around the world that will allow you to access your bank account while you're on the road, and that is certainly true of the more heavily touristed Virgin Islands like St. Thomas, St. Croix, and Tortola. But you may be headed for one of the more remote islands or you may just want the security of carrying traveler's checks. Either way, checks denominated in U.S. dollars are widely accepted throughout the U.S. and British Virgin Islands.

The U.S. Dollar & the British Pound

US$	UK£	US$	UK£
.25	.16	15.00	9.38
.50	.31	20.00	12.50
.75	.47	25.00	15.63
1.00	.625	50.00	31.25
2.00	1.25	75.00	46.88
3.00	1.88	100.00	62.50
4.00	2.50	150.00	93.75
5.00	3.13	200.00	125.00
6.00	3.75	250.00	156.25
7.00	4.38	300.00	187.50
8.00	5.00	350.00	218.75
9.00	5.63	400.00	250.00
10.00	6.25	500.00	312.50

What Things Cost in St. Thomas	U.S. $
Taxi from airport to an East End hotel	10.00
Local bus from Charlotte Amalie to Red Hook ferry	1.00
Local telephone call	.25
Double at Marriott's Frenchman's Reef (deluxe)	275.00
Double at Blackbeard's Castle (moderate)	140.00
Double at Island View Guesthouse (budget)	65.00
Lunch for one at Greenhouse (moderate)*	18.00
Lunch for one at Eunice's (budget)*	8.00
Dinner for one at Hotel 1829 (deluxe)*	50.00
Dinner for one at Alexander's (moderate)*	35.00
Dinner for one at East Coast (budget)*	15.00
Pint of beer in a bar	3.50
Coca-Cola in a cafe	1.25
Cup of coffee in a cafe	1.00
Glass of wine in a restaurant	3.75
Roll of ASA 100 color film, 36 exposures	6.25
Admission to Magens Bay Beach	1.00
Movie ticket	5.00
*Includes tax and tip but not wine	

Below is a list of agencies that issue checks and will refund them if lost or stolen, provided you produce sufficient documentation:

American Express (☎ **800/221-7282** in the U.S. and Canada) is one of the largest and most immediately recognized issuers of traveler's checks. No commission is paid by members of AAA, but the checks must be purchased at AAA offices. Also, the 1% commission fee is waived for gold and platinum American Express cardholders.

Citicorp (☎ **800/645-6556** in the U.S. and Canada, or 813/623-1709 collect from other parts of the world) is another major issuer. **Thomas Cook** (☎ **800/223-7373** in the U.S. and Canada, or 609/987-7300 collect from other parts of the world) issues MasterCard traveler's checks, and **Interpayment Services** (☎ **800/221-2426** in the U.S. and Canada, or 212/858-8500 collect from other parts of the world) sells Visa traveler's checks.

ATM NETWORKS

You'll find ATMs in the more commercial islands: St. Thomas, St. Croix, and Tortola. HONOR, CIRRUS, NICE, and PLUS networks operate in **St. Thomas;** look for machines at all banks, the major shopping malls, and at the Pueblo Supermarkets. In **St. Croix,** ATMs are less prevalent, with units located at K-mart, the two Pueblo Supermarkets, and all banks; CIRRUS, NICE, and PLUS are accepted here. On **Tortola,** there are only two ATMs (they accept CIRRUS, NICE, and PLUS), one at the Chase Manhattan Bank and the other at the Banco Popular. Before departing, check with your bank to see if your pin number for either your ATM card or credit card must be reprogrammed for use in the Virgin Islands. Also, determine what the frequency limits for withdrawals and cash advances are for your cards.

CREDIT CARDS

Credit cards are widely accepted in both the U.S.V.I. and the B.V.I. Visa and MasterCard are the cards of choice among local businesses, although American Express and, to a lesser extent, Diners Club are also popular. We've noted which credit cards are accepted at each hotel and restaurant recommended throughout this book.

MONEY GRAMS

If you run out of money on the road, an American Express wire service can help you tap willing friends and family for emergency funds. Through **MoneyGram,** 6200 S. Québec St., P.O. Box 5118, Englewood, CO 80155 (☎ **800/926-9400**), you can send or receive money around the world in less than 10 minutes. Here's how it works: Senders call AmEx to learn the address of the closest office (you don't have to go to an American Express office; often locations are pharmacies or convenience stores). Cash, credit cards, or the occasional personal check (with ID) are acceptable forms of payment. AmEx charges a $10 commission fee for the first $300 with a sliding scale for larger sums (sending $5,000 costs an additional $2,000). Included in the transfer is a 10-word telex-style message and a 3-minute phone call from sender to recipient. Funds can be retrieved by the beneficiary at the most convenient location when proper photo ID is presented, and in some cases, a security code or password established by whomever provides the funds.

The program is now in place in the U.S. Virgin Islands, but not yet in the British Virgin Islands.

2 When to Go

CLIMATE

With each passing year, the Virgin Islands become more of a year-round vacation spot. Why? Sunshine is practically an everyday affair here. Temperatures climb into the 80s during the day and drop more comfortably into the 70s at night. You don't have to worry too much about rain—usually tropical showers come and go so quickly you don't have time to get off the beach.

Average Temperatures (°F) and Rainfall (Inches) in the U.S. Virgin Islands

		Jan	Feb	Mar	Apr	May	June	July	Aug	Sept	Oct	Nov	Dec
St. Thomas	Temp	76. 8	76.7	77.3	79	78.5	81.6	82.2	82.6	81.7	82.6	80.5	76.9
	Precip.	1.86	.95	.97	8.32	9.25	1.62	2.25	3.6	2.04	4.43	7.77	2.46
St. Croix	Temp.	75.9	75.8	77.5	78.7	79.3	81.9	83	83.3	82.6	82	79.8	78.3
	Precip.	2.72	.46	1.44	4.25	7.19	2.35	1.20	4.07	2.11	3.08	7.64	2.77
St. John	Temp.	75. 4	75.1	77.3	78.1	77.8	79.7	80.3	82.6	81.7	80.4	78.3	76.4
	Precip.	2.08	1.03	.81	8.02	10.6	1.92	2.55	4.61	1.86	4.02	8.42	3.44

THE HURRICANE SEASON

The curse of Caribbean weather, the hurricane season, officially lasts June through November. But, don't panic. Each year tropical cyclones pound the U.S. mainland more than hurricanes devastate the Virgin Islands. Hurricane Hugo in 1989 and Hurricane Marilyn in 1995 were the exceptions, however, causing the most widespread damage in years, especially on St. Croix.

Islanders hardly stand around waiting for a hurricane to strike. Satellite forecasts generally give adequate warning so that residents and visitors can take precautions. And of course, there's always prayer: Islanders have a legal holiday in the third week of July called Supplication Day, when they ask to be spared from devastating storms. In late October, they celebrate the end of the season on Hurricane Thanksgiving Day.

If you're heading here during hurricane season, call the nearest branch of the National Weather Service to check the forecast. You'll find a local number in your phone directory under the U.S. Department of Commerce. If you have Internet access, check The Weather Channel's Web site (**http://www.weather.com**) for up-to-date information.

THE "SEASON"

High season in the Virgin Islands, when hotel rates are at their highest, runs roughly from mid-December to mid-April. Winter is generally the dry season in the islands, but heavy rainfall can occur at any time of year.

If you're planning to visit during the winter months, make reservations as far in advance as possible. If you choose to contact hotels directly, you should fax or telephone the hotel of your choice (look for a toll-free number), agree on terms, and rush a deposit to hold the room.

THE "OFF-SEASON"

Off-season begins when North America starts to warm up, and vacationers, assuming that temperatures in the Virgin Islands are soaring into the 100s, head for places like Cape Cod or the Jersey shore. However, it's actually quite balmy all year long in the Virgin Islands—thanks to the fabled trade winds—with temperatures varying little more than 5° between winter and summer.

From mid-April to mid-December, there's an 8-month summer sale here, as hotel rates are slashed a startling 25% to 50%; it's a great time for cost-conscious travelers, especially families, to visit.

But, slashed prices aren't the only reason to visit the Virgin Islands off-season. An even slower pace prevails in spring, summer, and autumn, when you'll have a better chance to appreciate the local culture and cuisine. Plus, you're less likely to encounter crowds during the off-season at swimming pools, beaches, resorts, restaurants, or shops.

HOLIDAYS

In addition to the standard legal holidays observed in the United States, U.S. Virgin Islanders also observe the following holidays: Three Kings' Day (January 6); Transfer Day, commemorating the transfer of the Danish Virgin Islands to the Americans (March 31); Organic Act Day, honoring the legislation that granted them voting rights (June 20); Emancipation Day, celebrating the freeing of the slaves by the Danes in 1848 (July 3); Hurricane Supplication Day (July 25); Hurricane Thanksgiving Day (October 17); Liberty Day (November 1); and Christmas Second Day (December 26). The islands also celebrate two carnival days on the last Friday and Saturday in April: Children's Carnival Parade and the Grand Carnival Parade, which is for adults.

In the British Virgin Islands, public holidays include the following: New Year's Day; Commonwealth Day (March 12); Good Friday; Easter Monday; Whitmonday (sometime in July); Territory Day Sunday (usually July 1); Festival Monday and Tuesday (during the first week of August); St. Ursula's Day (October 21); Birthday of the Heir to the Throne (November 14); Christmas Day; and Boxing Day (December 26).

U.S. VIRGIN ISLANDS CALENDAR OF EVENTS

April

✪ **St. Thomas Carnival.** The most spectacular carnival in all the Virgin Islands, this annual celebration has roots in Africa. Over the years, the festivities have become

Christianized, but the fun and gaiety remain. Mocko Jumbies, people dressed as spirits, parade through the streets on stilts nearly 20 feet high. Steel and fungi bands, "jump-ups," and parades bring the event to life. **Where:** Islandwide, but most action is on the streets of Charlotte Amalie. **When:** After Easter, usually in April. **How:** Contact the visitors center in St. Thomas (☎ **809/774-8784**) for a schedule of carnival events.

July

• **Carnival of St. John.** Parades, calypso bands, and colorful costumes lead up to the selection of Ms. St. John and King of Carnival. First week of July. Call the St. John Tourist Office (☎ **809/776-6450**) for information.

August

• **U.S. Virgin Islands Open/Atlantic Blue Marlin Tournament.** The most prestigious event of its kind, this St. Thomas–centered charity event (proceeds go to the Boy Scouts) is also eco-friendly as trophies are based on the number of blue marlin caught, tagged, and released. The event is open to anyone who's interested, and sport fishers come from around the world, some from as far as Australia, to participate. Late August (weekend closest to the full moon). For more information, call the VI Council of the Boy Scouts of America (☎ **809/774-2752**).

December

✪ **Christmas in St. Croix.** This is a major event launching the beginning of a 12-day celebration that includes Christmas Day, the legal holiday on December 26, New Year's Eve—called "Old Year's Day"—and New Year's Day. It ends January 6, the Feast of the Three Kings, with a parade of flamboyantly attired merrymakers. **Where:** Christiansted and other island venues. **When:** December 25 to January 6. **How:** For information, call the U.S. Virgin Islands Department of Tourism office in Christiansted (☎ **809/773-0495**).

BRITISH VIRGIN ISLANDS CALENDAR OF EVENTS

April

✪ **BVI Spring Regatta.** When the islands are at their best in spring, they host this regatta, the third leg of the Caribbean Ocean Racing Triangles events. Puerto Rico and St. Thomas stage the first two legs. A range of talents, from the most dedicated racers to bareboat crews out for "rum and reggae," participate in the 3-day race. It's the event for the Caribbean boating set. **Where:** Tortola. **When:** April 4 to 6. **How:** For more information, contact the BVI Spring Regatta Committee, P.O. Box 200, Road Town, Tortola, B.V.I. (☎ **284/494-3286**).

August

✪ **BVI Summer Festival.** Many visitors from other Caribbean islands hop over to the B.V.I. for this 3-day party. Join locals as they dance to fungi and reggae bands and revel in the Unity Day Parade and other carnival activities and festivities. **Where:** Road Town fairgrounds. **When:** First week in August. **How:** Head for the fairgrounds, or call the BVI Tourist Board Office (☎ **284/494-3134**).

3 The Active Vacation Planner

There's no rule that says you have to confine yourself to a beach chair that's within arm's length of the bar while visiting the Virgin Islands—unless, of course, that's what you came here to do. While you will have endless opportunities to sit mindlessly by the crashing surf sipping rum drinks, remember that there are even more opportunities to actively explore the islands. Coral reefs and stunning beaches provide breathtaking backdrops for a variety of water sports from snorkeling to sea kayaking, but fear not, there's plenty of golf, tennis, hiking, and even horseback riding. This section presents an overview of all the sports you could ever want to pursue in the Virgin Islands. See individual chapters for more specific information on locations and outfitters.

CAMPING

The best campsites in the Virgin Islands are on St. John at **Maho Bay** and **Cinnamon Bay,** which is considered one of the finest campgrounds in the Caribbean. Both facilities are open year-round and are so popular that reservations for spots during the winter months need to be made far in advance.

In the British Virgin Islands, the best campsite is Tortola's **Brewers Bay Campground,** which rents tents and basic equipment and is open year-round.

GOLF

The golfing hub of the Virgin Islands is the challenging 18-hole **Carambola Golf Course** (☎ 809/778-0747) in St. Croix. Designed by Robert Trent Jones Sr., this public course took a beating from Hurricane Hugo in 1989, but has since been completely restored. Also on St. Croix is the reputable 18-hole course at **The Buccaneer** (☎ 800/255-3881) in Christiansted.

On St. Thomas's north shore is the 18-hole **Mahogany Run** (☎ 809/777-6006), a 6,350-yard, par-70 course with spectacular vistas. Designed by Tom and George Fazio, it boasts a tricky trio of cliffside holes known as "Devil's Triangle."

HORSEBACK RIDING

Equestrians will definitely want to head for St. Croix. **Paul and Jill's Equestrian Stables** (☎ 809/772-2880 or 809/772-2627) at Sprat Hall Plantation are the premier stables not only in the Virgin Islands, but also in the Caribbean. The outfit is known for the quality of both its horses and riding trails, which take you through lush forests. You can also go for a ride along the coast or participate in one of their memorable moonlit rides. Neophytes and experts are welcome.

SAILING & YACHTING

The Virgin Islands are a sailor's paradise offering crystal-clear turquoise waters, secluded coves and inlets, and protected harbors for anchoring.

If you're qualified, you can sail your own craft. If you don't feel like hauling your boat down here or simply have no nautical knowledge, you can **charter** a boat. For details, see the "Chartering Your Own Boat" feature below.

Most visitors, however, are content with **day sails,** which are easy to organize, especially at the harbors in St. Thomas, Tortola, and Virgin Gorda. Regardless of where you decide to cruise, you really shouldn't leave the islands without spending at least one day on the water, even if you have to load up on Dramamine before you go.

The most popular cruising area in both the U.S. Virgin Islands and the British Virgin Islands encompasses the 45 miles or so between St. Thomas and the North Sound off Virgin Gorda. Although the waters surrounding St. Croix are appealing, especially near Buck Island, the island itself lies relatively far from the more interesting sailing routes within the deep and incredibly scenic **Sir Francis Drake Channel.** Named after the 16th-century English explorer, it's surrounded by mountainous islands and boasts crisp breezes year-round. In heavy weather, this network of tiny islands shelters yachties from the brute force of the open sea.

Outside the channel, the Virgin archipelago contains reefy areas that separate many of the islands from their neighbors. To navigate such areas, you need to use a depth chart (available from charter companies or any marine supply outlet) and have some nautical knowledge of the area. (Tip: Free advice, often enough to last a couple of drinks, is willingly offered by locals and temporarily anchored sailors at almost any dockside watering hole.)

For more than a quarter of a century, *The Yachtsman's Guide to the Virgin Islands* has been the classic cruising guide to this area (don't worry, it's updated periodically). The detailed 240-page text is supplemented by 22 sketch charts, more than 100 photographs and illustrations, and numerous landfall sketches showing harbors, channels, landmarks, and such. Subjects covered include piloting, anchoring, communication, weather, fishing, and more. The guide also covers the eastern end of Puerto Rico, Vieques, and Culebra. Copies of the guide are available at major marine outlets, bookstores, and direct from Tropic Isle Publishers, P.O. Box 610938, North Miami, FL 33261-0938 (☎ **305/893-4277**), for $15.95 postpaid.

Except for Anegada, which is a low-lying atoll of coral limestone and sandstone set off to the archipelago's northeast, all the Virgin Islands are high and easily spotted. Water clarity is another advantage for sailors. Specific distances between the islands can be misleading because often you may need to take round-about routes from one point to another. The shortest distance, however, between St. Thomas and St. Croix is 35 nautical miles; from St. John to St. Croix, 35 nautical miles; from St. Thomas to St. John, 2 nautical miles; from Tortola to St. Thomas, 10 nautical miles; from Virgin Gorda to Anegada, 13 nautical miles; and from St. John to Anegada, 30 nautical miles. Virgin Gorda to St. Croix is about the longest run at 45 nautical miles.

If you don't know how to sail but would like to learn, sailing schools operate on St. Croix. One recommendable school is **Annapolis Sailing School,** 1215 King Cross St., Christiansted, St. Croix, U.S.V.I. 00820 (☎ **800/638-9192** or 809/773-4709). Using three 24-foot day-sailers, they charge $125 per person daily, plus $50 for each additional person (up to four guests per boat).

Womanship, The Boat House, 410 Severn Ave., Annapolis, MD 21403 (☎ **800/342-9295** in the U.S., or 410/267-6661) offers a sailing program for women of all ages and levels of nautical expertise in the British Virgin Islands. Groups consist of a maximum of six students with two female instructors. Participants sleep aboard the boat, and most courses last a week. The cost is $1,396 from December through April; off-season, $1,254.

The B.V.I. are also the headquarters of the **Offshore Sailing School,** Prospect Reef Resort, Road Town (☎ **284/494-3311**). The school offers sailing instruction year-round. For information before you go, write or call Offshore Sailing School, 16731 McGregor Blvd., Ft. Myers, FL 33908 (☎ **800/221-4326,** or 941/454-1700 in the U.S.).

SEA-KAYAKING/ISLAND-CAMPING TOURS

Arawak Expeditions, Cruz Bay, St. John (☎ **800/238-8687,** or 809/693-8312 in the U.S.), is the only outfitter in the Virgin Islands offering multiple-day sea-kayaking/island-camping excursions. Full-day and half-day trips are also available. You can cruise through the islands much like the Arawaks did, except that they used dugout canoes. Today's vessels are two-person fiberglass kayaks, complete with foot-controlled rudders. The outfit provides all the kayaking gear, healthful meals, camping equipment, and two experienced guides. The cost of a full-day trip is $65, half-day, $40; multiple-day excursions range in price from $750 to $1,195.

Chartering Your Own Boat

There may be no better way to experience the Virgin Islands than on the deck of your own yacht. Impossible? Not really. No one said you had to *own* the yacht.

Experienced sailors and navigators with a sea-wise crew might want to rent a **bareboat charter,** that is, a fully equipped boat with no captain or crew. You'll have to prove you can handle the task before you're allowed to set sail, and even if you're the skipper, you may want to take along an experienced sailor who's familiar with the sometimes tricky local waters.

If you're not nautically inclined, but still yearn to hit the high seas, consider a **fully crewed charter** with captain and cook. The cost of a crewed boat is obviously more expensive than a bareboat, and varies according to crew size and experience.

Four to six people, maybe more, often charter yachts measuring from 50 to more than 100 feet. Most are rented on a weekly basis and come with a fully stocked kitchen (or a barbecue) and bar, fishing gear, and water sports equipment. More and more bareboaters are saving money on charters by buying their own provisions, rather than relying on the charter company.

The best outfitter in the Virgin Islands is **The Moorings,** P.O. Box 139, Wickhams Cay, Road Town, Tortola, B.V.I. (☎ **284/494-2331**), which offers both bareboat and fully crewed charters equipped with barbecue, snorkeling gear, dinghy, and linens. Windsurfers come with crewed boats, but cost extra for bareboats. The experienced staff of mechanics, electricians, riggers, and cleaners is extremely helpful, especially if you're going out on your own. They'll give you a thorough briefing about Virgin Island waters and anchorages. In winter, bareboat rentals range from $2,380 to $6,776 weekly (for between 2 and 10 persons); in summer from $1,372 to $3,969.

The moment you add a crew to your chartered holiday, the size and cost of your yacht increase significantly. At The Moorings, the smallest yacht that's available with a crew (captain and cook) is a 50-footer (for bareboat charters the smallest craft is 32 to 35 feet in length). A weekly crewed charter on a 50-foot yacht costs $8,994 in high season (January through April) and $6,594 in low season (July through October). You can split the bill between up to six passengers and all meals and drinks are included, although crew members usually expect a tip at the end of the trip.

To make reservations in the United States or Canada, call **800/535-7289.** For information, write to The Moorings Ltd., 19345 U.S. 19 North, Suite 402, Clearwater, FL 34624 (☎ **813/530-5424**).

SNORKELING & SCUBA DIVING

The warm waters of St. Croix are particularly perfect for these sports. The most popular site is the underwater trails off **Buck Island,** easily accessible by day sails from the harbor in Christiansted. St. Croix is also known for its dramatic "drop-offs," including the famous Puerto Rico Trench. At 12,000 feet, the trench is the fifth-deepest body of water on earth. Scuba instruction, day and night dives, and equipment rentals are available on St. Croix.

On St. Thomas, all major hotels rent fins and masks for snorkelers, and most day-sail charters have this equipment on board. Many outfitters, like the St. Thomas Diving Club, also feature scuba programs.

The best snorkeling on Virgin Gorda is around its major attraction, **The Baths.** Lying off Anegada Island, Anegada Reef has been the "burial ground" for ships for centuries; an estimated 300 wrecks, including many pirate ships, have perished here. The wreckage of the **RMS *Rhone,*** near the westerly tip of Salt Island, is the most celebrated dive spot in the B.V.I. This ship went under in 1867 in one of the most disastrous hurricanes ever to hit the Virgin Islands.

SPORT FISHING

In the last 25 years or so, more than 20 sport fishing world records have been set from the Virgin Islands, mostly for the mega blue marlin. Other abundant fish in these waters include bonito, tuna, wahoo, sailfish, and skipjack. But you needn't go way out to sea to fish. On St. Thomas, St. John, and St. Croix, the U.S. government publishes lists of legal shoreline fishing spots (contact local tourist offices for more information). Closer inshore, you'll find kingfish, mackerel, bonefish, tarpon, amberjack, grouper, and snappers. Sport fishing charters, led by experienced local captains, abound in the islands—both half-day and full-day trips are available.

TENNIS

Tennis is a becoming a major sport in the Virgin Islands, and most courts are all-weather or Laykold. Because of intense midday heat, many courts are lit for night games. Pro shops, complete with teaching pros, are available at all the major tennis resorts, especially on the islands of St. Croix and St. Thomas.

St. Thomas has six public (and free) tennis courts that operate on a first-come, first-served basis. If the courts at the major hotels aren't booked by resident guests, most hotels will allow you to play for a minimal fee as long as you call a day in advance. Both **Bolongo Bay** and **Marriott's Frenchman's Reef Beach Resort** have four courts.

On St. Croix, **The Buccaneer** has the best tennis facilities in the Virgin Islands with eight meticulously maintained courts and a state-of-the-art pro shop. The island also has seven public courts, but they're rather rough around the edges.

On Tortola, **Prospect Reef** has six courts, which often open up to nonguests for a fee. If you're a serious tennis buff and are planning to stay on Virgin Gorda, consider **Little Dix Bay,** which has seven beautiful courts reserved for guests only.

4 Getting Married in the Virgin Islands

In recent years, the high cost of traditional weddings and the greater incidence of second or third weddings has led to an increased demand for less showy (and less expensive) weddings in warm-weather settings. If you yearn to tie the knot on a sun-dappled island, here are some basics for planning a wedding in the Virgin Islands. Also, take a look at our list of the "The Best Honeymoon Resorts" in chapter 1.

U.S. VIRGIN ISLANDS

No blood tests or physical examinations are necessary, but there is a $25 license fee, a notarized application for another $25, and an 8-day waiting period, which is sometimes waived, depending on circumstances. A civil ceremony before a judge of the territorial court costs $200; a religious ceremony by a member of the clergy is equally valid. Fees and schedules for church weddings must be negotiated directly with the officiant. More information is available from the **U.S. Virgin Island Division of Tourism,** 1270 Ave. of the Americas, New York, NY 10020 (☎ **212/ 332-2222**).

The guide *Getting Married in the U.S. Virgin Islands* is distributed by the U.S.V.I. tourism offices; it gives information on all three islands, including wedding planners, places of worship, florists, and limousine services. The guide also provides a list of island accommodations that offer in-site wedding services.

Couples planning on getting married in St. Thomas or St. John should begin their nuptial arrangements by applying for a marriage license. Write to the **Territorial Court of the Virgin Islands,** P.O. Box 70, St. Thomas, U.S.V.I. 00804 (☎ **809/ 774-6680**). To obtain an application for a wedding on St. Croix, write to the **Territorial Court of the Virgin Islands,** Family Division, P.O. Box 929, Christiansted, St. Croix, U.S.V.I. 00821 (☎ **809/774-6680**).

There are several wedding planning services available in the U.S. Virgin Islands, including **Fantasia Weddings and Honeymoons,** Suite 310, 168 Crown Bay, St. Thomas, U.S.V.I. 00802 (☎ **800-FANTASA** or 809/777-6588); **Weddings the Island Way,** P.O. Box 11694, St. Thomas, U.S.V.I. 00801 (☎ **800/582-4784** or 809/777-6505); and **Weddings by IPS,** 9719 Estate Thomas, Suite 1, St. Thomas, U.S.V.I. 00802 (☎ **800/937-1346**).

BRITISH VIRGIN ISLANDS

There is no requirement of island residency, but a couple must apply for a license at the attorney general's office, and stay on the B.V.I. for at least 3 days while the paperwork is processed. You'll need to present a passport or original birth certificate and photo identification, plus certified proof of your marital status, including any divorce or death certificates pertaining to former spouses. Two witnesses must accompany the couple. The fee is $110. Local registrars will perform marriages, or you can choose your own officiant. For information and an application for a license, contact the **Registrar's Office,** P.O. Box 418, Road Town, Tortola, B.V.I. (☎ **284/ 494-3701** or 284/494-3492).

5 Health & Insurance

STAYING HEALTHY

Finding a good doctor in the Virgin Islands is not a problem, and all of them speak English. See "Fast Facts" later in this chapter and also in individual island chapters for specific names and addresses.

If your medical condition is chronic, talk to your doctor before leaving home. He or she may have specific advice to give you, depending on your condition. For conditions such as epilepsy, a heart condition, or diabetes, wear a **Medic Alert's Identification Tag;** Medic Alert's 24-hour hotline enables a foreign doctor to obtain your medical records. For a lifetime membership, the cost is a well-spent $35 to $60, plus a $15 annual fee. Contact **Medic Alert,** 2323 Colorado Ave., Turlock, CA 95382 (☎ **800/825-3785**).

Although tap **water** is generally considered safe to drink, it's better to drink mineral water. Also, avoid iced drinks. Stick to beer, hot tea, or soft drinks.

If you experience **diarrhea,** moderate your eating habits, and drink only mineral water until you recover. If symptoms persist, you should consult a doctor.

The Virgin Islands sun can be brutal. Wear sunglasses and a hat, and use **sunscreen** (15 SPF and up) liberally. Limit your time on the beach the first few days. If you do overexpose yourself, stay out of the sun until you recover. If your sunburn is followed by fever, chills, a headache, or a feeling of nausea or dizziness, see a doctor.

Mosquitoes do exist in the Virgin Islands, but they aren't the malaria-carrying mosquitoes that you might find elsewhere in the Caribbean. Nevertheless, they are still a nuisance. But, **no-see-ums,** which appear mainly in the evening, are the bigger menace. Screens can't keep these critters out, so carry your favorite bug repellent.

Vaccinations are not required to enter either the U.S. Virgin Islands or the British Virgin Islands if you're coming from the United States, Britain, Canada, Australia, or New Zealand.

INSURANCE

Always review your present policies before traveling internationally—you may already have adequate coverage with your existing policies and what is offered by credit-card companies if the trip tickets were purchased with their card. Fraternal organizations sometimes have policies that protect members in case of sickness or accidents abroad.

Many homeowners' insurance policies cover theft of luggage during foreign travel and loss of documents (for instance, your airline ticket), although coverage is usually limited to about $500.

Some policies (and this is the type you should have) provide cash advances or transferals of funds so that you won't have to dip into your precious travel funds to settle medical bills.

If you've booked a charter flight, you'll probably have to pay a cancellation fee if you cancel a trip suddenly, even if it is due to an unforeseen crisis. It's possible to get insurance that will cover such a fee, either through travel agencies or through a credit-card company, when such insurance is written into tickets paid for by the card.

Several companies offer special travel insurance policies. **Travel Guard International,** 1145 Clark St., Stevens Point, WI 54481 (☎ **800/826-1300** or 715/345-0505), offers a comprehensive 7-day policy for around $60, including trip cancellation, lost luggage, emergency assistance, medical coverage, and accidental death.

Travelers Insurance PAK, Travel Insured International, Inc., P.O. Box 280568, East Hartford, CT 06128 (☎ **800/243-3174** or 860/528-7663), offers illness and accident coverage costing from $10 for 6 to 10 days. For lost or damaged luggage, $500 worth of coverage costs $20 for 6 to 10 days. You can also purchase trip cancellation insurance from $5.50 per $100 of coverage to a limit of $10,000 per person.

Access America, 6600 W. Broad St., Richmond, VA 23230 (☎ **800/284-8300**), offers comprehensive travel insurance 24-hour emergency assistance. One call to their center, staffed by multilingual coordinators, connects travelers to a worldwide network of professionals able to offer specialized help in reaching the nearest doctor, hospital, or legal advisor, and in obtaining emergency cash or the replacement of lost travel documents. Varying coverage levels are available.

Mutual of Omaha (Tele-Trip), Mutual of Omaha Plaza, Omaha, NE 68175 (☎ **800/228-9792**), offers insurance packages priced from $49 per person for a tour valued at $1,000, including travel-assistance services, and financial protection against trip cancellation, trip interruption, flight and baggage delays, accident-related medical costs, accidental death and dismemberment, and medical evacuation coverages. A deluxe package costing $213 per couple offers double the coverage of the standard policy mentioned above. Applications for insurance can be made over the phone for major credit-card holders.

INSURANCE FOR BRITISH TRAVELERS

Most big travel agents offer their own insurance and will probably try to sell you their package. Think before you sign. Britain's Consumers' Association recommends that you insist on reading the policy before buying it. You should also shop around for deals. You might contact **Columbus Travel Insurance Ltd.** (☎ **0171/375-0011**) in London, or, for students, **Campus Travel** (☎ **0171/730-3402**), also in London. Columbus Travel will only sell insurance to travelers who have been official British residents for 1 year.

6 Tips for Travelers with Special Needs

FOR TRAVELERS WITH DISABILITIES

You can obtain a free copy of **"Air Transportation of Handicapped Persons,"** published by the U.S. Department of Transportation, by writing to U.S. Department of Transportation, Subsequent Distribution Office, SVC-121.23, Ardmore East Business Center, 3341 Q 75th Ave., Landover, MD 20785 (☎ **301/322-4961;** fax 301/386-5394). Only written requests for publications will be accepted.

For names and addresses of operators of tours specifically for disabled travelers, and other relevant information, contact the **Society for the Advancement of Travel for the Handicapped (SATH),** 347 Fifth Ave., Suite 610, New York, NY 10016 (☎ **212/447-7284;** fax 212/725-8253). Yearly membership costs $45 ($25 for senior citizens and students). Send a stamped self-addressed envelope for information with $5 for a list of operators.

For the blind or visually impaired, the best source is the **American Foundation for the Blind,** 11 Penn Plaza, Suite 200, New York, NY 10011 (☎ **212/502-7600,** or 800/232-5463 for ordering of information kits and supplies). It acts as a referral source for travelers and can offer advice on the transport and border formalities for seeing-eye dogs. SATH will also provide hotel/resort accessibility for Caribbean destinations.

Travelers with a hearing impairment can contact the **American Academy of Otolaryngology,** 1 Prince St., Alexandria, VA 22314 (☎ **703/836-4444;** TTY 703/519-1585).

The **Information Center for Individuals with Disabilities,** Fort Point Place, 27–43 Wormwood St., Boston, MA 02210 (☎ **800/462-5015** or 617/727-5540), is another good source. It has lists of travel agents who specialize in tours for persons with disabilities, and provides travel-tip fact sheets for many Caribbean destinations.

One of the best organizations serving the needs of persons with disabilities (wheelchairs and walkers) is **Flying Wheels Travel,** 143 West Bridge, P.O. Box 382, Owatonna, MN 55060 (☎ **800/535-6790** or 507/451-5005), offering various all-inclusive vacation packages in the Caribbean.

For a $35 annual fee, consider joining **Mobility International USA (MIUSA),** P.O. Box 10767, Eugene, OR 97440 (☎ **541/343-1284** voice and TDD). It answers questions on various destinations and also offers discounts on videos, publications, and programs it sponsors.

TIPS FOR BRITISH TRAVELERS WITH DISABILITIES

RADAR (Royal Association for Disability and Rehabilitation), Unit 12, City Forum, 250 City Rd., London EC1V 8AF (☎ **0171/250-3222;** fax 0171/250-0212), publishes vacation "fact packs," which provide information on trip planning, travel insurance, specialized accommodations, and transportation abroad.

FOR GAY & LESBIAN TRAVELERS

The Virgin Islands are, along with Puerto Rico, one of the most gay-friendly destinations in the Caribbean. This is in part due to the barrage of multicultural influences, from both the U.S. mainland and Britain, that constantly permeate the archipelago. Here are some organizations that specialize in gay travel and can help you plan your trip:

Men can order *Spartacus,* the international gay guide ($32.95), or *Odysseus 1997: The International Gay Travel Planner,* a guide to international gay accommodations ($25). Both lesbians and gay men might want to pick up a copy of *Ferrari Travel Planner* ($16), which lists gay-friendly bars, hotels, and restaurants throughout the world. These books and others are available from **Giovanni's Room,** 1145 Pine St., Philadelphia, PA 19107 (☎ **215/923-2960**).

Our World, 1104 N. Nova Rd., Suite 251, Daytona Beach, FL 32117 (☎ **904/441-5367**), is a magazine devoted to options and bargains for gay and lesbian travel worldwide; it costs $35 for 10 issues. *Out and About,* 8 W. 19th St., Suite 401, New York, NY 10011 (☎ **800/929-2268**), has been hailed for its "straight" reporting about gay travel. It profiles the best gay or gay-friendly hotels, gyms, clubs, and other places, with coverage of destinations throughout the world. It's $49 a year for 10 issues. It aims for the more upscale gay male traveler, and has been praised by everybody from *Travel and Leisure* to *The New York Times.* Both of these publications are also available at most gay and lesbian bookstores.

The **International Gay Travel Association (IGTA),** P.O. Box 4974, Key West, FL 33041 (☎ **800/448-8550**), encourages gay and lesbian travel worldwide. With around 1,200 member agencies, it specializes in networking, providing the information travelers would need for an individual traveler to link up with the appropriate gay-friendly service organization or tour specialist. It offers quarterly newsletters, marketing mailings, and a membership directory that's updated four times a year. Travel agents, who are IGTA members, will be tied into this organization's vast information resources.

FOR SENIORS

Write for a free booklet called **101 Tips for the Mature Traveler,** available from **Grand Circle Travel,** 347 Congress St., Suite 3A, Boston, MA 02210 (☎ **800/ 221-2610** or 617/350-7500).

Golden Circle Travel, 347 Congress St., Boston, MA 02210 (☎ **800/248-3737**), offers escorted tours and cruises for retirees to many Caribbean destinations.

SAGA International Holidays, 222 Berkeley St., Boston, MA 02116 (☎ **800/ 343-0273**), is well known for its all-inclusive tours for seniors 50 years of age or older. Insurance and airfare are included in the net price of any of their tours, except for cruises.

AARP (American Association of Retired Persons), 601 E St., NW, Washington, DC 20049 (☎ **202/434-AARP**), is another great organization for seniors, offering discounts on car rentals and hotels. Call or write for information.

Elderhostel, 75 Federal St., Boston, MA 02110 (☎ **617/426-8056**), has an array of educational travel programs for seniors worldwide, including the Caribbean; trips include airfare, hotel accommodations in student dormitories or modest inns, meals, and tuition. Courses focus on liberal arts studies and last for around 3 weeks. Participants must be older than 55. Write for a free catalog.

FOR FAMILIES

The Virgin Islands have long been a popular family vacation destination. Toddlers can spend hours in the sand and shallow surf, while older kids might go boating, horseback riding, hiking, or even snorkeling. Plus, most resort hotels have baby-sitting services and organized children's programs; see chapter 1 for a list of the best family resorts.

Travel with Your Children (TWYCH), 40 Fifth Ave., New York, NY 10011 (☎ 212/477-5524), publishes a useful newsletter called *Family Travel Times,* which comes out 10 times a year. Subscriptions cost $40. TWYCH also publishes *Cruising with Children* for $22.

Families Welcome!, 92 N. Main St., Ashland, OR 97520 (☎ 800/326-0724), is a travel company specializing in worry-free family vacations to the Caribbean.

Another good resource is *The Family Travel Guide: An Inspiring Collection of Family Friendly Vacations,* a 410-page book filled with information. For a copy, contact **Carousel Press,** P.O. Box 6061, Albany, CA 94706 (☎ 510/527-5849).

FOR STUDENTS

The best travel service for students is **Council Travel,** 205 E. 42nd St., New York, NY 10017 (☎ 800/226-8624 or 212/822-2600), which provides details about budget travel (included discount airfares), insurance, and working permits. Be sure to ask about their valuable International Student Identity Cards ($19), which entitle bona fide students to travel discounts worldwide. In addition to its New York office, Council Travel has 37 other U.S. offices.

7 Flying to the Virgin Islands

The bigger islands, like St. Thomas, have regularly scheduled air service from North American carriers, and the smaller islands are tied into this vast network through their own carriers.

For information on how to reach each island by plane, refer to the "Getting There" section in the individual island chapters.

If you fly in summer, spring, or fall, you'll see substantial reductions on airfares to the Virgin Islands. It's usually cheaper to fly Monday to Thursday. Also, consider land-and-air packages, which offer considerably reduced rates.

SOURCES FOR DISCOUNT TICKETS
BUCKET SHOPS

Consolidators exist in many shapes and forms. A bucket shop acts as a clearing-house for blocks of tickets that airlines discount and consign during normally slow periods of air travel. In the case of the Virgin Islands, that means mid-April to mid-December.

Tickets are sometimes, but not always, discounted 20% to 35%. Terms of payment can vary from 45 days before departure to the last minute. Discounted tickets can be purchased through regular travel agents, but they usually mark up the ticket 8% to 10%.

A recent survey of flyers who used consolidator tickets found only one major complaint: You can't arrange for advance seat assignment. The survey revealed that *most* flyers received a savings off the regular ticket price. But, and here's the hitch, many reported no savings at all, as airlines will sometimes match the consolidator ticket with a promotional fare. The situation calls for some careful investigation on your part to determine just how much you're saving.

Bucket shops abound from coast to coast. Look for their ads in your local newspaper's travel section.

In New York try **TFI Tours International,** 34 W. 32nd St., 12th Floor, New York, NY 10001 (☎ 800/745-8000 or 212/736-1140). This tour company offers services to 177 cities worldwide.

CHARTER FLIGHTS

Many of the major airline carriers offer charter flights at rates that are sometimes 30% (or more) off the regular airfare. There are some drawbacks to charter flights, however. Advance booking of up to 45 days or more may be required, and there are hefty cancellation penalties, although you can take out insurance against emergency cancellations.

Since charter flights are so complicated, it's best to ask a good travel agent to explain the problems and advantages. Sometimes charters require ground arrangements, such as prebooking of hotel rooms.

One reliable charter flight operator is **Council Charter,** 205 E. 42nd St., New York, NY 10017 (☎ **800/800-8222** or 212/661-1450), which occasionally offers reduced fares to the Caribbean.

REBATORS

To confuse the situation even more, rebators have also begun to compete in the low-airfare market. These outfits pass along to the passenger part of their commission, although many of them assess a fee for their services. Although they are not the same as travel agents, they sometimes offer roughly similar services. They're not the same as travel agents, but they sometimes offer similar services, such as discounted land arrangements, including hotels and car rentals. Most rebators offer discounts averaging anywhere from 10% to 25% with a $25 handling charge.

Travel Avenue, 10 S. Riverside Plaza, Suite 14041, Chicago, IL 60606 (☎ **800/ 333-3335** or 312/876-1116), is one of the oldest of its kind. It offers up-front cash rebates on every airline ticket over $300 it sells. It sells airline tickets to independent travelers who have already worked out their travel plans. Also available are tour and cruise fares, plus hotel bookings.

Another major rebator is **The Smart Traveller,** 3111 SW 27th Ave., P.O. Box 330010, Miami, FL 33133 (☎ **800/448-3338** or 305/448-3338), which offers discounts on packaged tours, Caribbean cruises, and dive packages.

TRAVEL CLUBS

Travel clubs supply an unsold inventory of tickets that are discounted from 20% to 60%. After you pay an annual fee, you are given a "hotline" number to call to find out what discounts are available. Some of these discounts become available a few days before departure, some a week in advance, and some as much as a month. Of, course, you're limited to what's available, so you have to be flexible.

Following is a list of some of the best of these clubs. **Moment's Notice,** 7301 New Utrecht Ave., Brooklyn, NY 11204 (☎ **718/234-6295**), charges $25 per year for membership which allows spur-of-the-moment participation in dozens of tours. Its discounted land-and-air packages to the Virgin Islands sometimes represent substantial savings over what you've paid through more conventional channels. Members can call the company's hotline (☎ **212/873-0908**) to learn what options are available. Most of the company's best-valued tours depart from New Jersey's Newark airport, La Guardia, or JFK.

Travelers Advantage, 3033 S. Parker Rd., Suite 900, Aurora, CO 80014 (☎ **800/ TEL-TRIP**), offers a 3-month trial offer for $1. The annual membership fee of $49 includes the HalfPrice HotelCard, which grants you 50% off room rates at more than 3,000 hotels and motels worldwide. Members also get 5% cash bonuses on travel purchases made through Travelers Advantage. For travel membership, call **800/548-1116.**

FLIGHTS FROM THE UNITED KINGDOM

Although there are no direct flights from the United Kingdom to either the U.S. Virgin Islands or the British Virgin Islands, **British Airways** (☎ **0181/897-4000** in London, or 800/247-9297 in the U.S.) flies directly to San Juan, Puerto Rico. Once a week (Sundays), flights leave Gatwick Airport at 11am for San Juan, where several airlines connect with St. Thomas, St. Croix, Tortola, and Virgin Gorda.

8 Cruises

Some 300 passenger ships sail the Caribbean routes each month (in January and February that figure may reach 400), and St. Thomas in the U.S.V.I. is one of the major ports of call. Most cruise-ship operators suggest the concept of the "total vacation." Some promote activities sunup to sundown, while others suggest nothing but relaxation.

For those who don't want to spend all their time at sea, some lines offer fly-and-cruise vacations, where you spend one week on the boat and the next week at a hotel. Other good-value cruise packages include your airfare to the ship's departure point. You can purchase your airline ticket and cruise tickets separately, but you'll save more by going with a package.

Miami is the cruise capital of the world, but ships also leave from San Juan, New York, Port Everglades, Los Angeles, and other points. Most cruise ships travel at night, arriving the following morning at ports of call, where passengers can go ashore for sightseeing and shopping.

A high percentage of Caribbean cruises make at least one stop in the Virgin Islands. Charlotte Amalie in St. Thomas is the most popular port, followed by historic Christiansted in St. Croix, and Road Town in Tortola.

Two great resources for choosing a cruise line are *Frommer's Caribbean Cruises* and *Frommer's Caribbean Ports of Call* (Macmillan Travel). Here's a rundown of various ships cruising the Virgin Islands:

American Canadian Caribbean (☎ **800/556-7450** or 401/247-0955) is a Rhode Island–based cruise outfit whose shallow-draft, small-scale, and rather bare-boned coastal cruisers embark on 7- to 12-day excursions through complicated shoals and landmasses where larger ships cannot go. Although itineraries are likely to change, at least one of its trio of ships cruises around the Virgin Islands in winter.

Carnival Cruise Lines (☎ **800/438-6744** or 305/599-2600) is the richest, boldest, brashest, and most successful mass-market cruise line in the world. Eight of its mega-ships depart from Florida or Caribbean ports, including Miami, Tampa, New Orleans, and San Juan; four offer 7-day tours with stopovers at selected U.S.V.I. ports. Carnival's new supermega-ship, *Destiny,* weighs in at 101,000 tons—the largest cruise ship in the world today. Most cruises in and around the Virgin Islands last 7 nights and feature lots of partying—the atmosphere has been compared to a floating theme park.

Celebrity Cruises (☎ **800/437-3111** or 305/262-8322) maintains five newly built, medium- to large-sized ships, each offering cruises of 7 to 17 nights. In addition to stops at such ports as Key West, San Juan, Grand Cayman, Ocho Rios, Antigua, and Curaçao, among others, at least four of its ships dock in St. Thomas. It's an unpretentious but classy line, with surprisingly competitive prices. Accommodations are roomy and well equipped, and many passengers compare their vessels to all-inclusive resorts. While strong on cuisine, the ships lack wraparound promenade decks. In winter most passengers—typical age about 48 to 50—fall in the upper-middle-class bracket. On board, entertainment and recreation are emphasized, but shore excursions can be quite dull.

Costa Cruise Lines (☎ 800/462-6782 or 305/358-7325) maintains fairly large and new vessels that hold around 1,300 passengers each. Ships follow both eastern and western Caribbean itineraries; the only Virgin Islands stop is St. Thomas. On board, there's an Italian atmosphere and flair, with entertainment resembling Carnival in Venice. Cruises last from 7 to 11 nights.

Cunard (☎ 800/221-4770), despite recent fiscal and managerial problems, is still famous for its transatlantic journeys and its very British flagship, the *QE2*. The line's smallest and most opulent vessels, *Sea Goddess I* and *II,* look more like private yachts than cruise ships, and both list St. Thomas as their home port during parts of the winter. On board, the atmosphere is high class, although some complain it can be somewhat staid.

Dolphin Cruise Lines (☎ 800/222-1003 or 305/358-5122) operates a trio of older ships and offers low-cost, no-frills cruises. *SeaBreeze* spends its winter cruising the eastern and western Caribbean, with regular stops at St. Thomas.

Holland America Line-Westours (☎ 800/426-0327 or 206/281-3535) boasts eight hefty and good-looking ships, four of which make regular stops in the Virgin Islands. On board you can expect a solid, well-grounded clientele of mature travelers who expect value for their dollar, and usually get it. Most cruises are 7 days.

Norwegian Cruise Line (☎ 800/327-7030 or 305/445-0866) appeals to all ages and budgets, with Scandinavian officers, an international staff, and a pervasive Viking theme. Two of the company's five ships (the relatively informal *Seaward* and the line's dignified flagship, the *Norway*) stop in St. Thomas, as well as Santo Domingo, St. Lucia, and St. Kitts. The line's strongest features are its recreational and fitness facilities and its dining. Even the regular cabins are spacious, and the staff is extremely helpful.

Princess Cruises (☎ 800/421-0522 or 310/553-1770) introduced its newest mega-ship, *Dawn Princess,* in the spring of 1997; it stops in St. Thomas once every 2 weeks on its eastern Caribbean routes. They also own nine other ships, all of which feature luxury accommodations and upscale service. Cruises last 7 to 10 days, and the average passenger age in winter is 55 or over.

Royal Caribbean Cruise Line (☎ 305/539-6000) leads the industry in the development of mega-ships, and remains one of the most popular and best-run lines. These ships tend to feel like a floating house party, though some of them are aging and in need of refurbishment. Although not upscale, accommodations and accoutrements are more than adequate. Using either Miami or San Juan as their home port, RCCL ships call regularly at St. Thomas and other ports in the Virgin Islands.

Seabourn Cruise Line (☎ 800/929-9595 or 415/391-7444) is considered a desirable and expensive outfit whose *Seabourn Pride* offers luxury cruises—the kind Henry and Nancy Kissinger might opt to board if they decided to go cruising. Cruises last 10 to 14 days, and, depending on the itinerary, stops might include St. Thomas, Jost Van Dyke, and Virgin Gorda. Ships are relatively small, but feature an amazing amount of space per passenger; the food is nothing less than superb.

Tall Ship Adventures (☎ 800/662-0090 or 303/755-7983) has only one ship, a tall-masted reconfiguration of a circa-1917 schooner originally built to carry copper ore from the coast of Chile to the Baltic ports of Germany. Today, after extensive refittings, it meanders through the Virgin Islands, focusing more intently on the waters of the B.V.I. than any other cruise line. The vessel spends most of its winter exploring remote outposts like Peter Island, Norman Island, Cooper Island, Marina Cay, Long Bay, and sites off Virgin Gorda. The 1-week cruises depart from Road Town, on Tortola.

Windjammer Barefoot Cruises (☎ 800/327-2601 or 305/672-6453) operates seven sailing ships, most of which are faithful renovations of 19th-century schooners. It's an informal affair, where most passengers sport shorts and T-shirts. Although the entire fleet visits remote islands throughout the Caribbean, one ship, *Flying Cloud*, cruises through the scattered reefs and cays of the Virgin Islands; tours originate in Tortola and last 7 days.

Windstar Cruises (☎ 800/258-7245 or 206/281-3535) features luxury-level sailing ships that combine 19th-century designs and 21st-century materials. In fall, winter, and spring, one of the line's twin vessels, *Wind Spirit,* defines Charlotte Amalie as its home port, making 7-day excursions with stops in St. Croix, St. John, Jost Van Dyke, and Virgin Gorda. It's a unique experience unlike any offered by a diesel-driven cruise ship.

9 Package Tours

If you want everything done for you, and want to save money as well, consider traveling to the Virgin Islands on a package tour. The cost of airfare, a hotel room, meals, and sometimes sightseeing and car rentals are combined in one package, neatly tied up with a single price tag. Sound too good to be true?

Well, maybe. There are some drawbacks to package tours. First, you usually have to pay the entire cost up front. Then, you may find yourself in a hotel you dislike immensely, yet you are virtually trapped there. Also, the single traveler, regrettably, suffers too since most of these deals are based on double occupancy.

Nevertheless, package tours to the Virgin Islands and the Caribbean abound. Choosing the right one can be a bit of a problem. It's best to go to a travel agent, tell him or her what island or islands you want to go to, and see what's currently available.

You may also consider hiring the services of **TourScan, Inc.,** P.O. Box 2367, Darien, CT 06820 (☎ 800/962-2080 or 203/655-2841). Every season, the company gathers and computerizes the contents of most of the travel brochures to the Caribbean, The Bahamas, and Bermuda. TourScan selects the best value at each hotel and condo.

TourScan prints two catalogs each year listing a wide choice of hotels on most of the Caribbean islands, in all price ranges. (The scope of the islands and resort hotels that are included is amazing.) Write to TourScan for its catalogs, which cost $4 each.

Another good deal might be a combined land-and-air package offered by one of the major U.S. carriers. Call their toll-free numbers: **American Airlines Fly-Away Vacations** (☎ 800/321-2121) and **Delta's Dream Vacations** (☎ 800/872-7786). **TWA Getaway Vacations** (☎ 800/GETAWAY) specializes only in packages to Jamaica and San Juan, and **United Airlines Vacations** (☎ 800/328-6877) only covers San Juan.

Other tour operators include the following: **Caribbean Concepts Corp.,** 575 Underhill Blvd., Syosset, NY 11791 (☎ 800/423-4433 in the U.S., or 516/496-9800; fax 516/496-9880), offers all-inclusive, low-cost land-and-air packages to the islands, including apartments, hotels, villas, or condo rentals.

Other options for general independent packages include: **Renaissance Vacations,** 2655 Lejeune Rd., Suite 400, Coral Gables, FL 33134 (☎ 800/874-0027 in the U.S.), offering all-inclusive deals to Ocho Rios, Jamaica; St. Thomas; Santo Domingo; and Grenada. **Horizon Tours,** 1010 Vermont Ave. NW, Suite 202, Washington, DC 20005 (☎ 800/395-0025 in the U.S., or 202/393-8390; fax

202/393-1547), specializes in all-inclusive upscale resorts on the islands of The Bahamas, Jamaica, Antigua, Aruba, Barbados, and St. Lucia.

Club Med (☎ **800/258-2633** in the U.S.) has various all-inclusive options throughout the Caribbean and The Bahamas for families and singles.

Finally, advertising more packages to The Bahamas and the Caribbean than any other agency is **Liberty Travel** (☎ **800/216-9776**), with offices in many states.

PACKAGES FOR BRITISH TRAVELERS

Package tours can be booked through **British Virgin Islands Holidays,** a division of Wingjet Travel Ltd., 11–13 Hockerill St., Bishop's Stortford, Herts, England CM23 2DW (☎ **01279/656111**). This company is the major booking agent for all the important hotels in the B.V.I. Stays can be arranged in more than one hotel if you'd like to visit more than one island. The company also offers staffed yacht charters and bareboat charters.

Caribbean Connection, Concorde House, Forest Street, Chester CH1 1QR (☎ **01244/341131**), offers all-inclusive packages (airfare and hotel) to the Caribbean and customizes tours for independent travel. Other Caribbean specialists operating out of England include: **Kuoni Travel,** Kuoni House, Dorking, Surrey RH5 4AZ (☎ **01306/740-888**). **Caribtours,** 161 Fulham Rd., London SW3 6SN (☎ **0171/581-3517**), a small, very knowledgeable outfit that focuses on Caribbean travel and tailors individual itineraries.

10 Getting Around the Islands

Once you arrive, getting around the islands or the one you're on becomes a top priority. Below is a rundown of the different ways to go about it, but be sure to check out the "Getting Around" sections in the individual island chapters.

BY PLANE

Airplanes provide the best link between St. Thomas and St. Croix and between St. Thomas and Tortola's airport at Beef Island. To reach St. John by air, passengers usually land first at St. Thomas, then travel to St. John by boat. **American Airlines** (☎ **800/433-7300**) provides frequent daily service from the U.S. mainland to St. Thomas, with continuing service to St. Croix. **American Eagle** (☎ **809/778-1140**) offers seven daily flights from St. Thomas to St. Croix; a one-way fare is $60. **Virgin Islands Seaplane** (☎ **809/777-4491**) also makes this 30-minute trip eight times daily for $50 round-trip.

Nonstop air service is not available between the U.S. mainland and the B.V.I. Most visitors fly to St. Thomas or Puerto Rico, where you can then connect to either Tortola (at Beef Island) or Virgin Gorda. **American Eagle** (☎ **800/433-7300** or 284/778-1140), **St. Thomas Air** (☎ **800/522-3084**), and **LIAT** (☎ **800/468-0482**) provide these air links.

BY CAR

If you can afford it and don't mind driving on the left, a rented car is the best way to get around the Virgin Islands.

All the major car-rental companies are represented in the U.S. Virgin Islands, including **Avis** (☎ **800/331-2112**), **Budget** (☎ **800/472-3325**), and **Hertz** (☎ **800/654-3001**); many local agencies also compete in these markets (for detailed information, refer to "Getting Around" in specific island chapters). On **St. Thomas** and **St. Croix,** you can pick up most rental cars at the airport. On **St. John** there are car-rental stands at the ferry dock. During the high season, cars might be in short supply, so reserve as far in advance as possible.

Parking lots are found in Charlotte Amalie, in St. Thomas, and in Christiansted on St. Croix. In Frederiksted, you can generally park on the street. Most hotels, except those in the congested center of Charlotte Amalie, have free parking lots.

In the B.V.I., many visitors don't even bother renting a car. Be aware that some of the roads, like those on Tortola, are often compared to roller-coaster rides because of the many hairpin curves. Vehicles come in a wide range of styles and prices, including Jeeps, Land Rovers, minimokes, and even six- to eight-passenger Suzukis. Weekly rates are usually slightly cheaper. To rent a car on the B.V.I., you must purchase a local driver's license for $10 from police headquarters or at the car-rental desk, and you must be at least 25 years old. Major U.S. companies, such as Budget, are represented in the islands, and there are many local companies as well.

GASOLINE

There are plenty of service stations on St. Croix and St. Thomas, especially on the outskirts of Charlotte Amalie and at strategic points in the north and in the more congested East End. On St. Croix, most gas stations are in Christiansted, but there are some along the major roads and at Frederiksted. On St. John, make sure your tank is filled up at Cruz Bay before heading out on a motor tour of the island.

On the B.V.I. gas stations are not as plentiful as in the U.S. islands. Road Town, the capital of Tortola, has the most gas stations; fill up here before touring the island. Virgin Gorda has a limited but sufficient number of gas stations. Chances are you won't be using a car on the other British Virgin Islands.

DRIVING RULES

The most important rule is: **Drive on the left.** Highway codes and signs are generally the same as those used throughout the U.S. mainland. Take extra caution when merging. Speed limits on the U.S.V.I are 20 m.p.h. in town, 35 m.p.h. outside.

ROAD MAPS

Adequate maps are available for free on the islands at the individual tourist offices. If you arrive by plane, go to the tourist information office at the airport and request a map. If you plan to drive your rental car to your hotel, ask a staff member at the tourist office or car-rental desk to trace the best route for you.

BREAKDOWNS & ASSISTANCE

All the major islands, including St. Thomas, St. John, St. Croix, Tortola, and Virgin Gorda, have garages that will tow vehicles, but always call the rental company first—if your car requires extensive repairs because of a mechanical failure, a new one will be sent to replace it.

BY TAXI

Taxis are the main mode of transport on all of the Virgin Islands. On **St. Thomas,** taxi vans carry up to a dozen passengers to multiple destinations, and private taxis are also available. Rates are posted at the airport, where you'll find plenty of taxis upon arrival. On **St. John,** both private taxis and vans for three or more passengers are available. On **St. Croix** taxis congregate at the airport, in Christiansted, and in Frederiksted where the cruise ships arrive. Taxis here are unmetered, and you should always negotiate the rate before taking off.

On the **B.V.I.,** taxis are sometimes the only way to get around. Service is available on Tortola, Virgin Gorda, and Anegada, and rates are fixed by the local government.

BY BOAT

Ferry service forms the vital link between St. Thomas and St. John; private water taxis also operate between St. Thomas and St. John. Launch services link Red Hook (East End of St. Thomas) with both Charlotte Amalie and Cruz Bay in St. John.

You can also take a catamaran from St. Thomas to St. Croix. Try **Fast Cat** (☎ **809/773-3278**), which makes the quick crossing three times a day; the cost is $50 round-trip for adults, $30 for children under 12 (one-way fares are half price). Once on St. Croix, the most popular boat link is with Buck Island, a major offshore attraction.

In the B.V.I. ferries and private boats are the major modes of travel. Many ferries link Road Town, Tortola with the island's West End, and there is also service to and from Virgin Gorda, and some of the smaller islands, such as Anegada and Jost Van Dyke. However, on some of the really remote islands, boat service may only be once a week. Many of the private islands, such as Peter Island, provide launches from Tortola.

For details on specific ferry connections, including sample fares, see the "Getting Around" sections of the individual island chapters.

BY BUS

The only islands with a really recommendable bus service are St. Thomas and St. Croix. On St. Thomas buses leave from Charlotte Amalie and circle the island; on St. Croix, air-conditioned buses run from Christiansted to Frederiksted. Bus service elsewhere is highly erratic; it's mostly used by locals going to and from work.

BY BICYCLE

Much of the hilly terrain of St. Thomas and Tortola does not lend itself to extensive bicycling. St. John, however, is a better place for bike rides, and St. Croix is ideal. For specific information on bicycle or motor-scooter rentals, see the "Getting Around" sections of the individual island chapters.

11 Tips on Accommodations & Dining

ACCOMMODATIONS
HOTELS & RESORTS

Resorts and hotels in the Virgin Islands offer package deals galore, and though they have many disadvantages, the deals are always cheaper than rack rates. Therefore it's always best to consult a reliable travel agent to find out what's available in the way of land-and-air packages before booking accommodations.

There is no rigid classification of hotel properties on the islands. The word *deluxe* is often used, or misused, when *first class* might be more appropriate. First class itself often isn't what it claims to be. For that and other reasons, we've presented fairly detailed descriptions of the properties, so that you'll get an idea of what to expect. However, even in the deluxe and first-class properties, don't expect top-rate service and efficiency. Life here moves pretty slowly, and that can have its disadvantages: When you go to turn on the shower, sometimes you get water and sometimes you don't.

The choice of a hotel is often based upon facilities available. All the big, first-class hotels have swimming pools. Usually a beach is nearby if not directly in front of the property. To save money, you can book into one of the more moderate accommodations less desirably located. Then, often for a small fee, you can use the facilities of the larger, more expensive resorts.

Meal Plans: What the Symbols Mean

If you plan to stay at a hotel or resort in the Virgin Islands, you'll have to determine beforehand the type of meal plan you want. Below are the symbols for the different plans offered and what they mean:

AP (American Plan): Includes three meals a day (sometimes called full board or full pension).

BP (Bermuda or Bahamas Plan): Popularized first in Bermuda, this option includes a full American breakfast (sometimes called an English breakfast).

CP (Continental Plan): A continental breakfast (bread, jam, and coffee) is included in room rates.

EP (European Plan): This rate is always cheapest, as it offers only the room, not meals.

MAP (Modified American Plan): Sometimes called half board or half pension, this room rate includes breakfast and dinner (or lunch if you prefer).

In **winter,** what we consider very expensive hotels and resorts can command from $300 for a double, not including meals; expensive places charge from $200 to $300; moderately priced establishments get from $100 to $200; and inexpensive hotels and motels usually charge under $100 a night for a double. A 10% hotel tax and a 10% service charge are also added to the above rates. Keep in mind that hotels that offer meal plans add a surcharge of $35 to $60 per day to your tab. Of course, these are only estimated numbers for the Virgin Islands as a whole; each island has different rate structures. Hotel prices in the B.V.I., for example, tend to be on the expensive side due to the limited number of lodging options.

The good news: During the **off-season** (from mid-April to mid-December) hotels slash prices 25% to 50%.

RENTING YOUR OWN VILLA OR VACATION HOME

You might decide to rent a big villa, a good-sized condo or apartment, or even your own cottage on the beach while in the Virgin Islands.

Private apartments are more of a no-frills option than villas and condos, and they can be rented with or without chamber service. Cottages usually contain a simple bedroom with a small kitchen and bath. Many open onto a beach, while others are clustered around a communal swimming pool. In the high season, reservations should be made at least 5 to 6 months in advance.

Sometimes local tourist offices will advise you on vacation home rentals if you write or call them directly. Plus, dozens of agencies throughout the United States and Canada offer rentals in the Virgin Islands. Here are some recommendable ones:

At Home Abroad, Suite 6-H, 405 E. 56th St., New York, NY 10022 (☎ **212/ 421-9165**), has a roster of private homes, villas, and condos for rent in St. Thomas, St. John, Tortola, and Virgin Gorda; maid service is included in the price.

Caribbean Connection, P.O. Box 261, Trumbull, CT 06611 (☎ **203/ 261-8603**), offers island-hopping itineraries and a variety of accommodations, including condos and villas. It specializes in the less developed Caribbean islands, and will also customize itineraries. The best part about Caribbean Connection is that it caters to four different budgets, defined as: shoestring, comfortable, deluxe, and fantasy.

Hideaways International, 767 Islington St., Portsmouth, NH 03801 (☎ **800/ 843-4433,** or 603/430-4433 in the U.S.), publishes *Hideaways Guide,* a 148-page pictorial directory describing home rentals throughout the Caribbean. Rentals range from cottages to staffed villas to entire islands! In most cases, you deal directly with the owners. Other services include specialty cruises, yacht charters, airline ticketing, car rentals, and hotel reservations. Annual membership is $99; a 4-month trial membership is $39.

If you're interested in a condo rental, contact **Paradise Properties of St. Thomas,** P.O. Box 9395, St. Thomas, U.S.V.I. 00801 (☎ **809/775-3115**), which currently represents six condo complexes. Rental units range from studio apartments to four-bedroom villas. A minimum stay of 3 days is required in any season, 7 nights during Christmas.

Island Villas, Property Management Rentals, 6 Company St., Christiansted, St. Croix, U.S.V.I. 00820 (☎ **800/626-4512** or 809/773-8821; fax 809/773-8821), offers some of the best properties on St. Croix. The outfit specializes in villas, condos, and private homes; many are on the beach. One- to six-bedroom units are available, with prices from $1,200 to $5,000 per week.

Villas of Distinction, P.O. Box 55, Armonk, NY 10504 (☎ **800/289-0900,** or 914/273-3331 in the U.S.), is one of the best agencies, offering "complete vacations," including car rental and domestic help. Private villas have one to six bedrooms, and almost every villa has a swimming pool.

Ocean Property Management, P.O. Box 8529, St. Thomas, U.S.V.I. 00801 (☎ **800/874-7897**), rents accommodations in St. Thomas at the Secret Harbourview Villas, which are set on a hillside. Condo suites with private balconies and ocean views lie only a short walk from the beach. They also rent condo suites on other parts of St. Thomas.

THE WEST INDIAN GUEST HOUSE

Most of the Antilleans stay in guest houses when they travel to the Virgin Islands. Some are surprisingly comfortable, with private baths in each room, air-conditioning or ceiling fans, and swimming pools. Don't expect the luxuries of a first-class resort, but for the money the guest house can't be beat. (You can always journey over to a big beach resort, and use its seaside facilities, but you must first check with the reception desk). Although free of frills, the guest houses we've recommended in this book are clean, comfortable, and safe.

RENTING YOUR OWN ISLAND

For extremely well-heeled escapists, the British Virgin Islands offer the option of renting a private island. If you can't foot the bill yourself, organize a group of friends to share the cost (but even splitting it can be pricey). Here's what's up for grabs:

- **Guana Island:** For a negotiable fee, up to 30 guests can take over this privately owned island, the sixth largest of the British Virgin Islands. The 850-acre island is a nature sanctuary with seven pristine beaches and a network of hiking trails. See chapter 7 for more details.
- **Mosquito Island:** Guests usually sail their yachts to this sandy 125-acre island that's about a 5-minute jaunt north of Virgin Gorda. Once on land, they take over Drake's Anchorage Resort Inn, which has 12 units. With four deserted beaches, it's the perfect hideaway—we're talking no TVs, phones, or any other modern amenities. See chapter 7 for more details.
- **Necker Island** (☎ **800/557-4255,** or 212/696-4566 in New York City): This 74-acre hideaway is enveloped by its own unpolluted coral reef. It's owned by Richard Branson (of Virgin Atlantic Airways), who is well acquainted with its trio

of sugar-white beaches. When he's not around, he leases the entire island to friends like Eddie Murphy and Princess Di. At the core of the island is a 10-bedroom villa, surrounded by two one-bedroom guest houses. Sun pours into the lush tropical garden, which has a private freshwater pool and Jacuzzi. The daily rate is $11,000 to $16,000, depending on the number of guests, and includes food, drinks, and activities (tennis, snorkeling, windsurfing, boating, and sea kayaking to name a few) for up to 24 people.

DINING

Dining in the Virgin Islands is generally more expensive than it is in either the United States or Canada since, except for locally caught fish, virtually everything is imported. A 10% to %15 service charge is automatically added to most restaurant tabs, and if the service has been good, you should tip extra. For details on island cuisine see "The Cuisine: A Taste of the Virgin Islands" in chapter 2.

In some of the posh resorts such as Caneel Bay on St. John, it is customary for men to wear a jacket, but in summer, virtually no establishment requires it. If in doubt, always ask the restaurant, or check the policy of the hotel before going to a particular establishment. At the better places, women's evening attire is casual-chic. During the day it is proper to wear something over your bathing suit if you're in a restaurant.

Whenever possible, stick to regional food, which is fresher. For a main dish, that usually means Caribbean lobster or fish caught in the deep sea. Many world-class chefs cook in the Virgin Islands, but they are only as good as their ingredients, which are not always the freshest.

Nevertheless, the food is better than ever in the islands, and many fine talents, including many top-notch female chefs from California, now cook there. Many have adapted stateside recipes with the local ingredients available to come up with Caribbean/California cuisine.

Check to see if reservations are required before going to a restaurant. In summer, you can almost always get in, but in winter, all the tables may be taken at some of the famous but small places.

If you're going out in the evening, especially if you drink, it is a good idea to go by taxi and arrange for the taxi to pick you up or have the restaurant call a cab for you. It generally arrives in no more than 30 minutes.

Whatever you do, try to get out and eat at some of the local places. The prices are more reasonable, and the fare is more adventurous and interesting.

12 Tips on Shopping

With discount stores mushrooming in Canada and the United States, your hometown might offer better bargains than the fabled duty-free deals of St. Thomas and St. Croix, which are the top shopping destinations in the entire Caribbean. We've recommended numerous shops in the individual island chapters ahead, but we thought you might appreciate a few insider tips on shopping in the Virgin Islands, from bargain-hunting to bartering.

U.S. residents are entitled to $1,200 worth of duty-free exports from the **U.S. Virgin Islands** (not Puerto Rico) every 30 days—that's three times the exemption allowed from most foreign destinations. (For more details on Customs, see "Visitor Information, Entry Requirements & Money," earlier in this chapter.) One way to get the most out of your **duty-free allowance** is to send gifts home. You can ship up to $100 worth of unsolicited gifts per day without paying duty, and you don't have to declare such gifts on your Customs form when leaving the islands.

If you're in the market for a particular item, it's wise to check out prices at home before you go. The best buys are liquor (because of the generous U.S. allowance), jewelry, and china. You may find bargains on crystal, certain clothing, porcelain, leather goods, watches, and even furs. Cigarettes are cheaper, and imported beauty products such as perfume are generally excellent buys. (See also "The Best Shopping Buys" in chapter 1.)

In clothing, the best buys are woolen items, such as sweaters. Cashmere sweaters are sometimes good values. Fashions from the Far East, especially China, are usually inexpensive, and European and U.S. designer labels are often discounted. But, remember, you may find the same (or better) discounts back on the mainland.

Jewelry is the most common item for sale in St. Thomas. Look over the selections of gold and gemstones (emeralds are traditionally considered the finest savings) carefully. Gold that is marked 24K in the United States and Canada is marked 999 (99.9% pure gold) on European items. Gold marked 18K in the United States and Canada has a European marking of 750 (or 75% pure), and 14K gold is marked 585 (or 58.5% pure). You can often get deals on name-brand **watches,** which are sold throughout Charlotte Amalie and, to a lesser degree, St. Croix.

When shopping for **porcelain and crystal,** you'll find that the best European brands are *usually* priced lower than in the States; it pays to know what the going rate is at home before you leave. Most stores will arrange for items to be shipped.

The most popular island-made, duty-free items include leather sandals, paintings, island dolls, locally made clothing, pottery, boutique canvas bags, locally recorded music, straw products, batiks, and unusual handmade jewelry.

If you're only visiting and shopping in the **British Virgin Islands,** remember that goods will be taxed at the same rate as any other foreign destination. But, it's pretty much common knowledge that shopping selections and venues in the B.V.I. pale in comparison to those of St. Croix and especially St. Thomas. The smart shopper will still find some good buys in Road Town, Tortola, usually on English fabrics, china, and some other British goods. But, again, you will have to pay duty when you bring them back into the United States if their value exceeds the limit imposed by U.S. Customs.

Theoretically, **bartering** or bargaining is not the rule, but over the years we have found merchant after merchant willing to do so, particularly on expensive items such as jewelry and perfume. Obviously, the slow summer, late spring, and fall seasons are the best times to try to make deals with local vendors.

FAST FACTS: The U.S. Virgin Islands

American Express   Visitors to St. Thomas and St. John should contact **Caribbean Travel Agency/Tropic Tours,** 9716 Estate Thomas (☎ **809/774-1855**). On St. Croix, the AmEx rep is **Southerland,** Chandler's Wharf, Gallows Bay (☎ **809/773-9500**).

Area Code   The area code for all the U.S. Virgin Islands is **809,** which you can dial directly from the U.S. mainland.

Banks   Several major banks are represented; most are open Monday through Thursday from 9am to 2:30pm, Friday from 9am to 2pm and 3:30 to 5pm.

Business Hours   Typically, Monday through Friday from 9am to 5pm, Saturday from 9am to 1pm. On Sundays, businesses will open or close depending on how many cruise ships are in port.

Cameras and Film   Most name brand film, like Kodak, is sold, but it's not cheap, and neither is developing it so bring it home. Protect your camera, not only from theft, but also from sun, saltwater, and sand. For the best commercial camera stores in the U.S.V.I., see the individual island chapters.

Climate   See "When to Go," earlier in this chapter.

Currency   U.S. currency is used on the U.S. Virgin Islands.

Customs   See "Visitor Information, Entry Requirements & Money," earlier in this chapter.

Documents Required   See "Visitor Information, Entry Requirements & Money," earlier in this chapter.

Driving Rules   Drive on the left, and obey speed limits (20 m.p.h. in town, 35 m.p.h. outside).

Drugs   A branch of the federal narcotics strike force is permanently stationed in the U.S. Virgin Islands. If convicted of possession of marijuana, severe penalties are imposed, ranging from 2 to 10 years imprisonment. Possession of hard drugs like cocaine can get you 15 years in prison.

Drugstores   If you need medications, over-the-counter or prescription, you'll find many drugstore outlets in St. Thomas and St. Croix, with limited stores on St. John. See specific island "Fast Facts" for local drugstore recommendations.

Electricity   The electrical current in the Virgin Islands is the same as on the mainland: 110 volts AC, 60 cycles.

Embassies and Consulates   There are no embassies or consulates here.

Emergencies   Police, **915;** fire, **921;** ambulance, **922;** coast guard, **809/774-1911.**

Hitchhiking   It isn't illegal, but it isn't widely practiced. It might be more practical on St. Croix, because of longer distances, but we don't recommend it anywhere.

Holidays   See "When to Go," earlier in this chapter.

Hospitals   See "Fast Facts" for the individual islands.

Information   See "Visitor Information," earlier in this chapter, and in specific island chapters.

Laundry   See "Fast Facts" under the individual island listings for the names of Laundromats.

Liquor Laws   You must be 21 years of age or older to purchase liquor or order it out.

Mail   Postage rates are the same as on the U.S. mainland.

Maps   Tourist offices provide free maps of all three islands. If you plan on extensive touring, purchase a copy of the *Official Road Map of the United States Virgin Islands,* available in most bookstores.

Newspapers and Magazines   Daily U.S. newspapers are flown into St. Thomas and St. Croix, and local papers, such as the *Virgin Island Daily News,* available on St. Thomas and St. Croix, also carry the latest news. St. Croix has its own daily newspaper, the *St. Croix Avis;* St. John's paper is *Tradewinds.*

Passports   See "Visitor Information, Entry Requirements & Money," earlier in this chapter.

Pets   To bring your pet, you must have a health certificate from a mainland veterinarian, and show proof of vaccination against rabies. Very few hotels allow animals, so check in advance. If you're strolling with your dog through the national park on St. John, the dog must be on a leash. Pets are not allowed at campgrounds, picnic areas, or on public beaches. Both St. Croix and St. Thomas have veterinarians listed in the yellow pages.

Police   Call **915.** For local stations see "Police" under "Fast Facts" for the individual islands.

Radio and TV   All three islands receive both cable and commercial TV stations. Radio weather reports can be heard at 7:30pm and 8:30am on 99.5 FM.

Rest Rooms   You'll find public toilets at public beaches and airport terminals, and sometimes at the main town squares.

Taxes   There is no departure tax for the U.S. Virgin Islands. Hotels add an 8% tax to rates that is not always included in the rate quoted to you. Always ask.

Telephone, Telex, and Fax   Local calls at a telephone booth cost 25¢. From all points on the mainland you can dial direct to the Virgin Islands using the area code **809.** Cable service is available as well. Most hotels are equipped to send telex and fax. You can also do so at local post offices on the islands. See "Telephone, Telex, and Fax" under "Fast Facts" under individual island listings for specific addresses.

Time   The U.S. Virgins are on Atlantic Time, which places the islands one hour ahead of Eastern Time. However, during Daylight Saving Time, the Virgin Islands and the East Coast are on the same time. So when it's 6am in Charlotte Amalie, it's 5am in Miami; during Daylight Saving Time it's 6am in both places.

Tipping   Tip as you would on the U.S. mainland.

Tourist Offices   See "Visitor Information, Entry Requirements & Money," earlier in this chapter. In St. Thomas, the Visitors Center is at Emancipation Square (☎ **809/774-8784**); in St. Croix at the Old Scalehouse (☎ **809/773-0495**) on the waterfront at Christiansted, and also in the Customs House Building, Strand Street, Frederiksted (☎ **809/772-0357**); and in St. John at Cruz Bay (☎ **809/ 776-6450**).

Visas   U.S. and Canadian citizens do not need a visa to enter the U.S. Virgin Islands. Visitors from other nations should have a passport and a U.S. visa. Those visitors may also be asked to produce an onward ticket. See "Visitor Information, Entry Requirements & Money," earlier in this chapter.

Water   There is ample water for showers and bathing in the Virgin Islands, but you are asked to conserve. Many visitors drink the local tap water with no harmful after effects. Others, more prudent or with more delicate stomachs, should stick to bottled water.

FAST FACTS: The British Virgin Islands

American Express   Local representatives include Travel Plan, Ltd., Waterfront Drive (☎ **284/494-2347**), in Tortola; and Travel Plan, Ltd., Virgin Gorda Yacht Harbour (☎ **284/495-5586**), in Virgin Gorda.

Area Code   The area code is **284.** When calling from outside the islands, you must then dial **49** before all B.V.I. numbers.

Banks   Banks are generally open Monday through Thursday from 9am to 3pm, Friday from 9am to 5pm. To cash traveler's checks, try Bank of Nova Scotia, Wickhams Cay (☎ **284/494-2526**) or Barclays Bank, Wickhams Cay (☎ **284/ 494-2171**), both near Road Town.

Bookstores   The best bookstore on the island is the National Educational Services Bookstore, Wickhams Cay in Road Town (☎ 284/494-3921).

Business Hours   Most offices are open Monday through Friday from 9am to 5pm. Government offices are open Monday through Friday from 8:30am to 4:30pm. Shops are generally open Monday through Friday from 9am to 5pm and Saturday from 9am to 1pm.

Cameras and Film   The best place for supplies and developing on Tortola is Bolo's Brothers, Wickhams Cay (☎ **284/494-2867**).

Currency   The U.S. dollar is the legal currency, much to the surprise of British travelers.

Customs   You can bring items intended for your personal use into the B.V.I. For U.S. residents, the duty-free allowance is only $400, providing you have been out of the country for 48 hours. You may send unsolicited gifts home if they total less than $50 per day to any single address. You don't pay duty on items classified as handcrafts, art, or antiques. See "Visitor Information, Entry Requirements & Money," earlier in this chapter.

Dentist   For dental emergencies, contact **Dental Surgery** (☎ **284/494-3474**), which is in Road Town, Tortola, behind the Skeleton Building and next to the *BVI Beacon,* the local newspaper.

Doctor   See "Hospitals," below.

Documents Required   See "Visitor Information, Entry Requirements & Money," earlier in this chapter.

Driving Rules   You need a valid Canadian or American driver's license and must pay $10 at police headquarters for a 3-month British Virgin Islands driving permit. Some of the larger car-rental companies keep a supply of these forms. Remember to drive on the left.

Drug Laws   Illegal drugs—including use, possession, and sale—are strictly prohibited, and penalties are stiff.

Drugstores   The best place to go is J. R. O'Neal, Ltd., Main Street, Road Town (☎ **284/494-2292**), in Tortola; closed Sunday.

Electricity   The electrical current is 110 volts, AC, 60 cycles, as in the United States.

Embassies and Consulates   There are none in the B.V.I.

Emergencies   Thirteen doctors practice in Tortola, plus Peebles Hospital, Porter Road, Road Town (☎ **284/494-3497**), with X-ray and laboratory facilities. One doctor practices on Virgin Gorda. Your hotel can put you in touch with the island's medical staff.

Hitchhiking   Travel by thumb is illegal.

Holidays   See "When to Go," earlier in this chapter.

Hospitals   In Road Town, you can go to Peebles Hospital, Porter Road (☎ **284/494-3497**).

Information   See "Visitor Information, Entry Requirements & Money," earlier in this chapter.

Laundry and Dry Cleaning   In Tortola, one of the best places is Freeman's Laundry and Dry Cleaning, Purcell Estate (☎ **284/494-2285**).

Liquor Laws   The legal minimum age for purchasing liquor or drinking alcohol in bars or restaurants is 21.

Lost Property   Go to the police station. Sometimes they'll broadcast notice of your lost property on the local radio station.

Mail   Most hotels will mail letters for you, or you can go directly to the post office. Allow 4 days to 1 week for letters to reach the North American mainland. Postal rates in the BVI have been raised now to 30¢ for a postcard (airmail) to the United States or Canada, and 45¢ for a first-class airmail letter (¹/₂ ounce) to the United States or Canada, or 35¢ for a second-class letter (¹/₂ ounce) to the United States or Canada.

Maps   The best map of the British Virgin Islands is published by Vigilate and is sold at most bookstores in Road Town.

Newspapers and Magazines   Papers from the mainland, such as *The Miami Herald,* are flown into Tortola and Virgin Gorda daily, and copies of the latest issues of *Time* and *Newsweek* are sold at hotel newsstands and at various outlets in Road Town. The B.V.I. have no daily newspaper, but *The Island Sun,* published Wednesday and Friday, is a good source of information on local entertainment.

Nudity   Unlike in some parts of the Caribbean, nudity is an offense punishable by law in the B.V.I.

Passports   See "Visitor Information, Entry Requirements & Money," earlier in this chapter.

Police   The main police headquarters is on Waterfront Drive near the ferry docks on Sir Olva Georges Plaza (☎ **284/494-3822**) in Tortola. There is also a police station on Virgin Gorda (☎ **284/495-5222**) and on Jost Van Dyke (☎ **284/495-9345**).

Radio and TV   Hotels subscribe to cable TV and get such broadcasts as CNN. The B.V.I. has two local FM stations with nonstop music, including Z-HIT (94.3) and Z-WAVE (97.3).

Rest Rooms   You'll find public toilets at airports and ferry terminals; visitors usually rely on rest rooms at restaurants and hotels.

Taxes   There is no sales tax. A government tax of 7% is imposed on all hotel rooms. An $8 departure tax is collected from everyone leaving by air, $5 for those departing by sea.

Telephone, Telex, and Fax   You can call the British Virgins from the continental United States by dialing area code **284,** followed by **49,** and then five digits. Once here, omit both the 284 and the 49 to make local calls. Most hotels (not the small guest houses) will send a fax or telex for you.

Time   See "Fast Facts: The U.S. Virgin Islands," above.

Tipping   In general, tip 15%.

Tourist Offices   The headquarters of the BVI Tourist Board is in the center of Road Town (Tortola), close to the ferry dock, south of Wickhams Cay (☎ **284/494-3134**).

Visas   Visitors who stay for fewer than 6 months don't need a visa if they possess a return or onward ticket.

Water   See "Fast Facts: The U.S. Virgin Islands," above.

The U.S. Virgin Islands: St. Thomas

St. Thomas, the busiest cruise-ship harbor in the West Indies, is not the largest of the U.S. Virgins—St. Croix, 40 miles south, holds that title. But, bustling Charlotte Amalie at the heart of the island is the capital of the U.S. Virgin Islands, and remains the shopping hub of the Caribbean. Because of St. Thomas's thriving commercial activity and its ongoing drug and crime problems, the island is often referred to as the most "unvirgin" of the Virgin Islands.

Vacationers discovered St. Thomas right after World War II, and they've been flocking here ever since. Thanks to tourism, the standard of living is one of the highest in the Caribbean. St. Thomas is a boon for cruise-ship shoppers who flood Charlotte Amalie's Main Street; it's virtually a three- to four-block-long shopping center. While this area tends to be overcrowded, the island's beaches, major hotels, most restaurants, and entertainment facilities are, for the most part, removed from the cruise-ship chaos.

Condominium apartments and expensive villas continue to sprout up over the debris of bulldozed shacks. But, you can still find seclusion at a hotel in more remote sections of the island. Hotels on the north side of St. Thomas look out at the Atlantic, whereas those on the south side front the calmer Caribbean Sea.

St. Thomas is the most cosmopolitan of all the Virgin Islands, either U.S. or British. Its ports are not just for cruise-ships, but also for privately owned million-dollar yachts. The beaches here are renowned for their white sand and calm, turquoise waters, including the very best of them all, Magens Bay. *National Geographic* rated the island as one of the top destinations in the world for sailing, scuba diving, and fishing.

Charlotte Amalie, with its white houses and bright red roofs glistening in the sun, is one of the most beautiful towns in the Caribbean. Parts of it, however, are less than picturesque. The town is most synonymous with shopping, but it is also filled with historic sights like Fort Christian, an intriguing 17th-century building constructed by the Danes. The town's architecture reflects the island's culturally diverse past. You'll pass Dutch doors, Danish red-tile roofs, French iron grillwork, and Spanish-style patios.

And last, but not least, is the climate—the reason we've ventured here in the first place. St. Thomas enjoys sunshine all year round, with temperatures hovering in the 80s during the day, and dropping into the 70s at night. You don't have to worry too much about rain—most tropical showers come and go so fast you hardly have time to get off the beach.

1 Orientation

ARRIVING
BY PLANE

If you're flying to St. Thomas, you will land at the **Cyril E. King Airport** (☎ 809/774-5100), to the west of Charlotte Amalie on Route 30, where you can easily grab a taxi to your hotel or villa. Chances are you will be staying east of Charlotte Amalie, so keep in mind that getting through town often involves long delays and traffic jams, especially on heavy cruise-ship days.

Nonstop flights to the U.S. Virgin Islands from New York and Atlanta take $3^3/4$ and $3^1/2$ hours, respectively. Flight time from Miami is about $2^1/2$ hours. Flight time between St. Thomas and St. Croix is only 20 minutes. Flying to San Juan from mainland cities and connecting to St. Thomas may cost less than regular nonstop fares (see "Flying to the Virgin Islands" in chapter 3).

American Airlines (☎ 800/433-7300) offers frequent nonstop service to St. Thomas from the U.S. mainland, with five daily flights from New York (summer flights vary; call for schedules). Passengers coming from other parts of the world are usually routed through American hubs in Miami or San Juan, both of which offer daily nonstop service. Connections from Los Angeles or San Francisco to St. Thomas are usually through New York, San Juan, or Miami. American arranges discount land-and-air packages to St. Thomas and other Virgin Island destinations.

Flights from Puerto Rico to the U.S. Virgin Islands are usually on **American Eagle** (☎ 800/433-7300), with daily flights leaving every 30 minutes to an hour.

Delta (☎ 800/221-1212) offers two daily nonstop flights between Atlanta and St. Thomas, one in the morning, one in the afternoon. The later flight continues on to St. Croix. **TWA** (☎ 800/221-2000) does not fly nonstop to any of the Virgin Islands, but instead offers connections on other carriers through San Juan. TWA flies into San Juan twice daily from New York's JFK, once daily nonstop from Miami, and once daily from St. Louis with a touchdown in Miami. **USAir** (☎ 800/428-4322) now has two daily flights from Baltimore to St. Thomas—one is nonstop, the other originates in Philadelphia with a stop in Baltimore.

Bohlke (☎ 809/778-9177), a charter airline, flies to St. Thomas from San Juan and Miami. A one-way fare for one to eight passengers is $920. They also fly to the B.V.I. and offer day trips to St. Croix. **Prestige Airways** (☎ 800/299-USVI) offers nonstop flights from Miami to St. Thomas (and St. Croix) 5 days a week in winter, 2 days in the off-season.

A final hint: Bargain-seekers should ask their airline representative to connect them with the tour desk, which can arrange discounted hotel rates if a hotel reservation is booked simultaneously with airline tickets.

BY BOAT

Charlotte Amalie is the busiest cruise-ship port in the Caribbean. For details on cruise-ship travel, see the "Cruises" section in chapter 3.

St. Thomas maintains no ferry connections to St. Croix, some 40 miles to the south. The best way to get there is by plane.

Island Highlights: St. Thomas

Beaches

- **Magens Bay,** 3 miles north of Charlotte Amalie, one of the world's most beautiful beaches.
- **Stouffer Grand Beach,** on the North Side, a stunning strip of palm trees and white sand, with water sports galore.
- **Sapphire Beach,** on the East End, with a luxury hotel complex and great views of St. John; it's *the* place to be on Sunday afternoons.

Must-See Attractions

- **Coral World,** a marine complex featuring a three-story underwater observation tower 100 feet offshore.
- **Jim Tillett's Art Gallery and Boutique,** built around an old plantation-era sugar mill.

Great Towns/Villages

- **Charlotte Amalie,** the capital of St. Thomas and the U.S.V.I., one of the most beautiful port cities in the Caribbean.
- **Frenchtown,** a quainter satellite of Charlotte Amalie, famous for its "cha-chas," or straw hats.

Historic Buildings

- The **St. Thomas Synagogue,** second oldest in the Western Hemisphere, built by Sephardic Jews in 1833.
- **Fort Christian,** constructed by the Danes in 1671 and named for King Christian V.
- **Government House,** at Government Hill in Charlotte Amalie, the official residence of the U.S. Virgin Islands governor.

If you're in the British Virgin Islands, you can take a boat to Charlotte Amalie from Tortola. Trip time is only 45 minutes between these two capitals, and a one-way ticket is $19, $35 round-trip. The major carriers to and from Tortola are **Smith's Ferry** (☎ 809/775-7292) and **Native Son** (☎ 809/774-8685), which are both based in Charlotte Amalie on St. Thomas. Boats arrive and depart from Tortola's West End.

St. Thomas is also linked by boat to St. John, about 3 to 5 miles away. Ferries depart from Red Hook Marina on the East End of St. Thomas and arrive at Cruz Bay on St. John. Trip time is about 20 minutes; the cost is $3 one way. For complete ferry schedules, call **809/776-6282.**

A new ferry service from St. Thomas to Puerto Rico (with a stop in St. John), is available once every 2 weeks, maybe more if the demand increases. Trip time from Charlotte Amalie is about 2 hours; the cost is $60 one way, including ground transportation to the San Juan airport or Condado, Puerto Rico. For more information, call **809/776-6282.**

VISITOR INFORMATION

In St. Thomas, the **visitors center** at Emancipation Square (☎ 809/774-8784) dispenses a helpful booklet, **"St. Thomas This Week,"** which has maps of St. Thomas and St. John, plus up-to-date touring information and current event listings. Open Monday through Friday from 8am to 5pm, Saturday from 8am to noon.

CITY LAYOUT
MAIN STREETS & ARTERIES

Charlotte Amalie, the capital of St. Thomas, is the only town on the island. Bordering the waterfront, its seaside promenade is called **Waterfront Highway** or simply, the Waterfront. From here, you can take any of the streets or alleyways into town to **Main Street** or Dronningens Gade. Principal links between Main Street and the Waterfront include **Raadets Gade, Tolbod Gade, Store Tvaer Gade,** and **Strand Gade.**

Main Street is home to all the major shops. The western end (near the intersection with Strand Gade) is known as **Market Square,** once the site of the biggest slave market auctions in the Caribbean Basin. Today, it's an open-air cluster of stalls where native farmers and gardeners gather daily (except Sunday) to peddle their produce. Go early in the morning to see the market at its best.

Running parallel to and north of Main Street is **Back Street** or Vimmelskaft Gade, which is also lined with many stores, including some of the less expensive ones.

Note: It's quite dangerous to walk along Back Street at night, but it's reasonably safe for daytime shopping.

In the eastern part of town, between Tolbod Gade and Fort Pladsen (northwest of Fort Christian), lies **Emancipation Park,** commemorating the liberation of the slaves in 1848. Most of the major historical buildings, including the Legislature, Fort Christian, and Government House, lie within a short walk of this park.

Southeast of the park looms ✪ **Fort Christian.** Crowned by a clock tower and painted rusty red, it was constructed by the Danes in 1671. The **Legislative Building,** seat of the elected government of the U.S. Virgin Islands, lies on the harbor side of the fort.

Kongens Gade (or King's Street) leads to **Government Hill,** which overlooks the town and St. Thomas Harbor. **Government House,** a white brick building dating from 1867, stands atop the hill.

Between **Hotel 1829,** a former mansion built in that year by a French sea captain, and Government House is a staircase known as the **Street of 99 Steps.** Actually, someone miscounted: It should be called the Street of 103 Steps. Regardless, the steps lead to the summit of Government Hill.

Close by are the remains of the 17th-century **Fort Skytsborg** or Blackbeard's Tower, a reference to the notorious 18th-century pirate Edward Teach, who is said to have spied on treasure galleons approaching the harbor. Today a 22-room hotel, **Blackbeard's Castle,** stands here.

Blackbeard's, however, should not be confused with **Bluebeard's Tower,** which crowns a 300-foot hill at the eastern edge of town. This is the site of the best known (but not the best) hotel in the Virgin Islands, Bluebeard's Castle.

FINDING AN ADDRESS

Finding an address in Charlotte Amalie is relatively easy, even though many stores don't advertise or even display their street numbers. As in the States, even numbers run up one side of the street and odd numbers up the other.

St. Thomas This Week, distributed free by the visitors center and usually on cruise ships stopping on St. Thomas, contains a great **two-page map,** with a clear, easy-to-follow street plan of Charlotte Amalie, plus the locations of important landmarks and all of Charlotte Amalie's leading shops.

The U.S. Virgin Islands

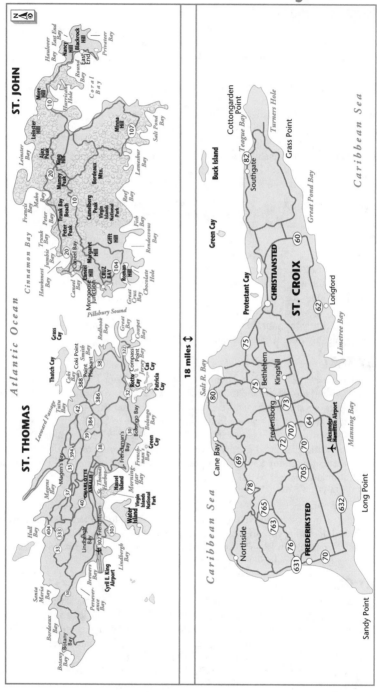

ST. JOHN

Haulover Bay
Nancy Hill
East End Bay
Blackrock Hill
Privateer Bay
Rosoal End
More Hill
Harmful Hole
Coral Bay
Leinster Bay
Leinster Hill
Ajax Peak
King Hill
Minna Hill
107
10
20
Maho Bay
Francis Bay
Peter Bay
Trunk Bay Beach
Camelberg Peak
Virgin Islands National Park
Bordeaux Mtn.
Salt Pond Bay
Lameshur Bay
Reef Bay
Cinnamon Bay
10
Peter Peak
Fish Bay
Jumbie Bay
Trunk Bay
Hawksnest Bay
20
Caneel Bay
Margaret Hill
Gifft Hill
Rendezvous Bay
Caneel Bay
CRUZ BAY
104
Mongoose Junction
Roman Hill
Great Cruz Bay
Chocolate Hole

Atlantic Ocean

Grass Cay

Thatch Cay

Redhook Bay
Great St. James Bay
Coupet Bay
Coki Point
Cabes Bay
Point Pleasant
Smith Bay
322
Rotto Cay
Compass Point
Cas Cay
388
38
386
32
Patricia Cay
Leeward Passage
42
384
39
35
394
38
Tutu Bay
Frenchman's Bay
30
Bolongo Bay
Bolongo Bay
Red Hook
Frenchman's Reef
Green Cay

ST. THOMAS

Pillsbury Sound

37
40
Magens Bay
St. Thomas Harbor
CHARLOTTE AMALIE
Hassel Island
Morning star
Virgin Islands National Park
Water Island

Magens Bay
Hull Bay
404
333
305
302
Frenchtown
Lindbergh Bay
Cyril E. King Airport
Lindbergh Bay

33
30
Santa Maria Bay
Brewers Bay
Perseverance Bay

Bordeaux Bay
Botany Bay
Botany Bay

↕ 18 miles

Buck Island

Green Cay

Cottongarden Point
Teague Bay
Turners Hole
82
Southgate
Grass Point
Great Pond Bay

Protestant Cay
CHRISTIANSTED
60
ST. CROIX
62
Longford
75
Limetree Bay

Caribbean Sea

Salt R. Bay
80
Bethlehem
Kingshill
75
Freidensborg
73
72
707
64
Manning Bay
Cane Bay
69
78
Alexander Hamilton Airport
70
705
765
763
Northside
76
FREDERIKSTED
632
631
70
Long Point
Sandy Point

Caribbean Sea

Caribbean Sea

NEIGHBORHOODS IN BRIEF

Charlotte Amalie is too small to be divided into several neighborhoods, and the only neighborhood of any significance is **Frenchtown.** Some of the older islanders still speak a distinctive Norman-French dialect here.

Since the heart of Charlotte Amalie is considered dangerous at night, Frenchtown, with its finer restaurants and interesting bars, has become the place to go after dark.

To reach Frenchtown, take Veterans Drive west of town along the Waterfront, turning left (shortly after passing the Windward Passage Hotel on your right) at the sign pointing to the Villa Olga.

The only other neighborhood worth mentioning is **Frenchman's Hill,** site of the famous Harbor View Hotel and restaurant. The Huguenots built many old stone villas here, which open onto panoramic views of the town and its harbor.

2 Getting Around

BY BUS

St. Thomas has the best public transportation of any island in the U.S. chain. Buses, called **Vitrans,** leave from street-side stops in the center of Charlotte Amalie, fanning out east and west along all the most important highways. They run between 5:30am and 10:30pm daily, and you rarely have to wait more than 30 minutes during the day. A ride within Charlotte Amalie is 75¢; anywhere else, $1. You may not be delivered to your door, but service is safe, efficient, and comfortable. For schedule and bus stop information, call **809/774-5678.**

BY TAXI

Taxis are everywhere on St. Thomas, and for good reason: They're the major means of transportation. Cabs are unmetered, and fares are controlled and widely posted; however, we still recommend that you negotiate a fare with the driver before you get into the car. A typical fare from Charlotte Amalie to Sapphire Beach is from $8 to $10 per person. Surcharges, from $1.50 to $2, are added after midnight. If you want to hire a taxi and a driver (who just may be a great tour guide) for a day, expect to pay about $30 for two passengers for two hours of sightseeing; each additional passenger pays $12. For 24-hour radio dispatch taxi service, call **809/ 774-7457.**

Taxi vans transport 8 to 12 passengers to multiple destinations on the island. It's cheaper to take a van if you're going from your hotel to the airport (or vice versa) instead of renting your own taxi. For example, a taxi from the airport to the Renaissance Grand Beach Resort costs $8 individually, but only $5 per person if there are passengers on board going in the same direction.

BY CAR

RENTING A CAR   Many of the big North American car-rental chains have offices at the airport in St. Thomas, and competition with local agencies is stiff. We recommend going with one of the larger companies. Before you go, compare the rates of: **Avis** (☎ 800/331-1084), **Budget** (☎ 800/626-4516), and **Hertz** (☎ 800/ 654-3001). There is no tax on car rentals in the Virgin Islands.

At press time, the cheapest cars at these firms were $227, $237, and $227.70, respectively, for 1 week (subject to change). All three companies offer cars with automatic transmission and air-conditioning.

St. Thomas has a high accident rate. Visitors are not used to driving on the left, the hilly terrain shelters blind curves and entrance ramps, roads are narrow and poorly lit, and drivers often get behind the wheel after too many drinks.

To be on the safe side, we recommend getting **collision-damage insurance,** which usually costs an extra $13 to $14 per day. But, be aware that even with this insurance, you could still get hit with a whopping deductible: The Hertz deductible is the full value of the car; at Avis it's $250; and Budget has no deductible.

PARKING   Because Charlotte Amalie is a labyrinth of congested one-way streets, don't try to drive within town looking for a spot. If you can't find a place to park along the waterfront (free), go to the large, sprawling lot to the east of Fort Christian, across from the Legislature Building. Parking fees are nominal here, and you can park your car and walk northwest toward Emancipation Park, or along the waterfront until you reach the shops and attractions.

DRIVING RULES   Always **drive on the left.** The speed limit is 20 m.p.h. in town, 35 m.p.h. outside town. Take extra caution when driving in St. Thomas, especially at night. Many roads are narrow, curvy, and poorly lit.

ON FOOT

Trust us: This is the only way to explore the heart of Charlotte Amalie. All the major attractions and the principal stores are within easy walking distances. However, other island attractions like Coral World or Magens Bay are long, hot hauls from the town center; it's better to take a bus or taxi to these places.

FAST FACTS: St. Thomas

Airport   Directly west of Charlotte Amalie, Cyril E. King Airport, Airport Road (☎ **809/774-5100**), is a modern terminal, with 11 major gates and five commuter gates. A line of taxis meets all arriving flights to take you to your hotel.

American Express   In St. Thomas, service is provided by the Caribbean Travel Agency/Tropic Tours, 9716 Estate Thomas, Havensight (☎ **809/774-1855**).

Area Code   The area code is **809.** You can dial direct from North America.

Baby-Sitters   Make arrangements through your hotel.

Banks   Several major U.S. banks are represented on St. Thomas. Hours vary, but most are open Monday through Thursday from 9am to 2:30pm, Friday from 9am to 2pm, 3:30 to 5pm.

Bookstores   Dockside Bookshop, Havensight Mall (☎ **809/774-4937**), where the cruise ships dock, also sells cards and maps.

Business Hours   Typical business hours are Monday through Friday from 9am to 5pm, Saturday from 9am to 1pm. Store hours are generally Monday through Friday, from 9am to 5pm, and Saturday, from 9am to 1pm. Some shops open Sunday for cruise-ship arrivals. Bars are usually open daily from 11am to midnight or 1am, although some hot spots stay open later.

Cameras and Film   Try Blazing Photos, Veterans Drive (☎ **809/774-5547**), in Charlotte Amalie, with a branch office at Havensight Mall (☎ **809/776-5547**), where cruise-ship passengers arrive. Other locations are at American Yacht Harbor at Red Hook (☎ **809/776-4587**), and Nisky Shopping Center (☎ **809/ 774-1005**).

Car Rentals   See "Getting Around," above.

Currency Exchange   Most major hotels will cash traveler's checks. You can also go to any of the major banks in Charlotte Amalie, including Chase Manhattan Bank, Veterans Drive (☎ **809/776-2222**) and Citibank, Veterans Drive (☎ **809/774-4800**). Citibank also issues Citicorp Traveler's Checks.

Dentist   The Virgin Island Dental Association (☎ **809/775-9110**) is a member of the American Dental Association and is also linked with various specialists. Call for information or an appointment.

Doctor   Doctors-on-Duty, Vitraco Park (☎ **809/776-7966**) in Charlotte Amalie, is a reliable medical facility.

Documents Required   See "Visitor Information, Entry Requirements & Money," in chapter 3.

Driving Rules   In St. Thomas motorists drive on the left. Road signs are similar to those on the U.S. mainland. Speed limit is 20 m.p.h. in town, 30 m.p.h. outside of town.

Drugstores   For over-the-counter and prescription medications, go to Apothecary, 19 Droningensgade (☎ **809/774-1341**).

Electricity   110 to 115 volts, 60 cycles, as on the U.S. mainland.

Embassies and Consulates   St. Thomas has no embassies or consulates.

Emergencies   Police, **911;** ambulance, **922;** fire, **921.**

Hospitals   The St. Thomas Hospital is at 48 Sugar Estate (☎ **809/776-8311**), Charlotte Amalie.

Hotlines   Call the police at **911** in case of emergency. If you have or witness a boating mishap, call the U.S. Coast Guard Rescue (☎ **787/729-6800,** ext. 140), which operates out of San Juan, Puerto Rico. Scuba divers should note the number of a decompression chamber (☎ **809/776-8311**) at the Roy Schneider Community Hospital on St. Thomas.

Laundry and Dry Cleaning   The major hotels provide laundry service, but it's more expensive than a Laundromat. For dry cleaning go to One-Hour Martinizing, Barbel Plaza (☎ **809/774-5452**), in Charlotte Amalie. A good full-service Laundromat is 4-Star Laundromat, 68 Kronprindsens Gade (☎ **809/774-8689**), in Charlotte Amalie.

Liquor Laws   Persons must be at least 21 years of age to patronize bars or purchase liquor in St. Thomas.

Maps   See "Orientation," earlier in this chapter.

Money   See "Visitor Information, Entry Requirements & Money," in chapter 3.

Newspapers and Magazines   Copies of U.S. mainland newspapers, such as *The New York Times, USA Today,* and *The Miami Herald,* arrive daily in St. Thomas and are sold at hotels and newsstands. The latest copies of *Time* and *Newsweek* are also for sale. *St. Thomas Daily News* covers local, national, and international events. Pick up *Virgin Islands Playground* and *St. Thomas This Week;* both are packed with visitor information and are distributed free all over the island.

Police   Dial **911** in an emergency.

Post Office   The main post office is at 9846 Estate Thomas (☎ **809/774-1950**), Charlotte Amalie, open Monday through Friday from 7:30am to 5:30pm and Saturday from 7:30am to 2:30pm.

Rest Rooms   You'll find public toilets at beaches and at the airport, but they are limited in town. Most visitors use the facilities of a bar or restaurant.

Safety   St. Thomas has an unusually high crime rate, particularly in Charlotte Amalie. Don't wander around town at night, particularly on Back Street. Guard your valuables. Store them in hotel safes if possible, and make sure you keep your doors and windows shut at night.

Taxes   The only local taxes are an 8% surcharge added to all hotel tariffs.

Taxis   See "Getting Around," earlier in this chapter.

Telephone, Telex, and Fax   All island phone numbers have seven digits. It is not necessary to use the 809 area code when dialing within St. Thomas. Numbers for all three islands, including St. John and St. Croix, are found in the U.S. Virgin Islands phone book. Hotels will send fax and telexes for you, often at cost, plus a small service charge. Make long distance, international, and collect calls as you would on the U.S. mainland.

Time   See "Fast Facts: The U.S. Virgin Islands," in chapter 3.

Tipping   Tip as you would on the U.S. mainland.

Transit Information   Call **809/774-7457** to order a taxi 24 hours a day. Call for airport information at **809/774-5100,** and dial **809/776-6282** for information about ferry departures for St. John.

Water   See "Fast Facts: The U.S. Virgin Islands," in chapter 3.

Weather   Call the U.S. Weather Service at **809/791-3490.**

3 Accommodations

Nearly every beach has its own hotel, and St. Thomas has more quaint inns than anyplace else in the Caribbean. You may want to stay in the capital, Charlotte Amalie, or at any of the far points.

If you want to stay in St. Thomas on the cheap, you'll have to stay at one of the guest houses in the Charlotte Amalie area. All the glittering, expensive properties lie in the East End. Remember that hotels in the Virgin Islands slash their prices in summer by 20% to 60%.

In our selection of hotels below, we've listed daily winter rates in double rooms with private baths. In general, **"Very Expensive"** indicates rooms charging from $325; **"Expensive,"** $195 to $325; **"Moderate,"** $135 to $195; and **"Inexpensive,"** under $135 (in this category, double rates can drop to as little as $65 per night for two people).

Unless otherwise noted, the rates listed do *not* include the 8% government tax. For an explanation of our symbols for rates with meal plans, see "Tips on Accommodations & Dining" in chapter 3.

CHARLOTTE AMALIE
EXPENSIVE

Bluebeard's Castle

Bluebeard's Hill (P.O. Box 7480), Charlotte Amalie, St. Thomas, U.S.V.I. 00801. ☎ **800/524-6599** in the U.S., or 809/774-1600. Fax 809/774-5134. 160 rms. A/C TV TEL. Winter, $195–$235 double. Off-season, $140–$175 double. Additional person $25 extra. MAP $50 per person extra. AE, DC, MC, V.

Bluebeard's is a popular resort overlooking Charlotte Amalie. In the 1930s, the U.S. government turned what had been a private home into a hotel that once hosted

Franklin D. Roosevelt. Its former position as the top hotel on the island has long been surpassed by deluxe East End resorts like Sapphire Beach. The hill surrounding the hotel is now heavily built up with offices and time-shares. Many guests prefer the rooms in the old tower, especially no. 139 or 140; some of the rooms in the newer unit, which also has conference rooms, have less charm. Guest rooms come in a variety of shapes and sizes—the decor in all is pleasant, but bland. After Hurricane Marilyn, the hotel reconfigured its rooms to give them a more suitelike appearance: They replaced twin beds with one queen-size bed, and turned the extra space into a sitting room.

Dining/Entertainment: The Terrace Restaurant commands a panoramic view and offers many delectable American and Caribbean specialties, open-air brunch, lunch, and late-night dining. Other dining choices include A Room with a View, an intimate bistro serving Caribbean and mostly Italian dishes, and Entre Nous (see separate listing in "Dining," below).

Services: Free transportation to Magens Bay Beach, a 15-minute drive away.

Facilities: Freshwater swimming pool, two Jacuzzis, championship tennis courts.

MODERATE

✪ Blackbeard's Castle

Blackbeard's Hill (P.O. Box 6041), Charlotte Amalie, St. Thomas, U.S.V.I. 00804. ☎ **800/344-5771** in the U.S., or 809/776-1234. Fax 809/776-4321. 18 rms, 3 junior suites, 3 full suites. A/C TV TEL. Winter, $140 double; $170 junior suite for 2; $190 full suite for 2. Off-season, $95 double; $120 junior suite for 2; $145 full suite for 2. Rates include continental breakfast. AE, MC, V. From the airport, turn right onto Rte. 30; when you get to Rte. 35, take a left and go ¹/₂ mile until you see the sign pointing left to the hotel.

Once a private residence, this castle has been transformed into a genuinely charming, hillside inn that enjoys one of the finest views of Charlotte Amalie and the harbor. Hurricane Marilyn shut the hotel in 1995, but it bounced back partially for the 1996 winter season.

In 1679 the Danish governor erected a soaring tower of chiseled stone here as a lookout for unfriendly ships. Legend says that Blackbeard himself lived in the tower 50 years later. Each bedroom has a semisecluded veranda, a flat-weave Turkish kilim, terra-cotta floors, simple furniture, and a private bath. Guests enjoy use of a swimming pool, and a lively bar and grill. In the Winter of 1997, the Hotel opened Cafe Lulu, featuring a cross-cultural cuisine. Magens Bay, a 15-minute taxi ride from the hotel, is the nearest beach. Blackbeard's is one of the most gay-friendly hotels on the island, and usually features a good-looking and lively clientele.

Hotel 1829

Kongens Gade (P.O. Box 1567), Charlotte Amalie, St. Thomas, U.S.V.I. 00804. ☎ **800/524-2002** in the U.S., or 809/776-1829. Fax 809/776-4313. 14 rms, 1 suite. A/C MINIBAR TV TEL. Winter, $90–$180 double; from $230 suite. Off-season, $70–$130 double; from $165 suite. Rates include continental breakfast. AE, DISC, MC, V.

Now a national historic site, this inn has serious island charm. Built by a French sea captain for his bride, it was designed by an Italian architect in a Spanish motif, with French grillwork, Danish bricks, and sturdy Dutch doors. Danish and African labor completed the structure in 1829 (hence the name), and since then it has entertained the likes of Edna St. Vincent Millay and Mikhail Baryshnikov.

After a major renaissance, this once-decaying historical site has become one of the leading small hotels in the Caribbean, attracting a small percentage of stylish gay clients. Right in the heart of town, it stands on a hillside about 3 minutes from Government House. It's a bit of a climb to the top of this multitiered structure, but you should note that there are many steps, but no elevator. Amid a cascade of flowering bougainvillea are the upper rooms, which overlook a central courtyard with a miniature swimming pool. The rooms, some of which are boxlike and small, are well designed, comfortable, and attractive, and most face the water. It's a 15-minute ride from the renowned beach at Magens Bay.

Villa Santana

Denmark Hill, St. Thomas, U.S.V.I. 00802. ☎ **809/776-1311.** Fax same as phone. 7 suites. TV TEL. Winter, $125–$195 suite for 2. Off-season, $85–$135 suite for 2. AE.

Built by Gen. Antonio López de Santa Ana of Mexico in the 1850s, this unique country villa boasts a panoramic view of ⌐   St. Thomas Harbor. It's a 5-minute walk from the sh‾

Beach. Accommodations co‾

can sleep in his former libra‾

equipped kitchens, private

vorite is La Mansion suite,

ing room and kitchen. Th

and intricate stonework. (

with hibiscus and bougair‾

Windward Passage Hot

Veterans Dr. (P.O. Box 640), S‾ 0.
Fax 809/774-1231. 151 rms, 0–
$230 suite. Off-season, $100‾ ‾k-
fast. AE, DC, MC, V. On Vitra

Even though its charm i‾ tel
enjoys one of the high‾ It's
the perfect place for b‾ t in
1968 and last renovate‾ ‾sive
atrium marked by a soaring concrete tount‾   iews
of some of the world's largest cruise ships and are subject to street‾   Many
frequent visitors request a bedroom overlooking the adjacent Emile Griffith Park, where baseball games provide entertainment. Rooms are comfortably modern and decorated in pastel colors—they're standard American motel rooms with marble-trimmed bathrooms.

The hotel restaurant, On the Bay, serves an eclectic cuisine, and the bar has a devoted local clientele. There's also a swimming pool and a variety of facilities for children. There is no beach nearby, but frequent shuttle buses run to and from Magens Bay, Morningstar Beach, and Sapphire Beach.

INEXPENSIVE

✪ The Admiral's Inn

Villa Olga (P.O. Box 306162), Frenchtown, Charlotte Amalie, St. Thomas, U.S.V.I. 00802. ☎ **800/544-0493** or 809/774-1376. Fax 809/774-8010. 16 rms. A/C TV TEL. Winter, $129–$149 double. Off-season, $89–$109 double. Children under 12 stay free in parents' room. Rates include continental breakfast. AE, DISC, MC, V. On Vitran bus line.

Set on a peninsula in Frenchtown, near the western entrance to Charlotte Amalie's harbor, this long famous little inn was battered by recent hurricanes, but is now up and running. Perched on the waterfront, a short walk from town, it often attracts divers and other travelers who aren't too particular about where they spend the night. Although the Admiral's Inn has had its share of admirers, it still disappoints many readers, who complain about lack of security and a sometimes hostile staff. Nevertheless, its fans continue to stay here.

Luckily, units that were in bad need of refurbishment before the hurricane received much-needed facelifts. A saltwater beach and sea pool lie a few paces from the lanai-style ocean-view units. There's a freshwater pool with a large sundeck, plus a poolside bar that remains open to hotel guests in the morning and afternoon. You can have dinner at the Chart House Restaurant (see "Dining," below), which is on the premises, but not affiliated with the inn.

Bunkers' Hill Hotel

7A Commandant Gade, Charlotte Amalie, St. Thomas, U.S.V.I. 00802. ☎ **809/774-8056.** Fax 809/774-3172. 16 rms, 4 suites. A/C TV TEL. Winter, $90 double; $105 suite. Off-season, $69 double; $79 suite. Rates include continental breakfast. MC, V.

This clean and centrally located guest lodge is ideal if you're on a tight budget and don't mind bare-bones accommodations and a little street noise. Four rooms have balconies, and some offer a view of the lights of Charlotte Amalie and the sea. In spite of some minor improvements, furnishings are simple and often threadbare. Guests share a communal kitchen, and there's a deli serving soups, sandwiches, and drinks. The closest beach is Lindbergh Bay, a 15-minute drive. Be aware that this is not the safest part of town, so take caution at night.

Danish Chalet Inn

9E-9J Nordsidevej (Solberg Rd.), P.O. Box 4319, St. Thomas, U.S.V.I. 00803. ☎ **800/635-1531** in the U.S. and Canada, or 809/774-5764. Fax 809/777-4886. 11 rms, 6 with bath. TEL. Winter, $75 double without bath; $85–$95 double with bath. Off-season, $70 double without bath; $80–$90 double with bath. Rates include continental breakfast. MC, V.

Set high above Charlotte Amalie on the western edge of the cruise-ship harbor, this inn is a 10-minute walk to the waterfront. A trio of buildings sits on a steeply inclined acre of land dotted with tropical shrubs and bougainvillea behind a facade of lattices and modern verandas. The heart and soul of the place is the panoramic terrace, which has a 180° view over the harbor and an honor bar. Bedrooms are neat, clean, and motel plain; all but the cheapest contain air-conditioning and refrigerators. The others have ceiling fans. Much of the hotel's business stems from its willingness to accept one-night guests (many other small island hotels insist on multiple-night bookings), making it popular with sailing buffs.

The establishment has no swimming pool, but it does have a semisecluded Jacuzzi spa for the relaxation of its guests. The nearest beaches are Morningstar and Beach-comber, about a 4-minute drive from here.

Galleon House

Government Hill (P.O. Box 6577), Charlotte Amalie, St. Thomas, U.S.V.I. 00804. ☎ **800/524-2052** in the U.S., or 809/774-6952. Fax 809/774-6952. 14 rms, 12 with bath. A/C TV TEL. Winter, $69 double without bath; $89 double with bath. Off-season, $59 double without bath; $69 double with bath. Rates include continental breakfast. AE, DISC, MC, V.

At the east end of Main Street, about a block from the main shopping section of St. Thomas, Galleon House is reached after a substantial climb, which can be down-right difficult in sweltering heat. The rates are among the most competitive in town, but some readers have complained about staff attitude and the lack of state-of-the-art maintenance. Nevertheless, it's an acceptable choice if your standards aren't too high.

At the top of the stairs is a concrete terrace that doubles as the reception area. Rooms are scattered in several hillside buildings, each with a ceiling fan, cable TV (HBO included), and so-so air-conditioning. There's a small freshwater pool and a sundeck. Breakfast is served on a veranda overlooking the harbor, and Magens Bay Beach is 15 minutes away by car.

Charlotte Amalie Accommodations

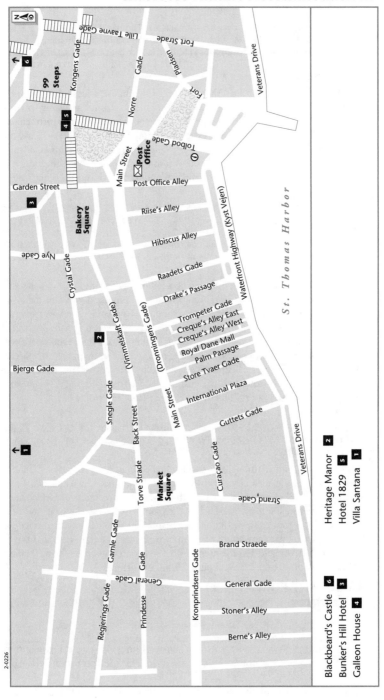

St. Thomas Harbor

99 Steps

Garden Street

Bakery Square

Market Square

Post Office

Heritage Manor 2
Hotel 1829 5
Villa Santana 1

Blackbeard's Castle 6
Bunker's Hill Hotel 3
Galleon House 4

2-0226

Heritage Manor

1A Snegie Gade (P.O. Box 90), Charlotte Amalie, St. Thomas, U.S.V.I. 00804. ☎ **800/ 828-0757** in the U.S., or 809/774-3003. Fax 809/776-9585. 8 rms, 3 with bath; 1 apt. A/C. Winter, $60–$80 double without bath; $95–$110 double with bath; $115 apt. Off-season, $40– $60 double without bath; $75–$80 double with bath; $85 apt. Rates include continental breakfast in winter only. AE, MC, V. Free parking.

This 150-year-old restored Danish merchant's town house is located in the historical district of Charlotte Amalie, about four blocks from the water. Intimate and personal, it offers well-furnished, comfortable bedrooms and one apartment with kitchens. The rooms contain many extras, including fans and refrigerator, and most have a view of the harbor. The tiny pool is only 4 feet deep—the manager calls it "very cute." A taxi, van, or bus will take you to the nearest beaches; the closest one is Brewer's, a 10-minute drive. Be careful walking back to the guest house at night.

Island View Guesthouse

11-C Contant (P.O. Box 1903), St. Thomas, U.S.V.I. 00803. ☎ **800/524-2023** for reservations only, or 809/774-4270. Fax 809/774-6167. 10 rms, 8 with bath; 1 suite. TV TEL. Winter, $65 double without bath; $95 double with bath; $115 suite. Off-season, $50 double without bath; $70 double with bath; $95 suite. Rates include continental breakfast. AE, MC, V. From the airport, turn right to Rte. 30; cut left and continue to the unmarked Scott Free Rd. where you turn left and look for the sign.

The Island View is located in a hilly neighborhood of private homes and villas about a 7-minute drive west of Charlotte Amalie and a 20-minute drive from the nearest beach at Magens Bay. Set on Crown Mountain, it has sweeping views over Charlotte Amalie and the harbor. Family owned and managed, it was originally built in the 1960s as a private home. Enlarged in 1989, it contains main-floor rooms (two without private bath) and some poolside rooms, plus six new units (three with kitchens and all with balconies). The bedrooms are cooled by breezes and fans, and the newer ones have optional air-conditioning. Furnishings are basic, although a major restoration was completed in 1997, following damage from Hurricane Marilyn.

Villa Blanca

4 Raphune Hill, Rte. 38 (P.O. Box 7505), Charlotte Amalie, St. Thomas, U.S.V.I. 00801. ☎ **809/ 776-0749.** Fax 809/779-2661. 16 rms. TV. Winter, $115–$135 double. Off-season, $75–$95 double. Honeymoon packages available. AE, DC, MC, V.

Small, intimate, and charming, this small-scale hotel lies 1 1/2 miles east of Charlotte Amalie on three secluded acres of panoramic, hilltop land. Owner Blanca Terrasa Smith converted her private residence, which was once the home of Dodge heiress Christine Cromwell, into a hotel. Each of the rooms contains a ceiling fan and/or air-conditioning, a well-equipped kitchenette, and a private balcony or terrace with sweeping views either eastward to St. John or westward to Puerto Rico and the harbor of Charlotte Amalie. On the premises is a freshwater swimming pool. The closest beach is Morningstar Beach, about a 20-minute drive.

FLAMBOYANT POINT
VERY EXPENSIVE

✪ Marriott's Morningstar Beach Resort

At Frenchman's Reef Beach Resort, Flamboyant Point, Charlotte Amalie, St. Thomas, U.S.V.I. 00802. ☎ **800/232-2425** or 809/776-8500. Fax 809/776-3054. 96 rms. A/C MINIBAR TV TEL. Winter, $325–$395 double. Off-season, $185–$235 double. MAP $58 per person extra. AE, DC, MC, V.

Both its public areas and its plush accommodations are among the most outstanding on the island—Hurricane Marilyn forced a major restoration in 1995. The resort was built on the landscaped flatlands near the beach of the Marriott's well-known Frenchman's Reef Beach Resort (see below). Each of the five buildings contains between 16 and 24 units, which have rattan furniture and views of the garden, beach, or the lights of Charlotte Amalie. Guests can enjoy the amenities and attractions of the larger hotel nearby, yet escape to the privacy of this more exclusive enclave.

Dining/Entertainment: The Oriental Terrace features Japanese exhibition cookery on a tennanyaki grill. The Raw Bar is an ideal spot for sunset cocktails, and Caesar's Ristorante, located on Morningstar Beach, serves rather standard American fare for lunch and dinner. A variety of restaurants and bars is also available at the adjoining Frenchman's Reef Beach Resort.

Services: Room service, baby-sitting, valet, plus all the services provided by the Frenchman's Reef next door.

Facilities: Two giant swimming pools; four tennis courts; water sports, including parasailing, dive shop, Jacuzzi, and private beach, which is one of the island's best.

EXPENSIVE

Marriott's Frenchman's Reef Beach Resort

Flamboyant Point (P.O. Box 7100), Charlotte Amalie, St. Thomas, U.S.V.I. 00801. ☎ **800/524-2000** in the U.S., or 809/776-8500. Fax 809/776-3054. 421 rms, 18 suites. A/C MINIBAR TV TEL. Winter, $275–$310 double; from $750 suite. Off-season, $160–$175 double; from $350 suite. MAP $60 per person extra. AE, DC, DISC, MC, V.

Frenchman's Reef, 3 miles east of Charlotte Amalie, has a winning southern position on a piece of land overlooking both the harbor and the Caribbean (though we find the rooms at its neighbor, Morningstar, more luxurious). Don't come here if you're looking for quaint and cozy island ambience. This is a full-service American-style mega-resort that will undergo an off-season $30 million renovation in 1997. It's a tour-group favorite, the darling of conventioneers, but also a popular choice among honeymooners.

Its facilities are devoted to the good life—you ride a glass-enclosed elevator to the private beach. The size and decor of the bedrooms vary greatly, but all are traditionally furnished in American-hotel taste.

Dining/Entertainment: Seafood with a continental flair is served in Windows on the Harbor, which resembles the inside of a cruise-ship and has a view of the harbor. The Lighthouse Cafe, once an actual lighthouse, serves up international fare. Caesar's Ristorante offers Italian cuisine and the Oriental Terrace features Japanese cooking. The Raw Bar serves light meals daily. At night the Wahoo Bar offers live entertainment.

Services: Room service (7am to 10:30pm), laundry, baby-sitting.

Facilities: Two swimming pools with poolside bar, tennis courts, water sports (snorkeling, scuba diving, sailing, deep-sea fishing).

EAST END
VERY EXPENSIVE

✪ Doubletree Sapphire Beach Resort and Marina

Rte. 36, Smith Bay Rd. (P.O. Box 8088), St. Thomas, U.S.V.I. 00801. ☎ **800/524-2090** in the U.S., or 809/775-6100. Fax 809/775-4024. 114 suites, 57 villas. A/C MINIBAR TV TEL. Winter, $355–$405 suite for 2; $435–$475 villa for 2. Off-season, $310–$360 suite for 2; $375–$415 villa for 2. Children 12 and under stay free in parents' room and eat for free when accompanied by a parent. MAP $70 per person extra. AE, DC, MC, V.

St. Thomas Hotels at a Glance	Access for disabled	A/C in bedrooms	Child-care facilities	Children are welcome	Convention facilities	Credit cards accepted	Directly beside beach	Fitness facility	Golf course nearby	Live entertainment	Marina facilities	Restaurant & bar	Spa facilities	Swimming pool	Tennis courts	TV in bedroom	Water sports
Admiral's Inn		•		•	•					•		•		•		•	
Bayside Inn Fitness		•		•		•	•	•				•		•		•	•
Blackbeard's Castle		•		•		•				•		•		•		•	
Bluebeard's Castle	•	•		•	•	•		•				•		•	•	•	•
Bolongo Beach Club	•	•	•		•	•	•		•		•	•	•	•	•	•	
Bunkers' Hill Hotel		•		•		•										•	
Danish Chalet Inn				•		•											
Doubletree Sapphire	•	•	•	•	•	•	•	•	•	•	•	•		•	•	•	•
Elisian Beach Resort		•		•	•	•	•	•		•		•	•	•	•	•	•
Galleon House																	
Heritage Manor				•		•								•		•	
Hotel 1829		•		•										•			
Island View Guesthouse		•		•		•				•		•		•		•	
Mariott's Frenchman	•	•	•	•	•	•	•	•		•		•		•	•	•	•
Mariott's Morningstar	•	•	•	•	•	•	•	•		•		•		•	•	•	•
Pavilions and Pools	•	•		•		•	•							•		•	•
Point Pleasant Resort	•	•		•		•	•			•		•		•	•	•	
Renaissance Grand	•	•	•	•	•	•	•	•			•	•	•	•	•		•
Ritz-Carlton	•	•	•	•	•	•	•	•	•	•		•		•	•	•	•
Secret Harbour	•	•	•	•		•	•	•				•		•	•	•	•
Villa Blanca				•		•								•		•	
Villa Santana				•		•								•		•	
Windward Passage	•	•	•	•	•	•				•		•		•		•	
Wyndham Sugar Bay	•	•		•	•	•	•	•				•		•	•	•	•

This secluded retreat, massively rebuilt in 1996, is one of the finest modern luxury resorts in the Caribbean. Guests can arrive by yacht, anchoring in the 67-slip marina, or else secure a suite or villa. Accommodations exude casual elegance and open onto a bay with one of St. Thomas's best and most sensuous beaches. The suites have fully equipped kitchens with microwaves, bedrooms with full bath, living/dining rooms with queen-size sofa beds, and large, fully tiled outdoor galleries complete with lounge furniture. The villas are on two different levels: The main, lower-level villas contain the same amenities as the suites, whereas the upper-level units feature a second full bath, a bedroom and sitting area with a queen-size sofa bed, plus a sundeck with out-door furniture. The suites accommodate one to four guests; the villas, up to six. The resort boasts a fantastic children's program, which makes this a good choice for families.

Dining/Entertainment: The Seagrape is one of the island's finest restaurants (see "Dining," below). A five-piece band often swings by for dancing under the stars. For casual dining, try the Sailfish Café.

Services: Beach towels, daily chamber service, guest-services desk, baby-sitting. The Little Gems Kids Klub offers supervised activities for kids.

Facilities: A one-acre freshwater pool, snorkeling equipment, Sunfish sailboats, windsurfing boards, four all-weather tennis courts, waterfront pavilion with snack bar, complete scuba-diving center.

Renaissance Grand Beach Resort

Rte. 38, Smith Bay Rd. (P.O. Box 8267), St. Thomas, U.S.V.I. 00801. ☎ **800/468-3571** in the U.S., or 809/775-1510. Fax 809/775-2185. 297 rms, 23 suites. A/C MINIBAR TV TEL. Winter, $325–$435 double; $595 one-bedroom suite; $895 two-bedroom suite. Off-season, $225–$325 double; $450 one-bedroom suite; $550 two-bedroom suite. MAP $60 per person extra. AE, DC, MC, V.

Perched on a steep hillside above a beautiful, though small, beach, this resort, which has a wide array of sports facilities, occupies 34 acres on the northeast shore of St. Thomas. Following 1995 hurricane damage, the newly renovated accommodations are in two separate locations: poolside and hillside. The two-story town-house suites and one- or two-bedroom suites have whirlpool spas, and all units are stylishly out-fitted. Each unit has satellite color TV with HBO and Spectravision, a hair dryer, a robe, a safe, and an open balcony or patio. This is another good family resort—the year-round children's program is free for guests 3 to 14 and supervised by trained counselors.

Dining/Entertainment: You can enjoy beachfront breakfast, lunch, and dinner at Baywinds, which features continental and Caribbean cuisine. Dinner and Sunday brunch are served in Smugglers Bar and Grill. There's a poolside snack bar and live entertainment/dancing in the Baywinds Lounge.

Services: Concierge, daily children's program, baby-sitting, laundry service, tropi-cal garden tour, 23-hour room service, twice-daily chamber service, newspaper and coffee with wake-up call.

Facilities: Two swimming pools (and a kiddie pool); daily scuba and snorkel les-sons; free Sunfish sailboats, kayaks, Windsurfers, snorkel equipment; on-site full-service dive shop; water sports center, where you can arrange for day sails, deep-sea fishing, and other island excursions; six lit tennis courts; exercise facility; newsstand; gift shop; beauty salon. There's an 18-hole golf course 10 minutes away.

✪ The Ritz-Carlton

Great Bay, St. Thomas, U.S.V.I. 00802. ☎ **800/241-3333** or 809/775-3333. Fax 809/775-4444. 148 rms, 4 suites. Winter, $400–$525 double; $925 suite. Off-season, $200–$395 double; from $475 suite. AE, DC, DISC, MC, V.

Almost overnight St. Thomas went "ritzy" when this chic hotel chain took over the Grand Palazzo in 1992 at the eastern tip of St. Thomas on a 15-acre oceanfront estate. It immediately became the island's toniest property, edging out Doubletree's Sapphire Beach and the Marriott resorts. The property is 4¹/₂ miles southeast of Charlotte Amalie and features landscaped gardens that open onto white sandy beaches.

Rooms and suites occupy six three-story villas designed with Italian Renaissance motifs and Mediterranean colors. Guests register in a reception *palazzo*, whose arches and accessories were inspired by a Venetian palace. From the monogrammed bathrobes to the digital room safes, the accommodations have more amenities than any others on the island.

Dining/Entertainment: The restaurant's international menu is exceptional, as are the views. There's also an outdoor cafe for more casual dining, plus weekly live local entertainment.

Services: Concierge, 24-hour room service, valet, in-room massages, hair salon.

Facilities: Private beach with windsurfing, Sunfish and Hobie Cat sailing, snorkeling, 125-foot free-form pool, complete fitness center, four lighted tennis courts, cruises on private catamaran. Diving and deep-sea fishing excursions can be arranged.

Secret Harbour Beach Hotel

6280 Estate Nazareth, Nazareth Bay, St. Thomas, U.S.V.I. 00802. ☎ **800/524-2250** or 809/775-6550. Fax 809/775-1501. 7 studios, 47 one-bedroom suites, 6 two-bedroom suites. A/C TV TEL. Winter, $265 studio double; $295 one-bedroom suite; $495 two-bedroom suite. Off-season, $169–$189 studio double; $199–$299 one-bedroom suite; $299–$319 two-bedroom suite. Rates include continental breakfast. AE, MC, V.

A favorite with honeymooners, this all-suite resort is on the beach at Nazareth Bay, just outside Red Hook Marina. Renovations, prompted by damage from Hurricane Marilyn, were completed in the summer of 1997. All four contemporary buildings have southwestern exposure, and each unit has a private deck or patio and a full kitchen. There are three types of accommodations: studio apartments with a bed/sitting-room area, patio, and dressing-room area; one-bedroom suites with a living/dining area, a separate bedroom, and a sundeck; and the most luxurious, a two-bedroom suite with two baths and a private living room.

Dining/Entertainment: The Sea Side Restaurant serves both continental and Caribbean cuisine, and the Secret Harbour Beach Cafe is a more informal place where you can eat breakfast and lunch on the outdoor terrace or gazebo. There's also a beachfront bar, where a manager's cocktail party is held weekly.

Services: Baby-sitting, daily maid service.

Facilities: Five-star PADI dive center and water sports facility on the beach, catamaran for sailing charters, two all-weather tennis courts, fitness center, freshwater pool, Jacuzzi.

EXPENSIVE

Bolongo Beach Club

7150 Bolongo, St. Thomas, U.S.V.I. 00802. ☎ **800/524-4746** or 809/775-1800. Fax 809/775-3218. 75 rms, 8 villas. A/C TV TEL. Winter, $235 double; $290 one-bedroom villa for up to 4 occupants; $390 two-bedroom villa for up to 6 occupants. Off-season, $195 double; $210 one-bedroom villa; $255 two-bedroom villa. AE, MC, V.

Few other hotels in St. Thomas have so frequently reconfigured their corporate structure. After unsuccessful linkages with nearby hotels, and devastation during the 1995 hurricanes, it finally reverted to the same beachfront, self-enclosed configuration that had earned it its initial success as one of the first hotels on the eastern side

St. Thomas Accommodations

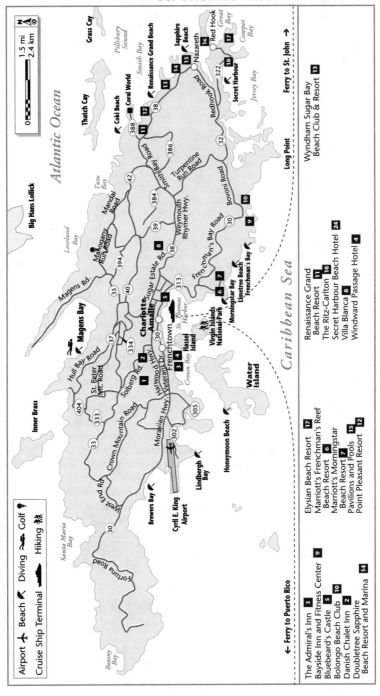

Atlantic Ocean

Caribbean Sea

0 1.5 mi
0 2.4 km

N

Airport ✈ Beach 🏖 Diving 🤿 Golf ⛳
Cruise Ship Terminal ⚓ Hiking 🥾

Grass Cay
Pillsbury Sound
Smith Bay
Thatch Cay
Coki Beach
Coral World
Renaissance Grand Beach
Sapphire Beach
Nazareth
Red Hook
Great Bay
Coupet Bay
Secret Harbour
Jersey Bay
Big Hans Lollick
Loveland Bay
Tutu Bay
Mandal Road
Smith Bay Road
Turpentine Run Road
Weymouth Rhymer Hwy.
Frenchman's Bay Road
Bovoni Road
Frenchman's Bay
Limetree Beach
Morningstar Bay
Long Point
Wyndham Sugar Bay Beach Club & Resort
Magens Rd.
Mahogany Run Road
Sugar Estate Rd.
Charlotte Amalie
St. Thomas Harbor
Hassel Island
Frenchtown
Virgin Islands National Park
Crown Bay
Water Island
Magens Bay
Hull Bay Road
St. Peter Mt. Road
Solberg Rd.
Harwood Hwy.
Veterans Dr.
Crown Mountain Road
Moravian Hwy.
West End Rd.
Brewers Bay
Cyril E. King Airport
Lindbergh Bay
Honeymoon Beach
Santa Maria Bay
Inner Brass
Fortuna Road
Botany Bay

← Ferry to Puerto Rico

The Admiral's Inn 3
Bayside Inn and Fitness Center 9
Bluebeard's Castle 5
Bolongo Beach Club 10
Danish Chalet Inn 2
Doubletree Sapphire Beach Resort and Marina 14

Elysian Beach Resort 17
Marriott's Frenchman's Reef Beach Resort 6
Marriott's Morningstar Beach Resort 7
Pavilions and Pools 15
Point Pleasant Resort 12

Renaissance Grand Beach Resort 11
The Ritz-Carlton 18
Secret Harbour Beach Hotel 24
Villa Blanca 8
Windward Passage Hotel 4

Ferry to St. John →

77

of St. Thomas. You'll find a half-moon–shaped beach, and a cement-sided, pink-walled series of two- and three-story buildings, plus some motel-like units closer to the sands. Outside is a smallish swimming pool and a raffish-looking beachfront bar replete with palm fronds.

Most clients check in on the semi-inclusive plan that includes breakfast and use of nonmotorized sports equipment. Others opt for all-inclusive plans whereby all meals and drinks are included, in addition to a sailboat excursion to St. John, and use of scuba equipment. Accommodations are simple, summery, and filled with undistinguished furniture that suits the unpretentious, often barefoot clientele. Villas (apartment-style condos with full kitchens) lie within a three-story building.

Dining/Entertainment: The relatively formal Lord Rumbottom's serves two-fisted portions of prime rib; the less formal, bistro-style Coconut Henry's features burgers, sandwiches, and salads. Although either venue serves cocktails, you may want to belly up to Iggie's Sing-Along and Sports Bar.

Services: Baby-sitting can be arranged. The gift shop (Beach Traders) on site is a registered outlet for Budget Rent-a-Car.

Facilities: Fitness Center, three swimming pools, two tennis courts, professional volleyball, basketball court, St. Thomas Diving Club (an independent outfit on their premises); *Heavenly Days,* a 49-passenger catamaran, is docked on the hotel's beach and makes frequent sails, depending on business, to St. John.

Elysian Beach Resort

6800 Estate Nazareth, Cowpet Bay, St. Thomas, U.S.V.I. 00802. ☎ **800/753-2554** or 809/775-1000. Fax 809/776-0910. 175 units. Winter, $225–$285 double; from $315 suite. Off-season, $175–$210 double; from $225 suite. Rates include continental breakfast. Special honeymoon packages available. AE, DC, DISC, MC, V.

This time-share resort on Cowpet Bay in the East End has European glamour, and it's within a 20-minute drive of Charlotte Amalie. The thoughtfully planned bedrooms have balconies, and 14 offer sleeping lofts reached by a spiral staircase. The decor is tropical, with white ceramic-tile floors, rattan and bamboo furnishings, and natural-wood ceilings. The rooms are in a bevy of four-story buildings connected to landscaped gardens. Rooms can be broken up into various configurations, with doors locked or shut, depending on the needs of a client. Of the various units, 43 can be converted into one-bedroom suites, 43 into two-bedroom suites, and 11 into three-bedroom suites.

Dining/Entertainment: The hotel offers elegant international dining at its Palm Court Restaurant, plus weekly barbecues on the terrace. Other dining options include the Oasis, right on the beach, serving a lighter continental fare. You can have drinks at the pool bar or in a first-class lounge. In season, there's live entertainment.

Services: Open-air shuttle to town, room service, masseur, baby-sitting.

Facilities: Fitness center, swimming pool, snorkel gear, canoes, Sunfish, tennis court.

Pavilions and Pools

6400 Estate Smith Bay, St. Thomas, U.S.V.I. 00802. ☎ **800/524-2001** or 809/775-6110. Fax 809/775-6110. 25 units. A/C TV TEL. Winter, $239–$259 double. Off-season, $175–$195 double. Rates include continental breakfast in winter only. AE, DISC, MC, V.

Ideal for a honeymoon, this is the ultimate in small-scale luxury—you have your own villa with floor-to-ceiling glass doors opening onto your own private swimming pool. The resort, 7 miles east of Charlotte Amalie, is a string of condominium units, tastefully rebuilt and furnished. Hurricane damage was so extensive from Marilyn that a massive reconstruction was necessary, with a reopening in 1997.

🏨 Family-Friendly Hotels

Doubletree Sapphire Beach Resort *(see p. 73)*   The resort does more for kids than most hotels on the island, and the expansive beach gives them plenty of room to play. Children under 12 stay and eat free when accompanied by their parents, and supervised activities are available through the Little Gems Kids Klub.

Renaissance Grand Beach Resort *(see p. 75)*   Special family rates and children's menus in the restaurants make this an especially appealing choice. Plus, baby-sitting can be arranged around the clock. The Kid's Club, offering a daily program of activities supervised by experienced counselors, operates year-round for kids 4 to 12.

Secret Harbour *(see p. 76)*   Children under 12 stay free at this Nazareth Bay hotel. Many units have kitchenettes where families can prepare light meals. Beach facilities are right at your doorstep.

After checking in and following a wooden pathway to your attached villa, you don't have to see another soul until you leave, if you so wish—the fence and gate around your space are that high. Your swimming pool is encircled by a deck and plenty of tropical greenery. Inside, a room divider screens a full, well-equipped kitchen. Each bedroom has its own style, with plenty of closets behind louvered doors. The bath has an outdoor garden shower where you can rinse off after a swim or trip to the beach. The resort adjoins Sapphire Bay, which boasts one of the island's best beaches and water sports concessions. Honeymooners should inquire about packages.

Dining/Entertainment: A small bar and barbecue area is set against a wall on the reception terrace, where rum parties and cookouts are held. Informal, simple meals are served nightly. Occasionally a musician or singer entertains.

Services: Helpful front desk, day sails, restaurant reservations.

Facilities: Free snorkeling gear.

Point Pleasant Resort

6600 Estate Smith Bay, St. Thomas, U.S.V.I. 00802. ☎ **800/777-1700** or 809/775-7200. Fax 809/776-5694. 130 rms. A/C TV TEL. Winter, $255–$360 double. Off-season, $170–$240 double. AE, DC, DISC, MC, V.

This is a very private, unique resort on Water Bay, on the northeastern tip of St. Thomas, just a 5-minute walk from lovely Stouffer's Beach. It's a series of condo units that are rented when owners are not in residence. From your living-room gallery, you look out on a group of islands: Tortola, St. John, and Jost Van Dyke. The complex is set on a 15-acre bluff with flowering shrubbery, century plants, frangipani trees, secluded nature trails, old rock formations, and lookout points. Some of the villa-style accommodations have kitchens, and the furnishings are light and airy, mostly with rattan and floral fabrics.

Dining/Entertainment: The restaurant, Agavé Terrace, is one of the finest on the island and offers three meals a day. The cuisine, featuring seafood, is a blend of nouvelle American dishes with Caribbean specialties. Local entertainment is provided several nights a week.

Services: Complimentary use of a car 4 hours per day, shopping, and dinner shuttle.

Facilities: Three freshwater swimming pools, lit tennis courts, snorkeling equipment, Sunfish sailboats.

Wyndham Sugar Bay Beach Club and Resort

6500 Estate Smith Bay, St. Thomas, U.S.V.I. 00802. ☎ **800/927-7100** in the U.S., or 809/777-7100. Fax 809/777-7200. 291 rms, 9 suites. A/C TV TEL. Winter, $250 double; $270–$290 suite. Off-season, $150 double; $170–$190 suite. Rates include all meals and drinks, plus nonmotorized activities. AE, DC, MC, V.

In a neck-and-neck race with the Renaissance Grand Beach Resort (see above), this East End hostelry is a 5-minute ride from Red Hook. Built in 1992 as an upscale Crowne Plaza Holiday Inn, it's now under the Wyndham wing. It's got stellar views, and bedrooms are equipped with balconies so guests can enjoy them. The rooms are often decorated with rattan pieces and tropical, pastel color schemes. Extra amenities include data ports, room safes, and hair dryers.

Dining/Entertainment: The main restaurant, Manor House, offers breakfast and dinner daily, with tables opening onto views of St. John and the British Virgin Islands. Casual meals are served poolside, entertainment is offered nightly, and there's an ice-cream parlor in the Main Grove Cafe.

Services: Room service (until 11pm), Kids Klub, baby-sitting, tour desk.

Facilities: Tennis, water sports, secluded beach (that's really too small for a resort of this size), three connected freshwater pools with a waterfall, fitness center; there's a golf course nearby.

INEXPENSIVE

Bayside Inn and Fitness Center

7140 Bolongo, St. Thomas, U.S.V.I. 00802. ☎ **800/524-4746** or 809/693-2600. Fax 809/775-3298. 6 rms. A/C TV TEL. Year-round, $65 double. AE, MC, V.

Bayside Inn is a restored 19th-century West Indian manor that was completely renovated and converted into a fitness center/guest house in early 1993. The quiet, comfortable rooms are just steps away from Bolongo Beach, where water sports concessions are available. Bayside Inn is the ideal way to combine relaxation, fitness, and fun into one vacation.

Facilities include a dry sauna, weight room, and cardiovascular equipment such as treadmills and stationary bikes. There is also a swimming pool.

4 Dining

The flavorful cuisines simmering in St. Thomas these days are among the best in the West Indies, but there are some drawbacks to eating out here. Fine dining, and even not-so-fine dining, tends to be expensive, and the best spots (with a few exceptions) are not right in Charlotte Amalie and so can only be reached by taxi.

You'll find an eclectic mix of cuisines on St. Thomas, including American, Italian, Mexican, and Asian. We recommend digging into some of the local Caribbean dishes at least once or twice, especially the seafood specialties like "ole wife" and yellowtail, which are usually prepared with a spicy Creole mixture of peppers, onions, and tomatoes. The winner among native side dishes is *fungi* (pronounced *foon*-gee), made with okra and cornmeal. Most local restaurants always serve johnnycake, a popular fried, unleavened bread.

Below is a list of our favorite restaurants on St. Thomas. We've broken them down by geography and by price (per person, not including tip or spirits). Those rated **"Expensive"** cost about $35 to $60 per person for dinner; **"Moderate,"** about $30 to $35; and **"Inexpensive,"** under $25.

CHARLOTTE AMALIE
EXPENSIVE

Entre Nous

In Bluebeard's Castle, Bluebeard's Hill. ☎ **809/776-4050.** Reservations recommended. Main courses $18.50–$31. AE, MC, V. Tues–Sun 6–9:30pm. Closed Sept. CONTINENTAL.

This long-established restaurant operates under independent management in one of St. Thomas's most famous hotels and serves some of the island's best cuisine. Although leaning heavily on the French and Italian side, the food is increasingly eclectic, with a strong emphasis on visual presentation. An open-air restaurant, it offers candlelit dinners and a sweeping view of the faraway harbor. Start with the Caesar salad, created at your table, followed perhaps by Caribbean lobster prepared any style—we like it simply with garlic butter. The seafood mélange with a fresh selection of fish and shellfish is one of the most appetizing main dishes, as is the sesame-crusted salmon, served on a bed of vanilla bean sauce. Desserts are excellent, especially the old-fashioned ones such as the baked Alaska, flambéed at the table.

✪ Hervé Restaurant and Wine Bar

Government Hill. ☎ **809/777-9703.** Reservations necessary. Main courses $17.75–$24.75; lunch $14.75–$16.75. AE, MC, V. Mon–Sat 11:30am–2:30pm and 6–10pm. CONTINENTAL/ AMERICAN/CARIBBEAN.

Next to Hotel 1829, Hervé has quickly become the hot new dining spot on St. Thomas, surpassing all competition in town, including its next-door neighbor. The panoramic view of Charlotte Amalie and the restaurant's historic ambience are delightful, but it's the cuisine here that stands out. Hervé P. Chassinis is a restaurateur with a vast, classical background, and, here, in his own unpretentious setting, he offers high-quality food at reasonable prices.

Before studying the menu, peruse the classic black-and-white photographs capturing St. Thomas at the turn of the century. There are two dining areas: a large open-air terrace and a more intimate wine room. Contemporary American dishes are served with the classic French and Caribbean touches. Start with the pistachio-encrusted brie, conch fritters with mango chutney, or shrimp in a stuffed crab shell. From here, try the red snapper poached with white wine, or a delectable black sesame–crusted tuna with a ginger-raspberry sauce. Nightly specials feature game, fish, and pasta. You'll rarely taste a creamier crème caramel or a lighter, fluffier mango or raspberry cheesecake.

Hotel 1829

Kongens Gade (at the east end of Main St.). ☎ **809/776-1829.** Reservations recommended, but not accepted more than 1 day in advance. Main courses $19.50–$32.50; fixed-price dinner $28.50. AE, DISC, MC, V. Daily 6–11pm. CONTINENTAL.

Hotel 1829 is graceful and historic, and its restaurant serves some of the finest food on St. Thomas. Before dining, guests like to linger at the attractive bar for a before-dinner drink. You'll then move into either the terrace or the main room, where the walls are made from ships' ballasts and the floor of Moroccan tiles. The cuisine has a distinctively European twist, and many dishes are prepared and served from trolleys beside your table. This is one of the few places in town with sublime caviar, but if fish eggs aren't your style, you may choose the goat-cheese bruschetta with roasted red pepper hummus. For dinner, try a ragout of swordfish with pesto, or sautéed snapper in brown butter. Mint-flavored roast rack of lamb and chateaubriand for two are other possibilities.

MODERATE

Beni Iguana's Sushi Bar

In the Grand Hotel Court, Veteran's Dr. ☎ **809/777-8744.** Reservations recommended. Sushi $4.50–$6 per portion (2 pieces); salads $5.50–$7; main courses $6–$13.75; combo plates for 4 to 5 diners $25–$60 each. AE, MC, V. Mon–Sat 11:30am–10pm. JAPANESE.

It's the only Japanese restaurant on St. Thomas, a change of pace from the Caribbean, steak, and seafood restaurants nearby. Along with a handful of shops, it occupies the sheltered courtyard and an old cistern across from Emancipation Square Park. Select a table outside, or go through the Danish colonial doors into the red- and black-lacquered dining room which has a sushi bar and a handful of tables. Todd Reinhard, an American carefully trained in the art of Japanese cuisine, is your host. Begin with a selection of sushi (freshwater eel, tuna, yellowtail, or amberjack), which the chefs dub "edible art," followed by a salad or a roll of seafood wrapped in rice. A perennial favorite is the "13" roll, stuffed with spicy crabmeat, salmon, lettuce, cucumbers, and scallions.

Virgilio's

18 Dronningens Gade (entrance on a narrow alleyway running between Main St. and Back St.). ☎ **809/776-4920.** Reservations recommended. Main courses $8.95–$19.95. AE, MC, V. Mon–Sat 11:30am–10:30pm. NORTHERN ITALIAN.

The best northern Italian restaurant in the Virgin Islands, Virgilio's is sheltered under heavy ceiling beams and brick vaulting, in a neo-Baroque dining room—stained-glass windows, crystal chandeliers, and soft Italian music for effect. Owner Virgilio del Mare and his well-trained staff serve everything from stuffed grape leaves to a delectable *cinco peche,* a house specialty of clams, mussels, scallops, oysters, and crayfish simmered in a saffron broth. Their lobster ravioli is excellent, and other dishes like rack of lamb filled with a porcini-mushroom stuffing and glazed with a roasted garlic aioli are also first class. You'll never go wrong with the fresh fish here.

INEXPENSIVE

Greenhouse

Veterans Dr. ☎ **809/774-7998.** Main courses $9.95–$19.95; breakfast $3.95–$4.95. AE, DISC, MC, V. Daily 8am–2am. AMERICAN/CARIBBEAN.

Fronted with big sunny windows, this waterfront restaurant attracts cruise-ship passengers on shopping breaks. The food is not the island's best, but it's perfectly satisfying if you're not too picky. Breakfast features different combinations of eggs, sausages, and bacon, plus some Jamaican-inspired dishes. At lunch, you might try the grilled mahimahi in a key lime, ginger butter, or Jamaican jerk sauce, or perhaps the house specialty, jerk-barbecued pork ribs. Happy hour (daily from 4:30 to 7pm) is usually lively here, and this is one of the safest places to be in Charlotte Amalie after dark.

Hard Rock Café

5144 International Plaza, the Waterfront, Queen's Quarter. ☎ **809/777-5555.** Reservations not accepted. Main courses $7.95–$16.95. AE, MC, V. Daily 11am–11pm, but hours can vary depending on business. AMERICAN.

Occupying the second floor of a pink-sided mall whose big windows overlook the ships moored in Charlotte Amalie's harbor, this restaurant belongs to the popular international chain. Entire walls are devoted to the memorabilia of such artists as John Lennon, Eric Clapton, and Bob Marley. The fare is the same as on the mainland—salads, sandwiches, burgers, and fresh fish—and there's live music on Friday nights.

Charlotte Amalie Dining

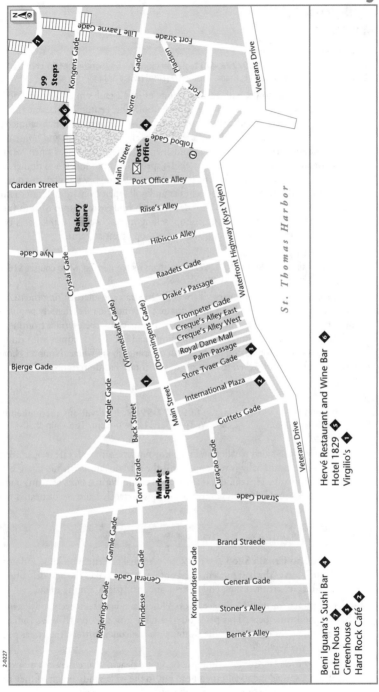

Beni Iguana's Sushi Bar 4
Entre Nous 3
Greenhouse 2
Hard Rock Café 2

Hervé Restaurant and Wine Bar 6
Hotel 1829 5
Virgilio's 1

FRENCHTOWN
MODERATE

Alexander's

Rue de St. Barthélemy. ☎ **809/776-4211.** Reservations recommended. Main courses $12–$24.95. AE, MC, V. Mon–Sat 11:30am–10pm. AUSTRIAN/GERMAN.

Alexander's, west of town, will seat you at one of its 12 tables in an air-conditioned room with picture windows overlooking the harbor. The Teutonic dishes are the best on the island, especially when they involve seafood—a delectable conch schnitzel is served on occasion. Other dishes include Wiener schnitzel, goulash, and homemade pâté. For dessert, try the homemade strudel, either apple or cheese. Lunch features a variety of crepes, quiches, and a daily chef's special. At both lunch and dinner, you can choose from 10 to 13 different pasta dishes, although we prefer the ones at Virgilio. Alexander's also has an adjacent bar and grill, open daily from 11am to midnight; a wine bar, Epernay, open Monday through Friday from 4pm to 1am (until 2am on weekends); and a deli/coffee shop, selling meats, cheeses, drinks, and pastries, open daily from 10am to 8pm (the coffee shop opens at 7am).

Chart House Restaurant

Villa Olga, Frenchtown. ☎ **809/774-4262.** Reservations recommended. Main courses $16.95–$29.95. AE, DC, MC, V. Daily 5:30–10pm. STEAKS.

This stripped-down 19th-century villa was the Russian consulate during the island's Danish administration, and lies a short distance beyond the most densely populated area of Frenchtown village. The dining gallery is a spacious open terrace fronting the sea. The Chart House features an outstanding salad bar, which comes with dinner. This chain is known for serving the finest cut of prime rib anywhere. Nonbeef choices range from Hawaiian chicken to Australian lobster tail. For dessert, order the famous mud pie.

✪ Craig & Sally's

22 Estate Honduras, Frenchtown. ☎ **809/777-9949.** Reservations recommended. Main courses $12.50–$27.50. AE, MC, V. Tues–Sat 11:30am–3pm, Tues–Sun 5:30–10pm. INTERNATIONAL.

Set in an airy, open-sided pavilion in Frenchtown, this Caribbean cafe is operated by a husband–wife team. Sally is responsible for the eclectic cuisine, while Craig is the host and coordinator. He confides that the food is not "for the faint of heart, but for the adventurous soul." He has compiled the most extensive and sophisticated wine

---

ⓗ Family-Friendly Restaurants

The Cream and Crumb Shop *(see p. 89)* is an eternal favorite with kids, and not just because it serves the best pizza on St. Thomas. It also makes the best deli sandwiches, and its ice cream, cakes, and pastries are unsurpassed on the island.

Eunice's Terrace *(see p. 89)*   Eunice loves children, and just about everybody seems to have a good time here. This place offers a tasty introduction to West Indian cooking. Little ones usually like the fishburgers, the conch fritters, the sweet potato pie, and the key lime pie.

Seagrape *(see p. 88)*   Kids love dining at Sapphire Beach, where they can quickly choose from a special menu and then head out to the wide sandy beach. If they're guests of the hotel and are 12 or under, they dine free when accompanied by their parents.

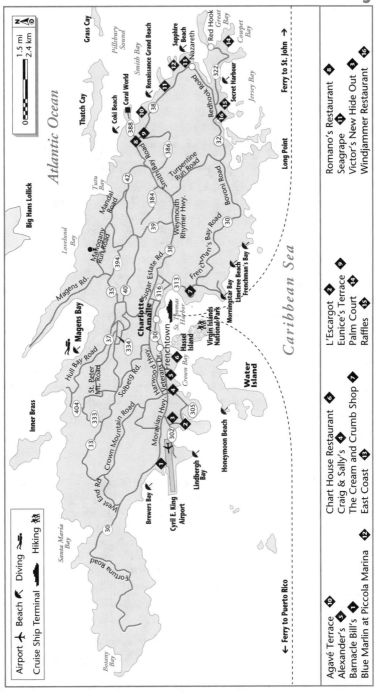

list on St. Thomas. Views of the sky and sea are complemented by meals that ranges from pasta to seafood, with flavors that range from European to Asian. Roast pork with clams, filet mignon with macadamia-nut sauce, grilled swordfish with fresh herbs and tomatoes, and lobster-stuffed twice-baked potatoes are examples from the creative and ever-changing menu.

SUB BASE
MODERATE

L'Escargot
12 Sub Base. ☎ **809/774-6565.** Reservations recommended. Main courses $15–$24. AE, MC, V. Daily 11:45am–2:30pm and 6–10pm. FRENCH.

This place has been in and out of fashion for so long it's a virtual island legend for its sheer endurance alone. But, it also serves a first-rate cuisine. Its focal point is a low-slung semioutdoor terrace with close-up views of Crown Bay Marina. Menu items include the standard repertoire of French dishes, including rack of lamb with rosemary sauce, scampi in pesto sauce with linguine, grilled swordfish with spicy mango sauce, onion soup, fresh mushroom salad, and chocolate mousse.

Victor's New Hide Out
103 Sub Base, off Rte. 30. ☎ **809/776-9379.** Reservations recommended. Main courses $9.95–$29.95. AE, MC, V. Mon–Sat 11:30am–3:30pm and 5:30–10pm, Sun 5:30–10pm. SEAFOOD/CARIBBEAN.

You never know who's going to show up here—maybe Bill Cosby, perhaps José Feliciano. Victor's is operated by Victor Sydney, who hails from the Caribbean island of Montserrat, and offers some of the best local dishes on the island. But, first you have to find it—if you're driving, call for directions; otherwise, take a taxi. Its dishes have much flair and zest, as opposed to the more down-home cookery found at other local restaurants like Eunice's Terrace. This large, airy restaurant serves fresh lobster prepared Montserrat style (that is, in a creamy sauce) or grilled in the shell. You might also opt for a plate of juicy barbecued ribs. For dessert, try the coconut, custard, or apple pie.

INEXPENSIVE

Barnacle Bill's
At the Crown Bay Marina, 16 Sub Base. ☎ **809/774-7444.** Reservations not required. Main courses $3–$15. AE, MC, V. Mon–Sat 11:30am–midnight. INTERNATIONAL.

Established by hardworking entrepreneur Bill Grogan, this restaurant is best known as a bar with live music. Its fans, however, also enjoy the view of Crown Point, and the food, particularly the pizzas. Other menu items include steak, lobster, burgers, sandwiches, pastas, and salads. This clapboard-sided house has lots of outdoor terraces and decks where you can watch yachts pull into the marina.

COMPASS POINT
MODERATE

Raffles
6300 Frydenhoj, Compass Point, off Rte. 32. ☎ **809/775-6004.** Reservations recommended. Main courses $13.50–$27.50. AE, MC, V. Tues–Sun 6:30–10:30pm. CONTINENTAL/SEAFOOD.

Named after the legendary hotel in Singapore, this establishment is filled with tropical accents more evocative of the South Pacific than of the Caribbean. Opened in 1972 beside the lagoon at Compass Point (1 mile west of Red Hook), it's one of the oldest restaurants on the island. Peacock chairs and ceiling fans set the mood here. The menu is split into sections: fresh seafood, beef, veal, lamb, chicken, and live Maine lobster. The fresh fish of the day, prepared in one of many savory sauces, is always a winner, and the chef's specialty is duck, which is marinated for two days then steamed and crisped. Another signature item is the curry and chutney dressing.

Windjammer Restaurant
41 Frydenhoj, Compass Point, off Rte. 32. ☎ **809/775-6194.** Reservations recommended. Main courses $7.75–$19.75. AE, MC, V. Mon–Sat 6–10pm. Closed Sept. SEAFOOD/GERMAN.

At the easternmost tip of the island, 1 mile west of Red Hook, this restaurant was destroyed by Hurricane Marilyn in 1995, but it's bounced back better and fresher than ever. The mahogany bar and paneling have been restored along with the oil lamps, which make for romantic dining. The extensive menu continues to reflect a German heritage, with a strong emphasis on seafood. Fresh fish arrives daily, including local favorites like mahimahi, wahoo, and grouper. Seafood dishes are prepared in several different ways. We prefer "island style," in a lime and ginger *buerre blanc* (white butter) sauce. The chef's specialty is chicken à la Bremen, a boneless breast of chicken wrapped in bacon in a casserole of mussels, shrimp, and asparagus. Appetizers are likely to include continental classics like escargots in garlic butter. Save room for the tasty devil's food cake, smothered in chocolate.

IN & AROUND RED HOOK
EXPENSIVE

Palm Court
In the Elysian Beach Resort, 6800 Estate Nazareth, Cowpet Bay. ☎ **809/775-1000.** Reservations recommended. Main courses $19.95–$25; lunch $6.95–$12.95; Sun brunch $10.95 adults, $12.95 children. AE, DC, DISC, MC, V. Mon–Sat 7:30–10:30am, Sun 7:30–10am; daily 11:30am–2:30pm and 6:30–9:30pm. INTERNATIONAL.

On the premises of a luxury resort, this restaurant offers cuisine, decor, and service that achieve a more subtle, European flare than any other on St. Thomas. At dinner tempt yourself with the shrimp cocktail or the savory conch fritters, followed by such main courses as Caribbean lobster tail, swordfish, rack of lamb, and an intriguing angel hair pasta studded with shrimp and flavored with ginger. Saturday is Caribbean night, with a live steel band and a generous buffet that includes everything from steaks to conch served with lemon butter. The cost is $22.95 for adults and $11.50 for children.

MODERATE

Blue Marlin at Piccola Marina
6300 Estate Smith Bay. ☎ **809/775-6350.** Main courses $15.50–$18.50. AE, MC, V. Daily 6–10pm, Sun 10:30am–2:30pm. Bar opens at 3pm. Take the Red Hook bus. INTERNATIONAL.

This popular dining spot is the definition of laid back. It's conveniently located beside the ferry dock where boats leave for St. John. The food is good, and much more imaginative than you might think. Everything is homemade, and local ingredients are used whenever possible. Only fresh fish is allowed in the kitchen, which also makes its own oils, including orange-pepper oil, basil oil, and various vinaigrettes. One of the more intriguing dishes is grilled wahoo with a pineapple and cucumber sambal. Grilled New York strip, along with Caribbean chicken, and zesty baby back ribs are also served. For dessert, stop by the ice-cream parlor and pastry shop on the premises.

FLAMBOYANT POINT
INEXPENSIVE

East Coast

In Red Hook Plaza, Rte. 38. ☎ **809/775-1919.** Main courses $6.75–$21.75. AE, MC, V. Daily 5:30–11pm. Bar, daily 4:30pm–4am. Take the Red Hook bus. CARIBBEAN.

Across the street from Red Hook Plaza, East Coast packs in visiting and local sports fans to see their favorite teams and players on TV. The adjacent restaurant, although often neglected, serves tasty Caribbean meals. You can dine in a denlike haven or on an outdoor terrace. A different fish of the day is prepared any way you like it: grilled, blackened, or even in a teriyaki glaze. Selections might include tuna, wahoo, dolphin, swordfish, or snapper, which is best in a garlic-cream sauce. The kitchen also turns out Cajun shrimp and its famous "Coast Burgers."

SAPPHIRE BEACH
EXPENSIVE

Seagrape

In the Doubletree Sapphire Beach Resort and Marina, Rte. 6, Smith Bay Rd. ☎ **809/775-6100.** Reservations recommended. Main courses $12.95–$24.95; Sun brunch $9.50–$15.95. AE, MC, V. Mon–Sat 7:30–10:30am, 11am–3pm, and 6–10pm; Sun 11am–3pm and 6–10pm. CONTINENTAL/AMERICAN.

This is one of the finest dining rooms along the eastern shore of St. Thomas. Seagrape opens onto the world-renowned Sapphire Beach. But the sound of the waves and the light seas breezes that permeate the restaurant are only part of Seagrape's allure—the staff is well trained and the food first class. The dinner menu includes traditional items like teriyaki chicken breast, veal marsala, and New York strip steak, which are prepared with extraordinary style and flair. The rib eye comes with garlic mashed potatoes, and chicken breast with a mushroom salsa. The popular Sunday brunch features favorites like Grand Marnier French toast and Belgian waffles with fresh fruit. For lunch, your best bets are the grilled catch of the day or one of the fresh salads; a children's menu is also available.

NORTH COAST
EXPENSIVE

Agavé Terrace

Point Pleasant Resort, 6600 Estate Smith Bay. ☎ **809/775-4142.** Reservations recommended. Main courses $17.50–$38. AE, MC, V. Daily 6–10pm. CARIBBEAN.

Perched high above a steep and heavily forested hillside on the eastern tip of St. Thomas, this restaurant, one of the island's best, offers a sweeping panorama and unparalleled romance. The house drink is a Desmond Delight, a combination of Midori, rum, pineapple juice, and a secret ingredient.

After a few Delights, you may opt for the house appetizer: an Agavé sampler prepared for two, which includes portions of crabmeat, conch fritters, and chicken pinwheel. For a main course, the preferred chef's specialty is seafood cardinale, served with lobster-flavored cream and fresh tomato sauce on a bed of angel hair pasta. Six different fish usually turn up as catches of the day; seafood can be prepared in seven different ways, including grilled with a choice of nine different sauces. The wine list is extensive, and a live steel drum band draws listeners Tuesday and Thursday nights.

✪ Romano's Restaurant

97 Smith Bay Rd. ☎ **809/775-0045.** Reservations recommended. Main courses $22.95–$26.95; pastas $15.95–$18.95. AE, MC, V. Mon–Sat 6:30–10:30pm. Closed Aug and 1 week in Apr for Carnival. Take the Vitran bus. ITALIAN.

Located on the sandy-bottomed flatlands near Coral World, this hideaway is owned by New Jersey chef Tony Romano, who specializes in a flavorful and herb-laden cuisine that some diners yearn for after too much Caribbean cooking. House favorites include linguine con pesto, four-cheese lasagna, osso buco, scaloppini marsala, and broiled salmon. All desserts are made on the premises. The restaurant, adorned in exposed brick and well-stocked wine racks, always seems full of happy, lively diners.

INEXPENSIVE

Eunice's Terrace

66–67 Smith Bay, Rte. 38. ☎ **809/775-3975.** Reservations not accepted. Main courses $5.25–$18.95. AE, MC, V. Mon–Sat 11am–10pm, Sun 5–10pm. Take the Red Hook bus. WEST INDIAN/AMERICAN.

A 30-minute taxi ride east of the airport, just east of the Coral World turnoff, this is one of the best-known West Indian restaurants in the Virgin Islands. It's devoid of any romance but oozes with local color. Visitors and islanders alike crowd into its confines for savory portions. Owner Eunice Best and her cuisine made international news on January 5, 1997, when Bill and Hillary Clinton popped in unexpectedly for lunch. Surrounded by secret-service agents, the president enjoyed a conch appetizer, followed by the catch of the day, "ole wife." Other lunch items, passed up by the First Couple, are fishburgers, sandwiches, and daily specials like Virgin Islands doved pork or mutton. (Doving, pronounced " *dough*-ving," involves baking sliced meat while basting it with a combination of its own juices, tomato paste, Kitchen Bouquet, and island herbs.)

For dinner, there's conch fritters, broiled or fried fish (try the dolphin if it's fresh), and sweet-potato pie, all of which are usually served with fungi, rice, or plantain. Key lime pie is a favorite dessert here, and the drink of choice is a concoction known as a Queen Mary, made with tropical fruit juices and dark rum.

PICNIC FARE & WHERE TO EAT IT

Because there are dozens of small restaurants and beachside cabanas selling burgers and beer, many would-be picnickers tend to forgo the picnic basket in favor of a quick bite on the sand.

But, if you crave a real American-style picnic, consult the culinary experts at **The Cream and Crumb Shop,** Building 6, Havensight Mall (☎ **809/774-2499;** open 6:30am to 6pm). Located where most cruise-ships dock for daytime excursions into St. Thomas, this cheerful, modern shop is easy to miss amid the cluster of tax-free jewelers and perfume shops.

The thickly layered deli sandwiches ($4.95 to $6.95), fresh salads (shrimp, chicken, potato, or crabmeat), and homemade pastries are all excellent options for take-out. The shop also specializes in pizza, and serves frozen yogurt and ice cream—these may not be the most practical picnic items but they're still awfully good.

With these ingredients, you can head for your favorite beach. We recommend Magens Bay Beach not just for its beauty but for its picnic tables too. Other ideal spots are Drake's Seat, and any of the secluded high-altitude panoramas along the island's western end.

High Society on the High Seas: Chartering Your Own Yacht for the Day

Most of the charter-boat business in the Caribbean is run by Virgin Islanders. In St. Thomas, most of the business centers around the Red Hook and Yacht Haven marinas.

Perhaps the easiest way to go out to sea is to charter your own yacht for the day from *Yacht Nightwind,* Sapphire Marina (☎ **809/775-4110** 24 hours a day), for only $90 per person. You're granted a full-day sail with champagne buffet lunch and open bar aboard this 50-foot yawl. You're also given free snorkeling equipment and instruction.

New Horizons, 6501 Red Hook Plaza, Suite 16, Red Hook (☎ **809/775-1171**), offers wind-borne excursions amid the cays and reefs of the Virgin Islands. This two-masted 60-foot ketch was built in 1969 in Vancouver. It has circumnavigated the globe and has been used as a design prototype for other boats. Owned and operated by Canadian Tim Krygsveld, it contains a hot-water shower, serves a specialty drink called a New Horizons Nooner (with a melon-liqueur base), and carries a complete line of snorkeling equipment for adults and children. A full-day excursion, with a "hot buffet Italian al fresco" and an open bar, costs $90 per person. Excursions depart every day, weather permitting, from the Doubletree Sapphire Beach Resort and Marina. Call ahead for reservations and information. Children aged 2 to 12, who must be accompanied by an adult, pay $45. The outfitter has recently expanded with another vessel, *New Horizons II,* a 44-foot custom-made speedboat taking you to some of the most scenic highlights of the British Virgin Islands, costing $100 for adults or $55 for children 2 to 12 for an all-day trip. New Horizons also operates Power Trip next door, renting out 25-foot Wellcrafts for $245 per day for up to eight people.

You can avoid the crowds by sailing aboard the *Fantasy* (☎ **809/775-5652**), at 6700 Sapphire Village (no. 253), which departs from the American Yacht Harbor at Red Hook at 9:30am daily. It sails to St. John and nearby islands, allowing a

5 Beaches, Water Sports & Other Outdoor Pursuits

Chances are, your hotel will be right on the beach, or very close to one, and this is where you'll spend most of your time. But in addition to all of its sand and surf, St. Thomas offers the biggest array of sports and outdoor activities in the West Indies, from golf and tennis to boating, scuba diving, and deep-sea fishing. So while you're kicking back on a lounge chair with a cold glass of rum punch in hand, just remember that no trip here is complete without a sail or snorkel.

BEACHES

Most of the beaches of St. Thomas lie from 2 to 5 miles from Charlotte Amalie; all beaches in the Virgin Islands are open to the public.

NORTH SIDE

✪ **Magens Bay**   Located 3 miles north of the capital, Magens Bay is one of the world's most beautiful beaches. Admission is $1 for adults and $1 per car. Facilities include changing rooms, snorkeling gear, lounge chairs, paddleboats, and kayaks. This white-sand beach, administered by the government, is ½ mile long and lies maximum of six passengers to go swimming, snorkeling, beachcombing, and trolling. Snorkel gear with expert instruction is provided, as is a champagne lunch. An underwater camera is available. The cost of a full-day trip is $95 per person. A full day trip to Jost Van Dyke is also offered for $90 per person, including a B.V.I. Customs charge of $15 (no lunch). A half-day sail, morning or afternoon, lasts 3 hours and costs $55. Sunset tours are also popular, with an open bar and hors d'oeuvres, costing $45 per person.

Remember Bing Crosby and Grace Kelly crooning a duet in *High Society*? The **True Love,** 6501 Red Hood Plaza, Suite 54 (☎ **809/775-6547**), a sleek 54-foot Malabar schooner, is the same yacht featured in the 1956 film. It sails daily at 9:30am from Doubletree Sapphire Beach Club Marina and costs $90 per person or $85 if paid in traveler's checks or cash. Bill and Sue Beer have sailed it since 1965. You can join one of the captain's snorkeling classes and later enjoy one of Sue's gourmet lunches with champagne.

American Yacht Harbor, Red Hook (☎ **809/775-6454**), offers both bareboat and fully crewed charters from a colorful yacht-filled harbor set against Heritage Gade, a Caribbean village reproduction. The harbor is home to numerous boat companies, including day-trippers, fishing boats, and long-term sailing charters. There are also five restaurants on the property, serving everything from continental to an island cuisine.

You may want to check out the *Yachtsman's Guide to the Virgin Islands,* available at major marine outlets, bookstores, through catalog merchandisers, or direct from **Tropic Isle Publishers,** P.O. Box 610938, North Miami, FL 33261-0938 (☎ **305/ 893-4277**). The guide, revised annually and costing $15.95, is supplemented by sketch charts, photographs, and landfall sketches and charts showing harbors and harbor entrances, anchorages, channels, and landmarks, plus information on preparations necessary for cruising the islands.

between two mountains. From Charlotte Amalie, take Route 35 north all the way. There is no public transportation to reach it. The beach is terribly overcrowded on cruise-ship days (which is virtually any day between December and April), but the crowds thin in the midafternoon.

If you'd like to go nude, as many locals do, you can follow a marked trail to Little Magens Bay. The gates to the beach are open daily from 6am to 6pm. After 4pm, you should use insect repellent to protect yourself from mosquitoes and sand flies.

Coki Beach Located on the northeast shore near Coral World, Coki Beach also gets crowded whenever cruise-ships are in port. Snorkelers and scuba divers love this beach for its abundance of reef fish. It is absolutely forbidden to remove coral or marine life from the water. Concessions at the beach can arrange everything from waterskiing to parasailing, not just snorkeling. Most people take a taxi from the center of Charlotte Amalie. The East End Vitran bus runs to Smith Bay, letting you off at the gate to Coral World and Coki Beach. Pickpockets are prevalent so protect your valuables.

Renaissance Grand Beach This gem lies on the north side of St. Thomas, along with its luxury hotel. This palm-lined strip of white sand opens onto Smith Bay, where you can try just about any water sport. The beach lies right off Smith Bay Road (Route 38) east of Charlotte Amalie, near Coral World. Take a taxi from town.

SOUTH SIDE

Morningstar   At this beach near Marriott's Frenchman's Reef Resort, about 2 miles east of Charlotte Amalie, you can appear in your most daring swimwear, as this is the premier gathering spot on the island for bikini wearers (and watchers). You can also rent sailboards, sailboats, snorkeling equipment, and lounge chairs. The beach is reached by a cliff-front elevator at Frenchman's Reef, which also owns the adjoining Marriott's Morningstar Resort. Because of its proximity to town, many residents of Charlotte Amalie use this beach, and the east side of the beach is often filled with young people who work in the hotels and restaurants of St. Thomas at night. There is no public transportation to the beach, but it's only a short taxi ride from Charlotte Amalie.

Limetree Beach   Set against a backdrop of sea grape trees and shady palms, Limetree lures those who want a serene spread of sand where they can bask in the sun and even feed hibiscus blossoms to iguanas. You can rent snorkeling gear, lounge and beach chairs, and towels. Cool drinks are served, including a Limetree green piña colada. There is no public transportation, but the beach can easily be reached by taxi from Charlotte Amalie.

Brewers Bay   One of the island's most popular beaches, Brewers Bay lies in the southwest part of the island, near the University of the Virgin Islands. This beach of white coral sand is almost as long as the beach at Magens Bay. Students often come here to swim between classes. Unfortunately, this is not the place to come for snorkeling. Light meals and drinks are served at stands along the beach. From Charlotte Amalie, take the Fortuna bus heading west. Get off at the edge of Brewers Bay, across from the Reichhold Center, the cultural center of St. Thomas.

Lindbergh Beach   With lifeguard, toilet facilities, and a bathhouse, Lindbergh lies at the Island Beachcomber Hotel and is used extensively by the locals, who sometimes stage political rallies here as well as carnival parties. Drinks, such as piña coladas, are served on the beach. It's not good for snorkeling. Take the Fortuna bus route west from Charlotte Amalie.

EAST END

Secret Harbour   Small and special, Secret Harbour lies near a number of condos whose owners frequent the beach. With its white sand, coconut palms, and tranquil waters, it is a cliché of Caribbean charm. Many residents of Charlotte Amalie visit on the weekends because of its proximity to town, so it is most crowded then. The snorkeling near the rocks here is some of the best around the island. No public transportation stops here, but it's an easy taxi ride east of Charlotte Amalie in the direction of Red Hook.

✪ **Sapphire Beach**   One of the finest beaches in St. Thomas is Sapphire Beach, extremely popular with windsurfers. There's a large reef near the white-sand shore, and good views of offshore cays and the island of St. John. Behind the beach is one of the most desirable hotels and condominiums in St. Thomas, Doubletree Sapphire Beach Resort and Marina, where you can lunch or order drinks. You can rent snorkeling gear and lounge chairs. To reach Sapphire Beach, take the East End bus from Charlotte Amalie via Red Hook. Get off at the entrance to Sapphire Bay.

DEEP-SEA FISHING

The U.S. Virgins have very good deep-sea fishing—some 19 world records (eight for blue marlin) have been set in these waters in recent years. Outfitters abound at the major marinas like Red Hook. We recommend angling off the **Fish Hawk** (☎ **809/ 775-9058**), which Capt. Al Petrosky of New Jersey sails out of Fish Hawk Marina Lagoon at the East End. His 43-foot diesel-powered craft is fully equipped with rods and reels. All equipment (but not meals) is included in the price: $400 per half day for up to six passengers. A full-day excursion, depending on how far the boat goes, ranges from $700 to $800.

GOLF

On the north shore, **Mahogany Run,** at the Mahogany Run Golf Course, Mahogany Run Road (☎ **800/253-7103** or 809/777-6006), is an 18-hole, par-70 course. Designed by Tom and George Fazio, it's one of the most beautiful courses in the West Indies. It rises and drops like a roller coaster on its journey to the sea, where cliffs and crashing sea waves are the ultimate hazards at the 13th and 14th holes. For 18 holes, greens fees are $85, reduced to $70 in the late afternoon, depending on the daylight available.Cart fees cost $15 year round. No cut-offs, tank tops, or swimwear are allowed in the SEA clubhouse or on the course.

KAYAKING

Virgin Island Ecotours (☎ **809/779-2155** for information) offers guided kayak trips through St. Thomas's Marine Sanctuary and Mangrove Lagoon on the southern coastline. Trips are 2¹/₂ hours and cost $50 per person. Ecotourists should be on the lookout for rays, herons, juvenile reef fish, and mangrove crabs; about 30 minutes of the paddling tour are set aside for snorkeling.

SCUBA DIVING & SNORKELING

With 30 spectacular reefs just off St. Thomas, the U.S. Virgins are rated as one of the "most beautiful areas in the world" for scuba diving and snorkeling by *Skin Diver* magazine. For snorkeling, we like the waters off **Coki Point,** on the northeast shore of St. Thomas; especially enticing are the coral ledges near Coral World's underwater tower. **Magens Bay** also has great snorkeling year-round. The best dive site off St. Thomas has to be **Cow and Calf Rocks,** off the southeast end (45 minutes from Charlotte Amalie by boat); you'll discover a network of coral tunnels riddled with caves, reefs, and ancient boulders encrusted with coral.

Here's a list of recommendable outfitters that can assist you with any underwater adventure:

St. Thomas Diving Club, 7147 Bolongo Bay (☎ **800/538-7348** or 809/ 776-2381), is the best on the island, and it's a full-service, PADI five-star IDC center. An open-water certification course, including four scuba dives, costs $330. An advanced open-water certification course, including five dives in 2 days, is $275. Every Thursday, the club runs an all-day scuba excursion that includes a two-tank dive off the wreck of the RMS *Rhone* in the British Virgin Islands; the cost is $110. You can also enjoy local snorkeling for $25 per day.

Dive In, Doubletree Sapphire Beach Resort and Marina, Smith Bay Road, Route 6 (☎ **809/775-6100**), is also a complete diving center, offering some of the finest diving services in the U.S. Virgin Islands. They provide professional instruction for all levels, daily beach and boat dives, custom dive packages, underwater photography and videotapes, snorkeling trips, and a full-service PADI dive center. An introductory course costs $55. Certified divers can enjoy a two-dive morning trip for $70 or a one-dive afternoon trip at $50. Evening dives cost $55. Serious divers can purchase a six-dive pass for $185.

TENNIS

Your best bet for great tennis on the island is **Wyndham Sugar Bay Beach Club,** 6500 Estate Smith Bay (☎ **809/777-7100**), which claims the Virgin Islands's first stadium tennis court (seats 220), plus six additional Laykold courts that are lit at night. There's also a pro shop, complete with teaching pro.

Another good resort for tennis is the **Bolongo Beach Club,** Bolongo Bay (☎ **809/ 775-1800**), which has two tennis courts that are lit until 10pm. It's free to members and hotel guests, except if you want a lesson, which costs $18 per hour.

Marriott's Frenchman's Reef Tennis Courts (☎ **809/776-8500,** ext. 444) keeps four courts lit until 10pm. Nonguests pay $10 per half hour per court and must reserve one day in advance.

WINDSURFING

This increasingly popular sport is available at the major resort hotels and at some public beaches, including Brewers Bay, Morningstar Beach, and Limetree Beach. The **Renaissance Grand Beach Resort,** Smith Bay Road, Route 38 (☎ **809/775-1510**), is the best hotel for windsurfing rentals and instruction. Hotel guests pay $25 for a lesson and use of the equipment. If you're not a guest, the cost is $35 per hour.

6 Touring St. Thomas: From Charlotte Amalie to Coral World

WALKING TOUR
Charlotte Amalie

Start: King's Wharf.
Finish: Waterfront.
Time: 2¹/₂ hours.
Best Times: Any day between 10am and 5pm.
Worst Times: When a cruise-ship is in port.

The color and charm of the Caribbean come to life in the waterfront town of **Charlotte Amalie,** capital of St. Thomas, where most visitors begin their sightseeing of the island. Seafarers from all over the globe used to flock to this old-world Danish town, as did pirates and members of the Confederacy, who used the port during the American Civil War. At one time, St. Thomas was the biggest slave market in the world.

Old warehouses, once used for storing stolen pirate goods, have been converted to shops. In fact, the main streets, called "Gade" (a reflection of their Danish heritage) now coalesce into a virtual shopping mall and are usually packed. Sandwiched among these shops are a few historic buildings, most of which can be covered on foot in about 2 hours.

The most interesting historic buildings can easily be covered on a walking tour of Charlotte Amalie (see below). Before starting your tour, stop off in the so-called **Grand Hotel,** near Emancipation Park. No longer a hotel, it contains shops and a visitors center (☎ **809/774-8784**).

Begin your tour along the eastern harbor front at:

1. King's Wharf, site of the Virgin Islands Legislature, which is housed in the apple-green military barracks dating from 1874. From here walk away from the harbor up Fort Pladsen to:

Walking Tour—Charlotte Amalie

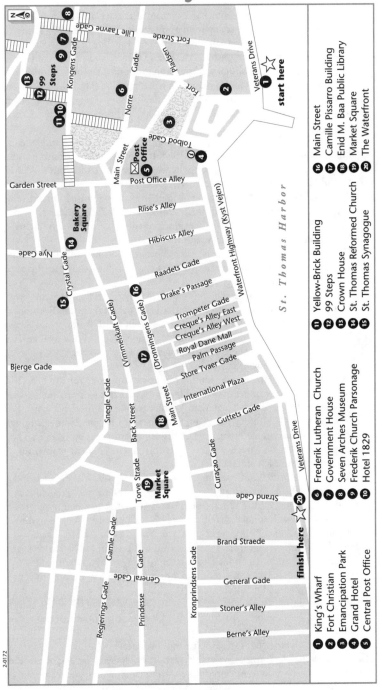

1 King's Wharf
2 Fort Christian
3 Emancipation Park
4 Grand Hotel
5 Central Post Office

6 Frederik Lutheran Church
7 Government House
8 Seven Arches Museum
9 Frederik Church Parsonage
10 Hotel 1829

11 Yellow-Brick Building
12 99 Steps
13 Crown House
14 St. Thomas Reformed Church
15 St. Thomas Synagogue

16 Main Street
17 Camille Pissarro Building
18 Enid M. Baa Public Library
19 Market Square
20 The Waterfront

St. Thomas Harbor

start here

finish here

2. ✪ **Fort Christian,** dating from 1672. Named after the Danish King Christian V, the structure has been everything from a governor's residence to a jail. The fort was a police station, court, and jail until it became a national historic landmark in 1977. A museum here demonstrates the history of the island culture and its people, including the Danes. Cultural workshops and turn-of-the-century furnishings are just some of the exhibits you can expect to see. A museum shop features local crafts, maps, and prints. The fort is open Monday through Friday from 8:30am to 4:30pm, Saturday from 9:30am to 4pm, and Sunday from noon to 2pm. Continue walking up Fort Pladsen to:

3. **Emancipation Park,** where a proclamation freeing African slaves and indentured European servants was read on July 3, 1848. It's now mostly a preferred picnic area for local workers and visitors. Facing the west side of the park is the:

4. **Grand Hotel,** where a visitors center dispenses valuable travel information about the island. When this hotel was launched in 1837, it was indeed a grand address, but it later fell into decay, and finally closed in 1975. The former guest rooms upstairs have been turned into offices and a restaurant. Northwest of the park, at Main Street and Tolbod Gade, stands the:

5. **Central Post Office,** displaying murals by Stephen Dohanos, who became famous as a *Saturday Evening Post* cover artist. From the post office, walk east along Norre Gade to Fort Pladsen, to the:

6. **Frederik Lutheran Church,** built between 1780 and 1793. The original Georgian-style building, financed by a free black parishioner, Jean Reeneaus, was reconstructed in 1825 after a fire and rebuilt again in 1870 after it was damaged in a hurricane. Exiting the church, walk east along Norre Gade to Lille Taarne Gade. Turn left (north) and climb to Kongens Gade (King Street), passing through a neighborhood of law firms, to:

7. ✪ **Government House,** the administrative headquarters for the U.S. Virgin Islands. It's been the center of political life in the islands since it was built—around the time of the American Civil War. Visitors are allowed on the first two floors, Monday through Saturday from 8am to noon, and 1 to 5pm. Some paintings by former resident Camille Pissarro are on display, as are works by other St. Thomas artists. Turn left on Kongens Gade. After leaving Government House, turn immediately to your left and look for the sign for:

8. **Seven Arches Museum,** Government Hill (☎ **809/774-9295**). Browsers and gapers love glimpsing the private home of longtime residents Philibert Fluck and Barbara Demaras. This 2-century-old Danish house has been completely restored and furnished with antiques. Walk through the yellow ballast arches into the Great Room, which has a great view of the Caribbean's busiest harbor. The $5 admission fee includes a cold tropical drink served in a beautiful walled flower garden. Open Tuesday through Sunday from 10am to 3pm, or by appointment.

   After visiting the museum, return to Government House. Directly to your left, as you face the building, is:

9. **Frederik Church Parsonage,** dating from 1725, and one of the oldest houses on the island. It is the only structure in the Government Hill district to retain its simple 18th-century lines.

   Continue west along Kongens Gade until you reach:

10. **Hotel 1829.** The former Lavalette House, it was designed by one of the leading merchants of Charlotte Amalie. This is a landmark building and a charming hotel that has attracted many of the island's most famous visitors over the years.

🌀 **TAKE A BREAK**   **Hotel 1829,** Kongens Gade, provides the perfect veranda, including a spectacular view, for a midday drink or a sundowner. You may just fall in love with the place, abandon this tour, and stick around for dinner. The bar is open daily from 10am to midnight, serving drinks for $3 and up. (See "Dining," above.)

Next door (still on the same side of the street), observe the:

11. **Yellow-Brick Building,** built in 1854 in what local architects called "the style of Copenhagen." Go inside and browse through the many shops that now occupy the building.

At this point, you might want to double back slightly on Kongens Gade and climb the famous:

12. **99 Steps.** The steps, which were erected in the early 1700s, take you to the summit of Government Hill, from where you'll see the 18th-century:

13. **Crown House,** immediately to your right on the south side of the street. This was once a stately home where two former governors of the Virgin Islands resided. Notice the Chinese wall hangings, a crystal chandelier from Versailles, and the intricately carved West Indian furniture. It was also the home of von Scholten, the Danish ruler who issued the famous proclamation of emancipation in 1848 (see Emancipation Park, above).

Walk back down the steps and continue right (west) along Kongens Gade, then down a pair of old brick steps until you reach Garden Street. Go right (north) on Garden Street and take a left onto Crystal Gade. On your left, at the corner of Nye Gade and Crystal Gade, you'll see:

14. **St. Thomas Reformed Church,** dating from 1844. Designed like a Greek temple, much of its original structure has been preserved intact.

Continue up Crystal Gade. On your right (north side), you'll come to:

15. **St. Thomas Synagogue,** the oldest synagogue in continuous use under the American flag and the second oldest in the Western Hemisphere. It still maintains the tradition of sand on the floor, commemorating the exodus from Egypt. Erected in 1833 by Sephardic Jews, it was built of local stone along with ballast brick from Denmark and mortar made of molasses and sand. It's open to visitors from 9am to 4pm, Monday through Friday.

Retrace your steps (east) to Raadets Gade and turn south toward the water, crossing the famous Vimmelskaft Gade or "Back Street" of Charlotte Amalie. Continue along Raadets Gade until you reach:

16. **Main Street** (Dronningens Gade), the most famous shopping street on St. Thomas and its major artery. Turn right (west) and walk along Main Street until you come to the mid–19th-century:

17. **Camille Pissarro Building,** on your right, at the Amsterdam Sauer Jewelry Store. Pissarro, a Spanish Jew who became one of the founders of French Impressionism, was born in this building as Jacob Pizarro in 1830. Before moving to Paris, where he got involved with some of the greatest artists of his day, he worked for his father in a store along Main Street.

Continuing west along Main Street, you will pass on your right:

18. **Enid M. Baa Public Library,** the former von Bretton House, dating from 1818. Keep heading west until you reach:

19. **Market Square,** officially known as Rothschild Francis Square, at the point where Main Street intersects Strand Gade. This was the center of a large slave-trading

market before the 1848 emancipation was proclaimed. It's an open-air fruit and vegetable market today, selling, among other items, *genips* (break open the skin and suck the pulp off a pit). The wrought-iron roof covered a railway station at the turn of the century. It's open Monday through Saturday, its busiest day.

If the genip doesn't satisfy you, take Strand Gade down (south) to:

20. The Waterfront (Kyst Vejen), where you can purchase a fresh coconut. One of the vendors will whack off the top with a machete, so you can drink the sweet milk from its hull. Here you'll have an up-close preview of one of the most scenic harbors in the West Indies, though it's usually filled with cruise ships.

FRENCHTOWN, MOUNTAIN TOP & DRAKE'S SEAT

West of Charlotte Amalie, Route 30 (Veterans Drive) will take you to **Frenchtown.** (Turn left at the sign to The Admiral's Inn.) Early French-speaking settlers arrived on St. Thomas from St. Bart's after they were uprooted by the Swedes. Many island residents today are the direct descendants of those long-ago immigrants, who were known for speaking a distinctive French patois and wearing *cha-chas* or straw hats.

This colorful village, inhabited mostly by fishers, contains a bevy of restaurants and taverns. Because Charlotte Amalie has become a dangerous place at night, Frenchtown has picked up its after-dark business and is the best spot for dancing, drinking, and other local entertainment.

West of Charlotte Amalie, Harwood Highway (Route 308) will lead you to **Crown Mountain Road,** a scenic drive opening onto the best views of the hills, beaches, and crystal-clear waters around St. Thomas. Eventually, you arrive at a former hotel which is a popular pit stop. **Mountain Top,** Crown Mountain (☎ **809/774-2400**), is a modern building with a restaurant and bar, plus some 14 shops. Most people come here to enjoy the view and sip the world-famous banana daiquiris—the bar here is said to have invented them in 1949! It is the most scenic perch in St. Thomas, as it opens onto a view of Sir Francis Drake Channel, which separates the U.S. Virgin Islands from the British Virgin Islands.

Farther down the road, you'll usually see tour buses filled with cruise-ship passengers converging on another scenic vista. This will be **Drake's Seat,** which locals claim offers the best view on the island—the panorama includes just about every Virgin

---

Under the Sea: The *Atlantis* Submarine

If you really want to get to the bottom of it all, board the *Atlantis* **submarine,** which takes you on a 1-hour voyage (the whole experience is really 2 hours when you include transportation to and from the sub) to depths of 90 feet, where an amazing world of exotic marine life unfolds. You'll have up-close views of coral reefs and sponge gardens through 2-foot windows on the air-conditioned sub, which carries 30 passengers.

Passengers take a surface boat from the West Indies Dock, right outside Charlotte Amalie, to the submarine, which lies near Buck Island (the St. Thomas version, not the more famous Buck Island near St. Croix). *Atlantis* divers swim with the fish and bring them close to the windows for photos. The fare is $72 for adults, $36 for teenagers 13 to 17, and $27 for children 6 to 12. The *Atlantis* operates daily November through April, Tuesday through Saturday May through October. Reservations are a must. For tickets, go to the Havensight Shopping Mall, Building 6, or call **809/776-5650.**

An Expedition to Hassel Island

Despite the maritime mob scene at Charlotte Amalie, the harbor's nearest and most visible island, **Hassel Island,** is almost completely deserted—its membership in the National Parks network prohibits most forms of development. There are no hotels or services of any kind, and swimming is limited to narrow, rocky beaches. Even so, many visitors hire a boat to drop them off for an hour or two of relief from the cruise-ship congestion. One company that makes the trip is **Launch with Larry** (☎ **809/690-8071**). A hike along part of the island's shoreline provides a different perspective on the hustle and bustle of Charlotte Amalie. You'll need to make arrangements in advance with the skipper who drops you off for your return trip. We recommend bringing your own drinking water and food if you plan to spend more than 3 hours here.

Island, both U.S. and British. According to local legend, Sir Francis Drake sat here, charting the channels and passages of the Virgin Island waters.

CORAL WORLD & OTHER NEARBY ATTRACTIONS

The number-one tourist attraction on St. Thomas is the ✪ **Coral World Marine Park and Underwater Observatory,** 6450 Coki Point (☎ **809/775-1555**), a marine complex that features a three-story underwater observation tower 100 feet offshore. Destroyed by Hurricane Marilyn in 1995, it's still being rebuilt and should be fully functional some time in 1997—at press time, an official at the U.S. Virgin Islands Division of Tourism said that it will "hopefully" reopen by December of 1997. Coral World is about a 20-minute drive from Charlotte Amalie off Route 38.

Entrance to the park is through a waterfall. Inside, you'll see sponges, fish, coral, and other aquatic creatures in their natural state through picture windows. In Coral World's **Marine Gardens Aquarium,** saltwater tanks display everything from sea horses to sea urchins. An 80,000-gallon reef tank features exotic marine life of the Caribbean; another tank is devoted to sea predators, with circling sharks and giant moray eels. Activities include daily fish and shark feedings and exotic bird shows. The latest addition to the park is a **semisubmarine** that lets you enjoy the panoramic view and the "down under" feeling of a submarine without truly submerging.

Coral World's guests can take advantage of adjacent Coki Beach for snorkel rental, scuba lessons, or simply swimming and relaxing. Lockers and showers are available.

Also included in the marine park are the Tropical Terrace Restaurant, duty-free shops, and a nature trail. The complex is open daily from 9am to 6pm. Admission is $16 for adults and $10 for children, but these prices are subject to change in 1997.

The **Paradise Point Tramway** (☎ 809/774-9809), opened in 1994, affords visitors a dramatic view of Charlotte Amalie harbor with a ride to a 697-foot peak, although you'll pay dearly for the privilege. The tramway operates four cars, each with a 10-person capacity, for the 15-minute round-trip ride. The tramways, similar to those used at ski resorts, transport customers from the Havensight area to Paradise Point, where riders disembark to visit shops and the popular restaurant and bar. The tramway runs daily from 9am to 5pm, costing $10 per person round-trip. Children travel for half price. The $2.8 million tramway line is supported by seven towers and engineered to withstand all types of weather conditions.

The **Estate St. Peter Greathouse Botanical Gardens,** at the corner of Route 40 (6A St. Peter Mountain Road) and Barrett Hill Road (☎ 809/774-4999), consist of 11 acres set at the foot of volcanic peaks on the northern rim of the island. They are laced with self-guided nature walks that will acquaint you with some 200 varieties of West Indian plants and trees, including an umbrella plant from Madagascar. From a panoramic deck you can see some 20 of the Virgin Islands, including Hans Lollick, an uninhabited island between Thatched Cay and Madahl Point. The house itself is worth a visit, although the admission is rather steep; it's filled with local art. It's open daily from 9am to 5pm; the cost is $8 for adults and $4 for children.

ESPECIALLY FOR KIDS

Coral World *(see p. 99)*   This is *the* place on St. Thomas to take your children. It's a hands-on experience—kids can even shake hands with a starfish at the Touch Pond. Later they can discover exotic Marine Gardens, where 20 aquariums showcase the Caribbean's incredible natural treasures.

Magens Bay Beach *(see p. 90)*   If you can introduce your children to only one beach in the entire Caribbean, make it this one. It's one of the finest in the world, with calm waters, white sand and lots of facilities, including picnic tables.

Atlantis **Submarine** *(see p. 98)*   Children are thrilled by this unique underwater adventure. On board, they'll dive to depths of up to 150 feet and see exotic fish, colorful sea gardens, coral formations, and unusual marine creatures. Children must be at least four years old.

ORGANIZED TOURS

Tropic Tours, 14AB Estate Thomas (☎ **809/774-1855**), a representative of American Express, offers a tour of St. Thomas, including Mountain Top, Drake's Seat, and Charlotte Amalie shopping. The cost is $20 per person.

Far more interesting than this rather dull tour is a day trip to St. John, home of the world famous Trunk Bay Beach.

Take one of the many ferry services to St. John. Boats depart from Charlotte Amalie or, more frequently from Red Hook, and arrive in St. John's Cruz Bay. The one-way fare is $3 for adults, $1 for children under 11. Near the access ramp of the pier in Cruz Bay, you'll find rows of independently operated taxis and their drivers who will take you on a tour of the island. A 2-hour guided tour costs about $30 per person, for two passengers, or $12 per person for six passengers.

If you want to skip the tour of St. John and head right to the beach at Trunk Bay for the day, simply negotiate a fare with one of the taxi drivers at the pier. Be sure to arrange a time to be picked up at the end of the day too. The cost of a one-way trip is usually around $3 to $5 per person. If you want to call ahead and arrange for a driver to pick you up, call one of the more reliable island drivers, Mr. Alexander, at **809/776-6757,** before you leave St. Thomas.

After arriving on St. John by ferry, you're driven around the island, stopping to take in some of the most scenic views. The tour, costing $60 per person, includes lunch. There's also time allotted for snorkeling with equipment provided.

DRIVING TOUR
St. Thomas

Start: Fort Christian.
Finish: Magens Bay Beach.
Time: 2¹/₂ hours.
Best Times: Sunday, when traffic is lightest.
Worst Times: Wednesday and Saturday, when traffic is heaviest.

Driving Tour—St. Thomas

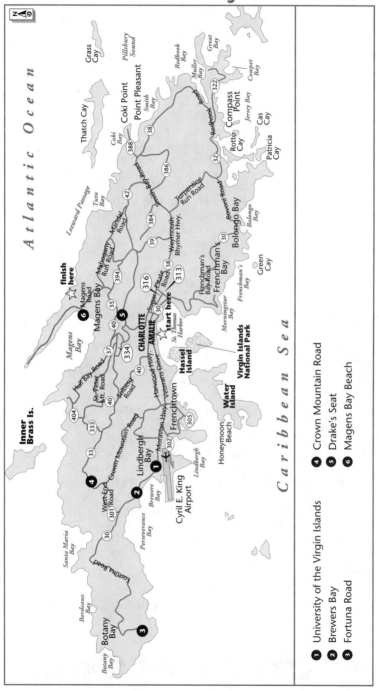

1. University of the Virgin Islands
2. Brewers Bay
3. Fortuna Road
4. Crown Mountain Road
5. Drake's Seat
6. Magens Bay Beach

Begin at Fort Christian in the eastern part of Charlotte Amalie and head west along the waterfront. To your left you'll see cruise ships anchored offshore and on your right all the stores. Continue west on Route 30 and pass the Cyril E. King Airport on your left. As the road forks toward the airport, keep right along Route 30, which runs parallel to the airport.

At about 2.4 miles from Fort Christian on your right will be:

1. **The University of the Virgin Islands,** which is the major university in the Virgin Islands. It is a modern complex with landscaped campus grounds. Continue west on Route 30 until you reach:

2. **Brewers Bay** on your left. You may want to park near here and go for a swim, as this is one of the more desirable beaches on the island.

    Continue 3.8 miles west, climbing uphill through scrub country along a hilly drive past the junction with Route 301. This far west Route 30 is called:

3. **Fortuna Road,** one of the most scenic areas of St. Thomas, with sweeping views of the water and offshore islands on your left. Along the way you'll come across parking areas where you can pull off and enjoy the view (the Bethesda Hill vista is particularly panoramic). The districts you pass through—Bonne Esperance and Perseverance—are named after the old plantations that once stood here. The area is now primarily residential. At Bordeaux Hill you descend sharply, and the road narrows until you come to a dead end.

    At this point, turn around and head back east along Route 30. The road is poorly marked at this point, and you'll probably need the *Official Road Map of the United States Virgin Islands,* available at bookstores in the U.S.V.I. Turn left and head northeast at the junction with Route 301. You will come to another junction at:

4. **Crown Mountain Road,** the most scenic road in the Virgin Islands. Turn left here onto Route 33. The road will sweep northward before it makes an abrupt switch to the east. You will be traversing the most mountainous heartland of St. Thomas. Expect hairpin turns during your descent. You'll often have to reduce your speed to 10 m.p.h., especially in the Mafolie district. The road will eventually lead to the junction with Route 37, where you should go left, but only for a short distance, until you reach the junction with Route 40. At one point routes 37 and 40 become the same highway. When they separate, turn right and stay on Route 40 to:

5. **Drake's Seat,** the legendary perch where Sir Francis Drake is said to have figured out the best routes for the colonial European powers to take their ships from the Atlantic into the Caribbean Sea. Continue left onto Route 35. The road will veer northwest. Follow it all the way to:

6. **Magens Bay Beach,** hailed as one of the most beautiful beaches in the world. Here you can arrange Sunfish, glass-bottom paddleboat, and windsurf rentals. Lounge chairs, changing facilities, showers, lockers, and picnic tables are also available.

🍵 **WINDING DOWN** **Magens Bay Bar and Grill,** Magens Bay Beach (☎ **809/777-6270**), is an ideal place for light meals on this heart-shaped beach. The snack bar overlooks the beach. You can order sandwiches from $3.95, salads from $4.95, and soft drinks from $1.75. Pizza is sold by the slice.

7 Shopping

The $1,200 duty-free allowance in the Virgin Islands (see "Entry Requirements," in chapter 3) makes every purchase a double bargain. If you go over the limit, duty is charged at a flat rate of 5% up to $1,000 rather than at the 10% imposed on goods

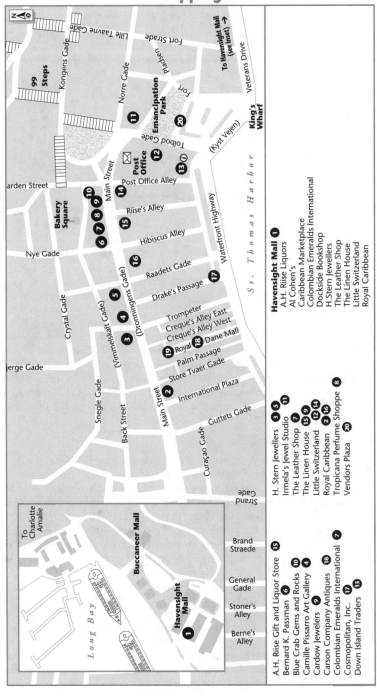

Shopping in Charlotte Amalie

Havensight Mall ❶
A.H. Riise Liquors
Al Cohen's
Caribbean Marketplace
Colombian Emeralds International
Dockside Bookshop
H.Stern Jewellers
The Leather Shop
The Linen House
Little Switzerland
Royal Caribbean

H. Stern Jewellers ❸ ❺
Irmela's Jewel Studio ⓫
The Leather Shop ❼
The Linen House ⓯ ❾
Little Switzerland ⓬ ⓮
Royal Caribbean ❷ ⓰
Tropicana Perfume Shoppe ❽
Vendors Plaza ⓴

A.H. Riise Gift and Liquor Store ❶
Bernard K. Passman ❻
Blue Crab Gems and Rocks ⓪
Camille Pissarro Art Gallery ❹
Cardow Jewelers ❾
Carson Company Antiques ⓲
Colombian Emeralds International ❼
Cosmopolitan, Inc. ⓱
Down Island Traders ⓭

from other countries. You can send as many gifts as you want to family or friends duty free—but not more than one per day up to $100. These items do not have to be declared on your exemption.

You can find some well-known brand names at savings of up to 60% off mainland prices. You often however, have to plow through a lot of junk to find the savings. You need to know the price back home of the item to determine if you are in fact saving money. Having sounded that warning, we'll mention some St. Thomas shops where we have found really good buys.

Most shops, some of which occupy former pirate warehouses, are open Monday through Saturday from 9am to 5pm. Some stores open Sunday and holidays if a cruise ship is in port. *Note:* Friday is the biggest cruise-ship visiting day at Charlotte Amalie (we once counted eight at once), so try to avoid shopping then.

It is illegal for most street vendors (food vendors are about the only exception) to ply their trades outside of the designated area called **Vendors Plaza,** at the corner of Veterans Drive and Tolbod Gade. Hundreds of vendors converge at 7:30am; they usually pack up around 5:30pm, Monday through Saturday. (Very few hawk their wares on Sunday, unless a cruise ship is scheduled to arrive.)

When you completely tire of French perfumes and Swiss watches, head for **Market Square** as it's called locally, or more informally, Rothschild Francis Square. Here under a Victorian tin roof, locals with machetes slice open fresh coconuts so that you can drink the milk; women wearing bandannas sell akee, cassava, or breadfruit.

THE BEST BUYS & WHERE TO FIND THEM

The **best buys** on St. Thomas include china, crystal, perfumes, jewelry (especially emeralds), Haitian art, fashions, and items made of wood. Cameras and electronic items, based on our experience, are not the good buys they're reputed to be.

St. Thomas is the best place in the Caribbean for discounts in porcelain. Look for the imported patterns for the biggest savings, but even U.S. brands may be purchased for 25% off the retail price on the mainland. There are also good deals on brand-name watches.

SHOPPING DISTRICTS

Nearly all the major shopping in St. Thomas is along the harbor of Charlotte Amalie. Cruise-ship passengers mainly shop at the **Havensight Mall** where they disembark at the eastern edge of Charlotte Amalie. The principal shopping street is called **Main Street** or Dronningens Gade (its old Danish name). North of this street is another merchandise-loaded street called **Back Street** or Vimmelskaft.

Many shops are also spread along the **Waterfront Highway** (also called Kyst Vejen). Between these major streets or boulevards is a series of side streets, walkways, and alleys, all filled with shops. Major shopping streets are Tolbod Gade, Raadets Gade, Royal Dane Mall, Palm Passage, Storetvaer Gade, and Strand Gade.

Other noteworthy shopping districts include **Tillett Gardens,** a virtual oasis of arts and crafts—pottery, silk screen fabrics, candles, watercolors, jewelry, and more—on the highway across from Four Winds Shopping Center. The Jim Tillett Gallery here is a major island attraction in itself (see listing below). **Vendors Plaza,** on the waterfront side of Emancipation Park, is an outdoor marketplace filled with vendors selling handmade jewelry, straw baskets, handbags, T-shirts, local foods, and pretty much everything under the sun. At **Mountain Top,** near the center of the island, there's also a modern shopping mall—a bit too tourist-tacky for us—that contains about a dozen shops; the views are much better than the merchandise.

All the major stores in St. Thomas are located by number on an excellent map in the center of the publication *St. Thomas This Week*, distributed free to all arriving plane and boat passengers and by the visitors center.

All of the stores recommended below can be reached on foot along the streets directly in the center of Charlotte Amalie. A lot of the stores don't have street numbers, or don't display them, so look for their signs instead.

SHOPPING A TO Z
ART

✪ Bernard K. Passman
38A Main St. ☎ **809/777-4580.**

Bernard K. Passman is the world's leading sculptor of black coral art and jewelry, famous for his *Can Can Girl* and his four statues of Charlie Chaplin. On Grand Cayman he learned to fashion exquisite treasures from black coral found 200 feet under the sea. After being polished and embellished with gold and diamonds, some of Passman's work has been treasured by royalty. There are also simpler and more affordable pieces for sale.

Camille Pissarro Building Art Gallery
Caribbean Cultural Centre, 14 Dronningens Gade. ☎ **809/774-4621.**

In the house where Pissarro, dean of Impressionism, was born in 1830, this art gallery, reached by climbing stairs, honors the illustrious painter. In three high-ceilinged and airy rooms, you'll discover all the available Pissarro paintings relating to the islands. Many prints and note cards of local artists are available, and the gallery also sells original batiks, alive in vibrant colors.

✪ Jim Tillett Art Gallery and Silk Screen Print Studio
Tillett Gardens, 4126 Anna's Retreat, Tutu. ☎ **809/775-1929.** Take Rte. 38 east from Charlotte Amalie.

Since 1959 Tillett Gardens, once an old Danish farm, has been the island's arts-and-crafts center. This tropical compound is a series of buildings housing arts-and-crafts studios, galleries, and an outdoor garden restaurant and bar. Prints in the galleries start as low as $10. The best work of local artists is displayed here—originals in oils, watercolors, and acrylics. The Tillett prints on fine canvas are all one of a kind. The famous Tillett maps on fine canvas are priced from $30.

BOOKSTORES

Dockside Bookshop
Havensight Mall. ☎ **809/774-4937.**

If you need a beach read, head for this well-stocked store near the cruise-ship dock, east of Charlotte Amalie. The shop has the best selection of books on island lore as well as a variety of general reading selections.

BRIC-A-BRAC

Carson Company Antiques
Royal Dane Mall, off Main St. ☎ **809/774-6175.**

Its clutter and eclecticism might appeal to you, especially if you appreciate small spaces loaded with merchandise, tasteless and otherwise, from virtually everywhere. Much of it is calibrated to appeal to the tastes of cruise-ship passengers looking for bric-a-brac that usually accumulates on shelves back on the U.S. mainland. Bakelite jewelry is cheap and cheerful, and the African artifacts are often especially interesting.

CAMERAS & ELECTRONICS

✪ **Royal Caribbean**

33 Main St. ☎ **809/776-4110.**

This is the largest camera and electronics store in the Caribbean. This store and its outlets carry Nikon, Minolta, Pentax, Canon, and Panasonic products. It's a good source for watches, too, including such brand names as Seiko, Movado, Corum, Fendi, and Zodiac. They also have a complete collection of Philippe Charriol watches, jewelry, and leather bags, and a wide selection of Mikimoto pearls, 14- and 18-karat jewelry, and Lladró figurines.

There are additional branches at 23 Main St. (☎ **809/776-5449**) and Havensight Mall (☎ **809/776-8890**).

CHINA, CRYSTAL & WATCHES

Little Switzerland

5 Main St. ☎ **809/776-2010.**

A branch of this shop seems to appear on virtually every island in the Caribbean. Its concentration of watches, including Omega and Rolex, is topped by no one. But it also sells a wide variety of other objects as well, including cuckoo clocks and music boxes. Its china, especially the Royal Worcester and Rosenthal collection, is outstanding, as are its crystal and jewelry. They also maintain the official outlets for Hummel, Lladró, and Swarovski figurines. There are several other branches of this store on the island, especially at the Havensight Mall, but the main store has the best selection.

✪ **A. H. Riise Gift and Liquor Stores**

37 Main St. at A. H. Riise Gift and Liquor Mall (perfume and liquor branch stores at the Havensight Mall). ☎ **800/524-2037** or 809/776-2303.

St. Thomas's oldest outlet for luxury items such as jewelry, crystal, china, and perfumes is still the largest. It also offers the widest sampling of liquors and liqueurs on the island. Everything is displayed in a 19th-century Danish warehouse, extending from Main Street to the waterfront. The store boasts a collection of fine jewelry and watches from Europe's leading craftspeople, including Vacheron Constantin, Bulgari, Omega, and Gucci, as well as a wide selection of Greek gold, platinum, and precious gemstone jewelry.

Imported cigars are stored in a climate-controlled walk-in humidor. Delivery to cruise ships and the airport is free. A. H. Riise offers a vast selection of fragrances for both men and women, along with the world's best-known names in cosmetics and treatment products. Featured in the china and crystal department are Waterford, Lalique, Baccarat, and Rosenthal, among others. Specialty shops in the complex sell Caribbean gifts, books, clothing, food, art prints, note cards, and designer sunglasses.

CLOTHING

Coki

Compass Point Marina. ☎ **809/775-6560.**

Coki of St. Thomas has a factory 1¹/₂ miles from Red Hook amidst a little restaurant row, so you might want to combine a dining tour with a shopping expedition.

From the factory's expansive cutting board come some of the most popular varieties of shoulder tote bags in the Virgin Islands. These include pieces of canvas and elegant cotton prints converted to beach bags, zip-top bags, and drawstring bags. All Coki bags are 100% cotton, stitched with polyester sailmaker's thread.

Cosmopolitan
Drakes Passage and the waterfront. ☎ **809/776-2040.**

Since 1973, this store has drawn a lot of repeat business. Its shoe salon features Bally of Switzerland, and Bally handbags are a popular addition. In swimwear, it offers one of the best selections of Gottex of Israel for women and Gottex, Hom, Lahco of Switzerland, and Fila for men. A menswear section offers Paul and Shark from Italy, and Burma Bibas sports shirts. The shop also features ties by Gianni Versace and Pancaldi of Italy (at least 30% less than the U.S. mainland price), and Nautica sportswear for men discounted at 10%.

GIFTS

Caribbean Marketplace
Havensight Mall (Building III). ☎ **809/776-5400.**

The best selections of Caribbean handcrafts are found here, including Sunny Caribbee products, a vast array of condiments (ranging from spicy peppercorns to nutmeg mustard). There's also a wide selection of Sunny Caribbee's botanical products. Other items range from steel-pan drums from Trinidad to wooden Jamaican jigsaw puzzles, from Indonesian batiks to bikinis from the Cayman Islands. Do not expect very attentive service.

Down Island Traders
Veterans Dr. ☎ **809/776-4641.**

The aroma of spices will lead you to these markets, which have Charlotte Amalie's most attractive array of spices, teas, seasoning, candies, jellies, jams, and condiments, most of which are packaged from natural Caribbean products. The owner carries a line of local cookbooks, as well as silk-screened T-shirts and bags, Haitian metal sculpture, handmade jewelry, Caribbean folk art, and children's gifts.

JEWELRY

Blue Carib Gems and Rocks
2 Back St. (behind Little Switzerland). ☎ **809/774-8525.**

For a decade, the owners scoured the Caribbean for gemstones; these stones have been brought directly from the mines to you. The raw stones are cut, polished, and then fashioned into jewelry by the lost-wax process. On one side of the premises you can see the craftspeople at work, and on the other, view their finished products. A lifetime guarantee is given on all handcrafted jewelry. Since the items are locally made, they are duty free and not included in the $1,200 Customs exemption.

✪ Cardow Jewelers
39 Main St. ☎ **809/776-1140.**

Often called the Tiffany's of the Caribbean, Cardow Jewelers boasts the largest selection of fine jewelry in the world. This fabulous shop, where more than 20,000 rings are displayed, offers savings because of its worldwide direct buying, large turnover, and duty-free prices. Unusual and traditional designs are offered in diamonds, emeralds, rubies, sapphires, and Brazilian stones, as well as pearls. Cardow has a whole wall of Italian gold chains, and also features antique-coin jewelry. The Treasure Cove has cases of fine gold jewelry all priced under $200.

Colombian Emeralds International
Havensight Mall. ☎ **809/774-2442.**

The Colombian Emeralds stores are renowned throughout the Caribbean for offering the finest collection of Colombian emeralds, both set and unset. Here you buy direct from the source, cutting out the middleperson, which can mean significant savings for you. In addition to jewelry, the shop stocks fine watches. There's another outlet on Main Street.

H. Stern Jewellers
Havensight Mall. ☎ **800/524-2024** or 809/776-1223.

This international jeweler is one of the most respected in the world, with some 175 outlets. In a world of fake jewelry and fake everything, it's good to know that there's still a name you can count on. It's a leading competitor on the island to Cardow (see above). Colorful gem and jewel creations are offered at Stern's locations on St. Thomas—there are two on Main Street, this one at the Havensight Mall, and a branch at Marriott's Frenchman's Reef. Stern gives worldwide guaranteed service, including a 1-year exchange privilege.

Irmela's Jewel Studio
In the Old Grand Hotel, at the beginning of Main St. ☎ **800/524-2047** or 809/774-5875.

Irmela's has made a name for itself in the highly competitive jewelry business on St. Thomas. Here the jewelry is unique, custom-designed by Irmela, and handmade by her studio or imported from around the world. Irmela has the largest selection of cultured pearls in the Caribbean, including freshwater Biwa, South Sea, and natural-color black Tahitian pearls. Choose from hundreds of clasps and pearl necklaces. Irmela has a large selection of unset stones.

LEATHER GOODS

The Leather Shop
1 Main St. ☎ **809/776-0290.**

Here you'll find the best selection from Italian designers such as Fendi, Longchamp, De Vecchi, Furla, and Il Bisonte. There are many styles of handbags, belts, wallets, briefcases, and attaché cases. Some of these items are very expensive, of course, but there is less-expensive merchandise like backpacks, carry-ons, and Mola bags from Colombia. If you're looking for a bargain, ask them to direct you to the outlet store on Back Street, selling close-outs at prices that are sometimes 50% off U.S. mainland tags.

LINENS

The Linen House
A. H. Riise Mall. ☎ **809/774-1668.**

The Linen House is considered the best store for linens in the West Indies. You'll find a wide selection of place mats, decorative tablecloths, and many hand-embroidered goods, much of them handmade in China. Other branches are at Havensight Mall (☎ **809/774-0868**), and 7A Royal Dane Mall (☎ **809/ 774-8117**).

LIQUOR

Al Cohen's
Long Bay Rd. ☎ **809/774-3690.**

In Al Cohen's big warehouse at Havensight, across from the West Indies Company dock where cruise-ship passengers come in, you can purchase discount liquor, fragrances, T-shirts, and souvenirs.

A. H. Riise Liquors
37 Main St. (☎ **809/774-2303**).

This store has almost every brand of liquor worth mentioning, along with a well-stocked supply of cigarettes and cigars. Fine ports, vintage Madeiras, rare cognacs and Armagnacs, and even "island flavor" favorites are sold here. The store will package your purchases for delivery to the airport or cruise ship. There's also a branch at Havensight Mall.

PERFUME

Tropicana Perfume Shoppe
2 Main St. ☎ **800/233-7948** or 809/774-0010.

This store at the beginning of Main Street is billed as the largest perfumery in the world, and it offers all the famous names in perfumes, skin care, and cosmetics. They carry Lancôme and La Prairie among other products. Men will also find Europe's best colognes and aftershave lotions here.

8 St. Thomas After Dark

St. Thomas has more nightlife than any other island in the Virgins, U.S. and British, but it's not as extensive as you might think. The big hotels, such as Marriott's Frenchman's Reef Beach Resort and Bluebeard's, have the most lively after-dark scene.

After a day of sightseeing and shopping in the hot West Indies sun, sometimes your best bet is to stay at your hotel in the evening, perhaps listening to a local fungi band. Big-time, big-name entertainment doesn't exist here.

Charlotte Amalie is no longer the rocking, swinging town it used to be at night. Many of the dark streets are dangerous, and muggings are frequent, so visitors have relatively abandoned it, except for a few places, such as the Greenhouse. Much of the action has shifted to Frenchtown, which has some great restaurants and bars. However, just as in Charlotte Amalie, some of these little hot spots are along dark, badly lit roads.

Note: St. Thomas is not an ideal place for single women travelers. Sexual harassment can be a problem in certain bars in Charlotte Amalie, where few single women would want to be alone at night anyway. Any of the major resort hotels is generally safe.

THE PERFORMING ARTS

Reichhold Center for the Arts
University of the Virgin Islands, 2 John Brewer's Bay. ☎ **809/693-1550.** Tickets $12–$40.

This artistic center, the premier venue in the Caribbean, lies west of Charlotte Amalie. Call the theater or check with the tourist office to see what's on at the time of your visit. The lobby displays a frequently changing free exhibit of paintings and sculptures by Caribbean artists. A Japanese-inspired amphitheater is set into a natural valley, with seating space for 1,196. The smell of gardenias adds to the beauty of the performances. Several different repertory companies of music, dance, and drama perform here. Performances begin at 8pm (call the theater to check).

THE CLUB & MUSIC SCENE

Barnacle Bill's

At the Crown Bay Marina, in the Sub Base. ☎ **809/774-7444.** No cover, except $3 on "Limelight Mondays," when several different bands are featured.

A restaurant during the day, this is one of the most desirable nightclubs on St. Thomas in the evening. Beginning around 9pm, a parade of local and imported musical talent plays to full houses until at least 1am. Although the bar is open nightly, live music is presented Tuesday through Saturday nights, January through March only. Cheap beer.

Cabaña Lounge

Blackbeard's Castle, Blackbeard's Hill. ☎ **809/776-1234.**

This lounge is one of the friendliest and most simpatico places to gather in St. Thomas any night but Monday from 5pm "until." Your hosts, Bob Harrington and Henrique Konzen, Blackbeard's owners, provide a limited but choice menu—nothing over $12—and an inviting atmosphere. On some nights, activities such as games are featured, perhaps a movie night, even an Ides of March toga party. After Hurricane Marilyn destroyed much of the property, this bar and pool area was converted into the Cabaña. Before that, it had been used strictly by Bob and Henrique as an extension of their own living quarters.

Courtyard Bar

Windward Passage Hotel, Veterans Dr. ☎ **809/774-5200.** No cover. Daily 11am–10:30 or 11pm.

You'd never know that the roar of Charlotte Amalie's coastal boulevard lies just outside the Courtyard Bar. Sheltered in semi-secluded cabaña, you can enjoy drinks like a "Paradise" (rum with cream of coconut, grenadine, and three kinds of fruit juice).

Dungeon Bar

Bluebeard's Hill. ☎ **809/774-1600.** No cover. Sun–Fri 11am–midnight, Sat 11am–1am.

Overlooking the pool and yacht harbor, the Dungeon Bar at Bluebeard's offers piano-bar entertainment nightly and is a popular gathering spot for both residents and visitors. You can dance from 8pm to midnight on Thursday and from 8pm to 1am on Saturday. Entertainment varies from month to month, but a steel band comes in on some nights whereas other nights such as Monday are devoted to karaoke or else jazz on Wednesday. Drink specialties are named after Bluebeard himself—Bluebeard's wench, cooler, and ghost.

Epernay

Rue de St. Barthélemy, Frenchtown. ☎ **809/774-5348.**

Adjacent to Alexander's Restaurant, this stylish watering hole with a view of the ocean adds a touch of Europe to the neighborhood. You can order glasses of at least six different brands of champagne, and vintage wines by the glass. Appetizers cost $6 to $10, and include sushi and caviar. You can also order tempting desserts, such as chocolate-dipped strawberries.

Fat Tuesday

26A Royal Dane Mall. ☎ **809/777-8676.** No cover. Daily 10am–midnight or 1am (later on Friday and Saturday).

Located on the waterfront in downtown Charlotte Amalie, this nightspot serves up frozen concoctions. In the partylike atmosphere of Fat Tuesday, patrons enjoy specialties like the Tropical Itch (a frozen punch made with bourbon and 151 rum) or the Moko Jumbi Juice (made with vodka, bourbon, 151 rum, and banana and cocoa liqueurs). There's also a wide variety of beer, highballs, and shooters, including the "Head Butt," which contains Jagermeister, Bailey's, and amaretto. Each night the bar has special events like Monday night football or T.G.I.F. night.

Greenhouse

Veterans Dr. ☎ **809/774-7998.** No cover Thurs–Tues, $5 Wed (including the first drink).

Set directly on the waterfront, this bar and restaurant is one of the few nightspots we recommend in Charlotte Amalie. You can park nearby and walk to the entrance. Each night different entertainment is featured, ranging from reggae to disco. Wednesday night is the "big blast."

Iggie's Bolongo

Bolongo Beach Club, 7150 Bolongo. ☎ **809/779-2844.**

During the day, Iggie's premises function as an informal open-air restaurant serving hamburgers, sandwiches, and salads. After dark, however, it turns into an entertainment venue featuring karaoke and occasional live entertainment. Call to find out what's happening.

Turtle Rock Bar

In the Mangrove Restaurant at the Wyndham Sugar Bay Beach Club, 6500 Estate Smith Bay. ☎ **809/777-7100.** No cover.

Set a few minutes' drive west of Red Hook, this is a popular bar where live music, steel bands, and karaoke provide diversions. Although there's lots of space on the premises if anyone should get the urge to dance, very few clients ever seem to take the opportunity, preferring instead to listen to the steel-pan bands (which play from 2pm to closing every night), or the more elaborate bands that play on Tuesday and Sunday nights. Thursday night is karaoke (for those of you who simply must—or those of you who want to stay away).

If you're hungry, burgers, salads, steaks, and grilled fish are available at the Mangrove Restaurant a few steps away. Entrance to the complex is free, and happy hour (when most drinks are half price) is 4 to 6pm every night.

Walter's

3 Trompeter Gade. ☎ **809/774-5025.** No cover Sun–Thurs, $3 Fri–Sat.

Dimly and rather flatteringly lit, this two-level watering hole attracts locals, often gay men, in season, drawing more off-island visitors in winter. Located about 100 yards from the island's famous synagogue, in a clapboard town house built around 1935, Walter's cellar bar features an intimate atmosphere with music from the 1950s, 1960s, and 1970s.

GAY & LESBIAN NIGHTLIFE

St. Thomas might be the most cosmopolitan of the Virgin Islands, but it is no longer the "gay paradise" it was in the 1960s and 1970s—the action has shifted mainly to San Juan. The major gay scene in the U.S. Virgins is in Frederiksted on St. Croix (see chapter 6).

That doesn't mean that gay men and lesbians aren't attracted to St. Thomas. They are, but many of the clubs that used to cater exclusively to them are gone. Today there are pockets of gay men and women who attend predominantly straight establishments.

These places include **Blackbeard's Castle, Hotel 1829,** and even the **Greenhouse** on Veterans Drive (see "St. Thomas After Dark," above).

9 An Excursion to Water Island

The fourth-largest of the U.S. Virgins with 500 acres of land, **Water Island** is only $^1/_2$ mile long and about $^1/_2$ to 1 mile wide. Its nearest point is about $^3/_8$ mile from St. Thomas.

It was only late 1996 that Water Island officially became the fourth U.S. Virgin Island. Ownership of 50 acres of the island was transferred from the U.S. Department of the Interior to the government of the U.S. Virgin Islands. The acreage includes a hotel site, catchment basin, two docks, a beach, and public roads which will require some maintenance. U.S.V.I. Gov. Roy L. Schneider and Interior Secretary Bruce Babbitt also agreed to spend more than $3 million on cleaning up the island. The transfer of remaining acres will occur as negotiations with island homeowners are finalized.

Visitors head for Water Island to spend the day on **Honeymoon Beach,** where they swim, snorkel, sail, water-ski, or just sunbathe on the palm-shaded beach and order lunch or a drink from the beach bar. The highest elevation is only 300 feet above sea level.

Originally inhabited by the Arawaks, the island was later a stopover for sailing vessels which used its freshwater ponds to replenish their casks. During World War I, the U.S. Army used Fort Segarra as a base.

Virgin Islanders seeking an escapist holiday often visit Water Island via private boat from St. Thomas. If you're not lucky enough to have access to a private yacht, you can take one of the public ferryboats maintained by Launch with Larry. Priced at $3 per person each way ($5 each way for evening passages), it runs from the Crown Bay Marina (part of St. Thomas's submarine base) to a pier opposite Tickles Restaurant. It departs from St. Thomas every day at 6:45, 7:15, 8am, noon, 2, 4, 5, and 6pm, with a return to St. Thomas scheduled for approximately 30 minutes later. On Monday, Friday, and Saturday nights, there are additional departures from St. Thomas at 9 and 10pm, with a return from Water Island to St. Thomas 30 minutes later.

If you happen to miss any of these departures, the ferryboat operator will sometimes schedule private departures for a minimum price of $20 for up to four passengers. Getting information about departure times of the individual boats is somewhat awkward; you must leave a beeper message for Launch with Larry by calling either **809/775-8071** or 809/779-6807 and hope for a return call. Although not associated with the ferryboat, the reception staff at Water Island's only hotel, the **Limestone Reef** (☎ **800/774-2148**), can also provide data and information about ferryboat transit to and from Water Island from St. Thomas.

The U.S. Virgin Islands: St. John

5

About 3 to 5 miles east of St. Thomas, across a glistening, turquoise-colored channel known as Pillsbury Sound, St. John, the smallest and least densely populated of the three main U.S. Virgin Islands, rises out of the Atlantic Ocean. At 7 miles long and 3 miles wide, its total landmass is only 20 square miles.

The United States purchased St. John from the Danes in 1917, but it wasn't until the 1940s that word of this island's rare natural beauty began to travel through yachting circles and among developers in the States.

Today St. John (unlike its neighboring U.S. islands) remains truly pristine, its preservation rigidly enforced by the U.S. Park Service. Thanks to the efforts of Laurance Rockefeller, who purchased acres of land here and donated them to the United States, the island's shoreline waters, as well as more than half of its surface area, comprise the Virgin Islands National Park.

St. John is ringed with a rocky coastline that forms crescent-shaped bays and white-sand beaches; the island array of bird and wildlife is the envy of ornithologists and zoologists around the world. There are miles of serpentine hiking trails, whose edges are dotted with panoramic views and the ruins of 18th-century Danish plantations. At scattered intervals along the trails, there are even mysteriously geometric petroglyphs of unknown age and origin incised into boulders and cliffs.

The pleasures and beauties of St. John, however, are not limited to land alone. Sailors and boaters have long cruised its sheltered coves for anchorages, swimming, and extended getaways. The hundreds of coral gardens that surround St. John are protected as rigorously as its land by the National Park Service—any attempt to damage or remove coral from these waters is punishable with large and strictly enforced fines.

The island's status as a national park does not preclude the presence of well-maintained roads, a scattering of hotels and restaurants, and a small commercial center, Cruz Bay, on the island's western tip. Growth and commercial development on the island are limited to the parcels of privately owned land that are not part of the park.

Despite the unspoiled beauty of much of St. John, the island manages to provide visitors with most modern amenities and travel services, including a sampling of restaurants, car-rental kiosks,

---

Island Highlights: St. John

Beaches

- **Trunk Bay,** wide and long, is one of the most beautiful beaches in the West Indies.
- **Caneel Bay,** site of the famous resort, has a string of seven beaches that stretch around Durloe Point to Hawksnest Caneel.
- **Cinnamon Bay,** doubles as one of the best campsites in the Caribbean.
- **Maho Bay,** largest beach on the north shore, was once the site of an old sugar plantation.
- **Hawksnest Bay,** is ideal for a beach party, with its white sand, picnic tables, and charcoal grills.

Must-See Attractions

- **Cruz Bay,** the capital, is a stage-set version of a little West Indian village, with pastel-painted houses.
- **The U.S. Virgin Islands National Park,** covers 9,500 acres of land filled with hiking trails and historical sites.
- **Annaberg Ruins,** site of a Danish sugar mill and plantation from the early 1700s, are an intriguing look into West Indian history.

---

yacht-supply facilities, hotels, and campgrounds—Cinnamon Bay, founded by the National Park Service in 1964, is the most famous campsite in the Caribbean.

One of the most exciting ways to see St. John is by Jeep or some other open-ended vehicle, which you can easily rent in town (in winter, it's best to reserve in advance). The endless roadside panoramas are dramatically steep, richly tinted with tones of forest green and turquoise, and liberally accented with flashes of silver and gold from the strong Caribbean sun.

1 Orientation

ARRIVING
BY BOAT

The easiest and most common way to get to St. John is by **ferryboat** (☎ 809/776-6282), which leaves from the **Red Hook** landing pier on St. Thomas's eastern tip and goes to Cruz Bay or St. John; trip time is 20 minutes each way. Beginning at 6:30am, boats depart more or less every hour, with minor exceptions throughout the day. The last ferry back to Red Hook departs from St. John's Cruz Bay at 11pm. Departures are so frequent that even cruise-ship passengers temporarily anchored in Charlotte Amalie for a short visit can visit St. John for a quick island tour. The one-way fare is $3 for adults, $1 for children under 11. Schedules can change without notice, so call in advance before your intended departure.

To reach the ferry at Red Hook Marina from Charlotte Amalie, grab a taxi or take the Vitran bus ($1 one way) from the stop near Market Square.

You can also board a boat for St. John at the **Charlotte Amalie waterfront,** but it costs more, $7 one way. The ride takes 45 minutes. The ferryboat departs from Charlotte Amalie at 9am and continues at intervals of between 1 and 2 hours until the last boat at around 7pm. (The last boat departing St. John's Cruz Bay for Charlotte Amalie is at 5:15pm.)

If you get stranded, you can call a **private launch service,** whose hours and priorities are less rigid than those of the publicly operated ferryboats. However, these services are expensive and are usually used for emergencies only. For up to four passengers, the private launches cost $56 per trip until midnight, when it goes up to $95.

VISITOR INFORMATION

The **St. John Tourist Office** (☎ **809/776-6450**) is located near the Battery, a 1735 fort that is a short walk from where the ferry from St. Thomas docks. You'll find plenty of travel information here, including a free map of Cruz Bay and the entire island that pinpoints all the main attractions, including restaurants, beaches, and campsites. Hours are Monday through Friday from 8am to noon and 1 to 5pm.

If you have Internet access, head to **http://www.stjohnusvi.com,** "The Complete Guide To Your St. John Vacation."

2 Getting Around

The 20-minute ferry ride from St. Thomas will take you to **Cruz Bay,** the capital of St. John, which seems a century removed from the life you left behind. Cruise ships are nonexistent here, and so you won't find hordes of milling shoppers. St. John is definitely sleepy, and that's why people love it. Don't come here looking for street addresses; they don't exist. In fact, Cruz Bay is so small its streets have no names.

Cruz Bay has a few shops—the **Mongoose Junction** shopping center (definitely worth a visit), a scattering of restaurants, and a small park. After a stroll around town, seek out the natural attractions of the island.

BY BUS OR TAXI

The **bus** service runs from Cruz Bay to Maho Bay and stops at Caneel and Cinnamon bays. A one-way fare is $10.

The most popular way to get around is by **surrey-style taxi.** Typical fares from Cruz Bay are $3 to Trunk Bay, $3.50 to Cinnamon Bay, or $7 to Mahoe Bay. Between midnight and 6am fares increase by 40%. For more information, call **809/776-8294.**

BY CAR OR JEEP

The extensive stretches of St. John's national park have kept the edges of the island's roads undeveloped and uncluttered, with some of the most panoramic vistas anywhere. Because of these views, many visitors opt to rent a vehicle (sometimes with four-wheel drive) to tour the island. Unless you have luggage, which should probably be locked away in a trunk, you might consider one of the open-sided, Jeep-like vehicles that allow a maximum view of the surroundings and a minimum of plush accessories. Sturdy, informal, with manual transmissions, and endlessly ventilated, they are the most fun way to tour St. John. Because of the island's relatively limited facilities, most visitors need a car for only a day or two.

Avis Rent-a-Car (☎ **800/331-2112** or 809/776-6374) has a branch at Cruz Bay. Avis charges $67 per day for a Suzuki Esteem. In winter, Avis tends to be fully booked for many weeks in advance so call ahead. Drivers must be 25 or older and must present a valid credit or charge card at the time of rental. A collision-damage waiver costs $11.95 per day.

Hertz (☎ **800/654-3001** or 809/776-6412) rents four types of vehicles, some of which have four-wheel drive. Depending on the model, the cost ranges from $69 to $80 per day; a collision-damage waiver is around $10 extra per day. Drivers must be at least 25 years old and must present a valid credit or charge card at the time of rental.

If you want a local firm, try **St. John Car Rental,** across from the post office in Cruz Bay (☎ **809/776-6103**). It offers daily or weekly rentals. A Jeep Wrangler rents for $60 per day, a Jeep Cherokee for $65, or a Suzuki Sidekick for $55.

PARKING　No problem on St. John. Parking is available in abundance in most places, and hotels have free parking.

DRIVING RULES　*Remember to drive on the left!* Otherwise, follow posted speed limits, which are generally very low, and traffic signs, which are the same as on the U.S. mainland.

ON FOOT

Walking is the only way to explore Cruz Bay and Mongoose Junction, but you'll need a taxi, scooter, motorcycle, or rented car to go to some of the faraway beaches or hidden coves. The national park has countless hiking trails, and most of its more interesting sections can be explored on foot.

FAST FACTS: St. John

American Express　See "Fast Facts: St. Thomas," in chapter 4.

Area Code　The area code is **809.** You can dial direct from the United States.

Business Hours　Banking hours are Monday through Thursday 9am to 2:30pm, Friday 9am to 2pm and 3:30 to 5pm. Typical business hours are Monday through Friday from 9am to 5pm, Saturday from 9am to 1pm. Stores are open Monday through Friday from 9am to 5pm, Saturday from 9am to 1pm.

Cameras and Film　To purchase film or have it developed, go to Sparky's, Cruz Bay Park (☎ **809/776-6284**).

Car Rentals　See "Getting Around," earlier in this chapter.

Currency Exchange　Go to the branch of Chase Manhattan Bank, Cruz Bay (☎ **809/776-6881**).

Dentists　See "Fast Facts: St. Thomas," in chapter 4.

Doctor　Call **922** for a medical emergency. Otherwise, go to St. John Myrah Keating Smith Community Health Clinic, 28 Sussanaberg (☎ **809/693-8900**).

Drugstores　Go to St. John Drugcenter, Boulon Shopping Center, Cruz Bay (☎ **809/776-6353**). The staff here not only fills prescriptions, but also sells film, cameras, magazines, and books. Hours are Monday through Saturday from 9am to 6pm and Sunday from 10am to 2pm.

Electricity　110 to 115V, 60 cycles, as in the mainland United States.

Emergencies　Police, **915;** ambulance, **922;** fire, **921.**

Holidays　See "When to Go," in chapter 3.

Laundry　Try Inn Town Laundromat, Cruz Bay (☎ **809/693-8590**), open Monday through Friday from 8:30am to 5:30pm; Saturday from 8:30am to 4pm. It shuts down for lunch from noon to 1pm. It's drop-off service only.

Liquor Laws　Persons must be at least 21 years of age to patronize bars or purchase liquor in St. John.

Maps　See "Visitor Information," earlier in this chapter.

Newspapers and Magazines Copies of U.S. mainland newspapers, such as *The New York Times* and *The Miami Herald* arrive daily and are for sale at Mongoose Junction, Caneel Bay, and Hyatt. The latest copies of *Time* and *Newsweek* are also for sale. Complimentary copies of *What to Do: St. Thomas/St. John* contain many helpful hints, although this publication is a commercial mouthpiece. It is the official guidebook of the St. Thomas and St. John Hotel Association and is available at the tourist office (see "Visitor Information," earlier in this chapter) and at various hotels.

3 Accommodations

The number of accommodations on St. John is limited, and that's how most die-hard fans would like to keep it. Your choices range from an elegant tropical haven to a no-frills campsite.

Prices are often slashed in summer by 30% to 60%. But in winter, hotels we've rated as **"Very expensive"** will cost from $350 to $750 per day for a double; **"Expensive,"** $195 to $235, and **"Moderate,"** from $135 and $195. Inns around Cruz Bay are rated **"Inexpensive"** if they offer either standard rooms or efficiencies (with small kitchens) for $75 to $80 per day.(See "Tips on Accommodations & Dining," in chapter 3, for an explanation of the meal plan abbreviations AP, CP, EP, and MAP.) **Campgrounds** (see below) are the most economical way to stay on St. John, not to mention a way to appreciate its natural wonders. Rates for two persons range from $95 to $105.

LUXURY RESORTS
VERY EXPENSIVE

Note: The **Hyatt Regency St. John** was still up for sale at press time; information about ownership, rates, and when the new resort will open was not available.

✪ Caneel Bay

U.S. Virgin Islands National Park, St. John, U.S.V.I. 00831. ☎ **800/928-8889** or 809/776-6111. Fax 809/693-8280. 166 rms. MINIBAR. Dec 20–Mar, $350–$750 double. Off-season, $250–$550 double. MAP $75 per person extra. AE, DC, MC, V.

Caneel Bay was the brainchild of megamillionaire Laurance S. Rockefeller. Built in 1956, it became the original eco-resort. The resort is actually part of the national park, containing some 350 species of trees. Long reigning as one of the premier resorts of the Caribbean, Caneel Bay is definitely not one of the most luxurious. One of its devoted fans once told us, "It's like living at summer camp." That means no phones, air-conditioning, and no TV sets in the rooms. Nevertheless, the movers and shakers of the world, including numerous celebrities like Michael J. Fox, have descended on this place. To attract more of a family audience, young children are now allowed at the resort, which can annoy some of the older guests.

In 1995 Hurricane Marilyn swept across the resort, canceling its winter season, but it reopened in November 1996. Operated by Rosewood Hotels and Resorts, it lies on a 170-acre portion of the national park, with a choice of seven beaches. The main buildings are strung along the bays, with a Caribbean lounge and dining room at the core.

Other, separate buildings housing guest rooms stand along the beaches, so all you have to do is step from your private veranda onto the sands. The savvy traveler requests one of the six rooms in cottage 7, overlooking two of the most idyllic beaches, Scott and Paradise. Not all rooms, however, are on the beaches; some are set back on low cliffs or headlands. The decor is understated, with Indonesian wicker furniture, handwoven fabrics, sisal mats, and plantation fans. Gardens surround all buildings. The rooms do not have phones or air-conditioning.

Dining/Entertainment: See "Dining," below, for descriptions of the Caneel Bay Beach Terrace Dining Room and Equator. The intimate Turtle Bay dining room has recently made a comeback. You can enjoy drinks at the Caneel Bay Bar, beneath the soaring ceiling of a stone-and-timber pavilion.

Services: An array of scheduled garden tours, diving excursions to offshore wrecks, deep-sea fishing, free snorkeling lessons, tennis clinics and lessons, baby-sitting, valet laundry.

Facilities: Full-service dive shop and water sports activities desk, fitness facility with free weight and cardiovascular training equipment, business center, children's play area, 11 tennis courts, free use of Sunfish sailboats and Windsurfers, swimming pool, snorkeling gear, kayaks, seven beaches, endless hideaways for solitary or romantic interludes.

VILLAS & CONDOS

Villa vacations are on the rise in St. John for travelers who want a home away from home. There are actually more villa and condo beds available on St. John than there are hotel beds. Private homes and condos offer spaciousness and comfort, as well as privacy and freedom, and come with fully equipped kitchens, dining areas, bedrooms, and such amenities as VCRs and patio grills. Rentals range from large multiroom resort homes to simply decorated one-bedroom condos. Villa rentals year-round average from about $1,200 to $2,000 per week, an affordable option for multiple couples or families looking for a large house. Condos generally range from $105 to $360 per night per unit. For information on privately owned villas and condos on St. John, call **800/USVI-INFO.**

EXPENSIVE

Caribbean Villas and Resorts Management Co.

P.O. Box 458, St. John, U.S.V.I. 00831. ☎ **800/338-0987** in the U.S., or 809/776-6152. 76 villas and condos, 45 private homes. Most condos are less than $210 per night (a Cruz view two-bedroom unit for 4 in winter is $220; $150 in summer). Private homes are more expensive. MC, V.

This is the island's biggest company and your best bet for value if you're seeking a villa or a condo on St. John. Private homes, ranging from two to six bedrooms, rent for around $200 to $1,500 per night, many with swimming pools, Jacuzzis, and ocean views. Children five and under stay free.

Estate Zootenvaal

Hurricane Hole, St. John, U.S.V.I. 00830. ☎ **809/776-6321** or 216/861-5337. 4 units. $175 one-bedroom for 2; $220 two-bedroom for 2. Each additional person $50–$65. No credit cards.

For a housekeeping holiday, you can stay within the boundaries of the U.S. National Park at the edge of a horseshoe-shaped bay. Local mariners know that this bay is usually safe from even the most violent hurricanes. It's a good choice for escapees from urban areas who want privacy. The cement-sided villas and the two-bedroom house,

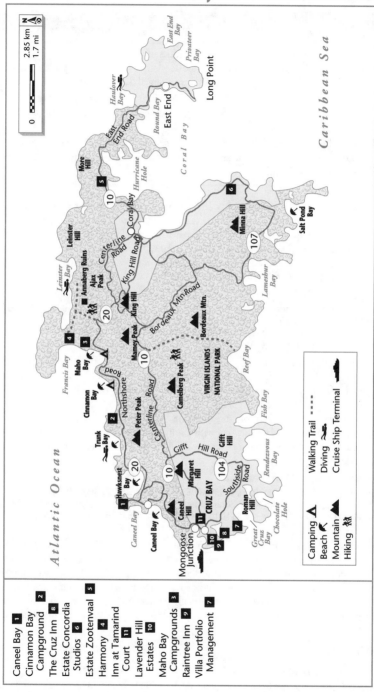

St. John Accommodations

Caneel Bay **1**
Cinnamon Bay Campground **2**
The Cruz Inn **8**
Estate Concordia Studios **6**
Estate Zootenvaal **5**
Harmony **4**
Inn at Tamarind Court **11**
Lavender Hill Estates **10**
Maho Bay Campgrounds **3**
Raintree Inn **9**
Villa Portfolio Management **7**

👪 Family-Friendly Hotels

Lavender Hill Estates *(see p. 120)*   Families often save money by staying at one of these condos. There's a swimming pool, and units have fully equipped kitchens. Children under 12 stay free; older kids are charged $25 extra per night.

Cinnamon Bay Campground *(see p. 122)*   Tents or cottages come with cooking gear at this National Park Service site. Families can even rent a bare site on a beachside campground.

Maho Bay Campground *(see p. 122)*   The tents here are really like small canvas houses with kitchen areas and sundecks. In this laid-back hideaway, children learn to be more eco-friendly.

---

each with exterior walls of driftwood gray with white trim, near what used to be a private estate called Zootenvaal. The accommodations have been renovated, with designer fabrics in muted tones. Each has its own color scheme, and comes with a fully equipped kitchen. Rooms have ceiling fans, but no air-conditioning, telephones, or televisions. Maid service can be arranged at an extra cost. Guests can use the private beach that's known for its great snorkeling.

Lavender Hill Estates

P.O. Box 8306, Lavender Hill, Cruz Bay, St. John, U.S.V.I. 00831-8306. ☎ **800/562-1901** or 809/779-4647. Fax 809/776-6969. 10 condo apts. TV TEL. Winter, $235 one-bedroom apt; $295 two-bedroom apt. Off-season, $140 one-bedroom apt; $175 two-bedroom apt. Additional person $20 extra. DISC, MC, V.

This outfit offers some of the best condominium values on the island, with a swimming pool with lounging deck. It's a short walk to the shops, markets, restaurants, and safari buses of Cruz Bay. Rates are midway between the campgrounds and inns and the upscale properties of Virgin Grand and Caneel Bay. The units, built in 1984, overlook Cruz Bay Harbor, and each one has a spacious central living/dining area opening onto a tiled deck, along with a fully equipped kitchen and one or two bedrooms. Laundry facilities are available. Units are furnished in a modern Caribbean style.

Villa Portfolio Management

P.O. Box 618, Cruz Bay, St. John, U.S.V.I. 00831. ☎ **800/858-7989** or 809/693-9100. Villas and studios. Winter, $175 to $269 per night for a one-bedroom unit, $1,330 to $2,033 per week. Off-season, it's more like $110 to $145 per night, $875 to $1,015 per week. No credit cards are accepted.

This well-run outfit offers three complexes of villas and studio apartments that many renters take for a week or more. Each has its own self-contained kitchen, as well as views over either the town and harbor of Cruz Bay or the faraway coastline of St. Thomas. Units include studios and one- and two-bedroom town houses, often on more than one level, and usually with verandas, terraces, ceiling fans, and patios. All units under the management of this company are a short walk south of Cruz Bay.

MODERATE

Estate Concordia Studios

20–27 Estate Concordia, Coral Bay, St. John, U.S.V.I. 00830. ☎ **800/392-9004** in the U.S. and Canada, or 212/472-9453 in New York City. Fax 212/861-6210 in New York City. 9 studios, 5 tents. Winter, $135–$190 studio for 2; $95 eco-tent for 2. Off-season, $95–$150 studio for 2; $60 eco-tent for 2. Additional person $15 extra. MC, V.

Opened in 1993, this environmentally sensitive, 51-acre development project was widely praised for its integration with the local ecosystem. The elevated structures were designed to coexist with the stunning southern edge of St. John. Nestled on a low cliff above a salt pond, surrounded by hundreds of acres of pristine national park land, the secluded location is recommended for those with a rental vehicle. Each building was designed to protect mature trees, and is connected to its neighbors with boardwalks.

The nine studios are contained in six postmodern cottages. Each comes with kitchen, bathroom, balcony, and ceiling fan. Some units have an extra bedroom or a larger-than-expected private bathroom. Five eco-tents, which are solar and wind powered, with large screened-in windows to lend a "tree house" atmosphere to guests, were recently added. There are two twin beds in each room, one or two twin mattresses on a loft platform, and a queen-size fold-out couch, allowing the tent-cottages to sleep five or six comfortably. Each kitchen comes with a stove and a running water sink, each tent with a toilet and private shower.

Estate Concordia also features a hillside swimming pool and guest laundry facilities. On-site management assists with activity suggestions.

Harmony

P.O. Box 310, Cruz Bay, St. John, U.S.V.I. 00831. ☎ **800/392-9004** in the U.S. and Canada, or 809/776-6226, or 212/472-9453 in New York City. Fax 809/776-6504, or 212/861-6210 in New York City. 12 studios. Winter, $150–$180 studio for 2. Off-season, $95–$125 studio for 2. Additional person $25 extra. Seven-night minimum stay in winter. MC, V.

Built on a hillside above the Maho Bay Campground, this is a small-scale cluster of 12 luxury studios in six two-story houses with views sweeping down to the sea. Designed to combine both ecological technology and comfort, it's one of the few resorts in the Caribbean to operate exclusively on sun and wind power. Its construction was adopted as part of the U.S. National Park Service *Handbook for Sustainable Design.* Most of the building materials are derived from recycled materials, including reconstituted plastic and glass containers, newsprint, old tires, and scrap lumber. The managers and staff are committed to offering educational experiences, as well as the services of a small-scale resort. Guests are taught how to operate a user-friendly computer telling them how their studio's energy is being spent.

The studios contain queen-size sofa beds and/or twin beds, tile bathrooms, kitchenettes, dining areas, and outdoor terraces. Guests can walk a short distance downhill to use the restaurant, grocery store, and water sports facilities at the Maho Bay campground.

INNS

Let's face it: Except for the campgrounds recommended below, the tab at most of the establishments on St. John is far beyond the budget of the average traveler. If you're willing to settle for few frills, the following places can provide a low-cost holiday on St. John.

INEXPENSIVE

The Cruz Inn

P.O. Box 566, Cruz Bay, St. John, U.S.V.I. 00831. ☎ **800/666-7688** in the U.S., or 809/693-8688. Fax 809/693-8590. 2 studios, 4 suites, 4 apts. Winter, $75 studio; $90 suite; $95–$105 apt. Off-season, $65 studio; $75 suite; $85–$95 apt. Rates include continental breakfast. Additional person $15 extra. Three-night minimum stay in apts. AE, DISC, MC, V.

This is hardly the most refined or elegant accommodation on St. John but it has its admirers who seek clean, reasonably comfortable accommodations at a fair price.

Overlooking Enighed Pond, Cruz Inn recently finished remodeling, and now all its rustic rooms have a private bath. The studios and suites also have a refrigerator and air-conditioning; the apartments have kitchenettes, but only two have air-conditioning. The Papaya Suite is airy with a wraparound deck; this unit sleeps up to six. Lying a few blocks from the Cruz Bay Dock, the inn has a convivial bar, a low-cost restaurant serving standard food, and an outdoor deck.

Inn at Tamarind Court

P.O. Box 350, Cruz Bay, St. John, U.S.V.I. 00831. ☎ **800/221-1637** or 809/776-6378. Fax 809/776-6722. 20 rms, 13 with bath; 1 apt; 2 suites. Winter, $73 double with bath; $98 apt; $108 suite. Off-season, $63 double with bath; $88 apt; $98 suite. Rates include continental breakfast. AE, DISC, MC, V.

Right outside Cruz Bay but still within walking distance of the ferryboat dock, this back-to-basics establishment consists of a small hotel (where the nonsmoking rooms have been renovated) and an even simpler West Indian inn. Baths in the single rooms at the inn are shared, whereas doubles within the hotel all have private baths. The establishment's social life revolves around its courtyard bar. From the hotel you can walk to shuttles taking you to the beaches; the staff will advise.

Raintree Inn

P.O. Box 566, Cruz Bay, St. John, U.S.V.I. 00831. ☎ **800/666-7449** or 809/693-8590. Fax 809/693-8590. 8 rms, 3 efficiencies. A/C TEL. Winter, $87–$92 double; $133.50 efficiency. Off-season, $70–$80 double; $111.60 efficiency. Three-day minimum stay in efficiencies. AE, DISC, MC, V.

One block from the ferry stop, next to the Catholic church, the Raintree Inn has simple no-smoking double rooms, some with high ceilings. Linen, towels, and soap are supplied upon request. The three efficiencies have full kitchens, and two twin beds in a slightly cramped loft. A small deck is attached. The inn adjoins a reasonably priced restaurant next door, the Fish Trap (see "Dining," below). Laundry service is available on the premises.

CAMPGROUNDS

Cinnamon Bay Campground

P.O. Box 720, Cruz Bay, St. John, U.S.V.I. 00831. ☎ **800/539-9998** in the U.S., or 809/776-6330. Fax 809/776-6458. 126 units, none with bath. Winter, $95–$105 cottage for 2; $75 tent site; $17 bare site. Off-season, $63–$68 cottage for 2; $48 tent site; $17 bare site (5-day minimum). Additional person $15 extra. AE, MC, V.

Established by the U.S. National Park Service in 1964, this is the most complete campground in the Caribbean, although security is minimal. The site is directly on the beach, and thousands of acres of tropical vegetation surround you. Life is simple here, and you have a choice of three different kinds of accommodations: tents, cottages, and bare sites. Bare sites, which include a picnic table and charcoal grill only, must be reserved at least 8 months in advance and can be secured by a credit card. The canvas tents are 10 by 14 feet. Cottages are 15 by 15 feet and consist of a room with two concrete walls, two screen walls, and four twin beds; maximum occupancy in a cottage is four. Cooking facilities are also supplied, but lavatories and showers are in separate buildings nearby. Linen is changed weekly, and camping is limited to a 2-week period in any given year. Near the road is a camp center office, with a grocery store and cafeteria.

✪ Maho Bay

P.O. Box 310, Cruz Bay, St. John, U.S.V.I. 00831. ☎ **800/392-9004,** or 809/776-6226, or 212/472-9453 in New York City. Fax 809/776-6504, or 212/816-6210 in New York City. 114 tent-cottages, none with bath. Mid-Dec to Apr, $95 tent-cottage for 2 (minimum stay of 7 nights required). May to mid-Dec, $60 tent-cottage for 2 (no minimum stay). Additional occupants: in winter, $15 for adults and children; after May 1, $12 for adults, $10 for children under 16. MC, V.

Maho Bay is an interesting concept in eco-travel, where you camp close to nature, but with considerable comforts—it's a great choice for families. The only problem is, the place is so popular you need to book a year in advance if you want to camp here in winter. Defined as a deluxe campground, an 8-mile drive northeast from Cruz Bay, it's set on a hillside above the beach surrounded by the U. S. Virgin Islands National Park. To preserve the existing ground cover, all tent-cottages are on platforms above a thickly wooded slope. Utility lines and pipes are hidden under wooden boardwalks and stairs.

The tent-cottages are covered with canvas and screens. Each unit has two movable twin beds, a couch, electric lamps and outlets, a dining table, chairs, a propane stove, and an ice chest (cooler). That's not all—you're furnished with linen, towels, and cooking and eating utensils. There's a store where you can buy supplies, and you can do your own cooking or eat at the camp's outdoor restaurant. Guests share communal bathhouses. The campground also offers an excellent water sports program.

Maho Bay has an open-air Pavilion Restaurant, which always serves breakfast and dinner. Lunches are offered in winter, and the international dinner menu is changed nightly depending on what food is fresh. Both meat and vegetarian selections are offered. The Pavilion doubles as an amphitheater and community center.

A GAY-FRIENDLY HOTEL

Oscar's Guesthouse, Estate Pastory 27, St. John, U.S.V.I. 00830 (☎ **800/854-1843** or 809/776-6193), lies only minutes from white sandy beaches opening onto Cruz Bay. Attracting a mixed gay and straight clientele, it offers a total of eight plainly furnished but clean rooms with queen-size beds, cable TV, ceiling fans, and color TVs. All rooms are smoke-free with private baths, but only four contain a refrigerator. In winter, rates are $90 double, dropping to $65 double off-season. Airline employees often stay here between flights. Within 5 minutes of the guest house, you can get in shape at a gym and also go swimming or play tennis. MasterCard, Discover, and Visa are accepted.

4 Dining

St. John has some posh dining, particularly at the luxury resorts like Caneel Bay, but it also has some West Indian restaurants with plenty of local color and flavor. Many of the restaurants here command high prices, but you can lunch almost anywhere at reasonable rates. Dinner is more like an event on St. John, since there's not much nightlife or organized entertainment in the evenings.

Restaurants categorized below as **"Very Expensive"** charge $60 and up per person for dinner without drinks; **"Expensive,"** from $40 to $60; **"Moderate,"** from $25 to $35; and **"Inexpensive,"** less than $25.

VERY EXPENSIVE

Caneel Bay Beach Terrace Dining Room

In the Caneel Bay Hotel. ☎ **809/776-6111.** Reservations required for dinner. Main courses $28–$38; Mon night grand buffet $50; lunch buffet $22. AE, DC, MC, V. Daily 11:30am–2:30pm and 7–9pm. INTERNATIONAL/SEAFOOD.

Right below the Equator (see below) is an elegant, open-air dining room, overlooking the beach. Start with an appetizer of papaya with prosciutto, and move on to one of their wonderful fresh salads, perhaps the marinated green bean or the tossed garden greens mimosa. Main dishes are likely to include baked fillet of red snapper or roast prime rib of blue-ribbon beef, carved to order with natural juices. For dessert, try strawberry cheesecake or Boston cream pie. Menus change nightly, and the self-service buffet luncheon is one of the best in the Virgin Islands. Although the cuisine here has varied over the years, the professional standards remain high. The resort's kitchen caters to elite palates, and it uses only first-rate, quality ingredients.

EXPENSIVE

✪ Asolare

Cruz Bay. ☎ **809/779-4747.** Reservations required. Main courses $20–$29. AE, MC, V. Daily 5:30–9:30pm. FRENCH/ASIAN.

This is the most beautiful and elegant restaurant in St. John, with the hippest and best-looking staff. Asolare sits on top of a hill overlooking Cruz Bay, where you can spy some of the British Virgin Islands. The word *Asolare* translates as "the leisurely passing of time without purpose," and that's what many diners prefer to do here. Chef Carlos Beccar Varela roams the world for inspiration, and cooks with flavor and flair, using some of the best and freshest ingredients available on island. To begin, try the prawn and coconut milk soup, or a spicy tuna tartare wrapped in somen noodles. For dinner, you may be tempted by a fillet of salmon awakened with a zesty Szechuan pepper crust, or roasted rack of lamb served with baby bok choy. The chef's specialty is Asolare pad thai, a medley of rice noodles, shrimp, chicken, and black soy beans. If you're into dessert, it's worth swimming across the channel to try the frozen mango guava soufflé or the chocolate pyramid cake with warm white chocolate ice cream hearts.

Ellington's

Gallows Point, Cruz Bay. ☎ **809/693-8490.** Reservations required only for seating upstairs. Main courses $13–$28. AE, MC, V. Daily 4:30–10pm. CONTINENTAL.

Ellington's is set near the neocolonial villas of Gallows Point, to the right after you disembark from the ferry. Its exterior has the kind of double staircase, fan windows, louvers, and low-slung roof found in an 18th-century Danish manor house. Drop in at sunset for a drink on the panoramic upper deck where an unsurpassed view of St. Thomas and its neighboring cays unfolds. The establishment is named after a local radio announcer ("The Fat Man"), a raconteur and mystery writer whose real-estate developments helped transform St. John into a stylish enclave for the American literati of the 1950s and 1960s. Named Richard "Duke" Ellington (not to be confused with the great musician), he entertained his friends, martini in hand, around a frequently photographed table painted with a map of St. John. Today the tabletop is a centerpiece at the Sunset Lounge.

The dinner menu changes often to accommodate the freshest offerings of the sea— sometimes wahoo or mahimahi with Cajun spices. Some other favorites include conch fritters, swordfish scampi, chilled mango soup, and chicken Martinique. The South American sea bass is especially zesty.

✪ Equator

In the Caneel Bay Hotel, Caneel Bay. ☎ **809/776-6111.** Reservations required. Main courses $12–$27. AE, MC, V. Winter, daily 6:30–10pm. Off-season, Wed–Thurs and Sun 6:30–10pm. CARIBBEAN/LATIN/THAI.

This restaurant lies behind the tower of an 18th-century sugar mill, where ponds with water lilies fill former crystallization pits for hot molasses. A flight of stairs leads to a monumental circular dining room, with a wraparound veranda and sweeping views of a park. In the center rises the stone column that horses and mules once circled to crush sugarcane stalks. In its center the restaurant grows a giant poinciana-like Asian tree of the *Albizia lebbeck* species. Islanders call it "woman's tongue tree."

The cuisine is the most daring on the island, and for the most part chefs pull off their transcultural dishes. The teriyaki tuna comes with a pickled lobster roll and tempura vegetables. The pepper-cured tandoori lamb with Egyptian-style couscous is another tasty winner, as is the wok-fried catfish with Polynesian ponzu and fried rice. The service, however, could be better.

Le Château de Bordeaux

Junction 10, Centerline Rd., Bordeaux Mountain. ☎ **809/776-6611.** Reservations recommended. Main courses $18–$28. MC, V. Mon–Sat with two nightly seatings, 5:30–6:30pm and 7:30–8:45pm. Closed Sun–Mon in summer. CONTINENTAL/CARIBBEAN.

Set 5 miles east of Cruz Bay near the geographical center of the island, and close to one of its highest points, this restaurant is known for its eastward-facing vistas and some of the best high-altitude views on St. John. A lunch grill on the patio serves burgers and drinks Monday through Saturday from 10am to 4:30pm. In the evening, amid a Victorian decor with lace tablecloths, appetizers might include a house-smoked chicken spring roll, or a velvety carrot soup. Move on to one of the saffron-flavored pastas or a savory West Indian seafood chowder. Smoked salmon and filet mignon bow to the international crowd, although the wild-game specials are usually more exquisite in flavor. There's a changing array of cheesecakes, among other desserts, and the drink of choice is a passion fruit daiquiri.

✪ Paradiso

Mongoose Junction. ☎ **809/693-8899.** Reservations recommended. Main courses $15–$25. AE, MC, V. Thurs–Tues 6–9:30pm. Bar, daily 5–10pm. ITALIAN/AMERICAN.

The most talked-about restaurant on St. John, other than Asolare, and the only one that's air-conditioned, is located in the island's most interesting shopping center, Mongoose Junction. The decor includes lots of brass, glowing hardwoods, and nautical antiques. Paradiso has the most beautiful bar on the island, crafted from mahogany, purpleheart, and angelique.

The Italian food here is the best on the island, including a selection of pastas. To start, opt for the Caesar salad. A platter of smoked seafood was also a winning appetizer, followed by seafood puttanesca, mussels and shrimp with tomatoes, capers, and garlic in a marinara sauce with linguini. Featured in *Bon Apetit,* the restaurant's chicken Picante Willie is a spicy, creamy picante sauce over crispy chicken with linguini and ratatouille. The house drink is Paradiso Punch, the bartender's version of plantation punch.

✪ Saychelles

4 Cruz Bay, Wharfside Village. ☎ **809/693-7030.** Reservations recommended in winter. Main courses $15.50–$24.50. AE, DC, MC, V. Daily 6–10pm. Closed Oct 1–15. SEAFOOD/CARIBBEAN.

Evoking a Riviera bistro, this hip, low-key hangout attracts a chic international crowd in winter that dresses up or down for dinner. Fortunately Chef Keith Seidner doesn't just depend on the view of the bay for inspiration. His delectable cuisine is first rate; we think he's one of the most creative chefs on island. After watching the sunset, dip into the beef carpaccio, calamari salad, or tuna tartare before working up an appetite for your main dish. Your best bet is the chef's specialty: sesame-seared tuna with wasabi and teriyaki sauce. Save room for the mango cheesecake or one of the freshly made sorbets, which come in island flavors like papaya, guava, or lime and are served in a waffle basket.

👪 Family-Friendly Restaurants

Café Roma *(see p. 126)*   This is a family favorite, where you can treat your child to a "white pizza" without tomato sauce.

Mongoose Restaurant *(see p. 126)*   The best choice for children if you're visiting Cruz Bay. Kids lover to munch on the well-stuffed sandwiches and island fish cakes here.

Pusser's *(see p. 128)*   Families like this place for its succulent barbecued chicken, and neither child nor adult can resist its frozen mud pie.

MODERATE

Café Roma
Cruz Bay. ☎ **809/776-6524.** Reservations not required. Main courses $8–$17. MC, V. Daily 5–10pm. ITALIAN.

Diners climb a flight of steps to reach this restaurant in the center of Cruz Bay. You might arrive early and have a strawberry colada, then enjoy a standard pasta dish, veal, seafood, or chicken. On most evenings, there are 30 to 40 vegetarian items on the menu that are a notch above most restaurants. The owner claims, with good reason, that his pizzas are the best on the island, praised by New Yorkers and Chicagoans who know their pizza. Ask for their white pizza, made without the red sauce. This is not a place for great finesse in the kitchen, but it's a long-standing favorite, and has pleased a lot of diners seeking casual, informal meals, not grand Italian cuisine. Italian wines are sold by the glass or bottle, and you can end the evening with an espresso.

Mongoose Restaurant and Deli
Mongoose Junction. ☎ **809/693-8677.** Reservations required during winter. Main courses $13.95–$18.95. AE, MC, V. Daily 8am–10pm. Bar, daily 8am–10pm. CARIBBEAN.

Some visitors compare the soaring interior design here to a large Japanese birdcage, because of the strong vertical lines and the 25-foot ceiling. Set among trees and built above a stream, it looks like something you might find in Northern California. Some guests perch at the bar for a drink and sandwich, whereas others sit on an adjacent deck where a canopy of trees filters the incoming sunlight.

Lunches include soups, well-stuffed sandwiches, salad platters, burgers, and pastas. Dinner is more formal, with such specialties as grilled steaks, fresh catch of the day, and surf and turf. More than the food, the setting, locale, long serving hours, and reasonable prices make this a winning choice. The Sunday brunch is mobbed with locals, who rate eggs Benedict the most popular dish.

Morgan's Mango
Cruz Bay. ☎ **809/693-8141.** Reservations recommended. Main courses $6.95–$21.95. AE, MC, V. Daily 6–10pm. Bar opens at 5:30pm. CARIBBEAN.

Across from the National Park dock, the chefs here roam the Caribbean for tantalizing flavors, which they adapt for their ever-changing menu. The restaurant is easy to spot with its big canopy, the only protection from the elements. The bar wraps around the main dining room and offers some 30 frozen drinks. Thursday is Margarita Night, when a soft rock duo plays. Although some critics claim the kitchen "overreaches" in trying to do too much with the nightly menu, they do emerge with some zesty fare—everything from Anegada lobster cakes to a spicy Jamaican

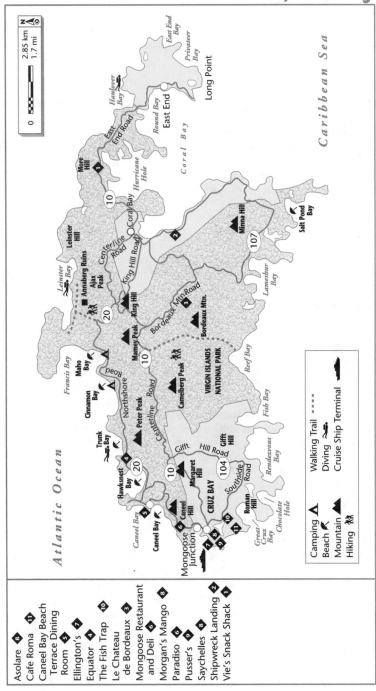

pickapepper steak. Try flying fish served as an appetizer, followed by Haitian voodoo snapper pressed in Cajun spices, then grilled and served with fresh fruit salsa. Equally delectable is mahimahi in a Cruzan rum and mango sauce. You can also order more standard steak, chicken, and vegetarian dishes. The knockout dessert is the mango-banana pie.

Pusser's

Wharfside Village, Cruz Bay. ☎ **809/693-8489.** Reservations recommended. Main courses $9.95–$24.95. AE, DISC, MC, V. Daily 11am–3pm and 6–10pm. INTERNATIONAL/CARIBBEAN.

A double-decker, air-conditioned store and pub in Cruz Bay, Pusser's overlooks the harbor and is near the ferry dock. These watering holes are unique to the Caribbean, and they serve Pusser's Rum, a blend of five West Indian rums that the Royal Navy has served to its men for 3 centuries. You face a choice of three bars: the Beach Bar where you can enjoy food while still in your bathing suit, the Oyster Bar (the main dining area), and the Crow's Nest. The same food is served at each bar. You can enjoy traditional English fare, including steak and ale; or try the jerk tuna loin; the jerk chicken with a tomato basil sauce over penne; or the spaghetti with lobster cooked in rum, wine, lemon juice, and garlic. Caribbean lobster is the eternal favorite here, but you might succumb to island fever and order the chicken Tropical (coconut encrusted, pan seared, and served up with a rum and banana sauce with macadamia nuts). Finish with Pusser's famous "mud pie."

INEXPENSIVE

The Fish Trap

In the Raintree Inn, Cruz Bay. ☎ **809/693-9994.** Reservations not accepted except for parties of 6 or more. Main courses $7.95–$22.95. AE, DISC, MC, V. Tues–Fri 11am–3pm and 4:30–9:30pm, Sat–Sun 10:30am–2:30pm and 4:30–9:30pm. SEAFOOD.

The Fish Trap attracts both locals and vacationers. It's known for its wide selection of fresh fish, but it also caters to the vegetarian and burger crowd. In the midst of coconut palms and banana trees, most diners begin with one of the nightly appetizers, such as seared scallops with stir-fried vegetables. We recently enjoyed an herb-crusted snapper with a Dijon tarragon cream sauce. On another occasion blackened swordfish with roasted red pepper aioli was the crowd-pleasing choice, or else grilled escolar and shrimp with papaya and kiwi salsa. In other words, it's not just another fish-and-chips joint.

✪ Shipwreck Landing

34 Freeman's Ground, Rte. 107, Coral Bay. ☎ **809/693-5640.** Reservations requested. Main courses $9.75–$15.25; lunch from $10. AE, MC, V. Daily 11am–10pm. Bar, daily 11am–11pm. SEAFOOD/CONTINENTAL.

Eight miles east of Cruz Bay on the road to Salt Pond Beach, Shipwreck Landing is run by Pat and Dennis Rizzo. You dine amid palms and tropical plants on a veranda overlooking the sea. The intimate bar specializes in tropical frozen drinks. Lunch isn't ignored here; there's a lot more than sandwiches, salads, and burgers—you might find a pan-seared blackened snapper in Cajun spices, or conch fritters. The chef shines even brighter at night, offering a pasta special along with such specialties as tantalizing Caribbean blackened shrimp. A lot of the fare is routine, including New York strip steak and fish-and-chips, but the grilled mahimahi in lime butter is worth the trip. Live music is featured on Friday, Saturday, and Sunday.

Vie's Snack Shack

East End Rd. ☎ **809/693-5033.** Reservations not required. Main courses $4.95–$6.50. No credit cards. Tues–Sat 10am–5pm, but call first! WEST INDIAN.

The owner of this plywood-sided hut on the island's East End is one of the best local chefs in St. John. Her famous garlic chicken is the best on the island. She also serves conch fritters, johnnycakes, island-style beef pâtés, and coconut and pineapple tarts. While the place is open most days, it's wise to call first, since, Vie warns, "Some days, we might not be here at all." Vie's is about 12^1/$_2$ miles east of Cruz Bay.

5 Beaches, Water Sports & Other Outdoor Pursuits

Don't visit St. John if golf is the only sport you wish to pursue during your vacation—you won't find any here. You can, however, expect to find some of the best snorkeling, scuba diving, swimming, fishing, hiking, and sailing in the Caribbean. The island is known for its coral-sand beaches; winding mountain roads; trails traversing old, bush-covered sugarcane plantations; and hidden coves.

BEACHES

✪ **Trunk Bay**   On the northwest coast of the island, against a backdrop of sea grape and palm, is St. John's biggest attraction and a sun-worshiper's dream come true. The only problem is that it's no secret—the beach is likely to be overcrowded, and pickpockets are prevalent. Lifeguards survey the waters and some water sport rentals are available, including snorkeling gear. Beginning snorkelers love the Underwater Trail (see below) near the shore. Both taxis and safari buses meet the ferry from St. Thomas at Cruz Bay, and shuttle beachgoers to Trunk Bay.

At Trunk Bay, you can take the ✪ **National Park Underwater Trail** (☎ 809/ 776-6201), stretching for 650 feet, allowing you to identify what you see, everything from false coral to colonial anemones. You'll pass lavender sea fans and felt schools of silversides. Equipment rental costs $4, and rangers are on hand to provide information.

Caneel Bay   A stomping ground of the rich and famous, Caneel has seven beautiful beaches, among which is **Hawksnest Beach,** a little gem of white sand, beloved by St. Johnians. The beach is a bit narrow and can be windy, but it's truly beautiful. Close to the road are barbecue grills, and there are portable toilets too. Safari buses and taxis from Cruz Bay will take you here along North Shore Road.

Cinnamon Bay and **Maho Bay**   Both of these campground areas (see "Accommodations," above) have their own pristine beaches where forest rangers sometimes have to remind visitors to keep their bathing suits on. Snorkelers find good reefs here too. Changing rooms and showers are available.

Salt Pond Bay   A favorite among locals but often missed by visitors, the remote beach here is tranquil, but there are no facilities. The Ram Head Trail, which begins here and winds for 1 mile, leads to a panoramic belvedere overlooking the entire bay.

SPORTS & OTHER OUTDOOR PURSUITS
BIKING

Bicycles are available for rent, at $25 per day, from the **Cinnamon Bay Watersports Center** on Cinnamon Bay Beach (☎ 809/776-6330). Whereas St. John's steep hills and off-road trails can challenge the best of riders, more moderate rides are to visit the ruins at Annaberg or the beaches at Maho, Francis, Leinster, or Watermelon Bay.

BOATING

Vacation Vistas and Motor Yachts (☎ 809/776-6462 or 809/771-3996) offers half- and full-day boat charters, including trips to the Baths at Virgin Gorda on Tuesday. The cost of this full-day adventure is $80 per person. On Wednesday and

Friday an "Around St. John Snorkel Excursion" costs $40 per person, and a sunset cocktail cruise also goes for $50 per person. Call for more details.

FISHING

You can take sportfishing trips with outfitters located on St. Thomas—they'll come over and pick up you and your party. Call the **St. Thomas Sportfishing Center** (☎ **809/775-7990**) at Red Hook. **St. John World Class Anglers** (☎ **809/ 775-4281**) offers light-tackle shore and offshore fishing for full or half days.

HIKING

Home of the ✪ **U. S. Virgin Islands National Park,** the largest U.S. National Park in the Caribbean, St. John is blessed with more than 120 clearly marked walking paths in a semitropical, moist setting. At least 20 of these trails originate from designated points along either the **North Shore Road** (Route 20) or from points along the island's main east-to-west artery, **Centerline Road** (Route 10). Each trail's origin is marked, and each has a preplanned itinerary that can take anywhere from 10 minutes to 2 hours.

Another series of hikes traversing the more arid eastern section of park land originates at clearly marked points along the island's southeastern tip off of Route 107. Many of the trails cross the grounds of 18th-century plantations, often circumnavigating ruined schoolhouses, rum distilleries, molasses factories, and great houses, many of them verdantly overgrown with encroaching vines and trees.

One of our favorite tours requires only about a $1/2$-mile stroll (about 30 minutes round-trip, not including stop) and departs from clearly marked points along the island's north coast, near the junction of routes 10 and 20. Identified by the National Park Service as **Trail no. 10** (The Annaberg Historic Trail), it crosses partially restored ruins of an 18th-century house overlooking the island's north coast. Signs along the way give historical and botanical data.

If you want to prolong your experience, **Trail no. 11** (The Leinster Bay Trail), begins near the point where Trail no. 10 ends. Following the edge of Watermelon Bay, it leads past Mangrove swamps and coral inlets rich with plant and marine life; markers identify some of the plants and animals.

Maps of the island's hiking trails are readily available from the **St. John National Park Service** (☎ **809/776-6201**) and at the visitors center at Cruz Bay.

SNORKELING & SCUBA DIVING

The best spots for snorkeling on St. John are: **Trunk Bay,** where you can follow a self-guided 225-yard-long trail that identifies species of coral and other marine life; **Leinster Bay,** which offers calm, clear, and uncrowded waters on the island's northern shore; and **Haulover Bay,** a favorite pocket among locals that's rougher than Leinster and is often deserted except, of course, for the exotic sea creatures that hang out here.

Snorkeling equipment can be rented from concessions at beaches like Trunk Bay and Cinnamon Bay, and also from outfitters in town like **Low Key Watersports** or **Cruz Bay Watersports** (see below for addresses and phone numbers). A daily rental will cost about $7.

For those interested in **scuba diving,** ask about dive packages at **Low Key Watersports,** Wharfside Village (☎ **800/835-7718** or 809/693-8999). All wreck dives are two-tank/two-location dives. A two-tank dive costs $75 per person, with night dives going for $65. Snorkel tours are also available at $25 per person, and parasailing is available at $50. The center uses its own custom-built dive boats and also offers and specializes in water sports gear, including masks, fins, snorkels, and "dive skins." It also arranges day sailing charters, kayaking tours, and deep-sea sport fishing.

Cruz Bay Watersports, P.O. Box 252, Palm Plaza, St. John, U.S.V.I. 00831 (☎ **800/835-7730** or 809/776-6234), is a PADI and NAUI five-star diving center on St. John. Certifications can be arranged through a divemaster, costing $225 to $350. Certification classes start daily, as well as two-tank reef dives with all the dive gear for $70 to $78. Beginner scuba lessons start at $68, and wreck dives (Wednesday and Friday), night dives, and dive packages are available at accommodations that range from budget to first class. Snorkel tours are given daily as well as trips to the British Virgin Islands (bring your passport).

TENNIS

Caneel Bay (☎ **809/776-6111**) has seven courts and a pro shop. The courts aren't lit at night, and nonguests are not allowed to play. There are two public courts near the fire station at Cruz Bay, available on a first-come, first-serve basis.

WATER SPORTS

The most complete line of water sports equipment available on St. John is offered at the ✪ **Cinnamon Bay Watersports Center** on Cinnamon Bay Beach (☎ **809/776-6330**). For the adventurous, there's windsurfing, kayaking, and sailing.

The **windsurfing** here is some of the best anywhere, for either the beginner or the expert. High-quality equipment is available for all levels, even for kids. You can rent a board at $15 an hour; a 2-hour introductory lesson costs $40.

Want to paddle to a secluded beach, explore a nearby island with an old Danish ruin, or jump overboard anytime you like for snorkeling or splashing? Try **kayaking.** One- and two-person kayaks are available for rent at $10 to $17 per hour.

You can also spend a day **sailing** the waters around St. John on a 12- or 14-foot Hobie monohull sailboat, renting for $20 to $30 per hour.

6 Touring St. John

DRIVING TOUR
St. John

Start: Ferry docks in Cruz Bay.
Finish: Ferry docks in Cruz Bay.
Time: 3 to 7 hours, depending on beach time, bar stops, and pedestrian detours.
Best Times: Any warm sunny day.
Worst Times: Any rainy day when you are likely to get stuck in the mud on bad roads.

Important note: Before you begin this tour, make sure you have at least three-quarters of a tank of gas, since there are only two gas stations on St. John, one of which is often closed. The more reliable of the two stations is in the upper regions of Cruz Bay, beside Route 104. Ask for directions when you pick up your rented vehicle. **Remember to drive on the left!**

Head out of Cruz Bay, going east on Route 20. Within about a minute, you'll pass the catwalks and verandas of:

1. Mongoose Junction. A sightseeing attraction as well as a shopping emporium, it contains some unusual art galleries and jewelry shops. (See "Shopping," below.)

Two miles northeast of Cruz Bay, you'll see a pair of unmarked stone columns on your left and an area of immaculate landscaping. This is the entrance to the island's most legendary resort:

2. **Caneel Bay.** Past the security guard, near the resort's parking lots, is a gift shop and a handful of bars and restaurants. In a mile, you'll see the first of many stunning vistas. Along the entire trajectory note the complete absence of billboards and electrical cables (a rule rigidly enforced by the National Park Service). In less than 3 miles, you'll come to:

3. **Hawksnest Beach,** whose palms and salt-tolerant wild figs are maintained by the National Park Service (NPS). Stop to read the ecological signs and perhaps wet your feet in the water. There are some squat toilets (with lots of flies) at this point if you need them. Continuing your drive, you'll pass, in this order, Trunk Bay, Peter Bay (private), and Cinnamon Bay, all of which have sand, palm trees, and clear water. A few steps from the entrance to the Cinnamon Bay Campground is a redwood sign marking the beginning of:

4. **The Cinnamon Bay Trail.** Laid out for hikers by the National Park Service, this 1.2-mile walk takes about an hour. Its clearly marked paths lead through shaded forest trails along the rutted cobblestones of a former Danish road, past ruins of abandoned plantations.

A short drive beyond Cinnamon Bay is the sandy sweep of Maho Bay, site of one of the most upscale campgrounds in the Caribbean.

Shortly after Maho Bay, the road splits. Take the left fork, which merges in a few moments with an extension of Centerline Road. Off this road, on your left, will appear another NPS signpost marked Danish Road, indicating a 5-minute trek along a potholed road to the ruins of an 18th-century school.

At the next fork, bear right toward Annaberg. (Make sure you don't go toward Francis Bay.) You'll pass the beginning of a .8-mile walking trail to the Leinster Bay Estate, which leads to a beach said to be good for snorkeling. Within less than a minute, you'll reach the parking lot of the:

5. **Annaberg Historic Trail.** The highlight of this driving tour, the Annaberg Trail leads pedestrians within and around the ruined buildings of the best-preserved plantation on St. John. During the 18th and 19th centuries, the smell of boiling molasses permeated the air here during the era of slavery. About a dozen National Park Service plaques identify and describe each building within the compound. The walk around the grounds takes about 30 minutes. From a terrace near the ruined windmill, a map identifies the British Virgin Islands to the north, including Little Thatch, Tortola, Watermelon Cay, and Jost Van Dyke.

After your visit to Annaberg, retrace your route to its first major division, and take the left fork. Soon a road sign will identify your road as Route 20 East. Stay on this road, forking left wherever possible, until you come upon many bends in the road to sandy bottomlands that contain an elementary school, a baseball field, and, on a hilltop, a simple barnlike building known as the:

6. **Emmaus Moravian Church,** with its yellow clapboards and red roof. (It's often closed to visitors.) Near its base yet another NPS walking trail begins (the $1^1/_2$-mile Johnny Horn Trail), known for its scenic views and steep hills. You will by now be about $12^1/_2$ miles east of Cruz Bay.

The roads at this point are not very clearly marked. Do not drive beyond the elementary school below the church. That road, although beautiful, is long and leads only to the barren and rather dull expanses of the island's East End. Instead,

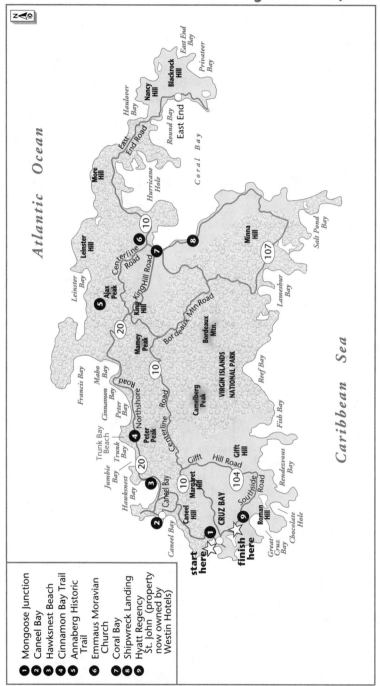

N

Atlantic Ocean

Caribbean Sea

East End Bay
Privateer Bay
Blackrock Hill
Nancy Hill
East Hanover Bay
East End Road
Round Bay
East End
Coral Bay
More Hill
Hurricane Hole
Salt Pond Bay
10
Leinster Hill
Leinster Bay
6
7
8
Minna Hill
107
Ajax Peak
5
King Hill Road
King Hill
Bordeaux Mtn. Road
Bordeaux Mtn.
Lameshur Bay
20
Mamey Peak
10
Centerline Road
VIRGIN ISLANDS NATIONAL PARK
Reef Bay
Francis Bay
Maho Bay
Cinnamon Bay
Peter Bay
Northshore Road
Peter Peak
4
Camelberg Peak
Fish Bay
Trunk Bay Beach
Trunk Bay
Centerline Road
Jumbie Bay
20
Caneel Bay
Gifft Hill Road
Gifft Hill
Rendezvous Bay
Hawksnest Bay
3
10
Margaret Hill
104
Southside Road
Caneel Bay
2
Caneel Hill
CRUZ BAY
Roman Hill
9
Chocolate Hole
start here
1
finish here
Great Cruz Bay

1 Mongoose Junction
2 Caneel Bay
3 Hawksnest Beach
4 Cinnamon Bay Trail
5 Annaberg Historic Trail
6 Emmaus Moravian Church
7 Coral Bay
8 Shipwreck Landing
9 Hyatt Regency St. John (property now owned by Westin Hotels)

133

backtrack a very short distance to a cluster of signs that point to the restaurant the Still and Shipwreck Landing. Follow these signs heading south about a mile to:

7. **Coral Bay.** Claimed by the Danes in the 1600s, the bay still contains a crumbling stone pier used to unload Danish ships. It was also the site of the first plantation on St. John. Established in 1717 (and long ago abandoned), it predated the far better developed facilities of Cruz Bay. Coral Bay was visited by a Danish princess in the early 1700s.

Prized by yachting enthusiasts, the bay shelters a closely knit community of boaters who moor and live on their yachts here between excursions to other parts of the Caribbean. Ringing the bay's perimeter is a widely spaced handful of restaurants and bars.

8. ☕ **TAKE A BREAK**   ✪ **Shipwreck Landing** (see "Dining," above) is an ideal place to drop in for a meal or else a tropical frozen drink. It lies 8 miles east of Cruz Bay on the road to Salt Pond Beach. You can drink or eat amid palms and tropical plants on a veranda overlooking the sea.

After your break, continue driving south along Coral Bay, perhaps stopping in at another of the two or three shops and bars beside the road.

The road is passable for only another 5 or 6 miles. If you want, you can continue for a few miles along the eastern coastline (there are some churches and houses along the way), but eventually you'll have to retrace your route.

Road signs on this end of the island are notoriously bad, so it's wise to ask directions at one of the Coral Bay bars, restaurants, or shops before making any firm conclusions about road conditions.

Backtrack north along Coral Bay to a point near the Emmaus Moravian Church, which you'll see in the distance. At the cluster of restaurant signs, turn left onto Route 10 West (Centerline Road), which has high-altitude views in all directions as you follow it back toward Cruz Bay. (An alternate, although much steeper, way is Route 108, which merges later with Route 10 West.)

Within 7 or 8 miles, Route 10 merges with Route 104 (Gifft Hill Road) just after the island's only hospital, the St. John Myrah Keating Smith Community Health Clinic. Take Route 104, and begin one of the steepest descents with the greatest number of blind curves of your driving tour. (Use low gear whenever possible, and honk around blind curves.) When the land levels off, you'll see, on your left, the entrance to one of the most imaginative pieces of modern architecture on the island, the deluxe postmodern:

9. **Hyatt Regency St. John.** The hotel is currently on the block so expect a name change. If you're a gardening or architecture enthusiast, stop in for a look at a hotel whose inspirations included ancient Mesopotamia, colonial Denmark, and the coast of California. What makes all of this even more impressive is the fact that it was built upon land that was unusable swampland only a few years ago.

From here, your return to Cruz Bay involves only a short drive along Route 104, through a slightly urbanized periphery of private homes.

ON YOUR OWN

The ferry from St. Thomas docks at the main town, **Cruz Bay.** In this West Indian village there are interesting bars, restaurants, boutiques, and pastel-painted houses. It's pretty sleepy, but it's a pleasant place to visit after the fast pace of St. Thomas. The **Elaine Ione Sprauve Museum** (☎ 809/776-6359) at Cruz Bay is small but contains some local artifacts that will teach you about the island's history. It's located in the public library; it's open from 9am to 5pm Monday through Friday.

Most cruise-ship passengers dart through Cruz Bay and head for the island's biggest attraction, **U.S. Virgin Islands National Park** (see "Hiking" above for suggested nature trails). But before going to the park, you may want to stop at the **Visitor Center** at Cruz Bay (see "Organized Tours," below), which is open daily from 8am to 4:30pm. There you'll see some exhibits and learn more about where to go and what to see in the park.

The U.S. Virgin Islands National Park is the only American national park in the Caribbean. It totals 12,624 acres, including submerged lands and waters adjacent to St. John, and has a 20-mile trail system.

If your time on St. John is limited, try at least to visit the **Annaberg Ruins,** Leinster Bay Road, where thriving under Danish rule a sugar plantation was maintained in the 1700s and 1800s. It's located at the end of North Shore Road, east of Trunk Bay. On varying days of the week, park rangers give guided walks of the area.

✪ **Trunk Bay** is one of the world's most beautiful beaches. It's also the site of one of the world's first marked underwater trails (bring your mask, snorkel, and fins, or rent them here). It lies to the east of Cruz Bay along North Shore Road. Beware of pickpockets.

Fort Berg (also called Fortsberg), at Coral Bay, dating from 1717, played a pivotal role during the 1733 slave revolt. The fort may be restored as a historic monument.

ORGANIZED TOURS

Park rangers conduct several different tours daily. You must make a reservation to participate in the 2¹/₂-mile Reef Bay Trail hike, which features old sugar mill ruins and mysterious petroglyphs. Call **809/776-6201** for reservations. Other conducted programs may include shore walks, a 3-hour historic bus tour, snorkel tours, and informal evening lectures.

The **St. John Taxi Association** (☎ **809/776-6060**) conducts a historical tour of St. John, and includes a swim at Trunk Bay and a visit to the Caneel Bay resort. The cost is $30 for two or $12 per person for three or more. Depending on demand, tours depart from Cruz Bay daily.

Visitors are encouraged to drop by the **Cruz Bay Visitor Center** upon their arrival on the island. At the center, you can pick up a park brochure, which includes a map, and the *Virgin Islands National Park News*, which has the latest information on activities in the park. For more information, call **809/776-6201.**

Maps of the island's hiking trails are readily available from the St. John National Park Service at Cruz Bay (see "Hiking" above).

7 Shopping

Compared to St. Thomas, the shopping on St. John isn't stellar, but it's interesting. The boutiques and shops of **Cruz Bay** are quite special. Most of the shops are clustered at **Mongoose Junction,** a woodsy area beside the roadway, about a 5-minute walk left (or northeast) from the ferry dock. In addition to shops, this complex also has some good restaurants (see "Dining," above).

Before you set sail for St. Thomas, you'll want to visit **Wharfside Village,** just a few steps from the ferry-departure point on the waterfront, opening onto Cruz Bay. Here in this complex of courtyards, alleys, and shady patios is a mishmash of all sorts of boutiques, along with some restaurants, fast-food joints, and bars.

Bamboula
Mongoose Junction. ☎ **809/693-8699.**

> Bamboula has an unusual and very appealing collection of gifts from the Caribbean, Haiti, India, Indonesia, and Central Africa. Its exoticism is unexpected and very pleasant. The store has added clothing for both men and women under its own label—hand-batiked soft cottons and rayons made for comfort in a hot climate. Many locally crafted items, ideal as gifts, are also sold.

The Canvas Factory
Mongoose Junction. ☎ **809/776-6196.**

> The Canvas Factory produces its own handmade, rugged, and colorful canvas bags in the "factory" at Mongoose Junction. Their products range from sailing hats to soft-sided luggage to cotton hats.

The Clothing Studio
Mongoose Junction. ☎ **809/776-6585.**

> The Caribbean's oldest hand-painted–clothing studio has been in operation since 1978. You can watch talented artists create original designs on fine tropical clothing, including swimwear, and daytime and evening clothing, mainly for babies and women, with a few items for men.

Coconut Coast Studios
Frank Bay. ☎ **809/776-6944.**

> A 5-minute stroll from the heart of Cruz Bay (follow along the waterfront bypassing Gallows Point) will lead you to the studio of Elaine Estern and Lucinda Schutt, one of the best watercolorists on the island. Especially known for her Caribbean landscapes, Elaine is the official artist for Westin Resorts, St. John; Lucinda is the artist for Caneel Bay. Note cards begin at $8, with unmatted prints costing $15 to $275.

Fabric Mill
Mongoose Junction. ☎ **809/776-6194.**

> This shop features silk-screened and batik fabrics from around the world. Vibrant rugs and bed, bath, and table linens add the perfect touch to your home if you like a Caribbean flair. Whimsical soft sculpture, sarongs, scarves, and handbags are also made in this studio shop.

R and I Patton Goldsmithing
Mongoose Junction. ☎ **809/776-6548.**

> On the island since 1973, this is one of the oldest tourist businesses here, and three-quarters of the merchandise is made on St. John. It has a large selection of island-designed jewelry in sterling silver, gold, and precious stones. Also featured are the works of goldsmiths from outstanding American studios, plus Spanish coins.

Pusser's of the West Indies
Wharfside Village, Cruz Bay. ☎ **809/693-8489.**

> This link in a famous chain was previously recommended for food and drink. The store/restaurant offers a large collection of classically designed old-world travel and adventure clothing along with unusual accessories. It's a unique shopping trip for the island. Clothing for women, men, and children is displayed, along with T-shirts carrying Pusser's emblem.

Donald Schnell Studio

Mongoose Junction. ☎ **809/776-6420.**

In this working studio and gallery, Mr. Schnell and his assistants have created one of the finest collections of handmade pottery, sculpture, and blown glass in the Caribbean. The staff can be seen working daily and is especially noted for its rough-textured coral work. Water fountains are a specialty item, as are house signs. The coral-pottery dinnerware is unique and popular. The studio will mail works all over the world. Go in and discuss any particular design you may have in mind.

The Shop at Caneel Bay

Caneel Bay Resort, Caneel Bay. ☎ **809/776-6111.**

The shop's location within a palatial outbuilding on the manicured grounds of the island's most legendary resort guarantees both an upscale clientele and an upscale assortment of merchandise. Scattered over two simple, elegant floors are the usual drugstore items, books, sundries, and handcrafts you'd expect at a Caribbean resort hotel, as well as some unusual artworks and pieces of expensive jewelry. There are also racks of resort wear and sportswear for men and women.

8 St. John After Dark

Bring a good book. St. John is not St. Thomas after dark, and everybody here seems to want to keep it that way. Most people are content to have a long leisurely dinner and then head home for bed. Occasionally there are special evening events or festivals featuring local entertainment. Call or stop by the visitors center for information.

Among the popular bars of Cruz Bay, **Pusser's** (see above) at Wharfside Village has the most convivial atmosphere. The **Caneel Bay Bar,** at the Caneel Bay Resort (☎ 809/776-6111), presents live music nightly from 8:30 to 11pm. The most popular drinks include a Cool Caneel (local rum with sugar, lime, and anisette) and the house specialty, a Plantation Freeze (lime and orange juice with three different kinds of rum, bitters, and nutmeg).

All of the places recommended above are very touristy. If you'd like to go where the locals go for drinking and gossiping, try **JJ's Texas Coast Café,** Cruz Bay (☎ **809/776-6908**), a real local dive lying across the park from the ferry dock. Your Texan host, JJ Gewels, makes everybody feel welcome—that is, if he likes you. The Tex-Mex food here is the island's best, and the margaritas are called lethal, and deservedly so!

Another Cruz Bay hot spot is **Bad Art Bar** (☎ **809/693-8666**), which is aptly named. Whoever selected this funky art had no taste at all, unless you're the type to go for a velvety Elvis (several locals claim to have spotted him on St. John, especially when they've had one drink to many). Find yourself a Day-Glo table and devour one of the frozen drink specials, like a "Witches Tit" or a "Busted Nut." Live entertainment is presented two nights a week, and if you go between 6 and 8pm daily you can order two-for-one frozen drink specials. The location is above the Purple Door Restaurant.

Also at Cruz Bay, check out the action at **Fred's** (☎ **809/776-6363**), which brings in island bands on Wednesday, Friday, and Sunday nights. The most laid-back bar on the island, it's also the best place to go to dance, at least on those nights. It's just a little hole-in-the-wall across from The Lime Inn, but it can get crowded fast.

The best sports bar on the island is **Skinny Legs,** Emmaus, Coral Bay, beyond the fire station (☎ 809/779-4892). It's only a shack made out of tin and wood, but it serves the best hamburgers in St. John. The chili dogs aren't bad either. The yachting crowd likes to hang out here—the richer they are, the poorer they dress, many looking like refugees as they step off their $1.5 million yachts. There's a satellite dish for major televised sporting events and live music at least once a week.

As a final option, check out **Sea Breeze,** 4F Little Plantation, Coral Bay on Salt Pond Road (☎ 809/693-5824), where you can both drink and eat. Each night a different chef demonstrates his/her specialties. The Sunday brunch is an island highlight, and the barbecued beef sandwich is the best on the island. A local dive and popular hangout, this place is very laid-back.

The U.S. Virgin Islands: St. Croix

6

Measuring 84 square miles, St. Croix is the largest of the U.S. Virgin Islands. Columbus named it *Santa Cruz* (Holy Cross) when he landed here on November 14, 1493. He anchored his ship off the north shore, but was quickly driven away by the spears, arrows, and axes of the Carib Indians.

Despite defensive efforts by the Caribs, settlers began arriving—first the Dutch, who were forced out by the English, then the Spanish, who were ousted out by the French, who laid claim to the island in 1650.

The Danes purchased St. Croix in 1773, and slave labor and sugarcane fields thrived during a golden era of both planters and pirates. The sugar boom, however, went bust in the 19th century, due to slave rebellions, the introduction of the sugar beet in Europe, and the emancipation of slaves in 1848. Even though seven different flags have flown over St. Croix, the nearly 1^1/$_2$ centuries of Danish influence still permeate the island and its architecture.

Today, visitors flock to St. Croix for its beaches and ideal weather. At the east end, which, incidentally, is the easternmost point of the United States, the terrain is rocky and arid. The west end is lusher, with a rain forest of mango, mahogany, tree ferns, and dangling lianas. Between the two extremes are rolling hills, pastures, and, increasingly, miles of condos.

1 Orientation

ARRIVING
BY PLANE

All flights to St. Croix land at the **Alexander Hamilton Airport** on the southern coast of the island.

American Airlines (☎ 800/433-7300) currently offers the most frequent and most reliable service to St. Croix. Passengers flying at night connect through San Juan from either New York's JFK or from Newark, New Jersey. From San Juan, **American Eagle** offers several daily nonstop flights to St. Croix.

There is one flight daily to St. Croix from Miami, with one stop (but no change of plane) in St. Thomas. The flight originates in Dallas/Fort Worth, American's biggest hub. A daily nonstop flight to St. Thomas departs from New York's JFK daily at 8:15am, with continuing service to St. Croix.

Island Highlights: St. Croix

Beaches

- **Cormorant Beach,** 5 miles northwest of Christiansted, has some 1,200 feet of white sands and palm trees.
- **Sandy Point,** is the biggest beach in the U.S. Virgin Islands, with shallow, calm waters.
- **Cane Bay,** adjoining Route 80 on the north shore, is a favorite among snorkelers and divers attracted to its rolling waves and coral gardens, with a "drop-off wall."

The Towns

- **Christiansted,** capital of St. Croix, is a seaport filled with restored 18th-century Danish Colonial buildings.
- **Frederiksted,** is a gingerbread monument to the former Danish mercantile prosperity.

Other Worthwhile Attractions

- **Government House,** in Christiansted, is the former seat of the Danish governor-general with a courtyard evocative of old-fashioned Europe.
- **Fort Christiansvaern,** built on the foundations of a 1645 French fortress, offers fine harbor views from the battlements.
- **Estate Whim Plantation Museum,** a unique sugar plantation great house, is a vestige of the slavery era.

Delta (☎ 800/221-1212) offers daily flights to St. Croix from Atlanta. Flights touch down in St. Thomas before continuing on to St. Croix. Convenient connections are available through San Juan. Fares are competitive with those of American and sometimes match their rival dollar for dollar.

Prestige Airways (☎ 800/299-8784) has nonstop flights to St. Thomas and St. Croix from Miami every day in winter except Tuesday and Saturday; they only fly on Thursday and Sunday in the off-season.

Trip time, including ground time, to St. Croix from New York is 4 hours, from Chicago $5^{1}/_{2}$ hours, from Miami $3^{1}/_{2}$ hours, and from the nearby island of Puerto Rico, 20 minutes.

Once you're on St. Thomas, there are easy air links between that island and St. Croix. **American Eagle** (☎ 809/778-1140) has seven daily flights, costing $60 per person one way. In addition, **Virgin Islands Seaplane** (☎ 809/777-4491) offers eight round-trip flights daily, at $50 per person one way. Flight time is only 30 minutes.

A final reminder: Often, an airline can arrange discounted hotel accommodations in conjunction with air passage if both are booked simultaneously. Ask an airline reservations agent to explain the various package options.

BY CATAMARAN

It's possible to take **Fast Cat** (☎ 809/773-3278), a catamaran that shuttles passengers from St. Thomas to St. Croix three times a day, costing $50 round-trip for adults and $30 for children under 12. A one-way fare is $25 for adults, $15 for children.

ISLAND LAYOUT

St. Croix has only two sizable towns: Christiansted on the north-central shoreline and Frederiksted in the southwest. The Alexander Hamilton Airport opens onto the south coast, lying directly west of the Hess Oil Refinery, the major industry on the island. There is no road that encircles St. Croix's coast.

To continue east from Christiansted, take Route 82 or the East End Road. Route 75 will take you west from Christiansted through the central heartland, then south to the Hess Oil Refinery. Melvin H. Evans Highway, Route 66, runs along the southern part of the island. You can connect with this route in Christiansted and head west all the way to Frederiksted.

FREDERIKSTED

Frederiksted is so tiny that it's almost impossible to get lost. Most visitors head for the central historic district, where the **Frederiksted Pier** juts out into the sea. The two major streets, both of which run parallel to the water, are **Strand Street** and **King Street.** Farther back are Queen Street, Prince Street, Hospital Street, and New Street, the last of which runs beside the cemetery. These streets are crisscrossed by such side streets as Queen Cross Street, King Cross Street, Hill Street, and Market Street. See the map of Frederiksted later in this chapter on page 168.

CHRISTIANSTED

The historic district—the only part of the capital of interest to most visitors—is in the center bordering **Veterans Drive,** which runs along the waterfront. The district is split by **Kronprindsens Gade** (Route 308), which runs completely through the district. Kronprindsens Gade (also called Main Street) is connected to Veterans Drive by a number of shop-filled little streets, including Gutters Gade, Trompeter Gade, and Raadets Gade. The **Visitor's Information Center** lies at the end of King Street (Kongens Gade) near the water. See the map of Christiansted on page 166.

Nearby **Fort Christiansvaern** also opens onto the water. The center of Christiansted can get very congested at times, and driving around is difficult because of the one-way streets. It is usually more practical to park your car and cover the relatively small district on foot. You will find open-air parking on both sides of Fort Christiansvaern.

FINDING AN ADDRESS

In both Christiansted and Frederiksted, buildings are numbered consecutively on one side, stretching all the way to the limits of these towns. Then the numbers "cross the street" and begin numbering on the opposite side. That means that even and odd numbers appear on the same side of the street. The numbering system begins in Christiansted at the waterfront. In Frederiksted, the first number appears at the north end of town for streets running north–south. Numbering begins at the waterfront for streets running east–west.

2 Getting Around

BY TAXI OR BUS

At Alexander Hamilton Airport you'll find official taxi rates posted. Per-person rates require a minimum of two passengers; a single person pays double the posted fares. Expect to pay about $10 for one or two riders from the airport to Christiansted and about $8.50 for one or two from the airport to Frederiksted. As the cabs are unmetered, agree on the rate before you get in.

The **St. Croix Taxicab Association** (☎ **809/778-1088**) offers door-to-door service.

Air-conditioned **buses** run between Christiansted and Frederiksted about every 30 minutes daily between the hours of 5:30am and 9pm. Originating at Tide Village to the east of Christiansted, buses go along Route 75 to the Golden Rock Shopping Center. Then they make their way to Route 70, with stopovers at the Sunny Isle Shopping Center, La Reine Shopping Center, St. George Village Botanical Garden, and Whim Plantation Museum before reaching Frederiksted. Bus service is also available from the airport to both Christiansted and Frederiksted. The fare is $1 or 50¢ for senior citizens. For more information, call **809/773-7746.**

BY CAR

This is a suitable means of exploring for some, but know that if you're going into the "bush country," you'll find the roads very difficult. Sometimes the government smoothes the roads out before the rainy season begins, but they deteriorate rapidly.

St. Croix offers moderately priced **car rentals.** Cars with automatic transmissions and air-conditioning are available, even among some of the lowest-priced rentals.

However, because of the island's higher than normal accident rate (which is partly the result of visitors who forget about driving on the left-hand side of the road), insurance costs are a bit higher than usual. **Avis** (☎ **800/331-2112**), **Budget** (☎ **888/227-3359** or 809/778-9636), and **Hertz** (☎ **800/654-3001** or 809/778-1402), all maintain their headquarters at the island's airport; look for their kiosks near the baggage claim areas.

Each of the three companies offers Suzuki Swifts, Suzuki Esteems, and Ford Escorts, usually with automatic transmission and air-conditioning. Rates vary from company to company. During a recent spot check, Budget was offering cars for $240 to $344 for 5 to 6 days; Hertz, $260 to $430 weekly; and Avis $178 to $350 weekly.

To rent a car at any of these companies, you must be between the ages of 25 and 70 or 75 years old and present a valid driver's license and a credit card at the time of rental.

Collision-damage insurance can be arranged for an additional fee of $13.95 a day, depending on the company, and we feel it's a wise investment. Some credit-card companies grant you collision-damage protection if you pay for the rental with their card. Verify coverage before you go.

Remember to **drive on the left** and to take more precautions than usual because of the unfamiliarity of the roads. In most rural areas, the speed limit is 35 m.p.h.; certain parts of the major artery, Route 66, the Melvin H. Evans Highway, are 55 m.p.h. In towns and urban areas, the speed limit is 20 m.p.h.

ON FOOT

St. Croix is too big to tour on foot; you'll need a rented car or taxi to get about since bus service is inadequate. The historic districts of Christiansted and Frederiksted, however, are relatively small and can only be explored on foot.

FAST FACTS: St. Croix

American Express   The American Express travel representative is Southerland, Chandler's Wharf, Gallows Bay (☎ **800/260-2682** or 809/773-9500).

Area Code   The area code is **809.** You can call direct from the U.S. mainland.

Banks   Several major banks are represented in St. Croix. Most banks are open Monday through Thursday from 9am to 3pm and Friday from 9am to 4:30pm. First Pennsylvania Bank has a branch at 12 King's St. (☎ **809/773-0440**), in Christiansted.

Bookstores The Bookie, 3 Strand St. (☎ **809/773-2592**), in Christiansted, will supply you with a selection of titles to read on the beach or around the pool.

Business Hours Typical business hours are Monday through Friday from 9am to 5pm, Saturday from 9am to 1pm.

Cameras and Film V.I. Express Photo, 2A Strand St. (☎ **809/773-2009**), in Christiansted, offers 1-hour photo finishing, as does Fast Foto, 1116 King St. (☎ **809/773-6727**), in Christiansted.

Car Rentals See "Getting Around," earlier in this chapter.

Crime At night, parts of Christiansted and Frederiksted are unsafe. Stick to the heart of Christiansted, exercise caution, and avoid wandering anywhere around Frederiksted at night.

Currency See "Visitor Information, Entry Requirements & Money," in chapter 3.

Customs See "Visitor Information, Entry Requirements & Money," in chapter 3.

Dentist Go to the Sunny Isle Medical Center, Sunny Isle (☎ **809/778-6356**). Call first for an appointment.

Doctors A good local doctor is Dr. Frank Bishop, Sunny Isle Medical Center (☎ **809/778-0069**). Call for an appointment.

Documents Required See "Visitor Information, Entry Requirements & Money," in chapter 3.

Drugstores Try the Golden Rock Pharmacy, Golden Rock Shopping Center (☎ **809/773-7666**), or People's Drugstore, Sunny Isle Shopping Center (☎ **809/778-5537**), which also has a more convenient branch at 1A King St. (☎ **809/778-7355**), in Christiansted.

Embassies and Consulates St. Croix has no embassies or consulates. Go to one of the local U.S. government agencies if you have a problem.

Emergencies Police, **915;** fire, **921;** ambulance, **922.**

Hitchhiking It isn't illegal, but it isn't commonly practiced. You'll probably wait a long time for a ride. We don't recommend it.

Hospitals The principal facility is St. Croix Hospital, Estate Ruby (☎ **809/778-6311**).

Information The U.S. Virgin Islands Division of Tourism has offices in Christiansted at 1AB Queen Cross St. (☎ **809/773-0495**), and at the Customs House Building, Strand Street (☎ **809/772-0357**), in Frederiksted.

Laundry Try Tropical Cleaners and Launderers, 16–17 King Cross St. (☎ **809/773-3635**), in Christiansted.

Liquor Laws You must be at least 21 years of age to purchase liquor.

Maps Tourist offices provide free maps to the island. *St. Croix This Week,* which is distributed free to cruise-ship passengers and air passengers, has detailed maps of Christiansted, Frederiksted, and the entire island, pinpointing individual attractions, hotels, shops, and restaurants. If you plan to do extensive touring of the island, purchase *The Official Road Map of the U.S. Virgin Islands,* available at island bookstores.

Newspapers and Magazines Newspapers, such as *The Miami Herald,* are flown into St. Croix daily. St. Croix also has its own newspaper, *St. Croix Avis. Time* and

Newsweek are widely sold as well. Your best source of local information is *St. Croix This Week,* which is distributed free by the tourist offices.

Police   The police headquarters (☎ **915**) is on Market Street in Christiansted.

Post Office   The U.S. Post Office is on Company Street (☎ **773-3586**), in Christiansted.

Rest Rooms   There are few public rest rooms, except at the major beaches and airport. Most people use the rest rooms in commercial establishments, which, technically, businesses have a right to reserve for customers. In Christiansted, the National Park Service maintains some rest rooms within the public park beside Fort Christiansvaern.

Safety   St. Croix is safer than St. Thomas. Possessions should never be left unattended, especially on the beach. Exercise extreme caution at night around Christiansted and Frederiksted. Avoid night strolls along beaches or drives along little-used roads.

Taxis   For an airport taxi call **809/778-1088;** otherwise, **809/773-5020,** the latter in Christiansted.

Telephone, Telex, and Fax   A local call at a phone booth costs 25¢. You can dial direct to St. Croix from the mainland by using the 809 area code. Omit the 809 for local calls. The bigger hotels will send telex and fax, or you can go to the post office (see above).

Water   Water is generally safe, but you are asked to conserve. If you have a delicate stomach, stick to bottled water.

3 Accommodations

St. Croix's charming old waterfront inns are mostly in Christiansted, whereas the deluxe resorts lie along the North Shore. You may also choose to stay at a former plantation, or in a condo complex. In general, rates are steep, and all rooms are subject to a 7.5% tax.

Hotels rated **"Very Expensive"** charge from $210 to $575 for a double room in winter; **"Expensive"** from $140 to $210; **"Moderate"** from $115 to $140; and **"Inexpensive"** from $69 to $115. For an explanation of the abbreviations AP, CP, EP, and MAP, see "Tips on Accommodations & Dining," in chapter 3.

In summer, you can get better deals on St. Croix accommodations, as hotels slash prices by about 20% to 50%.

NORTH SHORE
VERY EXPENSIVE

✪ **The Buccaneer**

Rte. 82 (P.O. Box 25200), Gallows Bay, St. Croix, U.S.V.I. 00824. ☎ **800/255-3881** in the U.S., or 809/773-2100. Fax 809/778-8215. 150 rms. A/C TEL. Winter, $210–$575 double. Off-season, $170–$240 double. Rates include continental breakfast. AE, DC, DISC, MC, V.

A large, luxury, family owned resort in operation since 1948, the Buccaneer is 2 miles east of Christiansted. Its 240 acres contain three of the island's best beaches, and it offers the best sports program on St. Croix. The property was once a cattle ranch and a sugar plantation, and its first estate house, dating from the mid-17th century, stands near a freshwater swimming pool. Pink and patrician, the hotel offers a choice of accommodations in its main building or in one of the beachside properties. The

St. Croix Accommodations

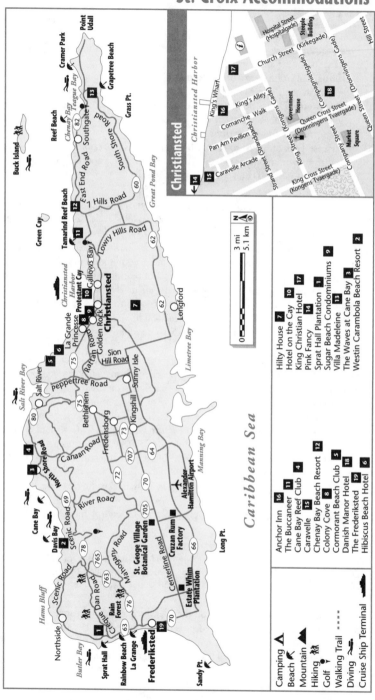

Christiansted

Hospital Street (Hospitalgade)
Steeple Building
Church Street (Kirkegade)
Hill street
King's Wharf
King's Alley
King Street (Kongens Gade)
Comanche Walk
Government House
Queen Cross Street (Compagniets Gade)
Queen Street (Dronningens Gade)
Pan Am Pavillion
Strand Street (Strandgade)
Queen Cross Street (Dronningens Tvaergade)
Caravelle Arcade
King Cross Street (Kongens Tvaergade)
Christiansted Harbor

Scale

N

3 mi
5.1 km

0

Hilty House **7**
Hotel on the Cay **10**
King Christian Hotel **17**
Pink Fancy **14**
Sprat Hall Plantation **1**
Sugar Beach Condominiums **9**
Villa Madeleine **13**
The Waves at Cane Bay **3**
Westin Carambola Beach Resort **2**

Anchor Inn **16**
The Buccaneer **11**
Cane Bay Reef Club **4**
Caravelle **15**
Chenay Bay Beach Resort **12**
Colony Cove **8**
Cormorant Beach Club **5**
Danish Manor Hotel **18**
The Frederiksted **19**
Hibiscus Beach Hotel **6**

Legend:
Camping
Beach
Mountain
Hiking
Golf
Walking Trail
Diving
Cruise Ship Terminal

Caribbean Sea

Point Udall
Cramer Park
Grapetree Beach
Reef Beach
Buck Island
Green Cay
Grass Pt.
Great Pond Bay
Chenay Bay
League Bay
Southgate
82
13
East End Road
South Shore Road
Tamarind Reef Beach
7 Hills Road
12
Lowry Hills Road
11
60
62
Galloways Bay
La Grande Princesse
Protestant Cay
10
9
8
Golden Rock
Christiansted
Christiansted Harbor
6
5
Salt River
Salt River Bay
80
Rattan Road
75
Peppertree Road
Sion Hill Road
Sunny Isle
7
62
Longford
Limetree Bay
Bethlehem
75
Kingshill
Fredensborg
73
707
64
Canaan Road
72
70
64
Alexander Hamilton Airport
Manning Bay
North Shore Road
4
3
River Road
69
78
705
Mahogany Road
St. George Village Botanical Garden
66
Cruzan Rum Factory
Long Pt.
Northside
Scenic Road
765
763
Creque Dan Road
Rain Forest
76
Centerline Road
70
Estate Whim Plantation
Sprat Hall
Rainbow Beach
La Grange
Frederiksted
19
1
63
Butler Bay
Hams Bluff
Davis Bay
2
Cane Bay
Sandy Pt.

baronially arched main building has a lobby opening toward drinking or viewing terraces, with a sea vista on two sides and Christiansted to the west. The comfortable rooms feature tropical furnishings and range from standard to deluxe (some of the standard rooms are a bit small).

Dining/Entertainment: Breakfast and dinner are served at the Terrace Dining Room and at the Little Mermaid Restaurant. Lunch is also served at the Mermaid and the Grotto. Dino's, long a popular St. Croix institution, has also opened here. There is entertainment nightly at the Terrace Lounge, with a variety of music ranging from jazz to island steel drums.

Services: Trips arranged to Buck Island; children's program.

Facilities: Swimming pool, eight championship tennis courts, fitness center and health spa, 18-hole golf course, 2-mile jogging trail.

Cormorant Beach Club

4126 La Grande Princesse, St. Croix, U.S.V.I. 00820. ☎ **800/548-4460** or 809/778-8920. Fax 809/778-9218. 34 rms, 4 suites. A/C TEL. Winter, $210–$230 double; $250–$265 triple; $295 suite. Off-season, $140–$190 double; $165–$230 triple; $300 suite. AE, DC, MC, V.

On a 12-acre site about 3 miles northwest of Christiansted on Route 75, this resort strikes a perfect balance between seclusion and accessibility. Long Reef, one of the better-known zoological phenomena of the Caribbean, lies a few hundred feet from the hotel's sandy beachfront. The hotel's social life revolves around a wood-sheathed, high-ceilinged clubhouse, whose walls were removed to give guests a firsthand taste of the salty sea breezes. Off the central area are a library, the largest freshwater pool on St. Croix, and an airy dining room that was rebuilt in the wake of Hurricane Marilyn.

The rooms are located in well-maintained outbuildings, and each contains a spacious bath, a tasteful decor of cane and wicker furniture, and bouquets of seasonal flowers. In winter, children under five are politely discouraged.

Dining/Entertainment: You can stay here on the Cormorant Beach Club (CBC) meal plan including breakfast, complete lunch, and all drinks until 5pm for only $37.50 per person per day. The all-inclusive plan (AIP) is the CBC plan, plus an open dinner menu and all beverages until closing for $77.50 per person per day. Thursday night is Caribbean Grill Night with a buffet and entertainment, and the Sunday brunch is well attended.

Services: Laundry; arrangements for golf, horseback riding, sailing, and scuba diving.

Facilities: Freshwater swimming pool, two tennis courts, snorkeling, dive shop, croquet, library.

Westin Carambola Beach Resort

P.O. Box 3031, Kingshill, St. Croix, U.S.V.I. 00851. ☎ **800/WESTIN** in the U.S. and Canada, or 809/778-3800. Fax 809/778-1682. 150 rms, 1 suite. A/C MINIBAR TV TEL. Winter, $245–$330 double; $540 suite. Off-season, $165–$250 double; $380 suite. AE, CB, DC, DISC, MC, V.

Set on 28 acres above Davis Bay, on the island's sparsely populated north shore, a 30-minute drive from Christiansted, this hotel reopened in 1993 after renovations and an ill-fated 3-year closing. It had originally opened with much fanfare in 1987, but was done in by Hurricane Hugo in 1989 and later damaged by the hurricanes of 1995. Today it's owned by the Kentucky-based Sargasso Corporation and has been operated since 1995 as a Westin.

The island's only chain hotel, and one of the largest hostelries on St. Croix, it's adjacent to an outstanding golf course designed by Robert Trent Jones. Guests are housed in red-roofed, two-story outbuildings, each of which contains six units. The accommodations are furnished in rattan and wicker, with pastel colors and a balcony overlooking either the garden or sea.

Dining/Entertainment: Diners face a trio of choices, all of which are open to non-residents. The Saman Room offers breakfast and lunch daily, with dinner served either here or at the Mahogany Room. Sandwiches and salads are offered daily in the New York Deli. The hotel's Sunday brunch is fast becoming an island tradition. Friday night features a pirate's buffet.

Services: 24-hour room service, baby-sitting, concierge who can arrange tours, car rentals.

Facilities: A large swimming pool, four hard-court tennis courts, 18-hole golf course.

EAST END
VERY EXPENSIVE

Villa Madeleine

Teague Bay (P.O. Box 3109), St. Croix, U.S.V.I. 00822. ☎ **800/548-4461** or 809/778-7377. Fax 809/773-7518. 43 villas. A/C TV TEL. Winter, $425 two-bedroom villa. Off-season, $300 two-bedroom villa. AE, DISC, DC, MC, V.

Eight miles east of Christiansted, Villa Madeleine was built in 1990 on 6¹/₂ acres and remains the island's poshest property. People arrive here and aren't heard from again until they show up at the airport to leave. Many of the well-heeled occupants are living here full time as retirees. The focal point is the Great House, whose Chippendale balconies and proportions emulate the Danish colonial era. Inside, a splendidly conceived decor incorporates masses of English chintz and mahogany paneling.

The hotel rents two-bedroom villas, each with its own privacy wall and plunge pool. Decorated with style, each unit has a four-poster bed, marble bathroom, and kitchen. The villas comprising the resort are individually owned, and different management companies handle some of them. Service and standards, it should be noted, can vary greatly depending on the villa you rent. Therefore, don't expect the standards and services of a typical Caribbean luxury resort. Beach-lovers willingly travel the ¹/₃ mile to the nearest beaches, Reef and Grapevine. Parents are discouraged from bringing children 11 and under.

Dining/Entertainment: Café Madeleine is a continental restaurant, with a piano bar and nautical accessories. No breakfast is served. A second restaurant, The Turf Club, is a New York–style steak house decorated with horse-racing memorabilia. They allow any kind of tobacco smoking, including cigars.

Services: Concierge, laundry, maid service every 3 days, baby-sitting (with advance notice).

Facilities: Small library with writing tables; game room for cards and billiards; laundry room; tennis courts; golf course below the property; a good beach 5 minutes away.

CHRISTIANSTED
MODERATE

Anchor Inn

58 King St., Christiansted, St. Croix, U.S.V.I. 00820. ☎ **800/524-2030** in the U.S., or 809/773-4000. Fax 809/773-4408. 30 rms. A/C MINIBAR TV TEL. Winter, $115–$145 double; $135–$165 triple. Off-season, $90–$105 double; $110–$125 triple. Additional person $20 extra. Scuba packages available. AE, DC, DISC, MC, V.

One of the few hotels in town directly on the waterfront, the Anchor Inn is set in a courtyard near Government House, in the heart of the national historic district and shopping belt. The space is so compact and intimate that you might not believe it holds 30 comfortably furnished although somewhat drab rooms, each with refrigerator, radio, bath, and a small porch. A few rooms (without porches) have king- and queen-size beds and dressing rooms.

A sundeck and small swimming pool sit directly on the waterfront, as does the Anchor Inn's own boardwalk, where catamarans and glass-bottom boats make daily trips to Buck Island. There are also deep-sea fishing boats, a scuba-dive shop, and honeymoon and family package tours. Dining is at Antoine's, on the harbor (see "Dining," below). To reach the nearest beach, you can take a $3 round-trip ferry ride across the harbor.

Caravelle

44A Queen Cross St., Christiansted, St. Croix, U.S.V.I. 00820. ☎ **800/524-0410** or 809/773-0687. Fax 809/778-7004. 43 rms, 1 suite. A/C TV TEL. Winter, $130–$140 double; $300 suite. Off-season, $100–$110 double; $225 suite. AE, CB, DC, DISC, MC, V.

The biggest hotel in the historic core of Christiansted, Caravelle usually caters to a clientele of international business travelers who prefer to be near the center of town. There's an Andalusian-style fountain in the lobby, and the restaurant, Banana Bay Club, is a few steps away. Many sports activities, such as sailing, deep-sea fishing, snorkeling, scuba, golf, and tennis, can be arranged at the reception desk. A swimming pool and sundeck face the water, and all the shopping and activities in town are close at hand. To reach the nearest beach requires a ferryboat ride from the harbor. Accommodations, which are generally spacious and comfortably furnished, are priced according to their views.

Hibiscus Beach Hotel

4131 La Grande Princesse, St. Croix, U.S.V.I. 00820. ☎ **800/442-0121** or 809/773-4042. Fax 809/773-7668. 36 rms, 1 two-bedroom efficiency. A/C MINIBAR TV TEL. Winter, $180–$190 double; $290 efficiency. Off-season, $130–$140 double; $220 efficiency. Honeymoon, dive, and golf packages available. AE, DISC, MC, V.

About a 10-minute ride from Christiansted, Hibiscus is located on one of the island's best beaches—lined with palm trees, next to the Cormorant—and is one of the most appealing properties to have opened in the mid-1990s. Its rates are also comfortably affordable to its lively clientele. Each of its beachfront rooms is complete with patios or balconies, and ceiling fans aid the air-conditioning. Furnishings are in the standard Caribbean motel style. Other amenities include an in-room safe and fresh flowers. The hotel also has a seaside swimming pool and a beachfront restaurant and bar, which offers good value theme buffets. Complimentary snorkeling equipment is provided.

Hilty House

P.O. Box 26077, Questa Verde Rd., Gallows Bay, St. Croix, U.S.V.I. 00824. ☎ and fax **809/773-2594.** 4 rms, 2 cottages. Winter, $110 double; $115–$135 cottage. Off-season, $95 double; $100–$110 cottage. Rates for regular rooms include continental breakfast. Honeymoon packages available. No credit cards.

Jacquie and Hugh Hoare-Ward own and manage this bed-and-breakfast in a 200-year-old building that was once a rum distillery. Hilty House is located on the east side of St. Croix atop a hill off Queste Verde Road, above Christiansted. The airport, 7 miles away, is a 15-minute drive; the nearest beach at Christiansted, a 10-minute drive.

Upon their arrival, guests pass through a shaded courtyard to a set of iron gates that lead through the inn's gardens to the main house. The plantation-style house is beautifully appointed with hand-painted Italian tiles. The interior has a high-ceilinged living room and an enormous fireplace that houses a spit. The bedrooms are uniquely

🅐 Family-Friendly Hotels

Anchor Inn *(see p. 147)* This inn is a good choice for families who don't want to spend money on a rental car, as it's located in the heart of Christiansted on the waterfront; children under 12 stay free in a room with their parents.

The Buccaneer *(see p.144)* Children get a big welcome at this family owned resort, and they stay free in their parents' room if 11 or under. During school holidays, the hotel has organized activities for kids of all ages.

Colony Cove *(see p. 152)* Families staying at Colony Cove have their own kitchens, clothes washers, and dryers. The hotel is near a beach and has a swimming pool.

Chenay Bay Beach Resort *(see p. 152)* Guests have their own cottages, with kitchenettes overlooking the Caribbean. The resort has a swimming pool and a fine beach nearby.

decorated, and some even have chandeliers. There are also two self-catering cottages that can be rented with a required minimum stay of 3 nights. The Danish Kitchen, one of the cottages, has an enclosed porch, TV, and telephone.

Dinner, a buffet meal with a set price of $25, is only served on Monday night. Guests can swim in the large pool decorated with hand-painted tiles. While the atmosphere is very homey, children 11 and under are not allowed, and no more than two people can share one room.

Hotel on the Cay

Protestant Cay, Christiansted, St. Croix, U.S.V.I. 00820. ☎ **800/524-2035** or 809/773-2035. Fax 809/773-7046. 52 rms, 3 suites. A/C TV TEL. Winter, $160 double; $190 suite. Off-season, $105 double; $135 suite. Additional person $25 extra. AE, DC, MC, V.

With its buff-colored stucco, terra-cotta tiles, and archways, this rather sterile looking hotel evokes Puerto Rico or the Dominican Republic, but it's the most prominent building on a 3-acre island set in the middle of Christiansted's harbor. Reaching it requires a 4-minute boat ride from a well-marked quay in the town center. (Hotel guests ride free; nonguests pay a $3 ferryboat charge, round-trip.) Its position in the clear waters of the harbor is both its main allure and its main drawback: Its wide sandy beaches provide the only pollution-free swimming in the town center, but it's the first hotel to be wiped off the map whenever a hurricane strikes.

In theory, this place should be a lavishly landscaped, upscale retreat; unfortunately, what you'll find doesn't meet those high expectations. But despite some drawbacks, it provides simple, unfrilly, and clean accommodations near the beach.

Dining/Entertainment: Breakfast, lunch, and tropical drinks are served daily from 7am to 5pm beneath a shed-style restaurant, the Harbormaster. Dinner is only served on Tuesday night, from 7 to 10:30pm; it's a beach barbecue, complete with steel band, and a "Moko Jumbi" floor show, priced at $23.50 per person.

✪ King Christian Hotel

59 King's Wharf (P.O. Box 3619), Christiansted, St. Croix, U.S.V.I. 00822. ☎ **800/524-2012** in the U.S., or 809/773-2285. Fax 809/773-9411. 39 rms. A/C TV TEL. Winter, $100 economy double; $140 superior double. Off-season, $85 economy double; $107 superior double. AE, DC, DISC, MC, V.

This three-story hotel is directly on the waterfront. Before its transformation into a hotel in the early 1960s, it had been a warehouse for 300 years; it's recently been restored. All its front rooms have two double beds, a bathroom, cable color TV,

St. Croix Hotels at a Glance	Access for disabled	A/C in bedrooms	Child-care facilities	Children are welcome	Convention facilities	Credit cards accepted	Directly beside beach	Fitness facility	Golf course nearby	Live entertainment	Marina facilities	Restaurant & bar	Spa facilities	Swimming pool	Tennis courts	TV in bedroom	Water sports
Anchor Inn		•		•		•				•		•		•		•	
The Buccaneer	•	•	•	•	•	•	•	•	•	•		•	•	•	•	•	•
Cane Bay Reef				•		•	•		•			•		•			•
Caravelle		•		•		•						•		•		•	
Chenay Bay		•		•			•			•		•		•	•		•
Colony Cove		•		•		•	•					•		•	•	•	•
Cormorant	•	•		•		•	•	•	•			•		•	•		•
Danish Manor		•		•		•						•				•	
The Frederiksted		•		•		•								•		•	
Hibiscus	•	•		•	•	•				•		•		•		•	•
Hilty House														•			
Hotel on the Cay		•		•	•	•	•			•	•	•				•	•
King Christian Hotel		•		•		•					•	•		•		•	•
Pink Fancy		•		•		•								•		•	
Sprat Hall Plantation	•	•		•		•						•				•	•
Sugar Beach Condos		•		•		•	•		•					•	•		
Villa Madeleine		•		•		•				•		•		•		•	
Waves at Cane Bay	•	•		•		•	•		•			•				•	•
Westin Carambola	•	•		•		•	•		•	•		•		•	•	•	•

refrigerator, room safe, and private balcony overlooking the harbor, and they're among the largest in town. The no-frills economy-wing rooms have a bath and two single beds or one double bed, but no view or balcony.

You can relax on the sundeck or shaded patio, or in the freshwater pool. The staff will make arrangements for golf, tennis, horseback riding, and sightseeing tours, and there's a beach just a few hundred yards across the harbor, reached by ferry. Mile Mark Charters water sports center offers daily trips to Buck Island's famous snorkeling trail as well as a complete line of water sports equipment. You can park in a public lot off King Street.

✪ Pink Fancy

27 Prince St., Christiansted, St. Croix, U.S.V.I. 00820. ☎ **800/524-2045** in the U.S., or 809/ 773-8460. Fax 809/773-6448. 13 rms. A/C TV TEL. Winter, $75–$120 double. Off-season, $65–$90 double. Additional person $15 extra. Rates include continental breakfast. Children 11 and under stay free in parents' room. AE, MC, V.

Pink Fancy was restored and turned into this small, unique private hotel located one block from the Annapolis Sailing School. The oldest part of the four-building complex is a 1780 Danish town house, now a historic island site. Years ago the building was a private club for wealthy planters. Fame came when Jane Gottlieb, the Ziegfeld

Follies star, opened it as a hotel in 1948. In the 1950s the hotel became a mecca for writers and artists, including, among others, Noël Coward. The spacious efficiency rooms, with ceiling fans, are in four buildings clustered around the swimming pool area. The bigger rooms contain a kitchenette with a two-burner stove and refrigerator. Other than the complimentary breakfast, you're on your own for meals.

INEXPENSIVE

Danish Manor Hotel

2 Company St., Christiansted, St. Croix, U.S.V.I. 00820. ☎ **800/524-2609** in the U.S., or 809/773-1377. Fax 809/773-1913. 34 rms, 2 suites. A/C TV. Winter, $69–$115 double; $115–$150 suite. Off-season, $59–$89 double; $89–$110 suite. Rates include continental breakfast. AE, DC, DISC, MC, V.

This is the best of the inexpensive hotels in the heart of Christiansted, painted in vivid shades of pink, blue, and violet, with hand-painted tropical friezes around the postage stamp swimming pool, plus art and mementos around the courtyard bar. The only drawback is that there's no view of the sea from most rooms. However, some rooms on the top (third) floor overlook the sands of Protestant Cay. An L-shaped three-story addition stands in the rear, with spacious but sterile rooms with air-conditioning, ceiling fans, and cable TV with HBO. The entrance to the courtyard is through old arches. You can park in a public lot off King Street. The hotel has a courtyard for guests where cool drinks and wine coolers are available, and the popular Italian/seafood restaurant, Tutto Bene (see "Dining," below), fronts the hotel. Guests can swim at the beach in Christiansted Harbor, about a 5-minute ferry ride from the hotel.

FREDERIKSTED
MODERATE

Sprat Hall Plantation

Rte. 63N, P.O. Box 695, Frederiksted, St. Croix, U.S.V.I. 00841. ☎ **800/843-3584** or 809/772-0305. 15 units. A/C TV. Winter, $130 double; $150 Great House room; $150 two-room efficiency; $200 cottage; $350 two-bedroom house for 4. Off-season, $110 double; $130 Great House room; $130 two-room efficiency; $160 cottage; $200 two-bedroom house for 4. AE, DC, DISC, MC, V.

This resort, 1 mile north of Frederiksted, is the oldest plantation great house (and the only French-built plantation house left intact) in the Virgin Islands. Dating from the island's French occupation of 1650 to 1690, the plantation, set on 20 acres, is fringed by private white sandy beaches. The plantation can house about 40 people, depending on how many guests use the cottage units.

The units in the great house have been designated for nonsmokers because of the value of their antiques. An annex originally built in the 1940s contains simply furnished units with ocean views. If you want a sense of the region's history, you should ask for a room in the great house. Some complain about the rooms in the rather plain and dingy cottages, so look at them before you decide to book.

Dining/Entertainment: Both the Beach Restaurant (which serves lunch) and the Sprat Hall Beach Restaurant serve good food often made with ingredients from the plantation's own gardens and fresh local fish. Dress is semiformal, and only people staying at the hotel and their guests can eat here. Lunches at the beach club (see below) are open to everyone.

Facilities: Equestrian stable (see "Sports & Other Outdoor Pursuits," below), hiking, bird-watching, snorkeling, swimming, shore fishing.

INEXPENSIVE

✪ The Frederiksted

20 Strand St., Frederiksted, St. Croix, U.S.V.I. 00840. ☎ **800/595-9519** in the U.S., or 809/772-0500 (and fax). 40 rms. A/C TV TEL. Winter, $95–$105 double. Off-season, $85–$95 double. AE, DC, DISC, MC, V.

For those who'd like to stay in the "second city" of St. Croix, historic Frederiksted, this contemporary four-story inn is the answer. It's located about 10 minutes by car from the airport in the center of town. Much of the activity takes place in the outdoor tiled courtyard, where guests enjoy drinks and listen to live music on Friday and Saturday nights. There's also a small swimming pool here. The average-size bedrooms, a bit tattered, are done in a tropical motif of pastels and are equipped with small refrigerators and a wet bar. The best (and most expensive) bedrooms are those with an ocean view, even though street noise can sometimes be a problem. A full breakfast is served at the poolside patio, and the bar is popular in the evening, as guests sip on rum punches. The nearest beach is Dorch Beach, a 1-mile walk along the water from the hotel or a 5-minute drive.

SELF-SUFFICIENT UNITS AROUND THE ISLAND
EXPENSIVE

Cane Bay Reef Club

P.O. Box 1407, Kingshill, St. Croix, U.S.V.I. 00851. ☎ **800/253-8534** in the U.S., or 809/778-2966. Fax 809/778-2966. 7 suites. A/C. Winter, $135–$175 suite for 1 or 2. Off-season, $90–$115 suite for 1 or 2. Additional person $15 extra. MC, V.

This is one of St. Croix's little gems, offering large suites, each with a living room, a full kitchen, a bedroom, a bath, and a balcony overlooking the water. The decor is breezy tropical, with cathedral ceilings, overhead fans, and Chilean tiles. It's on the north shore of St. Croix, about a 20-minute taxi ride from Christiansted, fronting the rocky Cane Bay Beach near The Waves at Cane Bay (see below). Guests enjoy a pool, and local rum drinks are served at the patio bar.

Chenay Bay Beach Resort

Rte. 82, East End Rd. (P.O. Box 24600), St. Croix, U.S.V.I. 00824. ☎ **800/548-4457** in the U.S., or 809/773-2918. Fax 809/773-2918. 50 cottages. A/C TV TEL. Winter, $195–$240 cottage for 1 or 2. Off-season, $140–$175 cottage for 1 or 2. Additional person $25 extra. Children under 18 stay free. $65 per person extra for all meals, drinks, and water sports. AE, MC, V.

With a quiet and barefoot-casual ambience, these West Indian–style cottages, new or newly renovated, are nestled on a 30-acre beach, with an open-air swimming pool. Home to one of the island's finest beaches for swimming, snorkeling, and windsurfing, Chenay Bay is just 3 miles east of Christiansted and is a terrific choice for families. Each cottage contains a fully equipped kitchenette, private bath, and ceiling fan. The 20 original cottages are smaller and more weathered than the newer duplexes.

The Beach Bar and Grille is open for Caribbean dining daily from 8am to 9pm. The hotel has a popular Tuesday West Indian buffet and pig roast and a Saturday night "Caribbean kaleidoscope" with a mélange of West Indian cuisine and entertainment. The resort also has one of the island's best children's programs during the summer and holiday periods. Tennis courts and kayaking are available.

Colony Cove

3221 Estate Golden Rock, St. Croix, U.S.V.I. 00820. ☎ **800/828-0746** in the U.S., or 809/773-1965. Fax 809/773-5397. 60 condos. A/C TV TEL. Winter, $185 apt for 1 or 2; $210 apt for 4. Off-season, $125 apt for 1 or 2; $150 apt for 4. Children under 6 stay free. Additional person $20 extra in winter, $10 in summer. AE, MC, V. Travel east on Rte. 75 going toward Christiansted as far as Five Corners, and then turn left and pass Mill Harbor; Colony Cove is the next driveway to the left.

Of all the condo complexes on St. Croix, Colony Cove is most like a full-fledged hotel. About a mile west of Christiansted next to a palm-dotted beach, it's composed of four three-story buildings that ring a swimming pool. Each apartment contains a washer and dryer (rare for St. Croix), a kitchen, an enclosed veranda or gallery, two air-conditioned bedrooms, and a pair of bathrooms. There's an on-site water sports center, plus two tennis courts.

Sugar Beach Condominiums

3245 Estate Golden Rock, St. Croix, U.S.V.I. 00820. ☎ **800/524-2049** in the U.S., or 809/773-5345. Fax 809/773-1359. 46 studios and apts. A/C TV TEL. Winter, $180 studio; $225 one-bedroom apt; $275 two-bedroom apt; $350 three-bedroom apt. Off-season, $110 studio; $145 one-bedroom apt; $180 two-bedroom apt; $250 three-bedroom apt. Maid service extra. AE, MC, V.

This row of modernized studios and one-, two-, and three-bedroom apartments is strung along 500 feet of sandy beach on the north coast off North Shore Road. Its location, however, near a housing development, is a turn-off for some visitors. When you tire of the sand, you can swim in the free-form freshwater pool nestled beside a sugar mill where rum was made 3 centuries ago. Under red-tile roofs, the apartments with enclosed balconies are staggered to provide privacy. All apartments open toward the sea, are tastefully decorated, and have completely equipped kitchens. The property has two Laykold tennis courts, and the Carambola golf course is minutes away.

The Waves at Cane Bay

Cane Bay (P.O. Box 1749, Kingshill), St. Croix, U.S.V.I. 00851. ☎ **800/545-0603** in the U.S., or 809/778-1805. Fax 809/778-4945. 12 rms. A/C TV. Winter, $140–$195 double. Off-season, $85–$125 double. Additional person $20 extra. AE, CB, MC, V. From the airport, go left on Rte. 64 for 1 mile, turn right on Rte. 70 for 1 mile, go left at the junction with Rte. 75 for 2 miles, and then turn left at the junction with Rte. 80 for 5 miles.

This intimate and tasteful property run by Suzanne and Kevin Ryan is about 8 miles from the airport, midway between the island's two biggest towns. It's set on a well-landscaped plot of oceanfront property on Cane Bay, which boasts some of the best scuba and snorkeling; Cane Bay Beach is rocky and tends to disappear at high tide. Accommodations are in two-story units with screened-in verandas, all directly on the ocean. The rooms are high-ceilinged, with fresh flowers, well-stocked kitchens, private libraries, and thick towels. A two-room villa next to the main building has a large oceanside deck. There's a beachside bar, and a restaurant on that's open 6 nights a week. A PADI dive shop also operates on the premises.

A GAY-FRIENDLY INN

Two or three inns in Frederiksted are popular among gay men and lesbians. The best of these is On the Beach Resort, Frederiksted Beach, P.O. Box 1908, Frederiksted, St. Croix, U.S.V.I. (☎ **800/524-2018** or 809/772-1205; fax 809/772-1757), a small hotel lying ¹/₂ mile from the town's shopping and dining areas. It has 20 bedrooms, all with kitchenettes, private baths, and chamber service. In winter, a single or double ranges from $95 to $195 daily; the price is lowered in summer to $50 to $110 (either single or double). Coffee and continental breakfast are provided free, and the very popular gourmet patio restaurant provides lunch, dinner, and a well-attended Sunday brunch. American Express, MasterCard, and Visa are accepted.

4 Dining

Don't limit yourself to your hotel for dining. Head for one of the island's many independently owned restaurants—they are among the best in the Caribbean.

Restaurants below rated **"Expensive"** charge $45 and up per person for dinner, not including drinks; **"Moderate,"** from $25 to $45; and **"Inexpensive,"** under $25.

CHRISTIANSTED
EXPENSIVE

✪ Indies

55–56 Company St. ☎ **809/692-9440.** Reservations recommended. Main courses $16–$21. AE, DISC, MC, V. Mon–Fri 11:30am–2:30pm and 6–9:30pm, Sat–Sun 6–9:30pm. CARIBBEAN/INTERNATIONAL.

Catherine Plav-Drigger is one of the most superlative chefs in the Caribbean, and you're likely to get your finest meal on St. Croix at her restaurant. Set in a 19th-century courtyard lined with antique cobblestone, Indies is a welcoming retreat. Catherine's fresh ingredients are first rate, and her menu reflects the produce and flavors of the Caribbean. You dine adjacent to a carriage and cookhouse from the 1850s in a sheltered courtyard protected from street noise.

The menu varies depending on what's fresh, including both fish and produce. The Thai green curry grilled shrimp with banana, chutney, and scallions, has a savory flavor, as does the lobster and corn quesadilla, both of which are often served as appetizers. For soup, you may have a choice between an excellent pumpkin-ginger soup with coconut or a West Indian seafood chowder. Main courses might feature a superb grilled wahoo with pepper sauce and grilled scallions, or perhaps a spicy Caribbean chicken with fresh pineapple chutney. Sushi, with a special emphasis on tuna, is a biweekly special.

✪ Kendrick's

12 Chandlers Wharf, Gallows Bay. ☎ **809/773-9199.** Reservations required at dinner upstairs. Main courses $14–$26; lunch $7–$17. AE, MC, V. Daily 11:30am–3pm and 6–9pm. FRENCH/CONTINENTAL.

The island's toniest restaurant has moved out to Gallows Bay, but its local fans are following it to this new location overlooking Christiansted Harbor. There are two dining rooms—the downstairs one is more informal, serving lunch as well as dinner. Some of the restaurant's recipes have been featured in *Bon Appétit* and deservedly so. You'll immediately warm up to specialties like homemade eggplant ravioli with a tomato-basil butter, or grilled filet mignon with black truffle in a bordelaise sauce. Our favorite dish—almost a signature, actually—is seared scallops and artichoke hearts in a lemon-cream sauce, which is served as an appetizer. Another dish that explodes with flavor is the pecan-crusted roast pork loin, served with a ginger mayonnaise. Friday is oyster and clam night, featuring live entertainment.

Top Hat

52 Company St. (opposite Market Sq.). ☎ **809/773-2346.** Reservations recommended. Main courses $20–$34, including access to a salad bar. AE, CB, DC, DISC, MC, V. Mon–Sat 6–10pm. Closed May–June. CONTINENTAL/DANISH.

Set on the second floor of an 18th-century merchant's house, 2 blocks inland from Christiansted's wharves, this is the only Danish restaurant in the Virgin Islands. A bit bourgeois and staid, it's a long-enduring favorite, despite its rather standard cuisine. Operated since 1970 by Bent and Hanne Rasmussen, two Scandinavians, it offers well-prepared dishes such as crisp roast duck prepared Danish-style with apples,

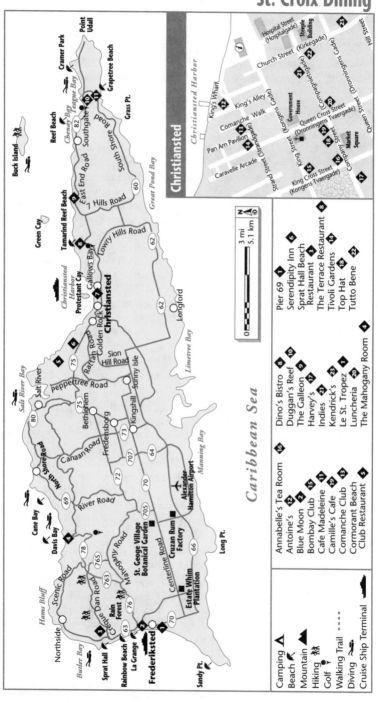

St. Croix Dining

Christiansted

Map Legend (Island features):

- Camping ▲
- Beach 👣
- Mountain ▲
- Hiking 🚶
- Golf ⛳
- Walking Trail - - - -
- Diving 🤿
- Cruise Ship Terminal ⚓

Dining List (left columns):

- Annabelle's Tea Room 16
- Antoine's 9
- Blue Moon 2
- Bombay Club 43
- Cafe Madeleine 11
- Camille's Cafe 19
- Comanche Club 13
- Cormorant Beach Club Restaurant 5

- Dino's Bistro 8
- Duggan's Reef 10
- The Galleon 9
- Harvey's 17
- Indies 21
- Kendrick's 23
- Le St. Tropez 7
- Luncheria 20
- The Mahogany Room 5

Dining List (right columns):

- Pier 69 1
- Serendipity Inn 6
- Sprat Hall Beach Restaurant 3
- The Terrace Restaurant 14
- Tivoli Gardens 18
- Top Hat 22
- Tutto Bene 22

Scale: 3 mi / 5.1 km

Caribbean Sea

155

prunes, red cabbage, sugar-brown Irish potatoes, and demiglace sauce; chilled cucumber soup; local dolphin simply sautéed with butter and lime; and an interesting version of Wiener schnitzel. This may be the only place around where you can order smoked eel and scrambled eggs, as well as frikadeller, those Scandinavian meatballs. The Top Hat platter comes with herring, roast beef, pâté, frikadeller, cheese, and fried fish.

MODERATE

Antoine's

58A King St. ☎ **809/773-0263.** Reservations required in winter. Main courses $13–$20. AE, MC, V. Daily 7:30am–2:30pm and 6:30–9:30pm. CARIBBEAN/INTERNATIONAL.

Set directly on King's Wharf, on the second floor of a building overlooking Christiansted's harbor and marina, this is an island institution. Many visitors come just for the bar, which mixes more than 35 different kinds of frozen drinks, and the island's largest selection of beer. In addition to the covered terrace, there's a satellite bar in back (the Aqua Lounge) decorated with a Windsurfer suspended from the ceiling, and a cubbyhole Italian restaurant (Pico Bello) serving lunch and dinner daily.

Regardless of where you decide to eat, a large selection of pastas and veal dishes is available, as well as Teutonic specialties like goulash, knockwurst salad, roulade of beef, and Wiener schnitzel. Local dishes such as fish chowder, lobster, and seafood specials are always on hand. In spite of its fame, dinners are only mediocre. Antoine's is more of a tradition for breakfast, when you can try one of the "creative" alpine omelets.

Blue Moon

17 Strand St. ☎ **809/772-2222.** Main courses $14–$18.50. AE, DISC, MC, V. Tues–Sun 11am–2pm and 6–10pm. Bar Tues–Sun 5pm–2am. Closed Aug to mid-Sept. INTERNATIONAL/CAJUN.

The best little bistro in Christiansted becomes a hot, hip spot on Thursday and Friday nights when it offers entertainment. A favorite of all visiting jazz musicians, the bistro is in a 200-year-old stone house on the waterfront. For 10 years, it's been going strong, building up a savvy local following. Visitors have recently discovered but not ruined it. It's decorated with funky, homemade American art and has a very casual, cafelike atmosphere. Begin with the "lunar pie," with feta cheese, cream cheese, onions, mushrooms, and celery in phyllo pastry, or the artichoke and spinach dip. This could be followed by the catch of the day, or else (on occasion) Maine lobster. Vegetarians opt for the spinach fettuccine, and there is the usual array of steak and chicken dishes. Save room for the yummy guava pie.

Bombay Club

5A King St. ☎ **809/773-1838.** Reservations recommended. Main courses, $10–$18. MC, V. Mon–Fri 11am–10pm, Sat–Sun 6–10pm. INTERNATIONAL.

Concealed from the street by the brick foundations of an 18th-century planter's town house, this Christiansted restaurant welcomes diners with some intriguing local art work. You enter through a low stone tunnel that leads to the bar and a courtyard with tables. The food, while simple, is plentiful, flavorful, and reasonably priced. Menu items include the catch of the day and regional dishes such as conch, veal, beef filet, and pasta. Pizza is also served.

Comanche Club

1 Strand St. ☎ **809/773-2665.** Reservations recommended. Main courses $8.95–$16.95. AE, MC, V. Daily 7–10:30am, 11:30am–2:30pm and 6–11pm. Closed June–Oct. WEST INDIAN/CONTINENTAL.

One of the most popular restaurants on the island, Comanche is relaxed yet elegant. It would be the ideal choice for the Graham Greene or Sydney Greenstreet of today. The specialties are eclectic—there's everything from fish and conch chowder to shark cakes. Each night, a different special is featured. There's also a good selection of Cruzan dishes, one for every night of the week. Salads and a cold buffet are traditionally featured; the Comanche curries have won over devotees. Island fish is generally sautéed with lemon butter and capers; typical West Indian dishes include conch Creole with fungi. You can also order standard international dishes such as filet mignon in a béarnaise sauce.

Tivoli Gardens

39 Strand St., upstairs in the Pan Am Pavilion. ☎ **809/773-6782.** Reservations recommended after 7pm. Main courses $14–$21. AE, MC, V. Mon–Fri 11:15am–2:30pm; daily 6–9:30pm. INTERNATIONAL.

This large second-floor porch festooned with lights affords the same view of Christiansted Harbor that a sea captain might have. The well-known local gathering place has white beams, trellises, and hanging plants that evoke its namesake, the pleasure gardens of Copenhagen. The menu lists everything from escargots Provençale to an Austro-Hungarian goulash. The Thai curry is excellent. For dessert, those in the know order a wicked, calorie-laden chocolate velvet cake. Often there is live music and dancing after 7pm.

Tutto Bene

2 Company St. ☎ **809/773-5229.** Reservations accepted only for parties of 6 or more. Main courses $12.95–$19.75. AE, V. Dinner only, daily 6–10pm. ITALIAN/SEAFOOD.

In the heart of town, Tutto Bene has more the allure of a bistro-cantina than of a full-fledged restaurant. The Connecticut-born owner, Tony Cerruto, believes in simple, hearty, and uncomplicated *paisano* dishes, the kind mama fed her sons long ago. At lunch you can enjoy bistro-style veggie frittatas, a chicken pesto sandwich, or spinach lasagna. If you don't feel like eating, there's a large mahogany bar in back that does a brisk business of its own. You'll dine on wooden tables covered with painted tablecloths, amid warm colors, and often lots of hubbub. Menu items are written on a pair of oversize mirrors against one wall. A full range of delectable pastas is offered nightly, along with carefully prepared seafood dishes. Fish might be served parmigiana or you can try something like seafood Genovese with mussels, clams, and shrimp in a white-wine/pesto sauce over linguine.

INEXPENSIVE

Annabelle's Tea Room

51–ABC Company St. ☎ **809/773-3990.** Reservations recommended. Sandwiches, salads, and platters $6.50–$12. No credit cards. Mon–Sat 9am–3pm. INTERNATIONAL.

This little nook occupies a quiet gingerbread courtyard filled with tropical plants, and surrounded with clapboard-sided buildings whose iron railings evoke New Orleans. Don't expect grand cuisine—what you get is a shady place to rest your feet; a warm welcome from Anna Deering or a member of her staff; a sense of Cruzan history; and a simple but refreshing assortment of sandwiches, salads, soups, and platters. Dolphin (the fish) in herb-flavored butter sauce, Cubano or "Lazy Virgin" sandwiches (no meat), and conch Creole are ongoing favorites.

Camille's Café

Queen Cross St. at 53B Company St. ☎ **809/773-2985.** Reservations not required. Main courses $10.95–$15.95; fixed-price dinner $15.95. MC, V. Mon–Sat 7:30am–3pm and 5–10pm. MEDITERRANEAN.

Across from Government House, Camille's, a wine bar, serves New York deli–type food during the day, along with a selection of Mediterranean dishes at dinner. It's one of the best dining values in town, especially for its fixed-price dinner, and the crowd is usually a mix of visitors and convivial locals. Starters include homemade soups and fresh salads, and main courses usually feature fresh fish, filet mignon, prime rib, lobster, and chicken.

Harvey's

11B Company St. ☎ **809/773-3433.** Main courses $7–$10. No credit cards. Mon–Wed 11:30am–6pm, Thurs–Sat 11:30am–9pm. CARIBBEAN/CONTINENTAL.

Forget the plastic and the flowery tablecloths that give this place the aura of a 1950s time warp, and try to grab one of its dozen or so tables. If you do, you can enjoy the thoroughly zesty cooking of island matriarch Sarah Harvey, who takes joy in her work and definitely aims to fill your stomach with her basic but hearty fare. Try one of her homemade soups, especially the callaloo or chicken. She'll even serve you conch in butter sauce as an appetizer. For a main dish you might choose from barbecue chicken, barbecue spareribs, boiled fillet of snapper, and even lobster when they can get it. Fungi comes with just about everything here. For dessert, try one of her delectable tarts made form guava, pineapple, or coconut.

Luncheria

Apothecary Hall Courtyard, 6 Company St. ☎ **809/773-4247.** Reservations not required. Main courses $5.25–$10.95. No credit cards. Mon–Fri 11am–9pm, Sat noon–9pm. MEXICAN.

In a historic courtyard in the center of town, this Mexican restaurant offers some of the best priced food on the island. You get the usual array of tacos, tostadas, burritos, nachos, and enchiladas. Specialties include chicken fajitas, enchiladas verde, and *arroz con pollo* (spiced chicken with brown rice). Daily specials feature both low-calorie and vegetarian choices, and the chef's refried beans are lard free. Whole wheat tortillas are offered. Check the board for specials, and indulge in the complimentary salsa bar.

Nolan's Tavern

5A Estate St. Peter, Christiansted East. ☎ **809/773-6660.** Reservations recommended only for groups of 6 or more. Burgers $7–$8.50; main courses $12.75–$16.25. AE, DC, MC, V. Kitchens open daily for dinner 5–9pm, bar at 3pm. INTERNATIONAL/WEST INDIAN.

Nolan's is the first place people in the know think of when you ask them for a warm, cozy, Antillean tavern with absolutely no social pretensions. It lies 2 miles east of Christiansted's harbor front, across from the capital's most visible elementary school, the Pearl B. Larsen School. Your host is Nolan Joseph, a Trinidad-born chef who makes a special point of welcoming guests and offering "tasty food and good service." No one will mind if you stop in just for a drink. Mr. Joseph, referred to by some diners as "King Conch," prepares the mollusk in at least half a dozen ways, including versions with curry, Creole sauce, and garlic-pineapple sauce. Reportedly, he experimented for 3 months to perfect a method of tenderizing the tough mollusk without artificial chemicals. His version of spareribs is equally delectable.

NORTH SHORE
EXPENSIVE

Cormorant Beach Club Restaurant

4126 La Grande Princesse. ☎ **809/778-8920.** Reservations recommended. Main courses $17.95–$22.95; lunch from $15. AE, DC, DISC, MC, V. Daily 11am–2pm and 6:30–9:30pm.

Although this place serves lunch, it is more romantic at night—the menu is more extensive and the service better too. Peruse the menu as you enjoy the sea breezes while dining near the beach. Although this restaurant no longer enjoys the prominence it once had, it is still a good choice. The menu isn't ambitious, but it still has a touch of the exotic, as exemplified by the curry dolphin topped with Cruzan coconut overlay. Tried-and-true favorites like blackened tuna steak or seafood linguine are also offered. Always ask about the specials of the day. Lunches feature sandwiches, vegetable stir-fries, ribs, and burgers.

✪ Dino's Bistro

In the Buccaneer, Gallows Bay. ☎ **809/773-2100.** Reservations recommended. Main courses $16–$30. AE, CB, DC, DISC, MC, V. Thurs–Mon 6–9:30pm. ITALIAN/MEDITERRANEAN.

In 1995, this successful Italian restaurant moved from independent premises to a location within St. Croix's most favored resort. Set close to the lobby, the restaurant offers views of the sea as well as of the lights of Christiansted. Chef Dino DiNatale is back, his fare zestier and better than ever. He serves the best and most flavorful Italian cuisine on the island, including hallmarks of modern Italian cookery. For example, you might begin with an array of antipasti delectably prepared from fresh ingredients. That old favorite of every Sicilian *paysano*, black linguine with squid, is given an original touch here. Mushroom fettuccine is another noteworthy choice, as is the local fish du jour prepared in several different ways; one of our favorites is with cilantro, tomato, and ginger. An innovative pasta is fettuccine Caribbean, with chicken, rum, black beans, ginger, cilantro, and both sweet and hot peppers.

✪ The Mahogany Room

Westin Carambola Beach Resort. ☎ **809/778-3800.** Reservations recommended. Main courses $24–$36. AE, DC, DISC, MC, V. Winter, Tues–Thurs and Sat 6–10pm. Off-season, Sat only 6–10pm. INTERNATIONAL.

An exclusive enclave in this previously recommended hotel, the setting here is elegant with wooden beams and stone walls inside. The restaurant seats 100 under a vaulted cathedral ceiling with mahogany and teak furniture. Tables lit by softly glowing lamps have a 180° view that includes the ocean. Ambience is important here, but it is the cuisine that continues to lure upscale patrons. Although chefs come and go at an alarming rate, the food remains consistently at a high level. The menu changes, but dishes like grilled wahoo with roasted pepper couscous, charcoal-grilled scallions, and a Hoisin sesame glaze appear often. For a touch of island flavor, their tuna is quickly seared and served with a papaya and mango chutney. Steaks are handled with care, and lamb and veal, although flown in frozen, still turn out tasty. Tangy appetizers include jumbo prawn cocktail with black bean salsa instead of the traditional cocktail sauce.

✪ The Terrace Restaurant

At the Buccaneer, Gallows Bay. ☎ **809/773-2100.** Reservations recommended. Main courses $10–$30. AE, DC, DISC, MC, V. Daily 6–9pm. INTERNATIONAL.

For years this was a humdrum hotel dining room with a predictable and not very noteworthy menu that virtually never changed. All that changed in the mid-1990s, however—the management poured time and energy into making a more creative and soothing open-air environment. Menu items vary with the availability of the ingredients, but are likely to include grilled local lobster cakes, a warm spinach salad, a selection of pasta dishes (bow ties with Caribbean lobster meat and broccoli is a favorite), fresh fish, grilled steaks, and a molasses-glazed plank roast fillet of salmon with a saffron-accented ginger-apple coulis. Lighter fare might feature a selection of pizzas, nachos, and cheeseburgers. There's also a full children's menu. Every Friday night Tommy Romano, a Trinidad-born bandleader, performs jazz, blues, and calypso from 8 to 11pm with four other musicians.

MODERATE

Serendipity Inn

Mill Harbour Condominiums, Mill Harbour. ☎ **809/773-5762.** Reservations recommended only for Fri night barbecue. Main courses $15–$21.50. AE, MC, V. Mon–Sat noon–2pm, Sun 10:30am–2:30pm; daily 6–9pm. Bar daily 11am–11pm. INTERNATIONAL.

This beach and poolside restaurant lies just west of Christiansted in the Mill Harbour Condominiums. Surrounded by iron gates and brick walls, the restaurant offers a spacious courtyard fronting the lagoon. At lunch you can enjoy light fare such as homemade soups, freshly made salads, and sandwiches. On Friday night a barbecue, including chicken and ribs, along with salad, costs only $12.50. For dinner, begin with calamari or crab cakes, then try the chef's fresh catch of the day, baked stuff shrimp, or perhaps steak au poivre.

IN & AROUND FREDERIKSTED
MODERATE

Le St. Tropez

Limetree Court, 67 King St. ☎ **809/772-3000.** Reservations recommended. Main courses $13.50–$22.50. AE, DISC, MC, V. Mon–Fri 11:30am–2:30pm and 6–10pm, Sat 6–10:30pm. FRENCH/MEDITERRANEAN.

At the most popular bistro in Frederiksted, you can dine on a covered terrace, presided over by Danielle and André Ducrot. Since it's small, it's always better to call ahead for a table. If you're visiting for the day, make this bright little cafe your luncheon stopover, and enjoy crepes, quiches, soups, or salads in the sunlit courtyard. At night the atmosphere glows with candlelight, and assumes more joie de vivre. Try the Mediterranean-inspired items, beginning perhaps with mushrooms aioli, escargots Provençal, or one of the freshly made soups. Main dishes are likely to include medallions of beef with two kinds of mushrooms, the fish of the day, or a magret of duck. Ingredients are always fresh and well prepared; if you're lucky, the daily special will be coq au vin.

INEXPENSIVE

Pier 69

69 King St. ☎ **809/772-0069.** Reservations not accepted. Sandwiches and platters $4.25–$17. AE, DC, DISC, MC, V. Mon–Thurs 10am–midnight, Fri–Sun 10am–4pm. AMERICAN/CARIBBEAN.

Although it will serve you a worthy but unfussy platter of food, this place is far more interesting for its resemblance to a funky bar in New York's Greenwich Village than for its reputation as a culinary citadel. New York–born Unise Tranberg is the earthmother/matriarch of the place, a warm and somewhat battered combination of a 1950s living room and a nautical bar sheathed in varnished tropical woods. Counterculture buffs from Christiansted make this their preferred hangout, sometimes opting for a mango colada or a lime lambada. If you're stepping off a boat and want something to eat, menu items include a predictable array of salads, sandwiches, and platters, ranging from American to Caribbean in their inspiration.

Sprat Hall Beach Restaurant

Rte. 63. ☎ **809/772-5855.** Reservations not required. Lunch $7–$15. No credit cards. Daily 9am–4pm (hot food 11:30am–2:30pm). CARIBBEAN.

One mile north of Frederiksted, this is an informal spot on the western coast of St. Croix near Sprat Hall Plantation. It's the best place on the island to combine lunch and a swim. The restaurant has been in business since 1948, feeding both locals and foreign visitors. Try such native dishes as conch chowder, pumpkin fritters, tannia soup, and the fried fish of the day. These dishes have authentic island flavor, perhaps more so than any other place on the island. If you'd like more standard fare, they also do salads and burgers. The bread is home baked daily. Cruzan-born Joyce Merwin Hurd and her husband, Jim, own Sprat Hall and charge $2 for use of the showers and changing rooms.

EAST END
MODERATE
Café Madeleine

Teague Bay. ☎ **809/778-7377.** Reservations recommended. Main courses $19–$33. AE, DC, MC, V. Wed–Sun 6–9:30pm. CONTINENTAL.

Located in the great house built by the Roncari family in 1990 in colonial style, Café Madeleine, 8 miles east of Christiansted, offers a mountaintop panorama of both the north and the south sides of the island. The lavish decor was created by a battalion of hardworking decorators. Diners have a choice of either indoor or terrace dining. Don't overlook a before-dinner drink at the mahogany-trimmed bar, where a scale model of a Maine schooner, bolted against mahogany paneling, creates a private club aura.

The eclectic menu might feature baked artichoke hearts, oysters Mario, fillet of red snapper Milanese, veal scaloppini alla Madeleine, and some of the most unusual pastas on island.

Duggan's Reef

East End Rd., Teague Bay. ☎ **809/773-9800.** Reservations required for dinner in winter. Main courses $14.50–$29; pastas $10–$24. AE, MC, V. Daily noon–3pm and 6–9:30pm. Bar, daily 11am–11:30pm. Closed for lunch in summer. CONTINENTAL/CARIBBEAN.

Set only 10 feet from the still waters of Reef Beach, and open to the sea breezes, Duggan's Reef is an ideal perch for watching the Windsurfers and Hobie Cats careening through nearby waters. The restaurant, owned for more than a decade by Boston-born Frank Duggan, is the most popular on St. Croix—all visitors seemingly dine here at least once during their stay on the island. At lunch, a simple array of salads, crepes, and sandwiches is offered. At night a more elaborate menu contains the popular house specialties: Duggan's Caribbean lobster pasta and Irish whiskey lobster. Begin with fried calamari or a conch chowder before sampling a pasta dish such as seafood Diavolo. The catch of the day is always fresh and can be baked, grilled, or blackened Cajun style; you can also order it island style (with tomato, pepper, and onion sauce). Other main dishes include New York strip steak or veal piccata. The cuisine remains consistently reliable.

The Galleon

East End Rd., Green Cay Marina, 50 Estate Southgate. ☎ **809/773-9949.** Reservations recommended. Main courses $15.50–$36. AE, MC, V. Daily 6–10pm. Proceed east on Rte. 82 from Christiansted for 5 minutes; after going 1 mile past the Buccaneer, turn left into Green Cay Marina. FRENCH/NORTHERN ITALIAN.

Overlooking the ocean, the Galleon is a local favorite, and deservedly so. Some of the best cooking in Europe is found in northern Italy and France, and that's what's offered here. Freshly baked bread, two fresh vegetables, and rice or potatoes accompany main dishes. The menu always includes at least one local fish, such as wahoo, tuna, swordfish, or dolphin, even fresh Caribbean lobster. You might order a perfectly done rack of lamb carved at your table or their osso buco that's straight from Milan. They have a nice wine list (including wines sold by the glass), and music from a baby grand accompanies dinner.

5 Beaches, Water Sports & Other Outdoor Pursuits

BEACHES

Beaches are the big attraction in St. Croix, but getting to them from Christiansted, where most hotels are, isn't always easy. It can also be expensive, especially if you want to go back and forth every day.

Hotel on the Cay   If you're staying in Christiansted, you can take the ferry to this great sandy beach on the hotel property, which occupies its own tiny island in the middle of the harbor. There's a bar, restaurant facilities, and lots of windsurfers.

Cramer Park   Located at the northeast end of the island, this public park is operated by the U.S. Department of Agriculture. Lined with sea grape trees, the beach has a picnic area, a restaurant, and a bar

✪ **Cane Bay** and **Davis Bay**—These are the kind of beaches you'd expect to find on a typical Caribbean Island (with palms, white sand, good swimming, and snorkeling). Cane Bay, which adjoins Route 80 on the north shore, attracts snorkelers and divers with its rolling waves, coral gardens, and drop-off wall. Davis Bay, which doesn't have any reefs to block the ocean swells, draws bodysurfers and has an alluring white sand beach. Changing facilities aren't available. It's located off the South Shore Road (Route 60), near the Carambola Beach Resort.

Reef Beach   Opening onto Teague Bay along Route 82, this beach, popular with windsurfers, is a half-hour ride from Christiansted. Food can be ordered at Duggan's Reef.

Rainbow Beach   On Route 63, a short ride north of Frederiksted, this beach lures people with its white sand and ideal snorkeling conditions. In the same vicinity, also on Route 63, about 5 minutes north of Frederiksted, La Grange is another good beach. Lounge chairs can be rented, and there's a bar nearby.

Cormorant Beach Club   About 5 miles west of Christiansted, some 1,200 feet of white sands are shaded by palm trees at this well-known resort (see "Accommodations," above). Since a living reef lies just off the shore, snorkeling conditions are ideal here.

Grapetree Beach   This stretch of white sand is located on the eastern tip of the island (Route 60). Follow the South Shore Road to reach it. Water sports are popular here.

✪ **Sandy Point**   Lying directly south of Frederiksted, this is the largest beach in the U.S. Virgin Islands. Its waters are shallow and calm, perfect for swimming. Sandy Point juts out from southwestern St. Croix like a small peninsula, and it's reached by taking the Melvin Evans Highway (Route 66) west from the Alexander Hamilton Airport.

SPORTS & OTHER OUTDOOR PURSUITS
FISHING

The fishing grounds at Lang Bank are about 10 miles from St. Croix. Here you'll find kingfish, dolphin fish, and wahoo. Using light-tackle boats gliding along the reef, you'll probably turn up jack or bonefish. At Clover Crest, in Frederiksted, Cruzan anglers fish right from the rocks.

Serious sportfishers can board the *Shenanigan's,* a 42-foot Ocean Super Sport convertible, available for 4-, 6-, or 8-hour charters with bait and tackle included. It's anchored at St. Croix Marina, Gallows Bay. Reservations can be made during the day by calling 809/773-7165, or 809/773-0917 at night.

GOLF

St. Croix has the best golf in the U.S. Virgins. In fact, guests staying on St. John and St. Thomas often fly over for a day's round. On the island are two 18-hole golf courses. ✪ **Carambola Golf Course** (☎ 809/778-0747), on the northeast side of St. Croix, was designed by Robert Trent Jones Sr., who called it "the loveliest course I ever designed." The course, formerly Fountain Valley, looks like a botanical garden with its bamboo, saman trees, and palms. Its collection of par-3 holes is known to golfing authorities as the best in the tropics. The course record at Carambola, site of "Shell's Wonderful World of Golf," is 65, set by Jim Levine in 1993. Greens fees are $77 per person for a day in winter ($47.50 in summer), which allows you to play as many holes as you like. Golf cart rentals are mandatory and cost $12.50 per 18 holes.

The other major course is at **The Buccaneer** (☎ 809/773-2100, ext. 738), 2 miles east of Christiansted (see "Accommodations," above). The Buccaneer is a challenging 6,200-yard, 18-hole course that allows players to knock the ball over rolling hills right to the edge of the Caribbean. The vistas are truly spectacular. Non-guests pay $40 greens fees, and carts rent for $14. A golf pro is available for lessons, and there's a pro shop. Three new holes have recently been added as a practice area.

The Reef, at Teague Bay (☎ 809/773-8844), is a 3,100-yard, 9-hole course, charging greens fees of $10 to $14, with carts renting for $5 to $8. On the east end of the island, its longest hole is a 579-yard par 5.

HIKING

Unlike the rest of St. Croix, a verdant portion of the island's western district is covered with dense forest—very different landscape than the scrub-covered hills covering other parts of the island. The area, although not an actual tropical rain forest is known as the "Rain Forest," and has a large network of footpaths that offers some of the best nature walks in the Caribbean. For more details on where to hike in this district see "Exploring the 'Rain Forest'" later in this chapter. Buck Island, just off St. Croix, offers some wonderful nature trails. For more details, see "An Excursion to Buck Island," at the end of this chapter.

St. Croix Environmental Association, 6 Company St. (☎ 809/773-1989), in Christiansted, offers regularly scheduled hikes from December through March. This is the most visible environmental group on St. Croix. They coordinate movements to restrict development in environmentally or culturally sensitive areas, test waters for sources of pollution, help reforest the land, and have ongoing in-school and public education programs. In addition to in-season hikes, their programs include lectures, slide shows, and films on environmental issues. Prices for events vary, and contributions are accepted.

HORSEBACK RIDING

Specializing in nature tours, **Paul and Jill's Equestrian Stables,** Sprat Hall Plantation, Route 58 (☎ 809/772-2880), are the only equestrian facilities in the Virgin Islands. Set on the sprawling grounds of the island's oldest plantation, Great House, it's operated by Paul Wojcie and his wife, Jill Hurd, a daughter of the establishment's original founders. The stables are known throughout the Caribbean for the quality of their horses. The scenic trail rides through the forests, past ruins of abandoned 18th-century plantations and sugar mills, to the tops of the hills of St. Croix's western end. All tours are accompanied by the operators, who give running commentaries on island fauna, history, and riding techniques. Beginners and experienced riders alike are welcome.

A 2-hour trail ride costs $50 per person. Tours usually depart daily in winter at 10am and 4pm and off-season at 5pm, with slight variations according to demand. Reservations at least a day in advance are important.

SNORKELING & SCUBA DIVING

Sponge life, black-coral trees (the finest in the West Indies), and steep drop-offs into water near the shoreline have made St. Croix a snorkeling and diving paradise.

Buck Island, with an underwater visibility of more than 100 feet, is the site of the nature trail of the underwater national monument, and it's the major diving target (see "An Excursion to Buck Island," at the end of this chapter). All the minor and major agencies offer scuba and snorkeling tours to Buck Island.

St. Croix is home to the largest living reef in the Caribbean, including the fabled north-shore wall that begins in 25 to 30 feet of water and drops to 13,200 feet, sometimes straight down. There are 22 moored sites, allowing the dive boats to tie up without damaging the reef. Favorite scuba-diving sites include the historic Salt River Canyon, the gorgeous coral gardens of Scotch Banks, and Eagle Ray, the latter so named because of the rays that cruise along the wall there. Pavilions is yet another good dive site, with a virgin coral reef that's in pristine shape.

Dive St. Croix, 59 King's Wharf (☎ **800/523-DIVE** in the U.S., or 809/773-3434), operates the 38-foot dive boat *Reliance.* The staff offers complete instructions from resort courses through full certification, as well as night dives. A resort course is $75, with a two-tank dive going for $70. Scuba trips to Buck Island are offered for $65, and dive packages begin at $190 for six dives.

V.I. Divers Ltd., in the Pam Am Pavilion on Christiansted's waterfront (☎ **800/544-5911** or 809/773-6045), is the oldest (1971) and one of the best dive operations on the island. In fact, *Rudales Scuba Diving* magazine rated its staff as among the top 10 worldwide. A full-service PADI five-star facility, it offers daily two-tank boat dives, guided snorkeling trips to Green Cay, night dives, and a full range of scuba-training programs from introductory dives through dive master. Introductory dives, which require no experience, are $95 for a two-tank dive, including all instruction and equipment. The outfitter offers a six-dive package for $195 and a 10-dive package for $295. A two-tank or beach dive is priced at $75, with night dives going for $55. A 2-hour guided snorkel tour costs $25, or else $35 for the boat snorkeling trip to Green Cay.

TENNIS

Some authorities rate the tennis at **The Buccaneer** (☎ **809/773-2100,** ext. 736) as the best in the West Indies. The eight courts, two of which are lit for night games, are open to the public. Nonguests pay $8 per person per hour. You must call one day in advance to reserve a court. A tennis pro is available for lessons, and there is a pro shop on the premises.

A notable selection of recently restored courts is also found at the **Carambola Golf Club** (☎ **809/778-0747**), which has five clay courts open to the public. The charge is $25 per hour for nonguests. Courts are no longer lit for night games. Both a pro shop and a teaching pro are available.

WINDSURFING

The best place for this increasingly popular sport is the **St. Croix Water Sports Center** (☎ **809/773-7060**), located on a small offshore island in Christiansted Harbor and part of the Hotel on the Cay. They give lessons and are open daily from 9am to 5pm in winter or 10am to 5pm in off-season. Windsurfing rentals are $25 per hour. They also offer Sea Doos renting for $50 per half-hour double, plus parasailing at $50 per person, and even snorkeling equipment at $12 per day.

6 Touring the Island: From Historic Towns to the "Rain Forest"

WALKING TOUR
Christiansted

Start: Visitors' Bureau.
Finish: Christiansted harbor front.
Time: 1 1/2 hours.
Best Times: Any day 10am to 4pm.
Worst Times: Monday through Friday 4 to 6pm.

Begin your tour at:

1. **The Visitors' Bureau,** a yellow-sided building with a cedar-capped roof near the harbor front. It was originally built as the Old Scalehouse in 1856 to replace a similar, older structure which burned down. In its heyday, all taxable goods leaving and entering Christiansted's harbor were weighed here. The scales that once stood could accurately weigh barrels of sugar and molasses up to 1,600 pounds each.

   In front of the scalehouse lies one of the most charming squares in the Caribbean. Its old-fashioned asymmetrical allure is still evident despite the masses of cars.

   With your back to the scalehouse, turn left and walk through the parking lot to the foot of the white-sided gazebo-inspired band shell that sits in the center of a park named after Alexander Hamilton. The yellow-brick building with the ornately carved brick staircase is the:

2. **Old Customs House** (currently the headquarters of the National Park Service). The gracefully proportioned 16-step staircase was added in 1829 as an embellishment to an older building. (There are public toilets on the ground floor.)

   Continue climbing the hill to the base of the yellow-painted structure which is:

3. **Fort Christiansvaern.** The best-preserved colonial fortification in the Virgin Islands, the fort is maintained as a historic monument by the National Park Service. Its original four-sided, star-shaped design was in accordance with the most advanced military planning of its era. The fort is the site of the St. Croix Police Museum, which traces police work on the island from the late 1800s to the present. Photos, weapons, and artifacts create the police force's past.

   Exit from the fort, and head straight down the tree-lined path toward the most visible steeple in Christiansted. It caps the appropriately named:

4. **Steeple Building** (Church of Lord God of Sabaoth), completed in 1753 as St. Croix's first Lutheran church, and embellished with a steeple in 1794–96. The building was deconsecrated in 1831, and served at various times as a bakery, a hospital, and a school. The building contains a museum devoted to local history.

   Across Company Street from the Steeple Building is a U.S. post office. The building that contains it was built in 1749 as:

5. **The West Indies and Guinea Warehouse.** The structure was once three times larger than it is today and included storerooms and lodgings for staff. Go to the building's side entrance, on Church Street, and enter the rear courtyard if the iron gate is open. For many years, this was the site of some of the largest slave auctions in the Caribbean.

Walking Tour—Christiansted

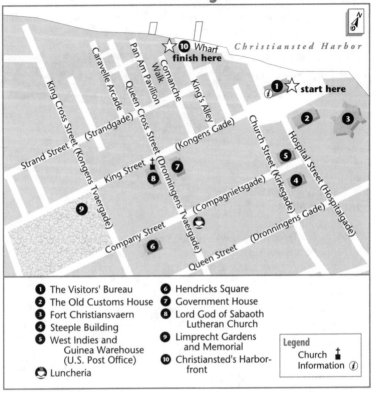

Christiansted Harbor

🏳 **⑩ Wharf finish here**

ⓘ **① 🏳 start here**

②

③

④

⑤

⑥

⑦

⑧

⑨

Caravelle Arcade
Pan Am Pavilion
Comanche Walk
Queen Cross Street
King's Alley
King Cross Street
Strand Street (Kongens Tvaergade)
(Strandgade)
(Kongens Gade)
King Street
(Dronningens Tvaergade)
Church Street (Kirkegade)
Hospital Street (Hospitalgade)
(Compagnietsgade)
Company Street
Queen Street (Dronningens Gade)

① The Visitors' Bureau
② The Old Customs House
③ Fort Christiansvaern
④ Steeple Building
⑤ West Indies and Guinea Warehouse (U.S. Post Office)
☕ Luncheria
⑥ Hendricks Square
⑦ Government House
⑧ Lord God of Sabaoth Lutheran Church
⑨ Limprecht Gardens and Memorial
⑩ Christiansted's Harbor-front

Legend
Church ✝
Information ⓘ

From the post office, retrace your steps to Company Street and head west for one block. On your left, you'll pass the entrance to Apothecary Hall, 2111 Company St., which contains a charming collection of shops and restaurants.

☕ **TAKE A BREAK**   If you need refreshment, try **Luncheria,** Apothecary Hall Courtyard, 6 Company St. (☎ **809/773-4247**). Housed in an extension of an 18th-century building, the bar's tables are grouped in a courtyard shaded by trees. The owners are the margarita specialists of the island, stocking more types of tequila (15-plus) than any other bar in the neighborhood. Specializing in Mexican fare, Luncheria serves burritos, tostadas, enchiladas, and tacos, as well as daily specials and vegetarian meals. See separate recommendation under "Dining."

Exit Apothecary Hall and turn left onto Company Street. Cross Queen Cross Street (Dronningens Tvergade). Half a block later, you'll arrive at the island's largest outdoor market:

6. Hendricks Square (Christian "Shan" Square), which was rebuilt in a timbered, 9th-century style after the 1989 hurricane. Fruits and vegetables are sold here Monday through Saturday from 7am to 6pm.

Retrace your steps half a block along Company Street, and turn left onto Queen Cross Street. Head downhill toward the harbor, walking on the right-hand side of the street. Within half a block, you'll reach an unmarked arched iron gateway, set beneath an arcade. If it's open, enter the charming gardens of:

7. Government House. Evocative of Europe, the garden contain a scattering of very old trees, flower beds, and walkways. The antique building that surrounds the gardens was formed from the union of two much older town houses in the 1830s.

Exit the same way you entered, turn right, and continue your descent of Queen Cross Street. At the first street corner (King Street), turn left, and admire the neoclassical facade of the:

8. Lord God of Sabaoth Lutheran Church, established in 1734. Continue walking southwest along King Street. Within two blocks is the:

9. Limprecht Gardens and Memorial. For 20 years (1888–1908) Peter Carl Limprecht served as governor of the Danish West Indies. Today, an occasional chicken pecks at seedlings planted near a Danish-language memorial to him.

At the end of the park, retrace your steps to Queen Cross Street, and go left. One very short block later, turn right onto Strand Street, which contains some interesting stores, including at least two different shopping arcades. The streets will narrow, and the pedestrian traffic will be more congested. Pass beneath the overpass belonging to a popular bar and restaurant, the Comanche Club (see "Dining," above).

Continue down the meandering curves of King's Alley and within one block you'll be standing beside:

10. Christiansted's harbor front, where you can end your tour by strolling on the boardwalk of the waterside piers.

OTHER SIGHTS IN CHRISTIANSTED

St. Croix Aquarium, Caravelle Arcade (☎ 809/773-8995), has expanded with many new exhibits, including "night creatures." In all it houses some 40 species of marine animals and more than 100 species of invertebrates. With constant rotation, each creature can adjust easily back to its natural habitat, as hundreds pass through the tanks each year. A touch pond contains starfish, sea cucumbers, brittle stars, and pencil urchins. The aquarium allows you to become familiar with marine life before you see it while scuba diving or snorkeling. It's open Tuesday through Saturday from 11am to 4pm, charging adults $4.50 and children $2.

Christiansted Apothecary Museum Exhibit, Queen Cross Street (☎ 809/772-0598), is located in a building dating from 1827. The Apothecary is fully stocked with all the medicine, supplies, and equipment needed to stock a pharmacy found on a small West Indian island in the late 19th century. It's open Monday through Saturday from 10am to 4pm, charging no admission.

FREDERIKSTED

This old Danish town at the western end of the island, about 17 miles from Christiansted, is a sleepy port that only comes to life when a cruise ship docks at its shoreline. In 1994, a 1,500-foot pier opened to accommodate the largest grade of cruise ship; the old pier had suffered damage from Hurricane Hugo in 1989. The pier facility is designed for two large cruise vessels and two minicruise vessels that run simultaneously.

The town is not new to natural disasters. Frederiksted was destroyed by a fire in 1879, and the citizens rebuilt it, using wood frames and clapboards on top of the old Danish stone and yellow-brick foundations.

Most visitors begin their tour at russet-colored Fort Frederik, next to the pier. Some historians claim that this was the first fort to sound a foreign salute to the U.S. flag, in 1776. It was here on July 3, 1848, that Governor-General Peter von Scholten emancipated the slaves in the Danish West Indies. The fort, at the northern end of

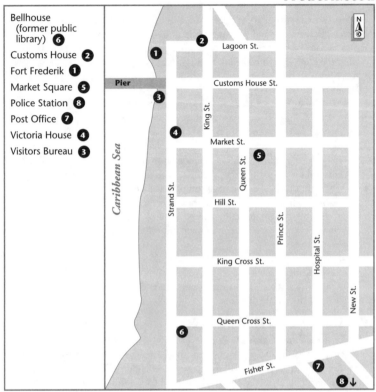

Bellhouse
  (former public
  library) **6**

Customs House **2**

Fort Frederik **1**

Market Square **5**

Police Station **8**

Post Office **7**

Victoria House **4**

Visitors Bureau **3**

Frederiksted, has been restored to the way it looked in 1840. You can explore the courtyard and stables, and an exhibit area has been installed in what was once the Garrison Room.

Just south of the fort, the Customs House is an 18th-century building with a 19th-century two-story gallery. Here you can go into the visitor's bureau and pick up a free map of the town.

Nearby, privately owned Victoria House, Market Street, is a gingerbread-trimmed structure built after the fire of 1879. Some of the original 1803 structure was preserved when it was rebuilt.

Along the waterfront Strand Street is the Bellhouse, once the Frederiksted Public Library. One of its owners, G. A. Bell, ornamented the steps with bells. The house today is an arts-and-crafts center and a nursery. Sometimes a local theater group presents dramas here.

Other buildings of interest include the Danish School, Prince Street, which was adapted in the 1830s into a building designed by Hingelberg, a well-known Danish architect. Today it's the police station and welfare department.

Two churches are of interest. St. Paul's Anglican Church, 28 Prince St., was founded outside the port in the late 18th century; the present building dates from 1812. St. Patrick's Catholic Church, 5 Prince St., was built in the 1840s.

OTHER ISLAND ATTRACTIONS

North of Frederiksted, you can drop in at Sprat Hall, the island's oldest plantation, or else continue to the rain forest, which covers about 15 acres, including the

150-foot-high Creque Dam. Mahogany trees and yellow cedar grow in profusion, as do wild lilies. The terrain is privately owned, but the owner lets visitors go inside to explore.

Most people want to see the jagged estuary of the northern coastline's Salt River, but other than bird life, there isn't much to see. This is where Columbus landed for a brief moment before being driven off by Caribs. A modest marker indicates the area, which is now a national park. In the area are burial grounds, extensive mangroves, an old earthworks fort, and Native American ceremonial ball court.

The St. Croix Environmental Association conducts tours of the area; call 809/773-1989 for details. Tours cost $15 for adults, $12 for children under 12.

Below are some other noteworthy attractions around St. Croix:

St. George Village Botanical Garden of St. Croix

127 Estate St., Kingshill. ☎ **809/692-2874.** Admission $5 adults, $1 children 12 and under; donations welcome. Nov–Apr, daily 9am–5pm; May–Oct, Tues–Sat 9am–4pm.

Just north of Centerline Road, 4 miles east of Frederiksted at Estate St. George, is a veritable 16-acre Eden of tropical trees, shrubs, vines, and flowers. Built around the ruins of a 19th-century sugarcane workers' village, the garden is a feast for the eye and the camera—from the entrance drive bordered by royal palms and bougainvillea to the towering kapok and tamarind trees. There's a gift shop and restrooms. Self-guided walking-tour maps are available at the entrance to the garden's Great Hall.

Cruzan Rum Factory

W. Airport Rd., Rte. 64. ☎ **809/692-2280.** Admission $3. Tours given Mon–Fri 9–11:30am and 1–4:15pm.

This factory distills the famous Virgin Islands rum, which is considered by residents to be the finest in the world. Guided tours depart from the visitors' pavilion; call for reservations and information. There's also a gift shop.

Estate Whim Plantation Museum

Centerline Rd. ☎ **809/772-0598.** Admission $5 adults, $1 children. Mon–Sat 10am–4pm.

About 2 miles east of Frederiksted, this museum was restored by the St. Croix Landmarks Society and is unique among the many sugar plantations whose ruins dot the island of St. Croix. This Great House is different from most in that it's composed of only three rooms. With 3-foot-thick walls made of stone, coral, and molasses, the house is said by some to resemble a luxurious European château.

A division of Baker Furniture Company used the Whim Plantation's collection of models for one of its most successful reproductions, the "Whim Museum—West Indies Collection." A showroom in the museum sells these reproductions, plus others from the Caribbean, including pineapple-motif four-poster beds, cane-bottomed planters' chairs with built-in leg rests, and Caribbean adaptations of Empire-era chairs with cane-bottomed seats.

Also on the museum's premises are a woodworking shop (that features tools and techniques from the 18th century), the estate's original kitchen, a museum store, and a servant's quarters. The ruins of the plantation's sugar-processing plant, complete with a restored windmill, remain.

ESPECIALLY FOR KIDS

Fort Christiansvaern (*see p. 165*)   Children are taken through dungeons and around battlements, and even shown how soldiers of yesteryear fired a cannon.

St. George Village Botanical Garden of St. Croix (*see p. 169*)   Kids wander this sunny spot built around the ruins of a sugarcane workers' village from the 1800s.

Buck Island *(see p. 179)* The boat ride to Buck Island's 850 mostly underwater acres is a great amusement for kids. Equally appealing are the island's white sandy beaches and its profuse wildlife; bring along a picnic.

ORGANIZED TOURS

Many visitors like to explore St. Croix on a **taxi tour** (☎ 809/778-1088), which for a party of two costs $30 for 2 hours or $40 for 3 hours. The fare should be negotiated in advance. Extra fees are charged for the following sights: $5 for the botanical gardens, $5 for the Whim Estate House, and $3 for the rum distillery.

Check with your hotel desk to see if you can go on an organized tour. The tours operate according to demand, with fewer departures in summer than in winter. A typical 4-hour tour costs $25 per person, and many are conducted at least three times a week during the winter. Tours usually go through Christiansted and visit the botanical gardens, Whim Estate House, the rum distillery, the rain forest, the St. Croix Leap mahogany workshop, and the site of the ill-fated Columbus landing at Salt River. Call **Travellers' Tours,** Alexander Hamilton Airport (☎ 809/778-1636), for more information.

If you're an independent traveler, consider taking our walking tour above or the driving tour below. However, if you'd like guidance, you can take a walking tour of both Christiansted and Frederiksted with **Take-a-Hike** (☎ 809/778-6997), which gives guided 1-hour walks of both towns. Tours leave Monday and Thursday at 10am from the Visitors' Bureau in Christiansted. The Christiansted tour costs $8, the Frederiksted tour is $7. Children are half-price.

DRIVING TOUR
East St. Croix

Start: The Buccaneer.
Finish: Fort Christiansvaern.
Time: 1½ hours.
Best Times: Early morning or late afternoon.
Worst Times: Any evening after 5pm.

Head east from Christiansted on Route 75. (Sometimes referred to as East End Road.) Within a few miles, it will become Route 82. If you get confused at any time during this tour, remember the ocean should always be on your left.

Landmarks you'll pass on your way out of town will include Gallows Point and:
1. **The Buccaneer,** a hotel where you might want to return for one of the nightly musical performances that are among the island's best (see "Accommodations," above).

Suddenly, the landscape will open onto verdant countryside. Cows graze peacefully on a rolling landscape that may remind you of the Scottish lowlands. Accompanying the cows are tickbirds, which feed on ticks buried in the cows' skin. An occasional traffic minijam might form as herds of goats cross the road.

Continue driving and you'll pass:
2. **Green Cay Marina,** identified by a road sign; you might want to visit the marina to admire the yachts bobbing at anchor or perhaps to have a swim at Chenay Bay. Nearby monuments include the Southgate Baptist Church and a handful of stone towers that once housed the gear mechanisms of windmills that crushed the juice from sugarcane.

Driving Tour—East St. Croix

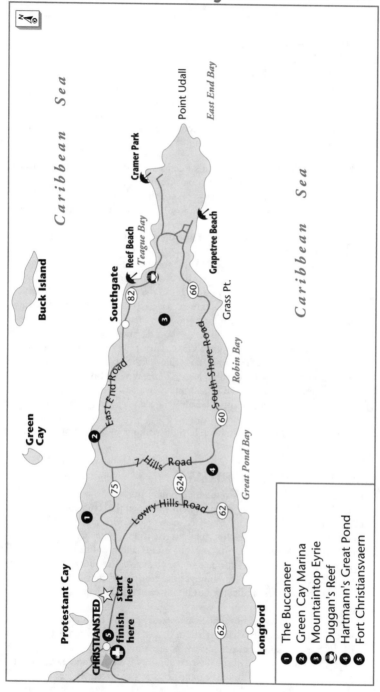

Caribbean Sea

Point Udall

East End Bay

Cramer Park

Caribbean Sea

Reef Beach
Teague Bay

Buck Island

Southgate

Grapetree Beach

Grass Pt.

82

60

3

Green
Cay

East End Road

60

South Shore Road

Robin Bay

2

7 Hills Road

Great Pond Bay

624

4

75

Lowry Hills Road

62

Protestant Cay

1

62

CHRISTIANSTED

start
here

5

finish
here

Longford

- 1 The Buccaneer
- 2 Green Cay Marina
- 3 Mountaintop Eyrie
- 4 Duggan's Reef
- 5 Hartmann's Great Pond
- 6 Fort Christiansvaern

As the vistas unfold, you'll pass by scatterings of bougainvillea-covered private villas.

About 7 miles along the route from Christiansted, you'll see the:

3. **Mountaintop Eyrie** of the island's most prominent socialite, the Contessa Nadia Farbo Navarro, the Romanian-born heiress to a great fortune. This opulent castle is the most outrageously unusual, most prominent, and most talked-about villa on St. Croix. Understandably, its privacy is rigidly maintained.

A couple of miles farther along East End Road, you'll reach one of the most popular windsurfing beaches in St. Croix, Teague Bay. This is a good spot to take a break.

🥄 **TAKE A BREAK   Duggan's Reef,** East End Road, Teague Bay (☎ **809/773-9800**), offers flavorful lunches, more formal dinners, fruit daiquiris, and a bar only 10 feet from the waves. Many guests claim this is the best way to experience windsurfing without getting on a sailboard. See "Dining," above, for details.

After your stop, continue driving east along Route 82 to the area that most residents consider the most peaceful and dramatic on the island. It is especially memorable at sunset, when the vistas are highlighted and the sun is against your back.

At Knight Bay, near the eastern tip of the island, turn right onto Route 60 (South Shore Road), and head west. One of the several lakes you'll pass is:

4. **Hartmann's Great Pond** (also known as Great Pond), a favorite of nesting seabirds. The sea vistas and the rolling grasslands are panoramic.

Route 60 merges with Route 624 a short distance north of Great Pond. Fork left onto Route 624, and, a short distance later, right onto Route 62 (Lowry Hill Road). You will travel the mountainous spine of the island through districts named after former farms, such as Sally's Fancy, Marienhøj, and Boetzberg.

Within 2 miles, Lowry Hill Road merges with Route 82 again. Fork left, and follow it as it turns into Hospital Gade and leads to the center of Christiansted.

To your right will appear:

5. **Fort Christiansvaern,** as you pull into the parking lot in front of Christiansted's tourist office (Old Scalehouse).

EXPLORING THE "RAIN FOREST"

Unlike the rest of St. Croix, a verdant portion of the island's western district is covered with dense forest—very different landscape than the scrub-covered hills covering other parts of the island. The area grows thick with mahogany trees, kapok (silk-cotton) trees, turpentine (red-birch) trees, samaan (rain) trees, and all kinds of ferns and vines. Sweet limes, mangoes, hog plums, and breadfruit trees, all of which have grown in the wild since the days of the plantations, are interspersed among the forest's larger trees. Crested hummingbirds, pearly eyed thrashers, green-throated caribs, yellow warblers, and perky but drably camouflaged banana quits nest in the trees.

Although the district is not actually a tropical rain forest, it's known as the "Rain Forest." To experience the charm of the area, some visitors opt to drive along Route 76 (which is also known as Mahogany Road), stopping beside the footpaths that meander off on either side of the highway into dry river beds and glens. (It's advisable to stick to the best-worn of the footpaths and to retrace your steps.)

You can also hike along the highways on the island's western sector, where few cars ever venture. Three of the most viable for hiking are the Creque Dam Road (routes 58/78), the Scenic Road (route 78), and the Western Scenic Road (routes 63/78).

Close Encounters of the Wildlife Kind

One of the most rarely visited parts of St. Croix, the island's southwestern tip is composed of salt marshes, tidal pools, and low vegetation inhabited by birds, turtles, and other forms of wildlife. More than 3 miles of ecologically protected coastline lie between Sandy Point (the island's most westerly tip) and the shallow waters of the Westend Saltpond.

Home to colonies of green and hawksbill turtles, the site is also a resting ground for leatherback turtles. It is one of only two such places in U.S. waters. The site is also home to thousands of birds, including herons, brown pelicans, Caribbean martins, black-necked stilts, and white-crowned pigeons. Sandy Point gave its name to a rare form of orchids, a brown and/or purple variety.

Part of the continued viability of the site as a wildlife refuge depends on its inaccessibility, except on Saturday and Sunday from 6am to 6pm. The site is most easily reached by driving to the end of Route 66 (Melvin Evans highway) and continuing down a gravel road. Earthwatch, a nonprofit organization staffed mostly by volunteers working cooperatively with advisors from universities around the world, maintains a monitoring program here. For inquiries about guided weekend visits to the site, call the St. Croix Environmental Association at 809/773-1989.

Consider beginning your trek near the junction of Creque Dam Road and Scenic Road. (Although cars can enter here, they rarely do.) Beginning at this junction, your trek will cover a broad triangular swath, heading north and then west along Scenic Road. First, the road will rise, and then it will descend toward the coastal lighthouse of the island's extreme northwestern tip, Hamm's Bluff. Most trekkers decide to retrace their steps after about 45 minutes of northwesterly hiking. Real diehards, however, will continue trekking all the way to the coastline, then head south along the coastal road (Butler Bay Road), and finally head east along Creque Dam Road to their starting point at the junction of Creque Dam Road and Scenic Road. Embark on this longer expedition only if you're really prepared for a prolonged hike lasting about 5 hours.

7 Shopping

Christiansted is the shopping hub of St. Croix, and the emphasis here is on hole-in-the-wall boutiques selling handmade goods.

All the shops are easily compressed into $^1/_2$ mile or so. On a day's tour (or half-day tours), you'll be able to inspect most of the stores. Following the hurricanes of 1995, a major redevelopment of the waterfront at Christiansted was launched. **King's Alley Complex** (☎ **809/778-8135**) opened as a pink-sided compound, packed with shops—it's worth a stop, even just for window shopping.

Of course, the same duty-free stipulations that apply in St. Thomas (see "Visitor Information, Entry Requirements & Money," in chapter 3) apply to shopping here.

SHOPPING A TO Z
ANTIQUES

Estate Mount Washington Antiques
2 Estate Mount Washington. ☎ **809/772-1026.**

If you can arrive on Sunday when Tony and Nancy Ayer are on site, this is a remarkable discovery: the best treasure trove of colonial West Indian furniture and "flotsam" in the Virgin Islands. After browsing through their shop and hopefully making a purchase, you can walk around the grounds of an 18th-century sugar plantation under restoration.

ARTS & CRAFTS

Folk Art Traders
1B Queen Cross St. ☎ **809/773-1900.**

Since 1985, the operators of this store have traveled throughout the Caribbean ("in the bush") to acquire a unique collection of local art and folk-art treasures—not only carnival masks, pottery, ceramics, and original paintings, but also hand-wrought jewelry. The assortment includes batiks from Barbados and high-quality iron sculpture from Haiti. There's nothing else like it in the Virgin Islands.

FASHIONS

Caribbean Clothing Co.
41 Queen Cross St. ☎ **809/773-5012.**

Hip sports clothing by top-name U.S. designers in all the latest styles is sold at this outlet. They carry Calvin Klein, Guess, Polo, and Dockers, among others. You get not only casual wear but some evening clothes for women, even jeans. They also sell a small stock of shoes for both men and women, along with a good selection of jewelry, belts, scarves, and purses.

Gone Tropical
55 Company St. ☎ **809/773-4696.**

About 60% of the merchandise in this unique shop is made in Indonesia (usually Bali). Prices of new, semiantique, or antique sofas, beds, chests, tables, mirrors, and decorative carvings are the same as (and sometimes less than) equivalent furniture you might have bought new at more conventional furniture stores. The store also sells worthy art objects and furniture (which can be shipped to wherever you want it) ranging in price from $5 to $5,000. Gone tropical also sells jewelry, batiks, candles, and baskets.

Java Wraps
In the Pan Am Pavilion, Strand St. ☎ **809/773-3770.**

Known for resort wear for women, men, and children, this shop is a kaleidoscope of colors and prints. You expect Dorothy Lamour, star of all those "Road" pictures, to appear at any minute. In fact, today's Dorothy (actually a local salesperson) demonstrates how to wrap and tie beach pareos and sarongs. Men's shirts are a collection of tropical and ethnic prints, and there's also a children's selection. The outlet also carries Javanese and Balinese art and antiquities.

Urban Threadz/Tribal Threadz
52C Company St. ☎ **809/773-2883.**

It's the most comprehensive clothing store in Christiansted's historic core, with a two-story, big-city scale and appeal that's different from the tropical-boutique aura of nearby T-shirt shops. It's the store where island residents prefer to shop, because of the hip, urban styles. Garments for men are on the street level, women's garments are upstairs, and the inventory includes everything from Bermuda shorts to lightweight summer blazers and men's suits. They carry Calvin Klein, Nautica, and Oakley among others.

GIFTS

Many Hands

In the Pan Am Pavilion, Strand St. ☎ **809/773-1990.**

Many Hands sells Virgin Islands handcrafts exclusively. The merchandise includes West Indian spices and teas, shellwork, stained glass, hand-painted china, pottery, and handmade jewelry. Their collection of local paintings is intriguing, as is their year-round "Christmas tree."

Only in Paradise

5 Company St. ☎ **809/773-0331.**

It's the largest store of its kind in Christiansted, and filled with merchandise you'll absolutely never need during your visit, but which you might want as intriguing dust collectors after you return home. The inventory includes cunningly crafted boxes, jewelry, and accessories for fashionable evenings out on the town. The outlet also sells a curious mix of leather products and lingerie. The taste is bourgeois and plush. Don't expect attentive service, however; the staff is inexperienced.

The Royal Poinciana

1111 Strand St. ☎ **809/773-9892.**

This is the most interesting gift shop on St. Croix. In what looks like an antique apothecary, you'll find such Caribbean-inspired items as hot sauces, seasoning blends for gumbos, island herbal teas, Antillean coffees, and a scented array of soaps, toiletries, lotions, and shampoos. There's also a selection of museum-reproduction greeting cards and calendars. Also featured are educational but also fun gifts for children.

HOUSEWARES

Green Papaya

Caravella Arcade no. 15. ☎ **809/773-8848.**

Shopkeepers here have assembled a unique collection of accessories for your home, including picture frames, lighting fixtures, and baskets. There are two rooms, one displaying these wares, another dedicated to their new interior design service, with fabrics on display.

JEWELRY

Colombian Emeralds

43 Queen Cross St. ☎ **809/773-1928.**

Along with stunning emeralds, called "the rarest gemstone in the world," rubies and diamonds also dazzle here. The staff will show you their large range of 14-karat gold jewelry, along with the best buys in watches, including Seiko quartz. Even though fake jewelry is peddled throughout the Caribbean, Colombian Emeralds is the genuine thing.

Crucian Gold

57A Company St. ☎ **809/773-5241.**

In this small West Indian cottage, you encounter the unique gold creations of island-born Brian Bishop. He designs all the gold creations himself, although cheaper versions of his work come in sterling silver. The most popular item is the Crucian bracelet, which contains a "True Lovers' Knot" in its design. The outlet also sells hand-tied knots (bound in gold wire), rings, pendants, and earrings.

Elegant Illusions Copy Jewelry
55 King St. ☎ **809/773-2727.**

This branch of a hugely successful chain based in California sells convincing fake jewelry. The look-alikes range in price from $9 to $1,000, and include credible copies of the baroque and antique jewelry your great-grandmother might have worn.

If you want the real thing, you can go next door to **King Alley Jewelry** (☎ **809/773-4746**), which is owned by the same company and specializes in fine designer jewelry, including Tiffany and Cartier.

Larimar
The Boardwalk/King's Walk. ☎ **809/692-9000.**

Everything sold in this shop is produced by the largest manufacturer of gold settings for larimar in the world. Discovered in the 1970s, larimar is a pale-blue pectolyte prized for its color. It's produced from mines in only one mountain in the world, which is located in the southwestern edge of the Dominican Republic, near the Haitian border. Objects range from $25 to $1,000. Although other shops sell the stone in imaginative settings, this emporium has the widest selection.

Little Switzerland
1108 King St. ☎ **809/773-1976.**

With branches throughout the Caribbean, this is the best source on the island for crystal, figurines, watches, china, perfume, flatware, and lots of fine jewelry. It specializes in all the big names, such as Paloma Picasso leather goods. For luxuries like a Rolex watch; an Omega; or heirloom crystal such as Lalique, Swarovski, and Baccarat, this is the place. At least a few items are said to sell for up to 30% less than on the U.S. mainland, but don't take anyone's word for that unless you've checked prices carefully.

Sonya Ltd.
1 Company St. ☎ **809/778-8605.**

Sonya Hough is the matriarch of a cult of local residents who wouldn't leave home without wearing one of her bracelets. She's most famous for her sterling-silver or gold (from 14- to 24-karat) interpretations of the C-clasp bracelet. Locals communicate discreet messages by how it's worn: If the cup of the "C" is turned toward your heart, it means you're emotionally committed. If the cup of the "C" is turned outward, it means you're available to whomever strikes your fancy. Prices range from $20 to $2,500. She also sells rings, earrings, and necklaces.

LIQUOR

Harborside Market and Spirits
59 King's Wharf. ☎ **809/773-8899.**

One of the best selections for duty-free liquors, wine, and beer, is sold at this outlet. The location is also one of the most convenient in town and saves a trip to Woolworth's which also has good prices in liquor but is inconveniently located outside of town.

Woolworth's
In the Sunny Isle Shopping Center, Centerline Rd. ☎ **809/778-5466.**

Although primarily a department store, this retail outlet contains the largest supply of liquor on the island. The liquor is duty free. Cruzan rum is in plentiful supply, along with a vast array of other brand-name liquors and liqueurs.

PERFUME

St. Croix Perfume Center

53 King St. ☎ **800/225-7031** or 809/773-76044.

Here you'll find the largest duty-free assortment of men's and women's fragrances on St. Croix, usually at 30% below U.S. mainland prices. For a minimum charge of $5, this store will ship perfumes anywhere in the world. The center recently added Iman cosmetics for women of color.

Violette Boutique

In the Caravelle Arcade, 38 Strand St. ☎ **809/773-2148.**

A small department store with many boutique areas carrying lines known worldwide, Violette includes many exclusive fragrances and hard-to-find toiletry items. It also has the latest in Cartier, Fendi, Pequignet, and Gucci. A wide selection of famous cosmetic names is featured, and Fendi has its own area for bags and accessories. A selection of gifts for children is also carried. Many famous brand names found here are located nowhere else on the island, but are definitely found elsewhere in the Caribbean.

AROUND THE ISLAND

If you're touring western St. Croix in the vicinity of Frederiksted, you might want to stop off at the following offbeat shops.

St. Croix Leap

Mahogany Rd., Rte. 76. ☎ **809/772-0421.**

On your tour of the island, especially if you're on western St. Croix near Frederiksted, stop off at St. Croix Leap for an offbeat adventure. In this open-air shop, you can see stacks of rare and beautiful wood being fashioned into tasteful objects. It's a St. Croix Life and Environmental Arts Project, dedicated to the natural environment through manual work, conservation, and self-development. The end result is a fine collection of Cruzan mahogany serving boards, tables, wall hangings, and clocks. Sections of unusual pieces are crafted into functional objects that are a form of art.

St. Croix Leap is 15 miles from Christiansted, 2 miles up Mahogany Road from the beach north of Frederiksted. Large mahogany signs and sculptures flank the driveway. Visitors should bear to the right to reach the woodworking area and gift shop. The site is open daily from 7am to 5:30pm. For inquiries, write to Leap, P.O. Box 245, Frederiksted, U.S.V.I. 00841-0245.

Whim Museum Store

In the Estate Whim Plantation Museum, east of Frederiksted on Centerline Rd. ☎ **809/772-0598.**

This unique store offers a wide selection of gifts, both imported and Cruzan. And if you buy something, it all goes to a worthy cause: the upkeep of the museum and the grounds.

8 St. Croix After Dark

St. Croix doesn't have as much nightlife as St. Thomas, which is just the way permanent residents like it. To find the action, you might have to go hotel- or bar-hopping.

Also, try to catch a performance of the Quadrille Dancers, a cultural attraction unique to St. Croix. Their dances have changed little since plantation days. The women wear long dresses, white gloves, and turbans, and the men are attired in flamboyant shirts, sashes, and tight black trousers. When you've learned their steps, you're invited to join the dancers on the floor. Ask at your hotel if and where they are performing.

THE PERFORMING ARTS

Island Center

Sunny Isle. ☎ **809/778-5272.** Tickets $5–$25.

This 1,100-seat amphitheater, half a mile north of Sunny Isle, continues to attract big-name entertainers to St. Croix. Its program is widely varied, ranging from jazz, nostalgia, and musical revues to Broadway plays, such as *The Wiz.* Consult *St. Croix This Week* or call the center to see what's going on. The Caribbean Community Theatre and Courtyard Players perform regularly. Call for performance times.

THE CLUB & MUSIC SCENE

Blue Moon

17 Strand St. ☎ **809/772-2222.**

The hottest spot in Christiansted on Thursday and Friday is this little dive, which is also a good bistro. Thursday's pianist Bobby Page (the Bobby Short of St. Croix) takes over the keys, and on Friday a five-piece ensemble entertains. The good news is there is no cover. It's not only hot, it's hip. Stick around to try some of the food from their eclectic menu.

✪ Cormorant Beach Club Bar

4126 La Grande Princesse. ☎ **809/778-8920.**

One of the most romantic bars on the island is found along La Grande Princesse northwest of Christiansted, opening onto one of the island's best beaches. It's a Caribbean cliché, but that's why people often come to the islands in the first place, to enjoy tropical drinks in a moonlit setting with palm trees swaying in the night winds. (For a hotel review, see "Accommodations," above). Guests sit at tables overlooking the ocean or around an open-centered mahogany bar, surrounded by an enlarged gazebo, wicker love seats, comfortable chairs, and soft lighting. Excellent tropical drinks are mixed here, including the house specialty, a Cormorant cooler made with champagne, pineapple juice, and Triple Sec.

Hondo's Nightclub

53 King St. ☎ **809/773-5855.** Cover $5.

Simply called "Hondo's" by the regulars, this local dive is a hot spot featuring mostly recorded music. Occasionally, the place heats up with live reggae, calypso, Latino, and international music. Locals usually outnumber visitors. Exercise caution going through the streets late at night to get here.

The Marina Bar

In The King's Alley Hotel, King's Alley/The Waterfront. ☎ **809/773-0103.**

This bar occupies a panoramic position on the waterfront, on a shaded terrace overlooking the deep-blue sea and Protestant Cay. Although the place remains open throughout the day, the most appealing activities begin here right after the last seaplane departs for St. Thomas from a position nearby (around 5:30pm) and continue until 8:30pm. Sunset-colored cocktails made with rum, mangos, bananas, papaya, and grenadine are the libations of choice. You can even stave off hunger pangs with

---

In the Wild on Buck Island

A radically different kind of walking tour than trekking through the "rain forest" (see "Exploring the 'Rain Forest'" in "Touring the Island," above) traverses Buck Island, a sunbaked, low-lying stretch of sand and coral rock off the island's northeastern coast. Here the climate is considerably drier than the rain forest, although the interest on this walk revolves around the marine life in the sun-flooded, shallow waters off the rocky coastline of this long and narrow offshore island.

During the 19th century, goats overgrazed the island's surface, reducing the land to the barren condition you'll find it in today. Despite its arid land, the island is eminently suitable for pedestrian hikes. Just don't rush to touch every plant you see. The island's western edge has groves of poisonous machineel trees, whose leaves, bark, and fruit contain toxins that cause extreme irritation if they come into contact with human skin.

Most visitors to Buck Island come for its ring of beaches and its offshore snorkeling; a circumnavigation of the island on foot will take about 2 hours. Although Buck Island is only accessible via chartered tours and boat trips (see below), it is one of the most-visited rock spits in the Caribbean.

Managed and protected by the National Park Service, Buck Island has a trail that meanders from several points along its coastline to its sun-flooded summit, which affords views over nearby St. Croix.

Of arguably greater interest on Buck Island is the underwater snorkeling trail that rings part of the island. With a face mask, swim fins, and a snorkel, you'll be treated to some of the most spectacular underwater views in the Caribbean. Plan on spending at least two-thirds of a day at this extremely famous ecological site.

---

burgers, sandwiches, and West Indian–style platters. The bar has live entertainment most nights, usually street bands. On Monday you can bet on crab races.

Mt. Pellier Hut Domino Club
Montpellier. ☎ **809/772-9914.**

Unique to the island, this club came into being as a battered snack shack established to serve players of a never-ending domino game. Gradually it grew into a drinking and entertainment center, although the game is still going strong. Today, the bar offers a beer-drinking pig (Miss Piggy), and has a one-man band, Piro, who plays on Sunday. The bartender will also serve you a lethal rum-based Mamma Wanna.

The Terrace Lounge
In the Buccaneer, Rte. 82, Estate Shoys. ☎ **809/773-2100.** Cover $5 for those who aren't staying in the hotel.

Every night this lounge off the main dining room of one of St. Croix's most upscale hotels welcomes some of the Caribbean's finest entertainers, often including a full band.

The Wreck Bar
5–AB Hospital St., Christiansted. ☎ **809/773-6092.**

The margaritas are "absolutely habit-forming," and the decor at this hole-in-the-wall is inspired directly by *Gilligan's Island*, with a retractable awning that extends over the open-air dance floor whenever it rains, and an indoor-outdoor space full of bamboo and thatch. The place has a sense of irreverent fun, especially when it offers live reggae.

9 An Excursion to Buck Island

The crystal-clear water and the white-coral sand of ✪ Buck Island, 1½ miles off the northeast coast of St. Croix, are legendary. Only ⅓ mile wide and 1 mile long, the island and much of its offshore reef have been administered by the National Park Service since 1948, much to the delight of environmental groups. The endangered brown pelican produces young here, and marine life in the outlying waters is thriving.

Today, the park covers about 850 acres of land and water surface. The island contains picnic tables, barbecue pits, and a hiking trail through tropical vegetation. Facilities include rest rooms and a small changing room. Offshore, there are two underwater trails for snorkeling above the coral, amazing schools of fish, and many other deeper labyrinths and underwater grottoes for more serious divers. Among the attractions are "forests" of elkhorn coral and thousands of colorful reef fish.

Mile Mark Watersports, in the King Christian Hotel, 59 King's Wharf, Christiansted (☎ 809/773-2628), has twice-daily tours of Buck Island. They offer two ways to reach the reefs. One is a half-day tour aboard a glass-bottom boat departing from the King Christian Hotel. Tours are daily from 9:30am to 1pm and 1:30 to 5pm, and cost $35 per person; all snorkeling equipment is included. A more romantic journey is aboard one of the company's wind-powered sailboats, which, for $45 per person, offers the sea breezes and the thrill of wind power to reach the reef. A full-day tour, offered daily from 10am to 4pm on the company's 40-foot catamaran, can take up to 20 participants to Buck Island's reefs. Included in the tour are a West Indian barbecue picnic on the isolated sands of Buck Island's beaches and plenty of opportunities for snorkeling. The full-day tour costs $60.

Captain Heinz (☎ **809/773-3161** or 809/773-4041) is an Austrian-born skipper with some 22 years or more of sailing experience. His trimaran, *Teroro II,* leaves Green Cay Marina "H" Dock at 9am and 2pm, never filled with more than 24 passengers. The snorkeling trip costs $45 in the morning or $40 in the afternoon. All gear and safety equipment are provided. The captain is not only a skilled sailor but is also a considerate host. He will even take you around the outer reef, which the other guides do not, for an unforgettable underwater experience.

The British Virgin Islands

In the northeast corner of the Caribbean, about 60 miles east of Puerto Rico, the British Virgin Islands embrace 40-odd islands, some no more than rocks or spits of land. Only a trio of the British Virgins is of any significant size—Virgin Gorda ("Fat Virgin"), Tortola ("Dove of Peace"), and Jost Van Dyke. These islands, craggy and volcanic in origin, are just 15 air minutes from St. Thomas. There is also regularly scheduled ferry service between St. Thomas and Tortola.

With its small bays and hidden coves, once havens for pirates, the British Virgin Islands are among the world's loveliest cruising grounds. Despite predictions that mass tourism will invade, these islands are still an escapist's paradise.

The smaller islands have colorful names such as Fallen Jerusalem and Ginger. Norman Island is said to have been the prototype for Robert Louis Stevenson's *Treasure Island.* On Deadman Bay, a barren islet, Blackbeard marooned 15 pirates and a bottle of rum, which gave rise to the well-known ditty.

Note: The British Virgin Islands use the U.S. dollar as their form of currency. British pounds are not accepted.

VISITOR INFORMATION

Before you go, you can obtain information about the British Virgin Islands from the **BVI Tourist Board,** 370 Lexington Ave., Suite 313, New York, NY 10017 (☎ **800/835-8530** or 212/696-0400); or from the **BVI Tourist Board,** 1686 Union St., San Francisco, CA 94123 (☎ **800/835-8530** or 415/775-0344). In the United Kingdom, contact the **BVI Tourist Board,** 110 St. Martin's Lane, London WC2N 4DY (☎ **0171/240-4259**).

If you have Internet access, try "The British Virgin Islands Welcome Tourist Guide On-Line," at **http://www.bviwelcome.com**.

GETTING THERE

Your gateway to the B.V.I. will most likely be either Tortola or Virgin Gorda, which have the most hotels and services. Supplies and services on the other islands are extremely limited.

BY PLANE

There are no direct flights from North America to Tortola or any of the other British Virgin Islands, but you can make easy connections through San Juan in Puerto Rico, St. Thomas, or St. Croix.

American Eagle (☎ 800/433-7300) has six daily flights from San Juan, Puerto Rico, to the airport at Beef Island/Tortola. San Juan is serviced by dozens of daily nonstop flights from North America, including Boston; Toronto; New York; Chicago; Miami; and Raleigh-Durham, North Carolina. You can also fly **American** (☎ 800/433-7300) to St. Thomas, then hop on an American Eagle flight to Tortola.

Four Star Aviation (☎ 284/495-4389 or 284/777-9000) also flies to Beef Island/Tortola and Virgin Gorda via San Juan and St. Thomas. Another choice, if you're on one of Tortola's neighboring islands, is **LIAT** (Leeward Islands Air Transport; ☎ 284/462-0701). This Caribbean carrier flies to Tortola from St. Kitts, Antigua, St. Maarten, St. Thomas, and San Juan, in small planes not known for their frequency or careful scheduling. **Air St. Thomas** (☎ 284/776-2722) flies to Virgin Gorda daily from San Juan, Puerto Rico.

Flying time to Tortola from San Juan is 30 minutes; from St. Thomas, 15 minutes; and from the most distant of the LIAT hubs (Antigua), 60 minutes.

BY BOAT

From Charlotte Amalie on St. Thomas **public ferries** run to Road Town and West End on Tortola via the Sir Francis Drake Channel; trip time is 45 minutes. Outfits offering this service include: **Native Son** (☎ 284/495-4617), **Smith's Ferry Service** (☎ 284/495-4495), and **Inter-Island Boat Services** (☎ 284/776-6597).

GETTING AROUND
BY BOAT

On Tortola, **Smith's Ferry** (☎ 284/495-4495) and **Speedy's Fantasy** (☎ 284/495-5240) operate ferry links to the Virgin Gorda Yacht Club (the trip lasts 30 minutes). The **North Sound Express** (☎ 284/495-2271), near the airport on Beef Island, has daily connections to the Bitter End Yacht Club on Virgin Gorda. **Peter Island Boat** (☎ 284/495-2000) also shuttles passengers between Road Town on Tortola and Peter Island at least seven times a day.

Island Highlights: The British Virgin Islands

Must-See Attractions

- **Guana Island,** just north of Tortola, boasts the richest fauna in the West Indies for an island of its size.
- **Sage Mountain National Park,** on Tortola, has the highest mountain in the Virgin Islands (1,780 feet).
- **The Baths,** on Virgin Gorda—clusters of massive prehistoric rocks forming cool, inviting grottoes ideal for swimming and snorkeling.
- **Wreck of the HMS *Rhone,*** off Salt Island—once a royal mail steamer from 1867, it's the most celebrated dive site in the West Indies.

Beaches

- **Cane Garden Bay,** on Tortola, ranks among the world's best, right up there with St. Thomas's Magens Bay Beach.
- **Apple Bay** (also called Cappoon's Bay), west of Road Town on Tortola, is a favorite among surfers.

Great Towns/Villages

- **Road Town,** capital of Tortola and of the B.V.I., is the place to stock up on supplies before heading for the more remote islands.

The British Virgin Islands

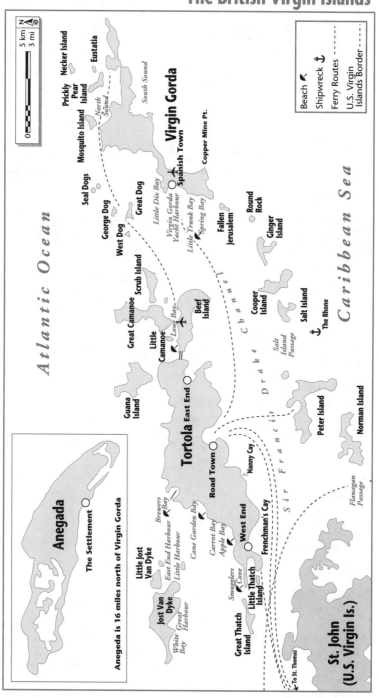

Area Code Change Notice

Please note that, effective October 1, 1997, the area code for the British Virgin Islands will change from **809** to **284.** All of the B.V.I. area codes in this book have been changed to 284. Prior to October 1, you will need to use the 809 area code for all B.V.I. phone numbers.

BY CAR, BUS, OR TAXI

Car-rental agencies are on the larger islands of Virgin Gorda and Tortola; taxis operate on these islands as well as some of the smaller ones. Bus service is available on Tortola and Virgin Gorda only. See the specific "Getting There" and "Getting Around" sections for each island for further details.

1 Tortola

On the southern shore of this 24-square-mile island, **Road Town** is the capital of the British Virgin Islands. It's the seat of Government House and other administrative buildings, but it seems more like a village. The landfill at Wickhams Cay, a 70-acre town center development and marina in the harbor, has brought in a massive yacht-chartering business and has transformed the sleepy capital into more of a bustling center.

The entire southern coast, including Road Town, is characterized by rugged mountain peaks. On the northern coast are white sandy beaches, banana trees, mangos, and clusters of palms.

GETTING THERE

Close to Tortola's eastern end is **Beef Island,** the site of the main airport for passengers arriving in Tortola and all of the British Virgins. The tiny island is connected to Tortola by the one-lane Queen Elizabeth Bridge.

Because Tortola is the gateway to the British Virgin Islands, the information on how to get here is covered just above in the first "Getting There."

GETTING AROUND
BY TAXI

Taxis meet every arriving flight. Government regulations prohibit anyone from renting a car at the airport; visitors must take a taxi to their hotels. The fare from the Beef Island airport to Road Town is $15 for one to three passengers. Your hotel can call a taxi for you. A tour lasting 2^1/$_2$ hours costs $45 for one to three people. To call a taxi in Road Town, dial **284/494-2322;** on Beef Island, **284/495-2378.**

BY CAR OR BUS

RENTING A CAR   Because of the volume of visitors to Tortola, you should reserve your rental car in advance, especially in winter. A handful of local companies rent cars, but we recommend using one of the U.S.–based giants, even if the cost is slightly higher. On Tortola, **Budget** (☎ **800/527-0700** in the U.S., or 284/494-5150) is at 1 Wickhams Cay, Road Town. **Avis** (☎ **800/331-2112** in the U.S., or 284/494-3322) maintains offices opposite the police headquarters in Road Town. **Hertz** (☎ **800/654-3001** in the U.S., or 284/495-4405) has offices outside Road Town, on the island's West End, near the ferryboat landing dock. Rental companies will usually deliver your car to your hotel. All three companies require a valid driver's license and a temporary B.V.I. driver's license, which the car-rental company can sell you (the cost is $10, and it's valid for 3 months).

Remember to **drive on the left.** Because the island roads are poorly lit, with few, if any, lines marking the shoulder of the sinuous and narrow roads, nighttime driving can be disturbing. It's a good idea to take a taxi to that difficult-to-find restaurant or nightspot.

BY BUS **Scato's Bus Service** (☎ 284/494-5873) operates from the north end of the island to the west end, picking up passengers who hail it down. Fares for a trek across the island are $1 to $3.

Because Tortola is the gateway to the British Virgin Islands, the information on how to get here is covered at the beginning of this chapter.

VISITOR INFORMATION

There is a **BVI Tourist Board Office** (☎ 284/494-3134) at the center of Road Town near the ferry dock. You'll find information about hotels, restaurants, tours, and more. Pick up a copy of *The Welcome Tourist Guide,* which has a useful map of the island.

WHERE TO STAY

Many of the island's hotels are small, informal family run guest houses offering only the most basic amenities. Others are more elaborate, boasting a full range of resort-related facilities. None of them, however, is as big, splashy, and all-encompassing as the hotels in the U.S. Virgin Islands. Many of the island's repeat visitors seem to like that just fine.

It is extremely difficult to divide hotels in the B.V.I. into rigid price classifications, because some "inexpensive" hotels have a few "very expensive" rooms. Therefore, the following classifications are arbitrary and have many variations. In general, hotels ranked **"Expensive"** charge from $190 to $330 per night for a double room; **"Moderate"** from $140 to $190, although some rooms in this classification fall into the expensive category; and **"Inexpensive"** less than $140 a night, although even in this category, there are some rooms in the "moderate" range.

All the tariffs quoted are winter (high-season) rates. In summer, rates are discounted by 20% to as much as 60%.

Note: All rates given within this chapter are subject to a 10% service charge and a 7% government tax.

EXPENSIVE

Frenchman's Cay Resort Hotel

West End (P.O. Box 1054), Tortola, B.V.I. ☎ **800/235-4077** in the U.S., or 800/463-0199 in Canada, or 284/495-4844. Fax 284/495-4056. 9 villas. Winter, $220 one-bedroom villa; $315 two-bedroom villa. Off-season, $125 one-bedroom villa; $180 two-bedroom villa. MAP $45 per person extra. AE, DISC, MC, V. From Tortola, cross the bridge to Frenchman's Cay, turn left, and follow the road to the eastern tip of the cay.

This intimate resort is tucked away at the windward side of Frenchman's Cay, a little island connected by bridge to Tortola. The 12-acre landscaped estate enjoys year-round cooling breezes and views of Sir Francis Drake Channel and the outer Virgins. The individual one- and two-bedroom villas, actually a cluster of condos, are well furnished, each with a shady terrace, full kitchen, dining room, and sitting room. The two-bedroom villas have two full baths.

Dining/Entertainment: The Clubhouse Restaurant and lounge bar is located in the main pavilion. The menu features a respectable continental and Caribbean cuisine.

Facilities: Beach with snorkeling, freshwater swimming pool, tennis court, Sunfish sailboats, kayaks, Windsurfers, day-sail trips, horseback riding, scuba diving, island tours; car rentals can be arranged.

❂ Long Bay Beach Resort

Tortola, B.V.I. ☎ **800/729-9599** in the U.S. and Canada, or 284/495-4252, or 0800/898-379 in Britain. Fax 914/833-3318 in Larchmont, N.Y. 62 rms, 20 villas. A/C. Winter, $220–$330 double; $450–$500 two-bedroom villa; $650–$700 three-bedroom villa. Off-season, $120–$195 double; $260–$350 two-bedroom villa; $360–$485 three-bedroom villa. MAP $40 per person extra. AE, MC, V.

On the north shore, about 10 minutes from the West End, is the only full-service resort on the island: a low-rise resort complex set in a 52-acre estate with a mile-long white-sand beach. The accommodations include hillside rooms and studios, the smallest and most basic with the simplest furnishings, as well as beachfront deluxe rooms and beachfront cabañas with balconies or patios. In addition, the resort offers two- and three-bedroom villas complete with kitchen, living area, and a large deck with a gas grill. Beachfront deluxe rooms and villas have cable TV. Even if you're not staying right on the beach, you'll still enjoy an ocean view.

Dining/Entertainment: The Beach Café offers breakfast and lunch as well as informal à la carte suppers. In the ruins of an old sugar mill, the restaurant serves regular evening buffets with live entertainment. The Garden Restaurant has dinner by reservation only, and the food is excellent.

Services: Daily maid service, laundry, baby-sitting, car rental; chef available on request for villa renters.

Facilities: Oceanside freshwater swimming pool, two championship tennis courts and one regular court, beach bar, shops, summer children's activity program (ages three to eight).

The Sugar Mill

Apple Bay (P.O. Box 425, Road Town), Tortola, B.V.I. ☎ **800/462-8834** or 284/495-4355. Fax 284/495-4696. 20 units, 1 villa. A/C. Winter, $190–$265 double; $280 triple; $295 quad; $585 two-bedroom villa. Off-season, $150 double; $195 triple; $210 quad; $400 two-bedroom villa. AE, MC, V. Closed Aug–Sept.

Set in lush foliage on the site of a 300-year-old sugar mill on the north side of Tortola, this cottage colony sweeps down the hillside to its own little beach, with flowers and fruits livening the grounds.

Comfortable but plain apartments climb up the hillside. At the center is a circular swimming pool for those who don't want to go down to the beach. The accommodations are contemporary, ranging from suites and cottages to studio apartments, all self-contained with kitchenettes and private terraces with views. Four of the units are suitable for families of four, but children nine and under are not allowed in winter.

Dining/Entertainment: Lunch or dinner is served down by the beach at The Islands, which offers dinner from 6:30 to 9pm Tuesday through Saturday January through May; it features Caribbean specialties along with burgers and salads. Dinner is also offered in the Sugar Mill Restaurant (see "Where to Dine," below). Breakfast is served on the terrace. The bars are open all day.

Facilities: Free snorkeling equipment.

Tortola

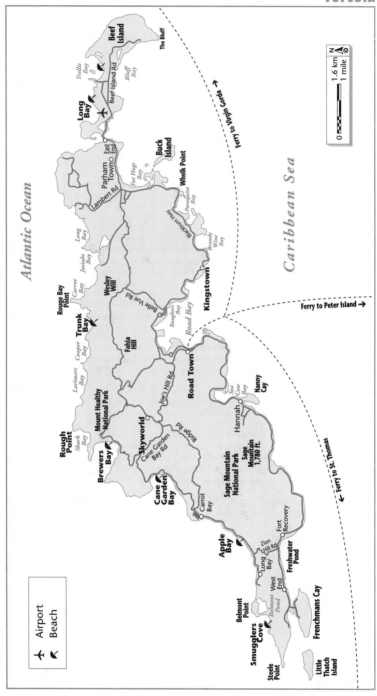

Atlantic Ocean

Caribbean Sea

Ferry to Virgin Gorda →

Ferry to Peter Island →

← Ferry to St. Thomas

Airport

Beach

N

1.6 km
1 mile
0

Beef Island

The Bluff

Trellis Bay

Bluff Bay

Beef Island Rd

Long Bay

East End

Parham Town

Buck Island

Whelk Point

Lambert Rd

Fat Hogs Bay

Paraquita Bay

Blackburn Hwy

Brandy Wine Bay

Long Bay

Josiahs Bay

Carrot Bay

Wesley Will

Belle Vue Rd

Kingstown

Rouge Bay Point

Trunk Bay

Cooper Bay

Baugher's Bay

Road Bay

Fahia Hill

Larimers Bay

Joe's Hill Rd

Road Town

Rough Point

Shark Bay

Mount Healthy National Park

Skyworld

Ridge Rd

Sea Cow Bay

Nanny Cay

Hannah

Brewers Bay

Cane Garden Bay Rd

Sage Mountain National Park

Sage Mountain 1,780 ft.

Cane Garden Bay

Carrot Bay

Apple Bay

Fort Recovery

Zion Hill Rd

Long Bay

Freshwater Pond

West End

Belmont Point

Belmont Pond

Frenchmans Cay

Smugglers Cove

Steele Point

Little Thatch Island

187

Sir Francis Drake: A Swashbuckling Adventurer

Sir Francis Drake (1543–96) was an English navigator and explorer famous for defeating the Spanish Armada in 1588. He's regarded as a notorious pirate throughout the Caribbean. Arriving in the West Indies as the young captain of *The Judith* and a favored subject of Elizabeth I, Drake brought the swashbuckling adventures of the Elizabethan age to the Virgin Islands. A channel on Tortola now bears his name. He was the first Englishman to circumnavigate the globe.

Born near Tavistock, England, he spent most of his life aboard ship, often in the Caribbean. Drake died aboard ship off Porto Bello on January 27, 1596, and was fittingly buried at sea.

MODERATE

The Moorings/Mariner Inn

Wickhams Cay (P.O. Box 139, Road Town), Tortola, B.V.I. ☎ **800/435-7289** in the U.S. for reservations, or 284/494-2332. Fax 284/494-2226. 39 rms, 2 suites. A/C TV TEL. Winter, $170 double; $230 suite. Off-season, $95 double; $125 suite. Additional person $15 extra. AE, MC, V.

The Caribbean's most complete yachting resort is outfitted with at least 180 sailing yachts, some worth $2 million or more. On an 8-acre resort, the inn was obviously designed with the yachting crowd in mind, offering not only support facilities and services but also shoreside accommodations (suites and air-conditioned hotel rooms), a dockside restaurant, Mariner Bar, swimming pool, tennis court, gift shop, and a dive shop that has underwater video cameras available for rent. The rooms are spacious; all have kitchenettes, and most of them open onto the water. Obviously the boaties get more attention here than the landlubbers. The nearest beach is Cane Garden Bay, about a 15-minute taxi ride.

Nanny Cay Resort and Marina

P.O. Box 281, Road Town, Tortola, B.V.I. ☎ **800/74-CHARMS** in the U.S., or 284/494-2512. Fax 284/494-0555. 42 studios. A/C TV TEL. Winter, $140–$255 studio for 2. Off-season, $45–$195 studio for 2. Additional person $20 extra. Children under 12 stay free in parents' room. Special diving, sailing, and windsurfing packages available. AE, MC, V.

On a 25-acre inlet adjoining a 180-slip marina, Nanny Cay is located 3 miles from the center of Road Town and 10 miles from the airport. It caters to self-sufficient, independent types rather than to those who want to be coddled in a full-service resort. All accommodations are studios with fully equipped kitchenettes. Standard studios have two double beds; deluxe studios are larger, with a sitting area and two queen-size beds. The studios have a West Indian decor, ceiling fans, and private balconies opening onto a view of the water, marina, or gardens. Note that the service is rather hit-or-miss.

The hotel's Pegleg Landing Restaurant serves both lunch and dinner daily, featuring international dishes with a Caribbean flair. More casual food is offered at the Plaza Café.

Prospect Reef Resort

Drake's Hwy. (P.O. Box 104, Road Town), Tortola, B.V.I. ☎ **800/356-8937** in the U.S., or 800/463-3608 in Canada, or 284/494-3311. Fax 284/494-5595. 131 units. TEL. Winter, $147–$190 double; $410 two-bedroom villa for 4. Off-season, $88–$117 double; $274 two-bedroom villa for 4. AE, MC, V.

Built by a consortium of British investors in 1979, this is the largest resort in the B.V.I. It rises above a small, private harbor in a series of two-story concrete buildings scattered over 44 acres of steeply sloping, landscaped terrain. The panoramic view of Sir Francis Drake Channel from the bedrooms is one of the best anywhere. (But note that there's no beach at the hotel.)

Each of the resort's buildings contains up to 10 individual accommodations and is painted in hibiscus-inspired shades of pink, peach, purple, or aquamarine. Initially designed as condominiums, there are unique studios, town houses, and villas, in addition to guest rooms. All include private balconies or patios; larger units have kitchenettes, good-size living and dining areas, plus separate bedrooms or sleeping lofts. About one-third of the rooms are air-conditioned; others are cooled by ceiling fans and the trade winds. All rooms are wired for TVs, which are available for rent.

Dining/Entertainment: Food at the hotel's Callaloo Restaurant (see below), offering a combination of continental specialties and island favorites, was recently praised by *Gourmet* magazine—the callaloo beef Wellington is exquisite. Light meals are served on the terrace of the Scuttlebutt Bar and Grill or around the Seapool Bar and Grill.

Facilities: Five pools including sand-terraced sea pools for snorkeling, plus a narrow, artificial beach. Six tennis courts are available, as well as a health and fitness center and a pitch-and-putt course. Guest services will advise you on harbor activities: day sailing, snorkeling, scuba diving, sport fishing.

Treasure Isle Hotel

Pasea Estate, east end of Road Town (P.O. Box 68, Road Town), Tortola, B.V.I. ☎ **800/ 334-2435** in the U.S. for reservations, or 284/494-2501. Fax 284/494-2507. 39 rms, 2 suites. A/C TV TEL. Winter, $170 double; $230 suite. Off-season, $95 double; $125 suite. Additional person $15 extra. AE, DISC, MC, V.

The most central resort on Tortola was built at the edge of the Road Town on 15 acres of hillside overlooking a marina (it's not on the beach). The core of the hotel is a rather splashy and colorful lounge and swimming-pool area. The motel-like rooms are on two levels along the hillside terraces; a third level is occupied by more elegantly decorated suites at the crest of a hill.

Dining/Entertainment: Adjoining the lounge and pool area is a covered open-air dining room overlooking the harbor. The cuisine is respected here, with barbecue and full à la carte menus offered at dinner. On Wednesday a West Indian "grill out" is served, and entertainment and dancing are part of the fun.

Services: Complimentary transportation to the nearest beach.

Facilities: The hotel has a fully equipped dive facility that handles beginning instruction up to full certification courses.

INEXPENSIVE

Fort Burt Hotel and Restaurant

P.O. Box 3380, Road Town, Tortola, B.V.I. ☎ **284/494-2587.** Fax 284/494-2002. 15 rms, 3 suites. Winter, $95–$120 double; $150–$200 suite with kitchen; $275 suite with private pool (but no kitchen). Off-season, $85–$110 double; $130–$180 suite. AE, MC, V.

Covered with flowering vines, Fort Burt rents rooms but devotes some of its energy to its popular pub and restaurant (see "Where to Dine," below). Built in 1960 upon the ruins of a 17th-century Dutch fort, the rooms are set at a higher elevation than any other hotel in Road Town, offering views of the waterfront from private terraces. Simple, sun-flooded, and cozy, the rooms have a colonial charm, although they are not as large and comfortable as the newer suites, which have marble-tiled bathrooms and rattan furnishings. There's a pool on the grounds or guests can walk to either Cane Bay or Smuggler's Cove beaches.

Sebastians on the Beach

P.O. Box 441, Little Apple Bay, West End Tortola, B.V.I. ☎ **284/495-4212.** Fax 284/495-4466. 26 rms. MINIBAR. Winter, $120–$190 double. Off-season, $85–$150 double. Additional person $15 extra. MAP $35 per person extra. AE, MC, V. Free parking.

Established in the 1970s, this hotel is located at Little Apple Bay, about a 15-minute drive from Road Town, on a long beach with the best surfing in the B.V.I. The rooms are housed in three buildings, only one of which is on the beach. The floral-accented units come with rattan furniture and have small refrigerators and private baths. Six units contain air-conditioning, balconies, and porches. The restaurant overlooks the bay and offers an international selection of cuisine; on Saturdays and Sundays, guests enjoy live entertainment in the bar. The hotel offers dive packages, as well as packages that include a MAP plan and other perks including a bottle of rum.

Village Cay Hotel

Wickhams Cay, Road Town, Tortola, B.V.I. ☎ **284/494-2771.** Fax 284/494-2773. 20 rms. A/C TV TEL. Winter, $125–$440 double. Off-season, $99–$330 double. AE, MC, V.

Village Cay is the most centrally located full-service lodging facility in the British Virgin Islands. Set in the heart of Road Town, all rooms have been recently refurbished and many directly overlook a marina filled with yachts from around the world. Some of the rooms have balconies and patios, and room service and laundry are provided; the least expensive is the standard room. The most expensive rooms are in the waterfront accommodations, which are costly, especially in winter. The dockside restaurant is open daily from 7am to 11pm, serving breakfast, lunch, and dinner. The standard menu is similar to that found almost anywhere in the Caribbean: lobster, catch of the day, barbecue chicken, and New York strip steak. Entertainment is featured during winter season.

Anything you need is within a 5-minute walk of the premises, including ferry service to other islands, secretarial services for traveling business clients, or taxi service to anywhere on Tortola.

WHERE TO DINE

Most guests dine at their hotels, but if you want to venture out, try one of our suggestions below.

Restaurants rated **"Expensive"** charge around $30 to $35 per person for dinner; **"Moderate,"** from $25 to $35; and **"Inexpensive,"** under $25.

EXPENSIVE

✪ Brandywine Bay Restaurant

Brandywine Estate. ☎ **284/495-2301.** Reservations required. Main courses $20–$28. AE, MC, V. Mon–Sat 6–9:30pm. Closed Aug–Oct. Drive 3 miles east of Road Town (toward the airport) on South Shore Rd. NORTHERN ITALIAN.

This restaurant is set on a cobblestone garden terrace along the south shore, overlooking Sir Francis Drake Channel. It's the most elegant choice for romantic dining. Davide Pugliese, the chef, and his wife, Cele, the hostess, have earned a reputation on Tortola for their outstanding Florentine food. Davide changes his menu daily, based on the availability of fresh produce. Typical dishes include beef carpaccio, homemade pasta, his own special calves' liver dish (the recipe is a secret), the typical *bistecca alla fiorentina,* and homemade mozzarella with fresh basil and tomatoes. If your fancy runs to game, you can order either pheasant or venison.

Callaloo

Prospect Reef Resort, Drake's Hwy. ☎ **284/494-3311.** Reservations recommended. Main courses $10–$28.50. AE, MC, V. Daily 7am–11pm. INTERNATIONAL.

One of the better hotel restaurants, this place gets rather romantic at night, especially if it's a balmy evening and the tropical breezes are blowing. It's the kind of cliché Caribbean setting that is forever a turn-on, and the food is quite good too. The menu is hardly imaginative, but the chefs do well with their limited repertoire. Begin with the conch fritters or shrimp cocktail, and don't pass on the house salad, which has a zesty papaya dressing. Main dishes include fresh lobster when available (not as good as the Maine variety) and also fresh fish like tuna, swordfish, or mahimahi. For dessert, make it the orange bread pudding if featured. If not, then the key lime pie. Downstairs is the less-expensive Scuttlebutt Bar and Grill (see below).

✪ SkyWorld

Ridge Rd., Road Town. ☎ **284/494-3567.** Reservations required. Main courses $16.50–$29. AE, MC, V. Daily 11am–3pm and 5:30–8:30pm. INTERNATIONAL.

Under new management, SkyWorld continues to be all the rage, one of the worthiest dining excursions on the island. On one of Tortola's loftiest peaks, at a breezy 1,337 feet, it offers views of both the U.S. Virgin Islands and the British Virgin Islands. Completely renovated, the restaurant is now divided into two sections: one more upscale with a dress code for men (shirts with collars and long trousers) and an enclosed garden section where you can dine in shorts. Both sections offer the same menu.

The fresh pumpkin soup is an island favorite, but you can also begin with seafood au gratin or, our favorite, mushrooms stuffed with conch. The fresh fish of the day is your best bet (we prefer to skip the steak with port and peaches). The best key lime pie on the island awaits you at the end of the meal, unless you succumb to chocolate fudge ice cream pie.

Sugar Mill Restaurant

Apple Bay. ☎ **284/495-4355.** Reservations required. Main courses $16–$28. AE, MC, V. Daily noon–2pm and 7–8:30pm. From Road Town, drive west for about 7 miles, take a right turn over Zion Hill going north, and then at the T-junction opposite Sebastians, turn right; Sugar Mill lies about ¹/₂ mile down the road. Closed Aug–Sept. CALIFORNIA/CARIBBEAN.

Here, you'll dine in an informal room that was transformed from a 3-century-old sugar mill (see "Where to Stay," above). Colorful works by Haitian painters hang on the old stone walls, and big copper basins once used in distilling rum have been planted with tropical flowers. Before going to the dining room, once part of the old boiling house, visit the open-air bar on a deck that overlooks the sea.

Your hosts, the Morgans, know a lot about food and wine. Jinx Morgan supervises the dining room and is an imaginative cook herself. One of their most popular creations, published in *Bon Appétit,* is a curried-banana soup. You may also begin with smoked conch pâté. Jamaican jerk pork roast with a green-peppercorn salsa or ginger-lime scallops with pasta and toasted walnut sauce are likely choices for dinner. Lunch can be ordered by the beach at the second restaurant, **Islands,** where dinner is also served Tuesday to Saturday from 6:30 to 9pm from January through May. Try jerk ribs or stuffed crabs here.

MODERATE

Captain's Table

Inner Harbour Marina, Wickhams Cay. ☎ **284/494-3885.** Reservations recommended for dinner. Main courses $18.50–$23.50; lunch from $12. DISC, MC, V. Mon–Fri 11:30am–2:30pm; daily 6:30–10pm. CARIBBEAN/FRENCH.

This restaurant is contained within a pastel-colored, low-slung building that was originally built as a disco in the early 1980s. Seating is available in a clean, high-ceilinged, and spacious dining room, which is mainly used in bad weather, but the more desirable tables are on a waterfront veranda with cane chairs and furnishings.

At lunch you find not only the best salads on the island (and the most varied) but the widest array of soups as well. On our last visit, we counted nine different soups, ranging from vichyssoise to pumpkin and ginger, from Bermudian fish chowder to chilled pear. The array of salads was equally impressive, including sliced marinated duck and Cajun cold poached salmon. You can also order hot dishes, including "honeystung" chicken or grilled lamb kidneys. The dinner fare is equally impressive. Begin perhaps with a smoked fish plate and carry on from here, perhaps the rack of lamb with mint or the sautéed scallops in a vegetable basket. There is also a large assortment of fresh fish; meat and poultry dishes are shipped in frozen to the island.

Fort Burt Restaurant and Pub

Fort Burt, Road Town. ☎ **284/494-2587.** Reservations recommended for dinner. English breakfast $8.75; dinner platters $15–$25; lunch sandwiches and platters $5–$8.50. AE, MC, V. Daily 8–10am, noon–3pm, and 6–11pm. Bar daily 10am–midnight. INTERNATIONAL.

This restaurant was built upon rocks mortared together with lime and molasses in the 17th century by the Dutch and the French. Lunches offer very standard fare such as a selection of soups, salads, grilled fish, and sandwiches. Dinners are candlelit and more elaborate, with such dishes as fresh asparagus with aioli sauce, conch fritters, shepherd's pie, pepper steak, and roast duck with orange and tarragon sauce. It's hardly the best food on the island—we chalk it up as a "local favorite."

Mariner Inn Restaurant/Moorings

Wickhams Cay. ☎ **284/494-2332.** Reservations recommended for dinner only. Main courses $13.95–$30. AE, MC, V. Daily 11:30am–2:30pm and 6:30–9:30pm. Transportation: Taxi. FRENCH/CARIBBEAN.

This is one of the more sophisticated restaurants in the B.V.I., attracting a nautical crowd. Its open-air tables overlook the Moorings Marina lying east of Road Town. At lunch, you can drop in and enjoy light food at the Marina Inn Bar, including sandwiches, hamburgers, roti, and a freshly made salad. At night the dinners, served by soft "lamplight," are more elegant, featuring such dishes as steak au poivre, dolphin, baby back ribs, grouper, and lobster served Virgin Islands style.

INEXPENSIVE

✪ Capriccio di Mare

Waterfront Dr., Road Town. ☎ **284/494-5369.** Reservations not accepted. Main courses $5–$12. No credit cards. Daily 8–10:30am and 11am–9pm. ITALIAN.

Small, casual, and laid-back, this local favorite was created by the owners of the Brandywine Bay restaurant (see above) in a moment of whimsy. It's the most authentic-looking Italian cafe in the Virgin Islands. When it opens for breakfast, many locals stop in for a refreshing Italian pastry along with a cup of cappuccino. You can come back for lunch or dinner too. If it's evening, you might order the mango Bellini, a variation of the famous cocktail served at Harry's Bar in Venice (which is made with fresh peaches). Begin with such appetizers as *tiapina* (flour tortillas with various toppings), and go on to fresh pastas with succulent sauces, excellent pizzas (best on the island, especially the one with grilled eggplant), or even well-stuffed sandwiches. If you arrive on the right night, you might even be treated to lobster ravioli in a rosé sauce. Be sure to try one of their freshly made salads: We go for the *insalata mista* with large leafy greens and slices of fresh Parmesan.

Mrs. Scatliffe's Restaurant

Carrot Bay. ☎ **284/495-4556.** Reservations required (call before 5:30pm). Fixed-price meal $20–$27. No credit cards. Daily 7–8pm (no later). WEST INDIAN.

Mrs. Scatliffe's offers home-cooked meals on the deck of her island home, and some of the vegetables come right from her garden, although others might be from a can. You'll be served soup (maybe spicy conch), which will be followed by curried goat, "old wife" fish, or perhaps chicken in a coconut shell. After dinner your hostess and her family will entertain you with a fungi-band performance (except on Sunday) or gospel singing. Be duly warned: This entertainment isn't for everyone, including one reader who compared the hymns to a "screeching caterwaul." Service, usually from an inexperienced teenager, is more to be tolerated than admired for its efficiency.

You might be exposed to Mrs. Scatliffe's gentle and often humorous form of Christian fundamentalism. A Bible reading and a heartfelt rendition of a gospel song might be served up with a soft custard dessert. She often serves lunch in winter but call ahead just to be sure.

Paradise Pub

Fort Burt Marina, Harbour Rd. ☎ **284/494-2608.** Main courses $9.50–$23. AE, MC, V. Daily 6:30am–midnight. INTERNATIONAL.

Contained within a low-slung timbered building on a narrow strip of land between the coastal road and the southern edge of Road Town's harbor, this establishment has a grangelike interior and a rambling veranda built on piers over the water. Many of the island's sports teams celebrate here after their victories. The pub also attracts the boating crowd. In inventory are more than 25 different kinds of beer. Live entertainment begins at 10pm. If you're here for a meal, you can order Bahamian fritters, Caesar or Greek salads, pasta, four kinds of steaks, and burgers, the type of food the regulars in *Cheers* would applaud. The chef also prepares a catch of the day, perhaps wahoo. Different nights of the week are devoted to theme dinners, including all-you-can-eat pasta night, prime rib night, and baby back ribs night. Call to find out what the theme is on the night of your visit.

Pegleg Landing

Nanny Cay Hotel and Marina, Road Town. ☎ **284/494-4895.** Reservations required. Main courses $18–$26. AE, MC, V. Winter, daily 11:30am–2pm and 6–10pm. Off-season, daily 6:30–9pm. Bar daily 10am until closing in winter, daily 4:30pm until closing off-season. INTERNATIONAL.

Built in 1980, this restaurant lies 1¹/₂ miles southwest of Road Town and overlooks the yachts of the Nanny Cay Marina. You'll find accents of stained glass, mastheads from old clipper ships, lots of rustic paneling, and a nautical theme enhanced by the views and breezes from the sea. Specialties include sautéed breast of chicken in a champagne and orange sauce, charbroiled New York strip steak with mushrooms, and fresh fillets of fish, such as dolphin, swordfish, tuna, and wahoo. This is the type of food that appeals to yachties in many parts of the western world—it's competent, but hardly exciting.

Pusser's Landing

Frenchman's Cay, West End. ☎ **284/495-4554.** Reservations recommended. Main courses $13–$25. AE, DISC, MC, V. Daily 11am–10pm. CARIBBEAN/ENGLISH PUB/MEXICAN.

This second Pusser's (see below for the first) is even more desirably located in the West End, opening onto the water. In this nautical setting you can choose a well-prepared dinner, including fresh grilled fish, or select some English-inspired dishes, such as a classic shepherd's pie. Begin with a hearty bowl of fresh soup with seasonal ingredients and follow it with filet mignon, West Indian roast chicken, or a fillet of mahimahi. "Mud pie" is the dessert of choice, or else you can try Pusser's rum cake. Some dishes occasionally miss the mark, but on the whole this is a good choice. Happy hour is daily from 4 to 6pm.

Pusser's Road Town Pub

Waterfront Dr. and Main St., Road Town. ☎ **284/494-3897.** Reservations not accepted. Main courses $7–$20. AE, DISC, MC, V. Daily 10am–10pm. CARIBBEAN/ENGLISH PUB/ MEXICAN.

Standing on the waterfront across from the ferry dock, Pusser's serves Caribbean fare, English pub grub, and good pizzas. This is not as fancy or as good as the previously recommended Pusser's but it's a lot more convenient and has faster service. The complete lunch and dinner menu includes English shepherd's pies and deli-style sandwiches. *Gourmet* magazine published the recipe for its chicken-and-asparagus pie. John Courage Ale is on draft, but the drink to have here is the famous Pusser's Rum, the same blend of five West Indian rums that the Royal Navy has served to its men for more than 300 years. Thursday is nickel beer night.

Quito's Gazebo

Cane Garden Bay. ☎ **284/945-4837.** Main courses $12–$26; lunch $4–$9. No credit cards. Tues–Sun 11am–3pm and 6:30–9:30pm. Bar Tues–Sun 11am–midnight. Transportation: Taxi. CONTINENTAL/WEST INDIAN.

Owned by Enri Quito and Janice Rymer, this is the most popular of the several restaurants located along the shoreline of Cane Bay. Quito, one of the island's best-known musicians, performs after dinner on Tuesday, Thursday, Friday, Saturday, and Sunday. Set directly on the sands of the beach and designed like an enlarged gazebo, the restaurant serves frothy rum-based drinks (ask for the house version of a piña colada, or a Bushwacker made with four different kinds of rum). Lunch consists of sandwiches and salads, while evening meals might include conch fritters, mahimahi with a wine-butter sauce, conch with Callwood rum sauce, chicken roti, or steamed local mutton served with a sauce of island tomatoes and pepper. Dishes have true island flavor and lots of zest.

Scuttlebutt Bar and Grill

Prospect Reef Resort, Drake's Hwy. ☎ **284/494-3311,** ext. 229. Sandwiches, platters, and salads $4.50–$10.50. AE, MC, V. Daily 7am–1am. INTERNATIONAL/CARIBBEAN.

This cafe's greatest asset is its location 1 mile west of the center of Road Town beside the smallest and most charming marina in Road Town. Order your meal at the counter, then carry it to one of the picnic tables, which are sheltered from the sun but not from the breezes off the water. The simple setting here keeps prices down, and the food, especially breakfast, is plentiful and good. Specialties include beef crepes or crabmeat salads, sandwiches, burgers, and a house drink that combines several kinds of rum into a lethal combination known as a Painkiller. The place is especially popular at breakfast, when eight different kinds of "rooster omelets" draw yachters and construction workers alike.

Sebastians on the Beach

West End. ☎ **284/495-4212.** Reservations required for dinner only. Main courses $15–$35; lunch from $12. AE, DISC, MC, V. Daily 8–11am, noon–3pm, and 6:30–9:30pm. Bar daily 7am– 10:30pm. INTERNATIONAL.

The wooden tables and rush-bottomed chairs here are scattered, Polynesian style, beneath a rustic yet comfortable pavilion a few feet from the waves of the island's West End. Sun lovers sit within the open courtyard nearby. Sebastian's is a good choice if you're in the area for lunch. Nothing is special, just hot sandwiches, West Indian fritters, and a homemade soup of the day, along with burgers—but it's

---

An Excursion to Cane Garden Bay

Cane Garden Bay II, one of the choicest pieces of real estate on Tortola (directly west of Road Town), was discovered long ago by the sailing crowd. Its white sandy beach with sheltering palms is a cliché of Caribbean charm, but it's sometimes crowded with cruise-ship passengers. The beach alone is reason to visit Cane Garden Bay.

    Rhymer's, Cane Garden Bay (☎ **284/495-4639**), is the place to go for food and entertainment. Skippers of any kind of craft are likely to stock up on supplies here, but you can also order cold beer and refreshing rum drinks. If you're hungry, try the conch or whelk, or the barbecued spareribs. The beach bar and restaurant is open daily from 8am to 9pm and serves breakfast, lunch, and dinner. On Thursday night a steel-drum band entertains the mariners. Ice and freshwater showers are available (you can rent towels). Ask about renting Sunfish and Windsurfers from concessions on the beach. American Express, MasterCard, and Visa are accepted.

---

all satisfying. At night, dishes often have more flair and flavor. Your best bet is the fresh fish of the day, which can be panfried, grilled, or blackened, with a choice of sauces, including a local blend of seasonings and spices. You might also try their Jamaican jerk chicken, or vegetable casserole. Surf-and-turf items are also available.

BEACHES, WATER SPORTS & OTHER OUTDOOR PURSUITS
BEACHES

Beaches are rarely crowded on Tortola unless a cruise ship arrives. You can rent a car or a Jeep to reach the beaches below, or else take a taxi (arrange for a return at an appointed time). There is no public transportation.

    The finest beach is ✪ **Cane Garden Bay,** which some aficionados have compared favorably to the famous Magens Bay Beach on the north shore of St. Thomas. Cane Garden Bay lies directly west of Road Town, up and down some steep hills, but it's worth the effort to get there.

    Surfers like **Apple Bay,** lying to the west of Road Town. A hotel on Apple Bay, Sebastians on the Beach (see "Where to Stay," above), caters to a surfing crowd. January and February are the ideal time to visit.

    Brewers Bay, site of a campground, lies northwest of Road Town. Both snorkelers and surfers are attracted to this beach.

    Smugglers Cove is at the extreme western end of Tortola, opposite from the offshore island of Great Thatch. The American island of St. John is directly south of Smugglers Cove. This beach, also known as Lowre Belmont Bay, also attracts surfers.

    Long Bay Beach is on Beef Island, east of Tortola, and the site of the major airport. This mile-long stretch of white-sand beach is reached by taking the Queen Elizabeth Bridge to a dirt road on the left that's just before the airport. From Long Bay, you'll have a good view of Little Camanoe, one of the rocky offshore islands around Tortola.

WATER SPORTS

SCUBA DIVING   The one dive site in the British Virgins that lures divers from around the world is the wreckage of the **HMS _Rhone_** (see box below), which sank in 1867 near the western point of Salt Island. _Skin Diver_ magazine called this "the world's most fantastic shipwreck dive." It teems with beautiful marine life and coral formations, and was featured in the motion picture *The Deep*. Although it's no *Rhone*, **Chikuzen** is another intriguing dive site off Tortola. It's a 270-foot steel-hulled refrigerator ship, which sank off the island's east end in 1981. The hull, still intact under about 80 feet of water, is now home to a vast array of tropical fish, including yellowtail, barracuda, black-tip sharks, octopus, and drum fish.

The best way for novice and expert divers to see these and other great dive sites is with one of the following outfitters:

Baskin in the Sun, a PADI five-star facility (☎ **800/233-7938** in the U.S., or 284/494-5854), on Tortola is a good choice with two different locations at the Prospect Reef Resort, near Road Town, and at Soper's Hole, on Tortola's West End. Baskin's most popular trip is the supervised "Half-Day Scuba Diving" experience for $95, catered to beginners, but there are trips for all levels of experience. Daily excursions are scheduled to the HMS *Rhone,* as well as to "Painted Walls," an underwater canyon in which the walls are formed of brightly colored coral and sponges, and the "Indians," four pinnacle rocks that divers trace down to coral reefs along the sea floor, 40 feet below the surface.

Underwater Safaris (☎ **800/537-7032** in the U.S., or 284/494-3235) takes you to all the best sites, including the HMS *Rhone,* "Spyglass Wall," and "Alice in Wonderland." It has two offices: "Safari Base," in Road Town, and "Safari Cay" on Cooper Island. Get complete directions and information when you call. The center, connected with The Moorings (see below), offers a complete PADI and NAUI training facility. An introductory resort course and one dive costs $95, and an open-water certification, with 4 days of instruction and four open-water dives, goes for $385, plus $40 for the instruction manual.

SNORKELING   If you plan on snorkeling by yourself, exercise due caution and consider driving to **Marina Cay,** off Tortola's East End; it's a good snorkeling beach. You may also want to head to **Cooper Island,** across Sir Francis Drake Channel. **Underwater Safaris** (see above) leads snorkel expeditions to both sites, weather permitting.

YACHTING   Tortola boasts the largest fleet of bareboat sailing charters in the world. The best charter company is ✪ **The Moorings,** Wickhams Cay (P.O. Box 139, Road Town), B.V.I. (☎ **800/535-7289** in the U.S., or 284/494-2332), whose

---

The Wreck of the HMS *Rhone*

At any Virgin Island bar frequented by scuba enthusiasts, the conversation will inevitably turn to one of the world's most unusual dive sites, the wreck of the HMS *Rhone*. The 310-foot steel-hulled steamship was built in Britain in 1865 and sank during a violent unexpected hurricane in 1867. Today, the steel wreckage, home to myriad species of fish and encrusting corals, rests on a steeply sloping underwater site off the western coast of Salt Island, southwest of Tortola.

Scuba instructors carefully predetermine whether divers will visit either the bow of the sunken wreck (80 feet underwater) or the stern (20 feet underwater) based on weather and water conditions. In either case, the experience is among the most eerie (and sometimes mystical) in the underwater world. The wreck's allure was captured by the 1977 film *The Deep,* which featured evocative underwater shots of Jacqueline Bisset. See "Scuba Diving" above for a list of dive outfitters.

8-acre waterside resort is also recommended in "Where to Stay," above. You can choose from a fleet of sailing yachts, which can accommodate up to four couples in comfort and style. Depending on your skill and inclination, you can arrange a bareboat rental (with no crew); a fully crewed rental with a skipper, a staff, and a cook; or any variation in between. Boats usually come equipped with a portable barbecue, snorkeling gear, dinghy, linens, and galley equipment.

The Moorings has an experienced staff of mechanics, electricians, riggers, and cleaners. In addition, if you're going out on your own, you'll get a thorough briefing session about Virgin Island waters and anchorages.

EXPLORING SAGE MOUNTAIN NATIONAL PARK

No visit to Tortola is complete without a trip to ✪ **Sage Mountain National Park** (on Ridge Road, west of Road Town), a national park rising 1,780 feet. On its slopes, you'll find traces of a primeval rain forest with ideal spots for picnicking as you gaze out at neighboring islets and cays.

Before you head out among the flora and fauna, stop by the tourist office and pick up a copy of a little brochure called *Sage Mountain National Park.* It has a location map, indicating directions to the forest (where there is a parking lot) and an outline of the park's main trails.

Covering 92 acres, the park was established in 1964 to protect the remnants of Tortola's original forests which were not burned or cleared during the island's plantation era. From the parking lot, a trail leads to the main entrance of the park. The two main trails are the Rain Forest Trail and the Mahogany Forest Trail.

ORGANIZED TOURS

Travel Plan Tours, Waterfront Plaza, Road Town (☎ **284/494-2872**), offers organized tours of Tortola. They will pick you up at your hotel (a minimum of four people is required) and take you on a $2^1/_2$-hour tour of the island for around $25. The agent also offers $2^1/_2$-hour snorkeling tours for $35 per person and glassbottom boat tours. A **taxi tour** lasting $2^1/_2$ hours costs $45 for up to three persons. To call a taxi in Road Town, dial **284/494-2322;** on Beef Island, **284/495-2378.**

DRIVING TOUR
Tortola's West End

Start: Harbour Drive, in the center of Road Town.
Finish: Harbour Drive, in the center of Road Town.
Time: 2 hours, not counting stops.
Best Times: Any day before 5:30pm.
Worst Times: Sunday, when many places close.

This tour concentrates on the West End, site of some of the lovelier beaches and vistas. Begin your tour at:

1. Wickhams Cay, which has the densest concentration of shops and restaurants in Road Town. Less carefully planned than many other Caribbean capitals, Road Town seems at first glance to be a scattered sprawl of modern buildings which form a crescent along the harbor front and up the hillsides. At Wickhams Cay, however, some of the town's charm is more apparent.

From Road Town, head southwest along the coastal road, passing the capital's many bars and restaurants, including Pusser's, a popular watering hole. You'll also pass St. Paul's Episcopal Church (established 1937) and the Faith Tabernacle Church.

Less than 2 miles away on your left is the sandy peninsula containing:

2. **Nanny Cay Hotel and Marina.** There's an attractive restaurant here called Pegleg Landing (see "Where to Dine," below) and the opportunity to view some fine yachts bobbing at anchor.

Along the same road, 2¹/₂ miles southwest of Road Town, panoramic views on your left reveal the 5-mile-wide Sir Francis Drake Channel, loved by yachters throughout the world. You'll now traverse a curvy expanse of uncluttered road, one of the loveliest on the island, dotted with rocks, cays, inlets, and uninhabited offshore islands.

The crumbling antique masonry on the right side of the road (look through the creeping vegetation) is the ruins of a stone prison built by the English for pirates and unruly slaves. Lush St. John will appear across the distant channel.

Keeping the water constantly on your left, you'll come to the unpretentious hamlet of:

3. **West End and the pier at Soper's Hole.** Yachters and boaters report to the immigration and Customs officer stationed here. Turn left on the hamlet's only bridge to:

4. **Frenchman's Cay,** where there's a scenic view and, to the west, Little Thatch Island.

Retrace your route toward Road Town. At the first major intersection, turn left up Zion's Hill. Tucked into a hollow in the hillside, is the:

5. **Zion Hill Methodist Church.** Boasting a devoted local following despite its rural isolation, it's one of many churches dotting the island.

You'll soon be driving parallel to the island's northern coast, site of many of its least-developed beaches, with imaginative names like Apple Bay, Little and Great Carrot bays, and Ballast Bay. Stop at any of them to swim or snorkel wherever it looks safe; if in doubt, ask a local. Continuing along the coast, you'll pass the Methodist Church of Carrot Bay and the Seventh-day Adventist Church of Tortola.

☕ **TAKE A BREAK**   On the island's north coast, **Quito's Gazebo** (☎ 284/495-4837) is at Cane Garden Bay. Owned by Quito Rymer, one of the island's best musicians, it serves piña coladas (either virgin or laced with liberal quantities of Callwood's local rum) in an enlarged gazebo built almost directly above the waves.

After Quito's, the road will cut inland, climbing dramatically through forests and fields; a sweeping view will unfold continuously behind you. Soon, you'll be forced to make a turn. Fork left, and continue for a short distance along the rocky spine that runs down the length of the island. A sign will point to a platform offering one of the finest views on Tortola:

6. **SkyWorld.** This eagle's-nest aerie has survived the most violent hurricanes. It offers unparalleled views of the entire island, as well as an array of food and drink. Many daytime visitors return to SkyWorld for a candlelit dinner.

After passing SkyWorld, continue east for about 1 mile, keeping right whenever possible. After the second right fork, the road will descend, passing houses, churches, suburbs, and schools, and eventually join the main road running beside the waterfront at Road Town.

SHOPPING

Most of the shops in the British Virgin Islands are on Main Street, in Road Town on Tortola. British goods are imported without duty, and the savvy shopper will be able to find some good buys among these imported items, especially in English china. In general, store hours are 9am to 4pm Monday through Friday and 9am to 1pm on Saturday.

Caribbean Corner Spice House Co.
Soper's Hole. ☎ **284/495-4498.**

This shop has the finest selection of spices and herbs on the island, along with a selection of local handcrafts and botanical skin-care products. There's also a selection of Cuban cigars, but you'll have to smoke them on the island, as U.S. customs does not allow their importation.

Caribbean Fine Arts Ltd.
Main St., Road Town. ☎ **284/494-4240.**

This store has one of the most unusual collections of art from the West Indies. Not only does it sell original watercolors and oils, but also offers limited-edition serigraphs and sepia photographs from the dawn of the century. It also sells pottery and primitive art.

Caribbean Handprints
Main St., Road Town. ☎ **284/494-3717.**

This store features island handprints, all by local craftspeople on Tortola. It also sells colorful fabric by the yard.

Flamboyance
Soper's Hole. ☎ **284/495-4699.**

This is the best place to shop for duty-free perfume. Fendi purses are also sold here.

Fort Wimes Gourmet
Main St., Road Town. ☎ **284/494-3036.**

For the makings of a picnic you'd otherwise have to fly to the mainland to top, stock up on provisions here, partaking of everything from Petrossian caviar to French champagne. Sample its full line of Hediard pâté terrines along with a wide selection of chocolates, including some of the best from Paris. There's also an elegant showcase of glassware, lacquered boxes, and handmade Russian filigree items plated in 24-karat gold.

Little Denmark
Main St., Road Town. ☎ **284/494-2455.**

Little Denmark is your best bet for famous names in gold and silver jewelry and china: Spode and Royal Copenhagen. Here you'll find many of the well-known designs from Scandinavian countries. It also offers jewelry made in the B.V.I., and there's a collection of watches. The outlet also offers a large selection of fishing equipment. They also sell Cuban cigars, which can't be brought back into the United States, but have to be smoked before you return.

J. R. O'Neal
Upper Main St., Road Town. ☎ **284/494-2292.**

Across from the Methodist church, this is a decorative and home accessories store, with the most extensive collection of items on the island. You'll find terra-cotta pottery, wicker and rattan home furnishings, Mexican glassware, dhurrie rugs, baskets, and ceramics. There's also a collection of fine crystal and China.

Exploring "Treasure Island"

Legend has it that Norman Island, a tiny isle south of Tortola and east of St. John, was the inspiration for Robert Louis Stevenson's *Treasure Island,* first published in 1883. It's only accessible by boat and has serviced smugglers and ruffians since the 1600s, when pirates used its hillocks to spot Spanish galleons. You can row a dinghy into the southernmost cave on the island—with bats overhead and phosphorescent patches—where Stevenson's Mr. Fleming supposedly stowed his precious treasure. Norman Island has a series of other caves whose waters are teeming with marine life. These caves are a well-known snorkeling spot in the B.V.I. Intrepid hikers climb through scrubland to the island's central ridge, Spy Glass Hill, to take in the panoramic views of land and sea. Be aware that hiking trails are either nonexistent or poorly maintained.

Most boat trips to Norman Island revolve around snorkeling. Try **King Charters** (☎ **284/494-5820**) or **Captain Roy** (☎ **284/495-2653**), a knowledgeable local skipper who runs half-day or full-day excursions to Norman Island and other snorkeling sites.

Pusser's Company Store
Main St., Road Town. ☎ **284/494-2467.**

Here you'll find a long, mahogany-trimmed bar accented with many fine nautical artifacts and a line of Pusser's sports and travel clothing and upmarket gift items. Pusser's Rum is one of the best-selling items here, or perhaps you'd prefer a Pusser's ceramic flask as a memento of your visit.

✪ Sunny Caribbee Herb and Spice Company
Main St., Road Town. ☎ **284/494-2178.**

This old West Indian building was the first hotel on Tortola, and its shop specializes in Caribbean spices, seasonings, teas, condiments, and handcrafts. You can buy two world-famous specialties here: West Indian Hangover Cure and Arawak Love Potion. A Caribbean cosmetics collection, Sunsations, is also available and includes herbal bath gels, island perfume, and suntan lotions. Most of the products are blended and packaged in an adjacent factory. With its aroma of spices permeating the air of the neighborhood, this factory is an attraction in itself. There's a daily sampling of island products, something different every day—perhaps tea, coffee, sauces, or dips. In the Sunny Caribbee Art Gallery, adjacent to the spice shop, you'll find an extensive collection of original art, prints, metal sculpture, and many other Caribbean crafts.

TORTOLA AFTER DARK

Ask around to find out which hotel has entertainment on a given evening. Steel bands and fungi or scratch bands appear regularly, and nonresidents are usually welcome. Pick up a copy of *Limin' Times,* available at your hotel, which lists local events.

✪ Bomba's Surfside Shack
Cappoon's Bay. ☎ **284/495-4148.** Free admission.

This the oldest, most memorable, and most uninhibited nightlife venue on the island, known for its hedonistic bashes, called "Full Moon Parties." It sits on a 20-foot-wide strip of unpromising coastline near the West End. By anyone's standards this is the junk palace of the island; it's covered with Day-Glo graffiti and laced into a semblance of structure with wire and scraps of plywood, driftwood, and abandoned rubber tires. Despite its appearance, the shack has the sound system to create a really great party. The place is at its wildest on Wednesday and Sunday nights, when there's live music and a $7 all-you-can-eat barbecue. Open daily from 10am to midnight (or later, depending on business).

The Moorings/Mariner Inn

Wickhams Cay. ☎ **284/494-2332.** Free admission.

This inn (see "Where to Stay," above) contains the preferred watering hole for some of the most upscale yacht owners in the islands. Open to a view of its own marina, and bathed in a dim and flattering light, the place is nautical and relaxed. A fungi band sometimes provides a backdrop to the socializing.

Spyhouse Bar

Treasure Isle Hotel, east end of Road Town. ☎ **284/494-2501.** Free admission.

This is one of the most popular bars on the island. Lying in a little house designed with Haitian gingerbread, it has a sunken bar, set on a terrace overlooking the swimming pool and faraway marina facilities of its popular hotel (see "Where to Stay," above). Specialties include Treasure Island rum punch with dark rum, orange juice, strawberry syrup, and apricot brandy, and "Windstorm," made with Galiano, rum, fruit punch, and 7-Up.

2 Virgin Gorda

The second-largest island in the British cluster, Virgin Gorda is 10 miles long and 2 miles wide, with a population of 1,400-odd people. It is located 12 miles east of Tortola and 26 miles from St. Thomas.

In 1493, on his second voyage to the New World, Columbus named the island Virgin Gorda or "Fat Virgin," after the mountain framing the island, which looks like a protruding stomach. Seen from a boat, its shape has also been compared to that of a pregnant woman lying on her back.

The island was a fairly desolate agricultural community until Laurance Rockefeller established the resort of Little Dix in the early 1960s, following his success with Caneel Bay during the 1950s.

He envisioned a "wilderness beach," where privacy and solitude reigned, and he literally put Virgin Gorda on the world map. Other major hotels followed in the wake of Little Dix, but privacy and solitude still reign supreme.

GETTING THERE & GETTING AROUND

Speedy's Fantasy (☎ **284/495-5240**) operates a ferry service between Road Town on Tortola and Virgin Gorda. Three ferries a day leave from Road Town Monday through Saturday; two run on Sunday. The cost is $10 one way or $19 round-trip. From St. Thomas to Virgin Gorda, there is service three times a week (Tuesday, Thursday, and Saturday); the cost is $25 one way and $45 round-trip.

Air St. Thomas (☎ **284/776-2722**) flies to Virgin Gorda daily from San Juan, Puerto Rico. A one-way fare costs $63, or else $129 round-trip.

You can rent and drive a car on Virgin Gorda although there are only a few roads. Taxi companies also rent cars; a four-wheel-drive vehicle is best for negotiating some of the island's rougher terrain. Try **Mahogany Rentals and Taxi Service** (☎ **284/ 495-5469**).

Area Code Change Notice

Please note that, effective October 1, 1997, the area code for the British Virgin Islands will change from **809** to **284.** All of the B.V.I. area codes in this book have been changed to 284. Prior to October 1, you will need to use the 809 area code for all B.V.I. phone numbers.

An aerial view of the island shows what looks like three bulky masses connected by two very narrow isthmuses. The most northeasterly of these three masses (which contains two of the most interesting hotels) is not even accessible by road at all, requiring ferryboat transit from the more accessible parts of the island.

One possibility for exploring Virgin Gorda by car is to drive from the southwest to the northeast along the island's rocky and meandering spine. This route will take you to **The Baths** (in the extreme southeast), **Spanish Harbour** (near the middle), and eventually, after skirting the mountainous edges of **Gorda Peak,** the most northwesterly tip of the island's road system, near North Sound. Here, a miniarmada of infrequently scheduled ferryboats depart and arrive from Biras Creek and the Bitter End Yacht Club.

Independently operated open-sided **safari buses** run along the main road. Holding up to 14 passengers, these buses charge upwards from $3 per person to transport a passenger, say, from The Valley to The Baths.

FAST FACTS

American Express   The local representative is Travel Plan, Virgin Gorda Yacht Harbour (☎ **284/495-5586**), open Monday through Friday 9am to noon and 1 to 3pm, Saturday from 9am to 1pm.

Cameras and Film   Try Kysk Tropix, Virgin Gorda Yacht Harbour (☎ **284/ 495-5636**), open Monday through Saturday from 9am to 5:45pm.

Laundry and Dry Cleaning   Stevens Laundry and Dry Cleaning, near the Virgin Gorda Yacht Harbour (☎ **284/495-5525**), is open daily from 8am to noon and 1 to 9pm.

Services and Supplies   In Spanish Town, opposite Beef Island, stands the Yacht Harbour Shopping Centre, where you can stock up on supplies and find various services. The shopping complex contains a supermarket, ice-cream parlor, a pub, a wine and liquor store, a dive shop, a bakery, a Laundromat, a drugstore, and a boutique.

Visitor Information   The **tourist office** in Virgin Gorda is in Virgin Gorda Yacht Harbor, Spanish Town (☎ **284/495-5182**).

WHERE TO STAY
VERY EXPENSIVE

Little Dix Bay Hotel
On the northwest corner of the island (P.O. Box 70), Virgin Gorda, B.V.I. ☎ **800/928-3000** in the U.S., or 284/495-5555. Fax 284/495-5661. 98 rms, 4 suites. TEL. Winter, $475–$725 double; $1,300 suite. Off-season, $250–$450 double; $650–$900 suite. MAP $70 per person extra. AE, DC, MC, V. Take the private ferry service from the Beef Island airport to the resort.

Completely renovated in 1996, this 1964 hotel is now run by the Dallas-based Rosewood chain of luxurious hotels. An embodiment of understated luxury, the Little Dix Bay Hotel is a resort discreetly scattered along a half-mile crescent-shaped private bay on a 500-acre preserve. Many guests find this resort pricey and stuffy, infinitely

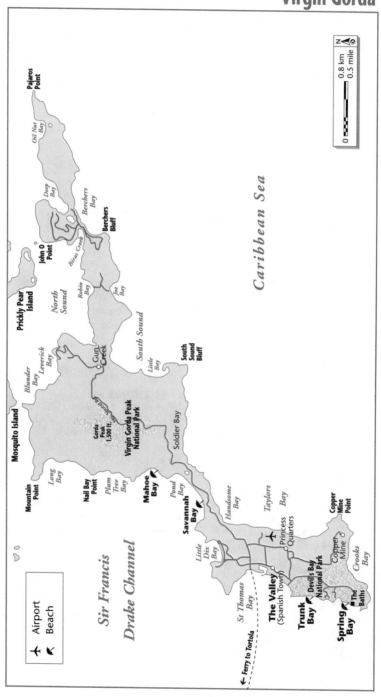

N

0.8 km
0.5 mile
0

Pajaros
Point

Oil Nut
Bay

Caribbean Sea

Deep
Bay

Berchers
Bay

Berchers
Bluff

John O
Point

Birea Creek

Prickly Pear
Island

Robin
Bay

Joe
Bay

North
Sound

Blunder
Bay

Leverick
Bay

Gun
Creek

South Sound

Little
Bay

South
Sound
Bluff

Mosquito Island

Gorda
Peak
1,500 ft.

Virgin Gorda Peak
National Park

Soldier Bay

Long
Bay

Mountain
Point

Nail Bay
Point

Plum
Tree
Bay

Mahoe
Bay

Pond
Bay

Savannah
Bay

Handsome
Bay

Taylors
Bay

Copper
Mine
Point

Little
Dix
Bay

Princess
Quarters

Copper
Mine

Crooks
Bay

Sir Francis
Drake Channel

Airport
Beach

St Thomas
Bay

The Valley
(Spanish Town)

Devil's Bay
National Park

Trunk
Bay

Spring
Bay

The
Baths

Ferry to Tortola

preferring the more casual elegance of Biras Creek Estate and the Bitter End Yacht Club (see below). It has the same quiet elegance as Caneel Bay on St. John in the U.S. Virgins.

All rooms, built in woods, have private terraces with views of the sea or of gardens. Trade winds come through louvers and screens, and the units are further cooled by ceiling fans or air-conditioning (in 44 of the rooms). Some units are two-story structures raised on stilts. All the guest rooms have been renovated with new furnishings and fabrics, evoking a Southeast Asia style with wicker or reed furniture, bamboo beds, Balinese boxes and baskets, along with ceramic objects of art. Telephones have been added to each room, providing guests with the option to reach out to the world or leave it at bay.

Dining/Entertainment: Four interconnected pyramids that face the sea comprise the roof of the Pavilion, venue for lunch buffets, afternoon teas, and candlelit dinners. The cuisine is international, with Caribbean specialties using fresh seafood, as exemplified by the red snapper with ratatouille drizzled with a curry infusion. For drinks, guests sit on the restaurant's terrace where a band performs nightly. The Sugar Mill is elegant but casual, specializing in fresh grilled fish, lobster, and steaks. On the edge of the beach, the Beach Grill serves light lunches and dinners.

Services: Unequaled service with a staff-to-guest ratio of one-to-one.

Facilities: Seven all-weather outdoor Laykold tennis courts, Sunfish sailboats, kayaks, snorkeling, scuba diving, waterskiing, boat rentals, deep-sea fishing, diving excursions, and the Virgin Gorda Yacht Harbor, half a mile from the resort (owned and operated by Little Dix Bay). The lack of a pool may bother some guests, but there is a fitness center.

EXPENSIVE

✪ Biras Creek Estate

North Sound (P.O. Box 54), Virgin Gorda, B.V.I. ☎ **800/608-9661** in the U.S., or 284/494-3555. Fax 284/494-3557. 32 suites, 1 two-bedroom villa. A/C. Winter, $495–$695 suite for 2; $795 villa for 2; $995 villa for 4. Off-season, $350–$425 suite for 2; $595 villa for 2; $795 villa for 4. Rates include all meals. AE, DISC, MC, V. Take the private motor launch from the Beef Island airport.

A private and romantic resort stands at the northern end of Virgin Gorda like a hilltop fortress, opening onto a good beach, much of which is artificial. Acquired by a former guest, Bert Houwer, the hideaway has vastly improved after a multimillion-dollar facelift. On a 150-acre estate with its own marina, it occupies a narrow neck of land flanked by the sea on three sides. To create their Caribbean hideaway, Norwegian shipping interests carved this resort out of the wilderness, but wisely protected the natural terrain. The greenhouse on the grounds keeps the resort supplied with foliage and flowers. Cooled by ceiling fans and air-conditioning, units have well-furnished bedrooms and divan beds with a sitting room and private patio, plus a refrigerator. Children five and under not allowed.

Dining/Entertainment: The food at the restaurant here has won high praise, and the wine cellar is also good. The two restaurants and drinking lounge are quietly elegant, and there's always a table with a view. A barbecued lunch is often served on the beach.

Services: Laundry, baby-sitting, taxi service for guests arriving in Virgin Gorda to the hotel's motor launch, free trips to nearby beaches.

Facilities: Swimming pool, snorkeling, Sunfish, paddleboards, tennis courts, kayaks, Hobie waves, unlimited use of motor dinghies.

○ The Bitter End Yacht Club

John O'Point, North Sound (P.O. Box 46), Virgin Gorda, B.V.I. ☎ **800/872-2392** or 312/
944-5855. Fax 312/944-2860. 46 beachfront villas, 38 Commodore Club suites, 9 hillside villas, 3 Freedom 30 Live-Aboard yachts. Winter (double occupancy), $520 beachfront villa; $570
Commodore Club Suite; $480 hillside villa; $480 Freedom 30 yacht. Off-season (double occupancy), $420 beachfront villa; $470 Commodore Club suite; $380 hillside villa; $350 Freedom
30 yacht. Rates include all meals. AE, DC, MC, V.

This rendezvous point for the yachting set has hosted the likes of treasure hunter Mel
Fisher and Jean-Michel Cousteau, but less well-known sailors or just lovers of the sea
have also been drawn to this family operated resort for the past 30 years. It opens onto
one of the most unspoiled and secluded deep-water harbors in the Caribbean, offering
the finest water sports program in the Virgin Islands. Guests have unlimited use of
the resort's million-dollar fleet, the Nick Trotter Sailing and Windsurfing School. The
Bitter End offers an informal yet elegant life, as guests settle into one of the hillside
chalets or well-appointed beachfront and hillside villas overlooking the sound and
yachts at anchor. Only the Commodore Suites are air-conditioned.

For something novel, you can stay aboard one of the 30-foot yachts, yours to sail,
with dockage and daily maid service, meals in the Yacht Club dining room, and overnight provisions.

Dining/Entertainment: Dining is in the Clubhouse Steak and Seafood Grille, the
English Carvery, or the Pub. Evening entertainment is provided by "The Reflections,"
a steel-drum band that gave a command performance for Princess Diana. On other
nights, local reggae and soca bands perform (soca music blends reggae rhythms with
popular Latino-American sounds).

Services: Laundry, free trips to nearby islands, ferry service from the Beef Island
airport at Tortola.

Facilities: Unlimited use of Lasers, Sunfish, Rhodes 19s, windsurfing equipment,
J-24s, Boston whalers, outboard skiffs; reef snorkeling; scuba diving; sport fishing;
fitness center; expeditions to neighboring cays; marine science participation; swimming pool.

MODERATE

Fischers Cove Beach Hotel

The Valley (P.O. Box 60), Virgin Gorda, B.V.I. ☎ **284/495-5252.** Fax 284/495-5820. 12 rms,
8 one-bedroom cottages. A/C. Winter, $145–$150 double; $170–$180 cottage. Off-season,
$100 double; $125–$135 cottage. MAP $40 per person extra. AE, MC, V.

There's swimming at your doorstep in this group of units nestled near the sandy
beach of St. Thomas Bay. Erected of native stone, each cottage is self-contained, with
one or two bedrooms and a combination living/dining room with a kitchenette. At
a food store near the grounds, you can stock up on provisions if you're doing your
own cooking. There are 12 pleasant but simple rooms with views of Drake Channel. Each has its own private bath (hot and cold showers) and private balcony. Jeep
rentals are available, as is a children's playground. There's often live entertainment.

○ The Olde Yard Inn

The Valley (P.O. Box 26), Virgin Gorda, B.V.I. ☎ **800/653-9273** or 284/495-5544. Fax 284/
495-5986. 14 rms. Winter, $195 double; $220 triple; $245 quad. Off-season, $110–$150
double; $130–$170 triple; $150–$190 quad. MAP $50 per person extra. Honeymoon packages
available. AE, MC, V.

This little charmer is a mile from the airport. Near the main house are two long bun-
galows with large renovated bedrooms, each with its own bath and patio. Four of the
rooms are air-conditioned, and all have ceiling fans and trade-wind breezes. Three

of the rooms also contain minirefrigerators. Scattered about are a few antiques and special accessories. You can go for a sail on a yacht or a snorkeling adventure at one of 16 beaches, with a picnic lunch provided.

Dining/Entertainment: Served under a cedarwood roof, the French-accented meals are one of the reasons for coming over. Lunch is served poolside at the Sip and Dip Grill. Dinners are from 6:30 to 8:30pm. There's live entertainment three times a week in the dining room.

Facilities: Off-site sailboat rentals, Jacuzzi, modern health club, one of the best hotel libraries in the Caribbean, huge freshwater pool, complimentary shuttle service to Savannah Bay Beach (a 20-minute walk).

INEXPENSIVE

Guavaberry Spring Bay Vacation Homes
Spring Bay (P.O. Box 20), Virgin Gorda, B.V.I. ☎ **284/495-5227.** Fax 284/495-5283. 18 houses. Winter, $142 one-bedroom house for 2; $200 two-bedroom house for 4. Off-season, $95 one-bedroom house for 2; $140 two-bedroom house for 4. Additional person $15–$20 extra. No credit cards.

Staying in one of these hexagonal white-roofed redwood houses built on stilts is like living in a tree house, with screened and louvered walls to let in sea breezes. Each home, available for daily or weekly rental, has one or two bedrooms, and all have a private bath, small kitchenette, dining area, and elevated sundeck overlooking Sir Francis Drake Passage. Within a few minutes of the cottage colony is the beach at Spring Bay, and the Yacht Harbour Shopping Centre is a mile away. The Baths, the island's top natural attraction, is also nearby.

The owners provide a complete commissary for guests, and tropical fruits can be picked in season or bought at local shops. They will make arrangements for day charters, scuba diving, or fishing, and will also arrange for island Jeep tours and sailing.

WHERE TO DINE
EXPENSIVE

Chez Bamboo
The Valley. ☎ **284/495-5963.** Reservations recommended. Main courses $16–$28. MC, V. Tues–Sun 6–10pm. CONTINENTAL/CARIBBEAN.

Chez Bamboo lies beside the main road, a short walk north of the yacht harbor at Spanish Town. On the ground floor of a clean and modern breeze-filled house, it is the most competent and urbanized of the privately owned restaurants on the island. The decor has been redone to look like a New York jazz club, and there's also a shaded outdoor patio. The menu serves many French-accented dishes, but also specializes in Carib/Creole dining, such as conch gumbo and lobster with curry sauce. Thursday and Saturday are prime rib and jazz nights.

MODERATE

Bath and Turtle Pub
Virgin Gorda Yacht Harbour, Spanish Town. ☎ **284/495-5239.** Reservations recommended. Main courses $16–$25. AE, MC, V. Daily 7am–midnight. INTERNATIONAL.

At the end of the waterfront shopping plaza in Spanish Town sits the most popular pub on Virgin Gorda, packed with locals during happy hour from 4 to 6pm. Even if you don't care about food, you might join the regulars over midmorning guava coladas or peach daiquiris. There's live music every Wednesday in summer only from 8pm to midnight (no cover charge). From its handful of indoor and courtyard tables, you can order fried fish fingers, nachos, very spicy chili, pizzas, Reubens or tuna melts, steak, lobster, and daily seafood specials such as conch fritters from the simple menu here.

Teacher Ilma's

The Valley. ☎ **284/495-5355.** Reservations required for dinner (call before 3pm). Full dinner $18–$25. No credit cards. Daily 12:30–2pm and 7:30–9:30pm. At Spanish Town, turn left at the main road past the entrance to the Fischers Cove Hotel; the sign to Teacher Ilma's is about 2 minutes ahead to the right. WEST INDIAN.

Mrs. Ilma O'Neal, who taught youngsters in the island's public school for 43 years, began her restaurant by cooking privately for visitors and island construction workers. Main courses, which include appetizers, might be chicken, local goat meat, lobster, conch, pork, or fish (your choice of grouper, snapper, tuna, dolphin, swordfish, or triggerfish), followed by such desserts as homemade coconut, pineapple, or guava pies. Teacher Ilma emphasizes that her cuisine is not Creole but local in its origins and flavors.

INEXPENSIVE

The Crab Hole

The Valley. ☎ **284/495-5307.** Reservations required for dinner. Main courses $10–$16. No credit cards. Mon–Sat 11:30am–2pm and 7–10pm. WEST INDIAN.

This is a clean and decent West Indian restaurant contained within the private home of Kenroy and Janet Millington. Built in 1986, it occupies the ground level of a concrete house surrounded by fields and other houses.

Order your food from the blackboard posted above the bar. The menu changes daily, but might include stewed whelk with a creole sauce made from local spices and tomatoes, bullfoot soup, curried chicken, fried fish, stewed oxtail, or hamburgers. Everything has a good, homemade flavor, but nothing is fancy here.

Mad Dog

The Baths, The Country. ☎ **284/495-5830.** Sandwiches $4; piña coladas $3.50. No credit cards. Daily 10am–7pm. PIÑA COLADAS/SANDWICHES.

Established in 1989, this is the most skillful and charming reconstruction of a West Indian cottage on Virgin Gorda. A wide veranda and the brightly painted 19th-century wooden timbers and clapboards create a cozy and convivial drink and sandwich bar where the piña coladas are absolutely divine. The owner and supervisor of this laid-back corner of heaven is London-born Colin McCullough, a self-described mad dog who sailed the B.V.I. for almost 30 years before establishing his domain here.

Thelma's Hideout

The Valley. ☎ **284/495-5646.** Reservations required for dinner. Lunch $8–$9; dinner $13–$15. No credit cards. Daily 7–10am, 11:30am–2:30pm; and (only upon notification before 3pm) 6–10pm. Bar daily 11am–midnight. WEST INDIAN.

Located in a concrete house whose angles are softened by ascending tiers of verandas, one of the most outspoken grandes dames of Virgin Gorda, Mrs. Thelma King (who worked in Manhattan for many years before returning to her native B.V.I.) runs a convivial gathering place for the island's West Indian community. Food choices include grilled steaks, fish filets, and West Indian stews containing pork, mutton, or chicken. Limeade or mauby are available, but many clients stick to rum or beer. There's live music presented on Saturday night in winter, and every other Saturday in off-season.

TOURING THE ISLAND
BEACHES

The best beaches are at **The Baths** (see below), where giant boulders form a series of panoramic pools and grottoes flooded with sea water. Snorkeling in this area is excellent. Neighboring The Baths is **Spring Bay,** one of the best of the island's beaches, with white sand, clear water, and good snorkeling. **Trunk Bay** is a wide sand beach accessible by boat or by a rough path from Spring Bay. **Savannah Bay** is a sandy beach north of Yacht Harbour. **Mahoe Bay,** at the Mango Bay Resort, has a gently curving beach with vivid blue water.

NATURAL ATTRACTIONS

Coppermine Point is the site of an abandoned copper mine and smelter. Because of loose rock formations, it can be dangerous, and you should exercise caution if you explore it. Legend has it that the Spanish worked these mines in the 1600s; however, the only authenticated document reveals that the English sank the shafts in 1838 to mine copper.

✪ **The Baths** is one of the most fascinating natural attractions in the B.V.I. and a world-famous snorkeling spot (equipment can be rented on the beach). They consist of tranquil pools and caves formed by gigantic house-size boulders. As these boulders toppled over one another, they formed saltwater grottoes, suitable for exploring. The pools among the boulders provide excellent places for swimming.

The **Devil's Bay National Park** can be reached by a trail from the Baths Roundabout. The walk to the secluded coral-sand beach through a setting of boulders and dry coastal vegetation takes about 15 minutes.

The Baths and surrounding areas are part of a proposed system of parks and protected areas for the B.V.I. The protected area encompasses 682 acres of land, including sites at Little Fort, Spring Bay, The Baths, and Devil's Bay on the east coast.

If you grow tired of sun, sea, and sand, consider hiking up the stairs and paths that crisscross Virgin Gorda's largest stretch of undeveloped land: the **Virgin Gorda Peak National Park.** To reach the best point of departure for your uphill trek, drive north of the valley on the only road leading to North Sound for about 15 minutes. (Use of a four-wheel-drive vehicle is preferable on these hilly roads.) Stop at the base of the stairway leading steeply uphill, where there's a sign pointing to the Virgin Gorda Peak National Park.

It takes between 25 and 40 minutes to reach the summit of ✪ **Gorda Peak,** the highest point on the island, where views of many scattered islets of the Virgin archipelago await you. There's a tower at the summit, which you can climb for enhanced views. Along the way, you're likely to encounter birds, lizards, and nonvenomous snakes. Consider bringing a picnic; there are picnic tables scattered amid the network of hiking trails.

ORGANIZED TOURS

The best way to see the island if you're over for a day trip is to call Andy Flax at the Fischers Cove Beach Hotel. He runs the **Virgin Gorda Tours Association** (☎ **284/ 495-5252**), which will give you a tour of the island for $20 per person. The tour leaves twice daily. You can be picked up at the ferry dock if you give them a 24-hour notice.

Kilbrides Underwater Tours is located at the Bitter End Resort at North Sound (☎ **800/932-4286** in the U.S., or 284/495-9638). Today Kilbrides offers the best diving in the B.V.I. at 15 to 20 dive sites, including the wreck of the ill-fated HMS *Rhone*. Prices range from $80 to $90 for a two-tank dive on one of the coral reefs.

A one-tank dive in the afternoon costs $60. Fees include use of all necessary equipment, and videos of your dives are available.

VIRGIN GORDA AFTER DARK

There's isn't a lot of action at night, unless you want to make some of your own. The previously recommended **Bath and Turtle Pub** (☎ 284/495-5239), at Yacht Harbour, brings in local bands for dancing. Most evenings in winter the **Bitter End Yacht Club** (☎ 284/494-2745), also recommended above, has live music. Call to see what's happening at the time of your visit. The biggest venue for island nightlife is:

Andy's Chateau de Pirate

Fischer's Cove Beach Hotel, The Valley. ☎ **284/495-5252.** No cover most nights, $5 Fri–Sun.

Built from poured concrete in 1985, this sprawling, sparsely furnished local hang-out has a simple stage, a very long bar, and huge oceanfront windows that almost never close. The complex also houses the Lobster Pot Restaurant, the Buccaneer Bar, and the nightclub EFX. The Lobster Pot is open from 7am to 10pm.

The place is a famous showcase for the island's musical groups, which perform Wednesday through Sunday from 8pm to midnight; lots of people congregate to listen and kibitz.

3 Jost Van Dyke

This rugged island (pop. 150) on the seaward (west) side of Tortola was named after a Dutch settler. On the south shore of this 4-square-mile mountainous island are some good beaches, especially at White Bay and Great Harbour. The island has just a handful of places to stay but has several dining choices, as it's a popular stopover point, not only for the yachting set but also for many cruise ships. The island is only tranquil when cruise ships aren't in port.

In the 1700s, a Quaker colony settled here to develop sugarcane plantations. One of the colonists, William Thornton, won a worldwide competition to design the Capitol in Washington, D.C. Smaller islands surround the place, including Little Jost Van Dyke, the birthplace of Dr. John Lettsom, founder of the London Medical Society.

GETTING THERE

Guests heading for any point on Jost Van Dyke usually arrive via **ferryboat** from either St. Thomas or Tortola. (Be warned that departure times can vary widely throughout the year and at times do not adhere very closely to what is printed in the timetables.) Ferryboats from St. Thomas depart from Red Hook 3 days a week (Friday, Saturday, and Sunday) about twice a day. More convenient (and more frequent) are the daily ferryboat shuttles from Tortola's isolated West End, where boats depart four times a day (25 minutes each way). The cost is $8 one way, or $15 round-trip. Call the **Jost Van Dyke Ferryboat Service** (☎ 284/494-2997) about departures from any of the points mentioned above. Of course, if all else fails, there is a handful of privately operated water taxis that for a fee will transport you, your entourage, and your luggage to Jost Van Dyke.

WHERE TO STAY

Very casual types consider the simple accommodations offered by Rudy's under "Where to Dine," below.

Impressions

Question: Where are the British Virgin Islands?
Answer: I have no idea, but I should think that they are as far as possible from the Isle
of Man.

—Sir Winston Churchill

Sandcastle Hotel

White Bay, Jost Van Dyke, B.V.I. ☎ **284/690-1611.** Fax 284/775-3590. 4 cottages. Winter, $160–$175 double. Off-season, $95–$115 double. Additional person $35–$45 extra. MAP $40 per person extra. Four-night minimum. MC, V. Take the private motor launch from Tortola (20-minute ride).

A retreat for escapists who want few neighbors and absolutely nothing to do, these four cottages are surrounded by flowering shrubbery and bougainvillea and have wonderful views. You mix your own drinks at the beachside bar, the Soggy Dollar, and keep your own tab. Visiting boaters often drop in to enjoy the beachside informality and order a drink called a "Painkiller." A line in the guest book proclaims, "I thought places like this only existed in the movies."

For reservations and information, call or write the Sandcastle, Suite 201, Red Hook Plaza, St. Thomas, U.S.V.I. 00802-1306 (☎ 284/775-5262). Don't send mail to Jost Van Dyke, as it could take months to reach there.

Sandy Ground

East End (P.O. Box 594, West End), Tortola, B.V.I. ☎ **284/494-3391.** Fax 284/495-9379. 8 villas. Winter, $1,400 per week villa for 2. Off-season, $980 per week villa for 2. Additional person $250 extra in winter, $150 extra off-season. MC, V. Take a private water taxi from Tortola or St. Thomas.

These self-sufficient housekeeping units are on a 17-acre hill site on the eastern part of Jost Van Dyke. The complex rents two- and three-bedroom villas. One of our favorites was constructed on a cliff that seems to hang about 80 or so feet over a small beach. If you've come all this way, you might as well stay a week, which is the way the rates are quoted. The airy villas, each privately owned, are fully equipped with refrigerators and stoves. Villa interiors vary widely, from rather fashionable to bare bones. The managers help guests with boat rentals and water sports. Diving, day sails, and other activities can also be arranged, and there are dinghies available. Snorkeling and hiking are among the more popular pastimes, and the beach is private.

WHERE TO DINE

Abe's by the Sea

Little Harbour. ☎ **284/495-9329.** Reservations recommended for groups of 5 or more. Dinner $12–$30; nightly barbecue $20. MC, V. Daily 8–11am, noon–3pm, and 7–10pm. Take a private motor launch or boat from Tortola; as you approach the east side of the harbor you'll see Abe's on your right. WEST INDIAN.

In this local bar and restaurant, sailors are satisfied with a simple menu of fish, lobster, conch, and chicken. Usually, the best item to order is West Indian steamed fish with onion and sweet pepper in a lime-flavored butter sauce. The barbecued spareribs are also the best in the area. Prices are low, too, and it's money well spent. For the price of the main course, you get peas and rice, along with coleslaw, plus dessert. On Wednesday night in season, Abe's has a festive pig roast.

Rudy's Mariner's Rendezvous

Great Harbour. ☎ **284/495-9282.** Reservations required by 6:30pm. Dinner $12–$25. MC, V. Daily 7pm–midnight. WEST INDIAN.

Rudy's, at the western end of Great Harbour, serves good but basic West Indian food and plenty of it. The place looks and feels like a private home with a waterfront terrace for visiting diners. A welcoming drink awaits sailors and landlubbers alike, and the food that follows is simply prepared and inexpensive. Conch always seems to be on the menu, and there's always a catch of the day.

The Sandcastle

On White Bay. ☎ **284/690-1611.** Reservations required for dinner by 4pm. Fixed-price dinner $32; lunch main courses $5–$8. MC, V. Daily 9:30am–3pm and one seating at 7:30pm. INTERNATIONAL/CARIBBEAN.

This hotel restaurant (see "Accommodations," above) serves food that has often been frozen, but, even so, the flavors remain consistently good. Lunch is served in the open-air dining room, whereas lighter fare and snacks are available at the Soggy Dollar Bar. Dinner is by candlelight, featuring four courses, including such dishes as mahimahi Martinique (marinated in orange-lemon-lime juice and cooked with fennel, onions, and dill). Sandcastle hen is another specialty likely to appear on the menu: It's a Cornish hen marinated in rum, honey, lime, and garlic before being grilled. But, I'd skip all that for the sesame snapper. Desserts are luscious, including a piña colada cheesecake or a mango mousse. Meals are served with seasonal vegetables and fresh pasta, along with a variety of salads and homemade desserts.

4 Anegada

The most northerly and isolated of the British Virgins, 30 miles east of Tortola, Anegada (pop. 250) has more than 500 shipwrecks lying off its notorious Horseshoe Reef. Many of the inhabitants of Anegada have looked unsuccessfully for legendary hidden treasures on sunken vessels, including the *Paramatta,* which has rested on the sea bottom for more than a century.

Anegada is different from the other British Virgins in that it's a flat coral-and-limestone atoll with a 2,500-foot airstrip. At its highest point, it reaches only 28 feet; Anegada hardly appears on the horizon, which explains why it has always been so notoriously dangerous for sailors. It is 11 miles long and 3 miles wide.

At the northern and western ends of the island, there are some good beaches, which might be your only reason for coming here. This is a remote little corner of the Caribbean. Don't expect any frills, and be prepared to put up with some nuisances, such as mosquitoes.

Most of the island is off-limits to development, and is reserved for birds and other wildlife. The BVI National Parks Trust has established a bird sanctuary, which is the protected home of a flamingo colony, a variety of herons, plus plenty of ospreys and terns. Thanks to the trust, the island's interior is also a preserved habitat for some 2,000 wild goats, donkeys, and cattle. The refuge is giving a new lease on life to the rock iguana, an endangered, fierce-looking, but actually harmless reptile that can grow to a length of 5 feet and weigh up to 20 pounds. Though rarely seen, these creatures have called Anegada home for thousands of years, and their surroundings have hardly changed a bit.

GETTING THERE & GETTING AROUND

Gorda Aero Service (☎ 284/495-2271) is the only carrier serving Anegada and it flies here from Tortola. Using six- to eight-passenger propeller planes, it operates four times a week. The fare is $56 per person round-trip. Flights run on Monday, Wednesday, Friday, and Sunday. In addition, **Fly BVI** (☎ 284/495-1747), operates a charter/sightseeing service to and from Anegada from Beef Island off Tortola. The one-way cost is $125 for two to three passengers.

Tony's Taxis, which you'll easily spot when you arrive, will take you around the island. It's also possible to rent bicycles. Just ask around.

WHERE TO STAY & DINE

The Anegada Reef Hotel is the only major accommodation on the island. Neptune's Treasure, below, rents tents.

Anegada Reef Hotel

Setting Point, Anegada, B.V.I. ☎ **284/495-8002.** Fax 284/495-9362. 16 rms. A/C. Winter, $200–$230 double. Off-season, $180–$215 double. Rates include all meals. MC, V.

The only major hotel on the island is 3 miles west of the airport, right on the beachfront. It's one of the most remote places in this guide—guests who stay here are in effect hiding out. It's a favorite of the yachting set, who enjoy the hospitality provided by Lowell Wheatley. He offers motel-like and very basic rooms with private porches, with either a garden or ocean view. Go here for tranquillity, not for pampering.

You can arrange to go inshore fishing, deep-sea fishing, or bonefishing (there's also a tackle shop); they'll also set up snorkeling excursions and secure taxi service and Jeep rentals. There's a beach barbecue nightly—the house specialty is lobster—and many attendees arrive by boat. Reservations for the 7:30pm dinner must be made by 4pm. Dinners begin at $16.50, $30 if you order the generous portion of lobster. Nonguests are also welcomed at breakfast or lunch. If you're visiting just for the day, you can use the hotel as a base. Call and they'll have a bus meet you at the airport.

Neptune's Treasure

Between Pomato and Saltheap points. VHF Ch. 16 or 68, or **284/495-9439.** Reservations required only for dinner. Breakfast $4–$7; lunch $6–$30; dinner $12–$30. AE, MC, V. Daily 8am–11pm. SEAFOOD.

While on Anegada, you may want to visit this seaside restaurant that serves fresh fish and lobster caught by the owners. They also serve burgers, sandwiches, baby back ribs, and chicken. The family that runs the restaurant helpfully explains how to explore the island. They also rent tents with single or double mattresses. Tents range from $15 to $25 a night, a bare site costing only $7. Tent rentals come with sheets, pillowcases, and solar showers. You can take a taxi to one of their sandy beaches and go snorkeling along their reefs.

SHOPPING

Hardly the reason to visit Anegada. But once you're here drop in at **Pat's Pottery** (☎ 284/495-8031), where islanders sell some interesting crafts, including dishes, plates, pitchers, and mugs in whimsical folk-art patterns.

5 Marina Cay

Near Beef Island, Marina Cay is a private six-acre islet. Its only claim to fame was as the setting of the 1953 Robb White book *Our Virgin Isle,* which was later filmed with Sidney Poitier and John Cassavetes. For 20 years after Robb White's departure, the island lay uninhabited until the hotel (see below) opened. The hotel has recently been taken over by Pusser's, the famous Virgin Islands establishment, which means that you'll always be able to sip the "Pusser's Painkiller." The island lies 5 minutes away by launch from Tortola's Trellis Bay, adjacent to Beef Island International Airport. The ferry running between Beef Island and Marina Cay is free. There are no cars on the island. We only mention the tiny cay at all because of the Marina Cay Resort.

WHERE TO STAY & DINE

Pusser's Marina Cay Resort

Marina Cay (mailing address: P.O. Box 626, Road Town, Tortola), B.V.I. ☎ **284/494-2174.**
Fax 284/494-4775. 4 rms, 2 villas. Winter, $125–$150 double; $350 villa. Off-season, $75–$95
double; $195 villa. Rates include continental breakfast. AE, MC, V. Take the private launch from
Beef Island.

This small cottage hotel, opened in 1960 and extensively renovated in 1995, attracts
the sailing crowd. It houses guests in simply furnished double rooms with king-size
beds, all overlooking a reef and Sir Francis Drake Channel, dotted with islands. Each
room has a private balcony. Marina Cay is a tropical garden.

Dining is casual in a beachside restaurant, with a cuisine featuring continental and
West Indian dishes. Activities include snorkeling, windsurfing, scuba diving (with
certification courses taught by a resident dive master), castaway picnics on secluded
beaches, kayaking, underwater safaris, and deep-sea fishing.

6 Peter Island

Half of this island, boasting a good marina and docking facilities, is devoted to the
yacht club. The other part is deserted. Beach facilities are found at palm-fringed
Deadman Bay, which faces the Atlantic but is protected by a reef. All goods and services are at the one resort (see below).

The island is so private that except for an occasional mason at work, about the only
company you'll encounter will be an iguana or a feral cat whose ancestors were abandoned generations ago by shippers (the cats are said to have virtually eliminated the
island's rodent population).

GETTING THERE

A hotel-operated ferry, **Peter Island Boat** (☎ 284/495-2000), picks up any overnight guest who arrives at the Beef Island airport. It departs from the pier at Trellis
Bay, near the airport. A round-trip costs $25. Other boats depart eight or nine times
a day from Baughers Bay in Road Town. Passengers must notify the hotel 2 weeks
before their arrival so transportation can be arranged.

WHERE TO STAY & DINE

✪ Peter Island Resort

Peter Island (P.O. Box 211, Road Town, Tortola), B.V.I. ☎ **800/346-4451** or 284/495-2000.
Fax 284/495-2500. 50 rms, 3 villas. A/C MINIBAR TEL. Winter, $395–$545 double; $695–$895
Hawk's Nest two-bedroom villa; $3,950 Crow's Nest four-bedroom villa. Off-season, $195–$385
double; $525–$675 Hawk's Nest two-bedroom villa; $1,400–$3,950 Crow's Nest four-bedroom
villa. MAP $75 per person extra. Crow's Nest rates include all meals. AE, MC, V.

This 1,800-acre tropical island is solely dedicated to Peter Island Resort guests and
yacht owners who moor their crafts here. The island's tropical gardens and hillside
are bordered by five private beaches, including Deadman's Beach (in spite of its name,
it's often voted one of the world's most romantic in travel magazine reader polls).

The resort contains 30 rooms facing Sprat Bay and Sir Francis Drake Channel
(ocean-view or garden rooms) and 20 larger rooms on Deadman's Bay Beach
(beachfront). Designed with a casual elegance, they have a balcony or terrace, ceiling fan, coffeemaker, clock radio, and hair dryer. The Crow's Nest, a luxurious four-
bedroom villa, overlooks the harbor and Deadman Bay and features a private
swimming pool, full kitchen, maid, gardener, personal steward, and island vehicle.
The Hawk's Nest villas are two two-bedroom villas situated on a tropical hillside.

Dining/Entertainment: The Tradewinds Restaurant serves breakfast and dinner throughout the year in fine Caribbean tradition. For a more casual setting, the Deadman's Beach Bar and Grill serves sandwiches and salads beside the ocean. The main bar, Drakes Channel Lounge, is also open throughout the day and evening.

Services: Room service (breakfast only), laundry, massage, baby-sitting, launch transport to/from Beef Island airport.

Facilities: Fitness center; gift shop; freshwater pool with a stunning view of the sea; four tennis courts (two lit for night play); scuba-diving base; library; spa; conference facility; basketball; mountain bikes; complete yacht marina with complimentary use of Sunfish, snorkeling gear, sea kayaks, Windsurfers, and 19-foot Squib day-sailers.

7　Mosquito Island (North Sound)

The sandy, 125-acre Mosquito (also spelled Moskito) Island just north of Virgin Gorda wasn't named for those pesky insects we all know and hate. It took its name from the tribe who inhabited the small landmass before the arrival of the Spanish conquistadors in the 15th century. Archaeological relics of these peaceful people and their agricultural pursuits have been found here.

GETTING THERE

You must take a plane to Virgin Gorda, then a taxi to Leverick Bay Dock. A boat will meet you and take you on the 5-minute ride from the dock to the resort. The island lies north of Virgin Gorda.

WHERE TO STAY

Drake's Anchorage Resort Inn
North Sound (P.O. Box 2510, Virgin Gorda), B.V.I. ☎ **800/624-6651,** or 284/494-2254, or 617/969-9913 in Massachusetts. 8 rms, 2 suites, 2 villas. Winter, $505–$526 double; $585–$615 suite; $695 villa. Off-season, $350–$425 double; $485–$515 suite; $595 villa. Rates include all meals. AE, MC, V.

The privately owned island is uninhabited except for Drake's, which many patrons consider their favorite retreat in the British Virgins. The hotel has comfortable rooms and suites with private baths and sea-view verandas. The resort's restaurant, attractively tropical in design, faces the water and offers a cuisine featuring local and continental dishes, including lobster and a fresh fish of the day.

Guests have free use of Windsurfers, snorkeling equipment, and bicycles. For additional fees, you can go scuba diving, deep-sea fishing, sailing, or to The Baths on Virgin Gorda. The snorkeling and scuba here are so good that members of the Cousteau Society spend a month each year exploring local waters. There are four beaches on the island, each with different wave and water conditions.

8　Guana Island

This 850-acre island, a nature sanctuary, is one of the most private hideaways in the Caribbean. Don't come here seeking action; come only if you want to retreat from the world. Guana Island lies right off the coast of Tortola. The small island contains seven virgin beaches and nature trails and an abundance of unusual species of plant and animal life. The island is ideal for hiking. Its highest point is Sugarloaf Mountain at 806 feet, which offers a panoramic view. Arawak relics have been found on the island. It is said that the name of the island came from a jutting rock that resembled the head of an iguana.

To get here, take the Guana Island Club boat, which meets visitors at Beef Island airport (10 minutes) near Tortola.

WHERE TO STAY

Guana Island Club

P.O. Box 32, Road Town, Tortola, B.V.I. ☎ **800/544-8262** in the U.S., or 284/494-2354. 16 cottages. For reservations, write or call the Guana Island Reservations Office, 10 Timber Trail, Rye, NY 10580 (☎ 800/544-8262 in the U.S., or 914/967-6050; fax 914/967-8048). Winter, $595 double; $960 North Beach cottage. Apr–Aug, $435 double; $720 North Beach cottage. Rent the island, $7,200–$9,525. Rates include all meals. No credit cards. Closed Sept–Oct. Take the private launch from Tortola.

Guana Island, the sixth or seventh largest of the British Virgin Islands, was bought in 1974 by Henry and Gloria Jarecki, dedicated conservationists who run this resort as a nature preserve and wildlife sanctuary. Upon your arrival on the island, a Land Rover will meet you and transport you up one of the most scenic hills in the region, in the northeast of Guana.

The cluster of white cottages was built as a private club in the 1930s on the foundations of a Quaker homestead. The stone cottages never hold more than 30 guests (and only two telephones), and since the dwellings are staggered along a flower-dotted ridge overlooking the Caribbean and the Atlantic, the sense of privacy is almost absolute. The entire island can be rented by groups of up to 30. Although water is scarce on the island, each airy accommodation has a shower. The decor is of rattan and wicker and each unit has a ceiling fan. North Beach cottage, the most luxurious, is like renting a private home. The panoramic sweep from the terraces is spectacular, particularly at sunset.

Dining/Entertainment: Guests will find a convivial atmosphere at the rattan-furnished clubhouse. Casually elegant dinners by candlelight are served on the veranda, with menus that include homegrown vegetables and continental and stateside specialties. A buffet lunch is served every day. The self-service bars operate on the honor system.

Services: Laundry.

Facilities: Seven beaches (some of which require a boat to reach), two tennis courts (one clay and one all-weather), fishing, snorkeling, windsurfing, kayaks, small sailboats, waterskiing.

General Index

ACCOMMODATIONS INDEX

BEACHES INDEX

OUTDOOR ACTIVITIES INDEX

FROMMER'S COMPLETE TRAVEL GUIDES

(Comprehensive guides to destinations around the world, with selections in all price ranges—from deluxe to budget)

Acapulco, Ixtapa & Zihuatenejo
Alaska
Amsterdam
Arizona
Atlanta
Australia
Austria
Bahamas
Barcelona, Madrid & Seville
Belgium, Holland & Luxembourg
Bermuda
Boston
Budapest & the Best of Hungary
California
Canada
Cancún, Cozumel & the Yucatán
Cape Cod, Nantucket & Martha's Vineyard
Caribbean
Caribbean Cruises & Ports of Call
Caribbean Ports of Call
Carolinas & Georgia
Chicago
Colorado
Costa Rica
Denver, Boulder & Colorado Springs
England

Europe
Florida
France
Germany
Greece
Hawaii
Hong Kong
Honolulu, Waikiki & Oahu
Ireland
Israel
Italy
Jamaica & Barbados
Japan
Las Vegas
London
Los Angeles
Maryland & Delaware
Maui
Mexico
Miami & the Keys
Montana & Wyoming
Montréal & Québec City
Munich & the Bavarian Alps
Nashville & Memphis
Nepal
New England
New Mexico
New Orleans
New York City
Northern New England
Nova Scotia, New Brunswick & Prince Edward Island
Paris

Philadelphia & the Amish Country
Portugal
Prague & the Best of the Czech Republic
Provence & the Riviera
Puerto Rico
Rome
San Antonio & Austin
San Diego
San Francisco
Santa Fe, Taos & Albuquerque
Scandinavia
Scotland
Seattle & Portland
South Pacific
Spain
Switzerland
Thailand
Tokyo
Toronto
Tuscany & Umbria
U.S.A.
Utah
Vancouver & Victoria
Vienna & the Danube Valley
Virgin Islands
Virginia
Walt Disney World & Orlando
Washington, D.C.
Washington & Oregon

FROMMER'S DOLLAR-A-DAY BUDGET GUIDES

(The ultimate guides to low-cost travel)

Australia from $50 a Day
Berlin from $50 a Day
California from $60 a Day
Caribbean from $60 a Day
Costa Rica & Belize from $35 a Day
England from $60 a Day
Europe from $50 a Day
Florida from $50 a Day
Greece from $50 a Day
Hawaii from $60 a Day

India from $40 a Day
Ireland from $45 a Day
Israel from $45 a Day
Italy from $50 a Day
London from $60 a Day
Mexico from $35 a Day
New York from $75 a Day
New Zealand from $50 a Day
Paris from $70 a Day
San Francisco from $60 a Day
Washington, D.C., from $50 a Day

FROMMER'S PORTABLE GUIDES

(Pocket-size guides for travelers who want everything in a nutshell)

Charleston & Savannah	New Orleans	San Francisco
Dublin	Puerto Vallarta,	Venice
Las Vegas	Manzanillo &	Washington, D.C.
Maine Coast	Guadalajara	

FROMMER'S FAMILY GUIDES

(The complete guides for successful family vacations)

California with Kids	New York City with Kids	Washington, D.C.,
Los Angeles with Kids	San Francisco with Kids	with Kids

FROMMER'S AMERICA ON WHEELS

(Everything you need for a successful road trip, including full-color road maps and ratings for every hotel)

California & Nevada	Mid-Atlantic	South-Central States
Florida	New England & New York	& Texas
Great Lake States &	Northwest & Great Plains	Southeast
Midwest		Southwest

FROMMER'S WALKING TOURS

(Memorable neighborhood strolls through the world's great cities)

London	San Francisco	Venice
New York	Spain's Favorite Cities	Washington, D.C.
Paris	Tokyo	

SPECIAL-INTEREST TITLES

Arthur Frommer's Branson!	New York Times Weekends
Arthur Frommer's New World of Travel	Outside Magazine's Adventure Guide
The Civil War Trust's Official Guide to	to New England
the Civil War Discovery Trail	Outside Magazine's Adventure Guide
Frommer's America's 100 Best-Loved	to Northern California
State Parks	Outside Magazine's Adventure Guide
Frommer's Caribbean Hideaways	to the Pacific Northwest
Frommer's Complete Hostel Vacation Guide	Outside Magazine's Guide
to England, Scotland & Wales	to Family Vacations
Frommer's Europe's Greatest	Places Rated Almanac
Driving Tours	Retirement Places Rated
Frommer's Food Lover's Companion	Wonderful Weekends from NYC
to France	Wonderful Weekends from San Francisco
Frommer's Food Lover's Companion to Italy	

FROMMER'S IRREVERENT GUIDES

(Wickedly honest guides for sophisticated travelers)

Amsterdam	Manhattan	Paris	U.S. Virgin Islands
Chicago	Miami	San Francisco	Walt Disney World
London	New Orleans	Santa Fe	Washington, D.C.

UNOFFICIAL GUIDES

(Get the unbiased truth from these candid, value-conscious guides)

Atlanta	The Great Smoky	Miami & the Keys	Walt Disney World
Branson, Missouri	& Blue Ridge	Mini-Mickey	Walt Disney World
Chicago	Mountains	New Orleans	Companion
Cruises	Las Vegas	Skiing in the West	Washington, D.C.
Disneyland			

BAEDEKER
(With four-color photographs and a free pull-out map)

Amsterdam	Crete	Lisbon	Scandinavia
Athens	Florence	London	Scotland
Austria	Florida	Mexico	Singapore
Bali	Germany	New York	South Africa
Belgium	Great Britain	New Zealand	Spain
Berlin	Greece	Paris	Switzerland
Brazil	Greek Islands	Portugal	Thailand
Budapest	Hawaii	Prague	Tokyo
California	Hong Kong	Provence	Turkish Coast
Canada	Ireland	Rome	Tuscany
Caribbean	Israel	San Francisco	Venice
China	Italy	St. Petersburg	Vienna
Copenhagen			

FROMMER'S BY NIGHT GUIDES
(The series for those who know that life begins after dark)

Amsterdam	Los Angeles	Manhattan	Paris
Chicago	Madrid	Miami	Prague
Las Vegas	& Barcelona	New Orleans	San Francisco
London			Washington, D.C.

FROMMER'S BEST BEACH VACATIONS
(The top places to sun, stroll, shop, stay, play, party, and swim, with ratings for each beach)

California	Florida	Mid-Atlantic
Carolinas & Georgia	Hawaii	New England

FROMMER'S BED & BREAKFAST GUIDES
(Selective guides with four-color photos and full descriptions of the best inns in each region)

California	Mid-Atlantic	The Rockies
Caribbean	New England	Southeast
Great American Cities	Pacific Northwest	Southwest
Hawaii		

FROMMER'S DRIVING TOURS
(Four-color photos and detailed maps outlining spectacular scenic driving routes)

America	California	Ireland	Scotland
Australia	Florida	Italy	Spain
Austria	France	New England	Switzerland
Britain	Germany	Scandinavia	Western Europe

FROMMER'S BORN TO SHOP
(The ultimate guides for travelers who love to shop)

Caribbean Ports	Great Britain	London	New York
of Call	Hong Kong	Mexico	Paris
France	Italy	New Egnland	

TRAVEL & LEISURE GUIDES
(Sophisticated pocket-size guides for discriminating travelers)

Amsterdam	Hong Kong	New York	San Francisco
Boston	London	Paris	Washington, D.C.

WHEREVER YOU TRAVEL, *H*ELP IS NEVER FAR AWAY.

From planning your trip to providing travel assistance along the way, American Express® Travel Service Offices are always there to help.

British Virgin Islands

Romney Associates Consultants (R)
Waterfront Plaza
Tortola, BVI
809/494-6239

Travel Plan Limited (R)
Virgin Gorda Yacht Harbour
Virgin Gorda, BVI
809/495-5586

U.S. Virgin Islands

Southerland Tours (R)
Chandlers Wharf Gallows Bay
St. Croix, USVI
809/773-9500

Caribbean Travel Agency Inc./
Tropic Tours (R)
14AB The Guardian Bldg.
St. Thomas, USVI
809/774-1855

Travel

http://www.americanexpress.com/travel

American Express Travel Service Offices are found in central locations throughout the Caribbean.